REFUGEES
A Third World Dilemma

REFUGEES
A Third World Dilemma

Edited by
John R. Rogge
UNIVERSITY OF MANITOBA

Rowman & Littlefield
PUBLISHERS

ROWMAN & LITTLEFIELD

Published in the United States of America in 1987
by Rowman & Littlefield, Publishers
(a division of Littlefield, Adams & Company)
81 Adams Drive, Totowa, New Jersey 07512

Library of Congress Cataloging-in-Publication Data

Refugees: a third world dilemma.

Bibliography: p. 343
Includes index.
1. Refugees—Congresses. 2. Refugees—Developing
countries—Congresses. 3. Refugees—Government
policy—Congresses. 4. Refugees—Government policy—
Developing countries—Congresses. I. Rogge, John.
HV640.R425 1987   362.8'7'091726   87-9605
ISBN 0-8476-7557-2

90 89 88 87
7 6 5 4 3 2 1

Printed in the United States of America

Contents

Tables and Figures

Figures

Abbreviations

ASEAN	Association of South East Asian Nations
BPEAR	Bureau of Placement and Education of African Refugees
CCSDP	Committee for Co-ordination of Services to Displaced Persons in Thailand
CEIC	Canada Employment and Immigration Commission
COMAR	Comision Mexicana de Ayuda a los Refugiados
COR	Commissioner of Refugees (Sudan)
CPH	Centres Provisoires d'Hébergement
CTD	Convention Travel Document
EDCOR	Economic Development Corps
EDU	Ethiopian Democratic Union
ELF	Eritrean Liberation Front
EPLF	Eritrean Peoples Liberation Front
FBIS	Foreign Broadcast Information Service
ICARA	International Conference on Assistant to Refugees in Africa
ICM	Intergovernmental Committee for Migration
ICMC	International Catholic Migration Committee
JMCDP	Joint Ministerial Committee for Displaced Persons
MCP	Malayan Communist Party
MNLF	Moro National Liberation Front
NATO	North Atlantic Treaty Organization
NGO	Non Governmental Organization
NPA	New People's Army
NWFP	North West Frontier Province
OAU	Organization of African Unity
ODP	Orderly Departure Programme
OPM	Free Papua Movement
PLF	Peoples Liberation Front
RCS	Refugee Counselling Service
RPC	Refugee Processing Centre
SAIRR	South African Institute of Race Relations
SCA	Sabah Chinese Association
TPLF	Tigrayan Peoples Liberation Front
UNBRO	United Nations Border Relief Organization
UNDP	United Nations Development Programme
UNHCR	United Nations High Commission for Refugees
UNRISD	United Nations Research Institute for Social Development
UNRWA	United Nations Relief Works Agency for Palestinian Refugees
UPKO	United Pasokmogum Kadazan Organization
USCR	United States Committee for Refugees
USIA	United Sabah Islamic Association
USNO	United Sabah National Organization

Acknowledgments

The majority of the papers in this volume are derived from the 1983 Symposium on the Problems and Consequences of Refugee Migrations in the Developing World, held at Hecla Island Provincial Park, Manitoba, Canada. Grants from a number of agencies permitted some 70 participants from twenty countries to assemble at Hecla for four days to discuss the refugee problem. These agencies were the Canadian International Development Agency, the International Development Research Centre, Employment and Immigration Canada, the Social Science and Humanities Research Council, the Government of Manitoba, and the University of Manitoba.

Following the decision to publish some of the symposium's papers, together with other relevant papers to be solicited, further funding was received toward publication costs from Employment and Immigration Canada, the United Nations High Commission for Refugees, and the International Geographical Union's Commission on Population Geography. The editor deeply appreciates the support received from all these sources, for without it, neither the symposium or this assembly of papers would have ever been possible.

Appreciation and thanks are also extended to Mrs. Hedy Chambers and Mrs. Jill Michalski, who undertook most of the typing; to Mrs. Marjorie Halmarson, who redrafted all the maps and diagrams; to Chowdhury Haque for assistance with compiling the bibliography; to Mark Lee and Ziarat Hossain, who helped with proofreading; and to Mrs. Nancy Pazner, who assisted with the final electronic formatting of the volume. To all the above I am deeply indebted.

J. R. Rogge
Winnipeg

1

Introduction

Over the past decade the volume of international migration has declined as major immigrant-receiving countries, such as the United States, Canada, and Australia, have steadily reduced their annual quotas for immigrants. The demand for emigration has also decreased in "traditional" immigrant source-areas of Europe. Yet, as the development gap between Third World nations and the industrialized world widens, the desire to emigrate from lesser developed regions to ones of greater economic opportunity increases annually. International labor migration is the manner in which most of these migratory aspirations manifest themselves, and some additional limited permanent migration from lesser developed to more developed countries is caused by changing immigration policies. But the contemporary volume of involuntary international migration—most of which is destined to become a permanent transfer of human resources—greatly supercedes these regular forms of international movement.

Although there are no comprehensive statistics on the total of involuntary migrants in the world, most sources place the number of refugees at somewhere between 10 and 12 million. These are the world's "political" refugees. There are also many other involuntary migrants, such as those displaced within their own countries by political events or by natural hazards, and an ever-growing population of so-called "economic" refugees: displacees who are induced to move by poverty and lack of economic opportunity. While the latter often share characteristics apparent among legally recognized "political" refugees, they are seldom received in the same manner by potential host states and, indeed, are generally denied the right of asylum that international protocols ascribe to legally recognized refugees.

The "regular" forms of migration, including labor migrations and urbanization, have all received much attention from social scientists, and much valuable research literature on these forms of migration is available. In contrast, relatively little research has been undertaken, until recently, on the causes, characteristics, and consequences of the world's involuntary migrations. For example, the arrival since the end of the Vietnam War in 1975 of some three-quarters of a million Indochinese refugees in the United States, and a further hundred thousand in Canada, has greatly stimulated aca-

demic inquiry into their absorption and economic assimilation. It has also
had the overall effect of sensitizing North Americans to the plight and needs
of refugees in general.

Yet although an awareness is developing of the needs of refugees
resettled in industrialized countries, considerable ignorance or misinformation persist about the problems, needs, and prospects of the many displacees and refugees who remain in exile throughout the Third World. Also,
our understanding of the refugee problem varies considerably depending
on the region: Southeast Asia has received much more attention than Africa,
which in turn has received more attention than Pakistan; and the problem in
Central America is only just beginning to be recognized. The relative
imbalance of the regional sections in this volume is in part a manifestation of
this situation.

The papers presented here are essentially an outgrowth of a symposium
that brought together researchers and professionals concerned with Third
World refugees. Not all of the papers presented there are included here. On
the other hand, a few additional papers have been added in an attempt to
provide more comprehensive coverage of the refugee problem in specific
regions.

The strong emphasis in this volume on Africa's and Southeast Asia's
refugees vis-à-vis the other regions is not intended to imply that these two
regions' refugee dilemma is more acute or of greater magnitude than that
prevailing in the other regions. It does suggest, however, that these two
areas have attracted the greater proportion of academic interest to date. In
contrast, research on issues related to the Afghan refugees in Pakistan and
Iran—the single largest refugee concentration in the world—remains relatively limited, albeit increasing over the past three years. The understanding
of the plight of Central American refugees is limited essentially to studies of
their absorption and integration in third countries of permanent resettlement, and virtually no research has yet been published to evaluate their
impact on areas of local settlement in Central America, or on the problems
they encounter in their countries of initial asylum. Even less is understood
about refugees and displaced populations existing on the Indian subcontinent. It is hoped therefore that one of the contributions of this volume will
be to direct potential researchers to areas and problems hitherto unrecognized or largely ignored.

Available statistics on refugees tell only part of the story, since many of
the world's involuntary migrants are not officially or legally recognized as
refugees. It is becoming increasingly more difficult to differentiate clearly
between bona fide refugees or asylum seekers and economic-motivated
migrants who use the umbrella of refugee status to emigrate to areas of
better economic opportunity. The limitations of the United Nations Convention and Protocol on refugees are well documented, and are referred to in
several of the essays in this volume. Moreover, this difficulty in determining
the status of refugees was recently demonstrated by UNHCR's response to
Ethiopian migrants in Sudan, where drought displacees—economic migrants in the strict sense of the term—were supported by the agency in

much the same manner as the "convention" refugees in the area had traditionally been supported.

There is also the problem of internal displacees vis-à-vis external (border crossing) migrants. In many refugee-generating regions, the number of internal displacees often exceeds those seeking refuge in neighboring states. While both groups of migrants are clearly refugees in the sense that they flee one area to seek refuge elsewhere, only the international migrants are ever recognized as refugees.

Lebanon and Cyprus are examples of states with major intranational refugee populations, and where UNHCR has decided to go beyond the constraints of its mandate to provide assistance to displacees. Internal displacees elsewhere have been less fortunate, and within Uganda, Ethiopia, and Mozambique, they remain beyond the protection and assistance normally afforded to other refugees.

The problem of numbers and definition of refugees is illustrated by two sets of data. Table 1.1 summarizes the world refugee population as recognized by UNHCR (UNHCR 1985), while Table 1.2 shows refugee numbers according to the U.S. Committee for Refugees (1980 and 1984). The former does not include any internally displaced population; the latter does. Also, UNHCR does not recognize the Palestinians as refugees, since they come under the orbit of another U.N. agency; the U.S. Committee for Refugees includes Palestinians in its summary statistics. A further difference lies in the way the two agencies view permanently resettled refugees. UNHCR continues to include refugees granted permanent asylum in such states as the U.S., Canada and Australia as refugees in its summary statistics. This is not done by the other data source. Also, a considerable time-lag often elapses between the migration and its subsequent recognition as a source of refugees (and thus their appearance in the statistics). Even though Sri Lankans have been seeking refuge in southern India for several years— there are now some 130,000 Sri Lanka Tamils in India—they do not appear in UNHCR summary statistics for December 1985.

A great need to refine enumeration methods clearly exists since, as Chambers (1979) has correctly emphasized, without a clear understanding of the size of affected populations, effective planning and execution of relief and rehabilitation programs will be limited. A need also exists for more attention to "nonrecognized" refugee movements. Most studies to date have focused upon refugees who fall under the UNHCR's mandate, yet more should be understood about many other displaced populations. Several of the essays in this volume focus on such displacees.

In organizing the thirty papers and reports that make up this volume, the editor was faced with the option of adopting one of two alternative approaches. On the one hand, the papers could have been organized systematically, divided into sections dealing with specific refugee issues such as problems associated with local integration, repatriation, or third-country resettlement. Or the papers could have been organized into sections based on the regional origin of the refugees. Given the diverse range of the papers and reports, neither option presented an ideal solution for the volume's

Table 1.1   The Geography of Exile: The World Refugee Population, According to UNHCR
            (December 1985)

Algeria	167,000	Rwanda	49,000
Angola	92,200	Somalia	700,000
Burundi	256,300	Sudan	690,000
Cameroon	13,700	Tanzania	179,000
Central African Rep.	42,000	Uganda	151,000
Djibouti	16,700	Zaire	317,000
Ethiopia	59,600	Zambia	96,500
Lesotho	11,500	Zimbabwe	46,500
Rest of Africa	42,200		

Total Africa: 2,930,200

China	179,800	Pakistan	2,500,000
Hong Kong	11,900	Papua New Guinea	10,000
Iran	1,900,000	Philippines	15,100
Malaysia	99,000	Thailand	128,500
Rest of Asia	25,600	Vietnam	21,000

Total Asia: 4,890,900

Argentina	11,500	Honduras	47,800
Costa Rica	16,800	Mexico	175,000
Guatamala	70,000	Nicaragua	18,500
Rest of Latin America	22,800		

Total Latin America: 362,400

Austria	20,500	Netherlands	15,000
Belgium	36,400	Norway	10,000
France	167,300	Sweden	90,600
Germany (FRG)	126,600	Switzerland	31,200
Italy	15,100	United Kingdom	135,000
Rest of Europe	26,700		

Total Europe: 674,400

Australia	89,000	New Zealand	4,500

Total Oceania: 93,500

Canada	353,000	USA	1,000,000

Total North America: 1,353,000

World Total (1985):   10,304,400

Source: UNHCR, December 1985.

Table 1.2   The Geography of Exile (Refugees and Displacees), According to U.S.
Committee for Refugees, 1980 and 1984

	1980	1984
Africa — refugees	2,655,200	2,633,000
—internally displaced	1,390,000	1,255,000–5,050,000
Asia — refugees	2,092,500	4,061,000
— internally displaced	5,200,000	230,000
Europe — refugees	229,750	27,000
Latin America — refugees	1,085,300	353,000
— internally displaced	—	535,000–1,300,000
Middle East — refugees	1,819,050	2,017,000
— internally displaced	1,493,450	600,000
Total — refugees	7,881,800	9,091,000
— internally displaced	8,083,450	2,620,000–7,180,000

Source: U.S. Committee for Refugees, *World Refugee Survey*, 1980 and 1984.

organization, since in each case a highly imbalanced series of sections emerged. Nevertheless, a regional organizational frame was adopted that permits the major issues in each refugee-generating arena to be brought into focus and, because of the resultant imbalance of the respective sections, suggests some of the research needs that prevail throughout the Third World.

The volume is divided into six sections, the first of which provides some overview of the refugee problem and introduces some of the responses that currently prevail. The five regional sections that follow deal with Africa, Central America, Western Asia, South Asia and Southeast Asia. The first and last of these are fairly extensive in comparison to the others, reflecting the relatively greater interests by academics in these areas or among refugees from these areas.

An extensive, comprehensive bibliography is included that melds the bibliographies from all of the individual papers. It will be a useful teaching and research resource for readers of this book.

Part One

Problems and Responses

The refugee problem in the Third World is not a new phenomenon; what is recent is the growing awareness among Western societies of the magnitude and consequences of the problem. Until the late 1970s, for most people in the Western industrialized world, "refugees" were essentially associated with the flight of East Europeans to the West. The end of the Vietnam War, and the diaspora of Southeast Asian refugees (Rogge 1985b) changed this situation. Since then, the refugee influx into Somalia, the astronomical exodus from Afghanistan to neighboring Iran and Pakistan, and the flight of Ethiopian refugees and drought displacees to Sudan have increasingly sensitized governments, voluntary agencies, and the general public to the plight of refugees in the Third World. This in turn is generating both positive and negative reactions: positive in the sense of generous responses to appeals for financial assistance and for volunteer sponsors, and negative in the sense that a backlash against permanent asylum in the West increases with each tide of asylum seekers.

It is important, however, to appreciate that the refugee problem in the Third World dates back to the early post–World War II years, if not even earlier. As Europe was attempting in the late 1940s and the early 1950s to resolve the massive problem of displacees and refugees resulting from World War II, other regions in the world also began to experience major population displacements. Both the partitioning of India in 1947 and the creation of Israel a year later unleashed a refugee problem of enormous dimensions, and which in the case of the Palestinians is no nearer to being resolved today than it was nearly forty years ago. Both internal and external displacements were generated in Indonesia as it threw off the yoke of Dutch colonialism, and in 1952, Tibetans were spread across the world as a consequence of China's annexation of Tibet. In the late 1950s, the first of Africa's many refugee crises began as Algerians fled to neighboring states because of the growing war for independence, and southern Sudanese were displaced both internally and externally as civil war erupted on independence (Akol 1986).

Although the Hungarian (1956) and Czechoslovakian (1968) refugee

7

crises continued to draw attention to European refugees, by the late 1960s
the bulk of the United Nations High Commission for Refugees' budget was
being allocated to refugee assistance in the Third World, primarily in Africa.
By 1985, UNHCR's general program expenditure was 36 percent in Africa,
24 in the Middle East and Southwest Asia, 21 percent in East and South
Asia, 14 percent in the Americas, and only 3 percent in Europe, which
clearly reflects the contemporary dynamics of the world's refugee situation.
An equally compelling statistic is that by 1985, the majority of funds
expended by UNHCR was for "care and maintenance" of refugees (57
percent) rather than for "durable solutions" (38 percent), which suggests
that much of the world's refugee population remains in a state of uncertainty, since "solutions" are often limited to keeping the refugees alive in
holding camps.

The first three essays in Part I focus on some of the problems and
responses associated with refugee movements. Alan Simmance, a senior
UNHCR administrator, examines some of the impacts of large-scale refugee
movements and the role of UNHCR. He outlines some of the needs of
refugees in first countries of asylum, and discusses, citing examples from
Somalia and Pakistan, the constraints placed upon UNHCR's activities by its
mandate and whether UNHCR's role should be limited to the provision of
relief and protection.

The second essay is Shelly Pitterman's detailed analysis of the determin-
ance of international refugee policy, with special reference to Africa. The
essay is the first in-depth review by an independent observer of the manner
in which UNHCR's assistance is distributed and of the external constraints
and pressures that influence decision-making within the UNHCR appa-
ratus.

The final essay focuses on the growing problem of asylum seekers who
are unable to find permanent refuge. Goran Melander examines the problem of "refugees in orbit," a phenomenon of concern to many European
states who currentiy find Third World refugees claiming asylum on their
doorsteps. Melander's review of the concept of asylum and of the refugees'
"right to asylum" focuses upon an issue of growing importance to all
refugee-receiving states. The issues raised in this and the two preceding
chapters apply equally to each of the refugee-generating regions covered in
the remaining sections of this volume.

2

The Impact of Large-Scale Refugee Movements and the Role of UNHCR

Alan J. F. Simmance

Of the world refugee population of approximately 10 million, the majority is the result, at least in countries of first asylum, of mass movements across national frontiers into the territory of neighboring states. The refugee prototype—the isolated individual or family fleeing from political persecution—has become numerically insignificant compared to the exodus of major population groups. In recent years such groups, whether of Latin American, Indochinese, African, Afghan, or other origin, have dominated the refugee landscape, with serious implications for development both in their countries of origin and, most immediately, in the countries in which they seek asylum.

UNHCR, as the nonpolitical, humanitarian arm of the international community, has a mandate to protect, to grant relief assistance, and to seek durable solutions only for refugees and for displaced persons who, as a result of so-called "man-made" disasters in their native lands, have been forced to flee across their borders to other states. As a result of successive General Assembly resolutions, these displaced persons are also of concern to the High Commissioner and can be assisted with the voluntary funds at his disposal. But here the mandate ends; UNHCR cannot involve itself directly with the underlying causes of refugee movements and can do nothing overtly to prevent them. Once they have taken place, UNHCR cannot act as a kind of developmental agency that sponsors country programs for the benefit of one sector or another of the national society to which the refugees have come.

How then can we act to ease the impact of a refugee influx on the development of a receiving state? That impact can be enormous and can take a variety of forms, whether social, economic, ecological or, since they are obviously interrelated, a combination of all three. The most dramatic effect is often the ecological or environmental one, which is illustrated below

9

with a summary of a report prepared by the Special Support Unit of UNHCR, illustrating specific examples from Somalia, Pakistan, and Sudan. It shows how the arrival of large numbers of refugees can have severe detrimental results in areas where physical resources are already scarce. A refugee influx can also seriously affect the local administrative infrastructure, the local market economy, health and social services, and transport and communications systems, and can even significantly alter the flow of goods and services within the society as a whole. The availability and pricing of commodities may be greatly altered, causing hardship among the local population and creating deep resentment against the refugees.

The first way in which UNHCR, its sister organizations within the United Nations system, and the voluntary agencies that assist in implementing so many of its programs can help governments to reduce the effects of refugee influxes on development is by providing a prompt and, where necessary, massive response to the need for emergency relief. The quicker this is done, the less the burden on local supplies of food, fuel, water, shelter, and transportation. The sooner adequate public health measures and decent sanitation can be provided, the smaller the chance of epidemics of infectious disease, which could afflict not only the refugees but the local populace as well.

Once the immediate emergency phase of refugee relief is over, the assistance program enters a more routine care and maintenance phase. For rural refugees or displaced persons, this usually involves the establishment of refugee settlements, which UNHCR tries to plan, site, and organize with the least possible disruption of local patterns of land usage and a minimum adverse effect on the physical environment and populations of the area. Associated with the settlement process is the inception of agricultural and/ or vocational programs, aimed at developing refugee self-sufficiency and reducing the burden of refugee support on the local community. These programs also directly help the refugees to not acquire habits of dependence, but rather to continue in as normally productive a way of life as possible pending a durable solution to their predicament. Indeed, UNHCR programs aim deliberately at the gradual phasing-out of international support and encourage the refugee community to become fully self-reliant as soon as it is in a position to do so.

Such communities and settlements may persist for many years while the refugees wait for a durable solution in the form, most commonly, of a return to their native land. In the event of a mass return once conditions permit, UNHCR programs may be mounted to help returnees rehabilitate themselves and reassimilate into national life. Such programs are emphatically not developmental; just as relief and self-sufficiency programs help societies of asylum to cope with refugee influxes with as little interference as possible in the development process, so returnee programs enable former refugees to be reabsorbed into that process with the basic necessities—seeds, agricultural implements, and domestic utensils—they must have to start contributing once again as human beings. Such programs have been carried out in countries as diverse as Burma, Ethiopia, Angola, Zaire, and Kampuchea, and their prospect can be a valuable incentive toward the most satisfactory solution for any refugee—a safe return home.

For many refugees, however, the prospect of returning home may be remote or nonexistent, as may be the hope of third-country resettlement in (most commonly) the developed countries of North America, Europe, or Oceania. If sufficient steps toward refugees' economic self-sufficiency have taken place, the country of first asylum may be prepared to let them take the final step of total integration, even progressing ultimately to naturalization as citizens of the asylum state. Where this is so and, as is almost always the case, the country of first asylum is a poor one, the problem of refugee integration usually cannot be solved by self-sufficiency programs alone, but requires a wider development-oriented approach aimed at the inception of schemes for the benefit of refugees and nationals alike. Such schemes typically will form part of regional economic development in major refugee-affected areas. They represent a bridge between relief and development and are certainly a major departure from the much more narrow, traditional approach.

As has been indicated earlier, UNHCR programs are directed specifically at refugees and do not have the character of country programs aimed at the development of one or another economic sector within society as a whole. But a growing school of thought advocates that UNHCR can and should contribute to the refugee-related aspects of development schemes, provided that these relate directly to a durable solution for the refugees concerned. UNHCR can also act as a catalyst among other appropriate agencies whose task is to specialize in economic development but for whom refugees are not a central preoccupation. UNHCR can take the initiative in encouraging such agencies to undertake programs that, by adopting an integrated approach to development within an area, will benefit refugees and nationals alike. Even now, we are really only beginning to explore these directions, but it is already possible to forecast that they will represent a major sphere of cooperation between UNHCR, developmental agencies, and governments over the years to come.

Most of what has been said above related directly to the relief and subsequently to the assimilation or voluntary repatriation of large-scale influxes of rural refugees. It is by no means as clear what assistance measures should—or, indeed, can—be taken when the influx is of urban dwellers who, instead of congregating in groups that can be settled on the land or housed in camps, infiltrate the towns and become merely an element in a larger-scale process of rural/urban drift. Some may find employment in the formal or informal sectors, depending on local legislation and job opportunity, while others have to be supported in the form of direct subsistence grants. Some lose any separate identity and merge into the urban mass, unsupported and eventually unknown. Many are a continuing burden on the development of the receiving state, but how best to assist them other than through education, vocational training, and identification (where possible) of employment openings is not always clear.

Finally, we may mention another largely unresearched area, the impact of a major outflow of refugees on the country of origin. The character of the exodus may represent a large-scale movement of simple, rural folk whose departure may temporarily relieve an overstrained, overgrazed, or over-cultivated environment, for mass exoduses are often precipitated by economic pressures in addition to political factors. But where the movement is significantly of middle-class urban origin, it may well constitute a major brain-drain of skilled manpower over a relatively short period of time. This has certainly been true of much of the exodus from Indochina, particularly during the years 1975 to 1979, when the proportion of doctors, nurses, teachers, and other professionals among refugees was high. It is impossible to quantify the adverse impact of population movements of this kind on the development process in their countries of origin, but it must be great. In the long run, no one gains from the involuntary shifts of population that refugee movements represent, and the interests of development would be best served everywhere if their root causes could be removed.

Ecological Impacts of Mass Movement

The balance of this essay summarizes a report prepared by the Special Support Unit of UNHCR on the ecological impacts of refugee migration. The ecological system of an area is the result of a complex relationship between land (geology, topography, climate, soils, water, vegetation), land use, habitation, and the socioeconomic-political context. Modifications to one or more of these factors may induce an imbalance of the whole system, which sooner or later results in the establishment of a new system. The kind and degree of disturbance of the ecological balance and the resulting new ecosystems depend on two factors: (a) the fragility of the existing system, which is highly related to natural conditions of the land such as climate, topography, soil, and vegetation; and b) the kind and degree of interference in the existing system.

Modification of ecosystem factors can be controlled or uncontrolled. If a modification of one or more factors is carried out to serve a special goal (for instance, land clearance for crop cultivation or land leveling for irrigation), and if this modification is based on sound planning, taking into account the impact on environmental conditions, the newly established ecosystem is not necessarily inferior to the old one. The development of the new system can in this case be called a controlled development. But, if an abrupt and unplanned change takes place, this may lead to serious, uncontrolled imbalancing with an impact on the whole system, both in the directly affected area and beyond. The mass movement of refugees is a good example of a situation where the impact on the ecology is not fully under control, because the emergency character of the movement does not allow for proper planning of the new habitat.

The ecological impact of mass movement can be well illustrated by the cases of Somalia, Pakistan, and the Sudan, where hundreds of thousands of refugees arrived within a short timespan. These three countries are all situated in arid and semiarid zones, where the ecological balance is extremely fragile. The impact of the refugee influx on the environment in these countries, leading to a process of desertification, stems mainly from the use of wood for the construction of huts or for fuel, and from agricultural overuse of the land, which results in soil depletion.

Somalia

During the period 1978 to 1980, an estimated 700,000 Ethiopian refugees settled in Somalia, in thirty-five camps concentrated in four regions: the Northwest, Hiran, Gedo, and Lower Shebelli. Food, water, health care, sanitation, and educational facilities are provided by the government with the assistance of UNHCR and voluntary agencies. The main concern in the selection of camp sites was the availability of water and the presence of agricultural land, and therefore sites near perennial river courses were used wherever possible.

Estimates of rural wood consumption in Somalia indicate that the wood requirement for a family of five for hut construction is 2.4 m^3, and for cooking is 1 m^3 per head per year. Assuming that the wood consumption of refugees would be modest, say half the normal consumption, a camp of four thousand refugees would consume approximately 10,000 m^3 of wood for hut construction and 20,000 m^3 of wood a year for cooking. The standing volume in the savanna-type woodlands of Somalia is estimated to be about 50 m^3 per hectare, which implies that the average refugee camp would deplete 600 hectares of land in the first year of its establishment and 400 hectares every year thereafter. In and around refugee camps, entire settlements have been completely cleared of all trees and shrubs, and the destruction of the surrounding woody vegetation progresses at a rate that confirms the above estimates. The inhabitants of three- or four-year-old camps have to walk for several hours to find trees and shrubs to cut. The presence of grazing livestock in the vicinity of the camps inhibits natural regeneration of the woodland and hampers reafforestation programs. The susceptibility of the land to wind and water erosion increases dramatically, as is clearly demonstrated by frequent sandstorms and by rills and gullies on the soil surface. Enormous quantities of soil are transported, resulting in sand dune formation and siltation of rivers, which increases risk of flooding. Soil fertility of the cleared and eroded land declines to a level that inhibits natural regeneration of vegetation and makes the land completely unsuitable for agricultural use.

If no measures are taken to stop land degradation, this process will accelerate and lead sooner or later to a state of emergency. The Somali government and UNHCR are very much aware of the problem, and programs are under way to diminish the process of land degradation and to restore the damage already done. These programs include reafforestation, controlled woodcutting, controlled cattle grazing, and introduction of alternative source of fuel and energy-saving cooking methods.

Pakistan

In Pakistan the impact of the large refugee influx from Afghanistan is best illustrated by the situation in the North West Frontier Province (NWFP), where by mid-1982 more than 2 million Afghan refugees were already registered, bringing with them approximately 1 million head of livestock. Refugees are settled in villages and receive much the same type of assistance from the government and UNHCR as in the case in Somalia.

The NWFP is endowed with relatively large areas of natural forest—the province is practically the only supplier of production timber to the whole of Pakistan. The impact of the refugee population on the environment is similar to the one in Somalia: deforestation and overgrazing cause bare land susceptible to wind and water erosion. Moreover, the magnitude of the problem is greater because of the larger number of refugees, the quantity of wood required (wood is also used for heating purposes), and the number of livestock. Damage done to scrubland, forests, and grazing lands in the vicinity of refugee villages is already clearly visible. Programs have also been initiated in Pakistan to stop land degradation and to restore the damage already done. These programs include afforestation and the distribution of oil, cooking stoves, and kerosene to relieve pressure on the bushlands. New projects for the introduction of more fuel-economic designs of cooking stoves are being planned.

Sudan

Since 1965, refugees from Zaire, Ethiopia, Uganda, and Chad have been arriving in the Sudan, which is now host to more than 600,000 refugees. The bulk of the refugees (440,000) are settled in eastern Sudan in the major cities and towns, along the Ethiopian border, and in twenty-two organized settlements in rural areas. In southern Sudan, Ugandan refugees are settled in some thirty agricultural settlements. The object of the settlements is to make refugees self-sufficient, primarily in their food needs. To this end, land allocated to each refugee family for farming in eastern Sudan is 10 feddan; in southern Sudan, 2–4 feddan. Soils in eastern Sudan are fertile, cracking, heavy clays; in southern Sudan, however, soils are less fertile, ferralitic soils. A plot of 2–4 feddan in southern Sudan cannot produce enough food to cover the needs of one family, so the farmers try to increase their production by intensification with no fallow period for soil regeneration. Consequently soil fertility declines drastically after the first two years of cultivation. In eastern Sudan this problem is not as acute, because larger family plots allow for fallowing, and the more fertile soils permit a shorter fallow period. A solution to the problem of soil depletion by overuse in southern Sudan would be the allocation of more land to each family. Access to land is, however, restricted by leasing arrangements with local chiefs.

The problems of soil depletion by overuse is a general problem in Africa in areas where the pressure of the population on the land is becoming too high. In areas where the ecological balance is fragile and the mass movement of refugees is likely to have a pronounced impact on the ecological system, the impact can and must be reduced by timely and adequate measures of control.

3

Determinants of International Refugee Policy: A Comparative Study of UNHCR Material Assistance to Refugees in Africa, 1963–1981

Shelly Pitterman

The challenges of managing and resolving the numerous refugee situations around the world today confront different international actors: governments, international organizations, voluntary agencies, the host populations, and of course the refugees themselves. A challenge also faces scholars, who have conscientiously endeavored to research and recommend.

Social science inquiries into social change and rural economy among refugees in Africa are made only rarely across time and space. Few authors have used basic case study/historical research as a foundation for more in-depth comparative study. Holborn's (1975) chronology of the institutional development of UNHCR and its assistance activities around the world is notable for its breadth, but proposes no explicit analytical framework for evaluating either the quality or impact of refugee aid. Betts (1966a, 1980), in contrast, wrote a series of comparative case studies concerning the orientation and adequacy of assistance to spontaneously settled refugees. Among the dominant concerns of Chambers's research on the administration of international assistance to rural refugees in Africa (1975, 1976c, 1979) are the costs and benefits of organized and spontaneous rural settlements.

An important reason for the lack of comparative refugee research is official sympathy for the contention that, because a host of factors distinguish all refugee situations, policy planning and comparative research are unlikely to be fruitful. Insofar as international policy is indeed responsive to refugee needs, this diversity should often generate considerable variations in the levels and types of assistance made available to African refugees by UNHCR.

This essay will explain the variations and identify the determinants of international assistance to refugees in Africa. Such an inquiry is warranted in light of the controversy concerning the extent to which refugee assistance is "humanitarian" or "politicized." Some critics argue that international assistance is directly influenced by the national interests of powerful donor states. One official of the UNHCR Secretariat, reflecting a not uncommon point of view, claimed that the organization is merely a "tool of U.S. foreign policy."

More abstractly, analysts disagree over the extent of "politicization" within the context of international organizations and over the reasons why states are more or less likely to intervene in the policy processes of those organizations. We hypothesize that government influence over resource allocation in UNHCR varies among recipient and donor states, and over time. Addressing this empirical issue will improve our understanding of the decision rules guiding the determination of refugee policy and will illuminate power relations within UNHCR.

Trends in UNHCR Assistance

The UNHCR is mandated to protect refugees and to assist governments and operational agencies to provide durable solutions to refugee problems, that is, to catalyze and coordinate efforts to assist them materially. While they are treated as conceptually distinct, the protection and assistance functions are inseparable insofar as the practicalities of an organized international response are concerned.

The protection of refugees is UNHCR's unique function; no other international agency is empowered with the binding authority to elicit government cooperation with the international covenants or to rebuke governments, however diplomatically, for betraying the word or spirit of these laws. Still, almost all of the money spent by the UNHCR is for material assistance. Its purpose is to guarantee for refugees the basic economic security and opportunity that laws alone cannot.

The level of international aid for refugees has changed dramatically, yet only UNHCR's African and Asian obligations constitute noteworthy proportions of the total pie, as shown in Figure 3.1. Since 1973, Asia has received, on average, more than a third of all monies, although the levels fluctuate between 20 percent in 1977 and 69 percent in 1979. African countries have received in proportion more UNHCR assistance than other regional groupings: in every year from 1967 through 1973, Africa received more than half of all international aid. The distribution within Africa is somewhat concentrated: six states each receive more than 10 percent of all funds assigned to the region. The largest recipients recently have been Somalia, Zaire, Cameroon, Angola, and Sudan.

Refugee policy in Africa, more than in the other regions, is characterized by a history of diversity. This facilitates empirical comparisons over time and across countries, the methodology used here. Only Africa has received

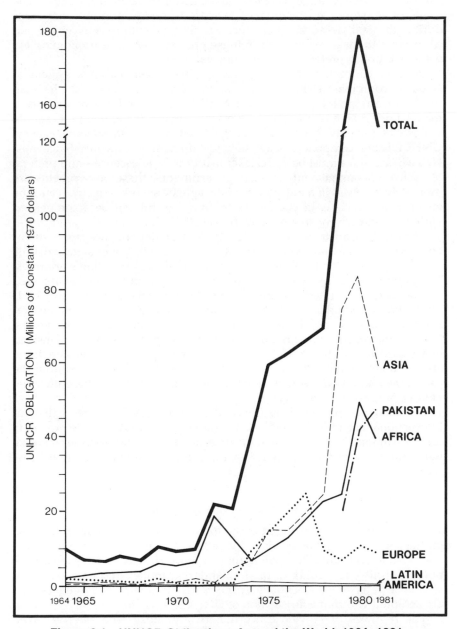

Figure 3.1   UNHCR Obligations Around the World, 1964–1981

uniformly high proportions of organized international assistance since the early 1960s, when thousands of Rwandans fled into neighboring states. The levels of assistance to Africa have increased greatly by global standards during the last decades. The larger number of countries receiving aid contributes to the diversity of the refugee problem, since the economic well-being and policy preferences of African states vary.

Policies, conceived of as the "striving by states within a system to actualize competing claims and demands" (Gordenker 1971:152), have an impact on the policy processes of UNHCR that should not be underestimated a priori simply because the work of UNHCR is defined in its statute as being of an "entirely non-political character." As an international agency, UNHCR is one component of a system still dominated by states. Since most UNHCR activities must be undertaken with the acquiescence—and preferably active encouragement—of state governments, these governments are intimately involved in many phases of the agency's work. "In any event, the government remains in charge and nothing useful can be accomplished without its consent or cooperation" (UNHCR 1965a).

The most distinctive feature of UNHCR is its dependence upon voluntary, as opposed to assessed, contributions. The major donor states are thus in a strategic position to influence the setting of the organization's priorities. The proportion of UNHCR's total budget coming from the pool of assessed payments to the United Nations was less than 3 percent in 1980 and 1981. Elmandjra argues that the U.N.'s reliance on voluntary contributions reflects the weakening of the concept of "collective responsibility." He writes: "The reinforcement of the trend in favor of voluntary contributions instead of assessed contributions has introduced a highly political dimension in the area of international economic and social cooperation, and has reduced the role of the majority of member states in the policy decisions which affect the volume of these activities" (1973:218).

A framework proposed by Cox and Jacobson (1975) suggests that, in international agencies dependent on voluntary contributions, the prospects for governmental intervention in the determination of aid priorities increase when the work of the agency is salient, and as resource constraints grow more severe.

A Model of Determinants

Two sets of factors are included in the model depicted in Figure 3.2. Those on the left side shape the needs of the refugees in asylum; on the right side are variables reflecting the politicizing, nonhumanitarian determinants of policy outputs. According to the humanitarian model, resource allocation should be determined essentially by the needs of the included refugees who are accepted within the jurisdiction of UNHCR.

The refugees of specific concern here are those who have received international assistance. Some do not actually qualify for refugee status in strict legal terms; the UNHCR, through its "good offices" in response to requests from the UN's Secretary General and the General Assembly, has

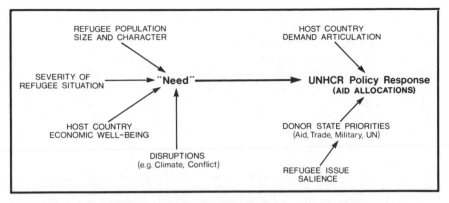

Figure 3.2   A Model of Determinants of International Assistance to Refugees

assisted displaced persons and returnees. In Africa in particular, the wide dispersion of refugees within countries of asylum has led to regional approaches to assistance, which necessarily involve host populations as well.

The competing model argues that political factors have greater weight when refugee policy is important to decision-makers in donor states. Alternative hypotheses are (a) that American policy priorities are critical determinants of resource allocation because the U.S. is the principle donor and (b) that the major donors in any given year, having "power of the purse," will guide resource allocation.

Factors concerning the refugees, the hosts, and the severity of the refugee situation are integrated within this model. A broad distinction is generally made between urban and rural refugees. The former are typically educated, young, and politically mobilized, although not necessarily employable given the pressing economic conditions in most African cities.

The vast majority of refugees in Africa and much of the Third World come from and flee to rural areas. Several considerations, such as desire to repatriate, factors of age and sex, or ethnic bonds with the host community, influence the operational aspects of the more broadly conceived policy response, three of which are common for rural refugees: spontaneous settlement, organized settlement, and maintenance aid.

The refugee needs to which UNHCR must respond are also defined to some extent by those of the host communities. It is a principle of refugee policy adminstration that aid to refugees should not raise their standards of living beyond the host communities' standards, to prevent resentments and conflicts between the two groups. The hospitality of African hosts has been widely acknowledged, and few cases have been documented of open conflict or of forced repatriation of refugees. Influxes of great magnitude have been accommodated swiftly, often at considerable expense to states already managing shaky economies, at best. African states are not uniformly poor, however, nor were the changes in economic achievement experienced over the last two decades. Therefore, the economic welfare of the host state influences the severity of need.

The recency and timing of the migration influence the needs of the refugees. Timing is especially relevant with regard to rural refugees, whose economic status depends critically upon the weather. The coincidence of refugee influxes with planting and harvest seasons can constrain policy choices. For example, even though plans for implementing and financing settlements for Zairan refugees in Tanzania were incomplete, the Executive Committee was warned that "the execution of the plan would be considerably delayed and even in some respects jeopardized if [its] decision was taken only at the autumn session" (UNHCR 1966). Although comparative data for change in the relative size of the refugee population are lacking, this particular variable will help to assess the impact of severity on resource allocation.

Nonhumanitarian factors also theoretically influence the mobilization of resources. The charge that refugee assistance is "politicized" most commonly refers to the influence that the major donor states, especially the U.S., have in setting agency priorities. This influence would be most directly manifested by the provision of more aid to politically sympathetic states.

Refugee migrations are politically sensitive issues. Acknowledging refugee status may involve implicit criticism of the political order in friendly states; it would be therefore logical to encourage the refugees to repatriate as soon as possible. Disproportionately generous assistance to friendly states would encourage regime maintenance by easing the hardships incurred by the host countries, perhaps by generating some infrastructural development, and even by increasing foreign exchange.

Assistance priorities can also be politicized by host states which are able to articulate demands for assistance effectively. Potential aid recipients can increase their attractiveness if management capabilities are cultivated and civil servants are skilled and well connected in the aid-giving establishments. Gordenker (1971) suggests that countries proficient in securing economic and technical assistance will over time improve their own administrative structures, which will enable them to become more influential in decision-making. Similarly, in refugee assistance, states already receiving U.N. aid and and those which are members of the Executive Committee are presumably in an advantageous position to push their demands.

Some argue that, since international organizations must operate within a nation/state-dominated system, their work is always largely politicized. Cox and Jacobson, referring to the 1960s, write: "the ultimate control of the powerful states was always there, even though it was seldom asserted directly. International organizations could provide only the services that governments would accept, and the levels were determined by a few of the most powerful states" (1975:433–34). We explore here the contention that the exertion of state influence is not static over time, but rather is related to the importance of an agency's primary activities to the powerful states.

Refugee policy is now politically important in the U.S. and Europe. This is primarily attributable to the dramatic increase in refugee demands placed upon the international community precisely at a time when donor states are suffering unfavorable changes in their economies. Also, the massive exodus of refugees from Indochina to North America, Europe, and Australia in the late 1970s brought home—in the most literal sense—the existence of refugees for the first time since World War II. Certainly, there were important refugee problems in the Third World in the intervening period, such as the tragic wars in Bangladesh, Cyprus, and Sudan; but none had the direct, tangible impacts of the Indochinese "boat people" resettling in Western communities.

The following hypotheses will be tested in subsequent sections:

1. Countries with larger refugee populations, especially urban-dominated ones, will receive more assistance.
2. As the severity of the refugee situation worsens, more assistance will be made available.
3. Countries which receive higher proportions of America's trade with Africa are likely to get disproportionately more UNHCR aid.
4. Countries which tend to agree with the U.S. in the General Assembly are likely to receive more aid, and those which disagree will get less aid.
5. Countries which receive a larger proportion of America's grant aid commitment will get relatively more aid from UNHCR.
6. Countries which receive larger proportions of American and NATO—as compared to Soviet and Warsaw Pact—military assistance to Africa are likely to get relatively more aid.
7. Countries in a strategic position to influence aid bureaucracies, either as members of the Executive Committee or as larger recipients of multilateral U.N. aid, will receive more UNHCR material assistance.
8. Nonhumanitarian considerations will act as increasingly important determinants of UNHCR allocation decisions over time.

The Need for Multivariate Analysis

The most straightforward approach to addressing a research problem is to analyze the variance of the means among groups. For example, during the years in which the size of the refugee population changes significantly, per capita levels of assistance also rise to accommodate new influxes or to assist in the often-expensive process of voluntary repatriation. As one would expect, the assistance made available per capita to countries also changes significantly, according to the size of their urban refugee population. The individual costs of maintenance are higher for urban refugees not only because of the higher costs of living in cities, but also because of the kinds of assistance the primarily young and educated refugees need. Counseling services and supplementary aid, for example, are more expensive on a per capita basis than the common forms of material assistance for rural refugees.

The data presented in Table 3.1 indicate that there is no appreciable difference between the average per capita levels of UNHCR aid allocated to

Table 3.1   Univariate Analysis of Variance of Means

Total population:	Average aid per refugee — $40.77		
	Number of cases — (280)		
Percent urban population:	Low	Medium	High
	$9.18	$34.39	$104.67
	(102)	(116)	(62)
Primary military aid source:	USSR/Pact	None	USA/NATO
	$20.78	$93.88	$24.41
	(97)	(71)	(112)
Proporation of U.S.-Africa trade:	Low	Medium	High
	$64.03	$28.15	$20.26
	(111)	(112)	(57)
Proportion of U.S. aid grants:	Low	Medium	High
	$60.27	$26.62	$19.02
	(127)	(112)	(41)
Severity of change in refugee population:	No Change	1%–50%	50%+
	$34.56	$21.80	$81.65
	(69)	(136)	(74)

Note: Numbers within parentheses indicate number of cases.

countries which depend on American and NATO, versus Soviet and War-saw Pact, military aid. In fact, countries which receive no military aid from either bloc receive far higher levels of UNHCR aid per refugee. The figures for mean differences among countries distinguished by their aid and trade linkages with the U.S. also do not empirically support the notion that aid from UNHCR is at all politically motivated.

Without sufficient controls, an analytical procedure provides very incon-clusive results. It can take only so many factors into account and also fails to examine the more dynamic linkages among variables. Nevertheless, these kinds of comparisons are frequently cited in the literature, and during public debates, to highlight what are considered apparent inequities in the distribution of resources among refugee groups, countries, and even conti-nents. At a recent meeting of the UNHCR Executive Committee, one African delegation lobbying for increased allocations to Africa took the unusual course of submitting, as evidence, budget-based statistics using differences in mean per capita expenditures.

The analysis of variance of means conducted here among theoretically significant groups does not confirm that political linkages with the U.S. generate inequalities in the distribution of UNHCR's resources. Instead, the reason that any one grouping of countries receives uniquely high per capita allocations might be that this group includes countries with high urban refugee populations. To account for this interaction effect, we will generate averages based on a further breakdown of countries according to this variable.

The breakdown for military aid and trade volume presented in Table 3.2 underlines this point. Sixty-two percent and 80 percent of the highest per capita categories of military aid and trade volume, respectively, have urban refugee populations. A characteristic interaction between the presence of urban refugees and the other independent variables results in distorting effects.

The problem of interpretation essentially remains because, once we have controlled for urban refugee population, a valid test would require additional controls for the size of the refugee population, the severity of the refugee situation, and the economic well-being of the host country. The time dimension also should be considered. In recent years the importance of refugee policy to the major donors, especially the U.S., has increased, and we therefore anticipate increased intervention in the allocation process.

Accordingly, multiple regression procedures will be used from now on to discern the strength and direction of the relationships among the hypothesized determinants and UNHCR aid commitments. An important method-

---

Table 3.2   Bivariate Analysis of Variance of Means

Total population	Average aid per refugee — $40.77		
	Number of cases — (280)		

Primary military aid source			
Percent urban	USSR/Pact	None	USA/NATO
None	$7.42	$12.03	$10.26
	(50)	(18)	(34)
Moderate	$62.16	$46.18	$16.72
	(14)	(48)	(54)
High	$23.23	$180.13	$66.02
	(8)	(24)	(30)

Proportion of U.S.–Africa trade			
	Low	Medium	High
None	$10.92	$7.27	$10.00
	(22)	(38)	(42)
Moderate	$43.11	$20.12	$0
	(72)	(44)	(0)
High	$221.36	$66.38	$48.99
	(17)	(30)	(15)

Proportion of U.S. aid grants			
None	$9.76	$15.30	$1.73
	(49)	(27)	(26)
Moderate	$52.84	$18.32	$0
	(54)	(62)	(0)
High	$180.13	$62.25	$48.09
	(24)	(23)	(15)

Note: Numbers within parentheses indicate number of cases.

ological point concerns the pooling of cross-sectional and longitudinal data. This research seeks generalizable inference about allocation decisions based on some 20 years of experience in twenty-four African countries. Although many countries have benefited from refugee aid, the duration of such aid varies considerably. The uneven country and year sample sizes documented in Table 3.3 preclude the application of common statistical techniques, such as regression, to otherwise straightforward cross-sectional or longitudinal designs. Significance levels would be depressed and the number of independent variables that could be included in any model for a given country or year would be limited by the few degrees of freedom.

The alternative is to pool the data and, in so doing, treat each country-year case as a data point independent of all others. The reality of the

Table 3.3   Length of UNHCR Aid (in years) and States Receiving Aid Each Year

State	Number of years	State	Number of years
Burundi	19	Lesotho	12
Central African Republic	18	Sudan	15
Egypt	15	Gabon	7
Kenya	16	Angola	7
Rwanda	10	Mozambique	7
Senegal	18	Algeria	7
Tanzania	19	Ghana	7
Uganda	19	Somalia	4
Zaire	19	Djibouti	5
Zambia	16	Swaziland	7
Botswana	14	Cameroon	4
Ethiopia	15	Morocco	7

Total number of cases: 287

States Receiving Aid Each Year of Study

Year	Number of states	Year	Number of states
1963	4	1973	14
1964	6	1974	14
1965	7	1975	21
1966	8	1976	21
1967	11	1977	22
1968	12	1978	24
1969	11	1979	24
1970	13	1980	24
1971	13	1981	24
1972	14		

Total number of Cases: 287

situation is that each data point is likely to be related to other years for a given country, or perhaps other countries for a given year (or both). Certain measures must therefore be taken to guard against bias, since the statistics otherwise derived from a pooled design are well-nigh impossible to interpret. The overall fit of the regression line—unless very high—might be underestimated, given systematically wide variations in aid among countries and over time. The approach adopted here is decomposition of the pool according to theoretically interesting criteria. By using ordinal measures for key variables, we can estimate the fit of the model for subgroups of the pooled set. This is conceptually similar to the analysis of variance approach introduced earlier, but allows for including multiple variables, investigating the interactions among them, and examining residuals.

The last factor is critically important for pooled data analysis, since we are confronted with the possibility of inefficient estimates due to variations among countries or systematic trends over time. Expenditure levels are indeed skewed: the residual output for equations using raw constant-dollar values for UNHCR expenditures show that countries with the highest values are most likely to have high residuals. This problem of heteroscedascity was resolved by using the logarithmic transformations of the UNHCR aid and refugee population variables.

Bargaining and Persistent Interests Approaches

Initial results indicate that humanitarian considerations are far and away the most significant and powerful determinants of aid. These results are informative because they show that decisions about expenditures to particular countries are largely based on information concerning the refugee situation during the year in question. On the other hand, annual fluctuations in the levels of economic, political, and military interactions with the U.S. have a very negligible effect on UNHCR expenditure levels.

An alternative model hypothesizes that, to the extent that nonhumanitarian considerations influence policy, they do so based on more persistent interests and images. While there might be fluctuations in a country's aid or trade interactions with a dominant donor country, bilateral foreign policy interests are more persistent over time. Whether this relationship is dependent, interdependent, or simply "sympathetic" is of secondary importance to the fact that the donor, the U.S. in this case, has stakes in promoting the well-being of the recipient country.

A decline in trade volume, for instance, may be due to circumstances that do not bear upon the essentially cooperative character of the foreign policy dyad. Similarly, military assistance to most countries tends to fluctuate from year to year considerably more than aid or trade relations. Arms sales and military grants are not maintained at annual base levels; rather, arms are purchased or grants are made periodically to replenish existing stocks. When there is a perceived need, large doses of military aid are transferred, and these generally decline as quickly as they rise. Still, countries getting military assistance from the major donors presumably have coinciding interests that endure such periodic fluctuations. Dramatic shifts in a country's market preference, such as occurred in Egypt, Ethiopia, and Somalia, are unusual. African states receiving military assistance most often get it from NATO countries. This reflects the continuing role of the former colonial powers in Africa, which until recently has been spared competitive superpower interest.

In lieu of a formula relying on discrete annual fluctuations in nonhumanitarian factors to explain decision-making priorities, we computed each country's average performance over the period during which it received refugee aid. Annual data for the humanitarian considerations are still used. Just because a country on average provides asylum to a large number of refugees, it does not follow that in any given year, perhaps after a mass repatriation, it will continue to receive large doses of multilateral refugee aid. If decision-makers are sensitive to the needs of the refugees, they must consider the size and character of the refugee population during the year for which authorizations are being made.

The same argument can be made for the extent of change in a country's refugee population. We have thus far used ordinal measures of change; in about half the cases considered here there was no change in the refugee population from one year to the next; the other half was divided between cases experiencing moderate change and those with very severe changes in the size of the refugee population. Thus, beginning in 1969 and over the course of three consecutive years, Rwanda was included first in the no change, then in the severe, and finally in the moderate change category.

The humanitarian model hypothesizes that the severity of change in a given year guides assistance decisions. Indeed, the data indicate that decision-makers give more consideration to the severity of the refugee situation during the year in question than to a country's overall experience, past or predicted, of change. Country officers may often foresee impending changes in the refugee situation and budget accordingly. Appropriations are proposed for the following year, but these are almost always radically revised based on the current needs estimates. Explicit projections, when they are made, are usually optimistic ones concerning improved resettlement opportunities or voluntary repatriation prospects.

On the other hand, the relative size of the urban population does not fluctuate dramatically from year to year. The southern African countries consistently provide asylum to an overwhelmingly urban refugee population. Those countries which had no urban refugees in 1970 and 1979 usually had none before or after. We have been forced to treat this variable less sensitively than warranted because of missing data for certain countries (notably Uganda), especially for 1977 and 1978. Urban population figures are usually very rough estimates anyway; using an ordinal measure does get at orders of magnitude. That the data are missing (as opposed to the conclusion that there are no urban refugees) is based on two considerations: first, that in previous years urban refugees were reported to be receiving aid; and second, that allocations for individual assistance, which is very often targeted to urban populations, are included in the budgetary breakdowns for that country-year case. More sensitivity to annual fluctuations in the urban refugee situation would certainly be desirable, since per capita allocations to urban refugees are very high.

The level of overseas development assistance from U.N. organizations proves to be a consistently important determinant of UNHCR allocations. This variable has been coded in interval and ordinal terms for years as well as according to country averages. Annual fluctuations on this variable do matter, and so the interval measures will be used from now on. Since U.N. aid correlates highly with U.S. bilateral aid, the U.N. variable was included in the final step of the regression equations in order to discern its independent effects on UNHCR aid priorities. The humanitarian considerations were included in the first steps of the equations to measure their cumulative effects and to allow for an examination of interactions between the two sets of variables. This stepwise inclusion is justifiable, insofar as critics of allocation priorities usually suggest that political factors account for inequities among otherwise equally deserving host states.

The data again provide strong evidence of humanitarian factors being the more important determinants of UNHCR allocations. The explanatory power of this revised model is stronger than the earlier one. Sixty percent of the variance in UNHCR expenditure levels can be accounted for, and many of the independent variables are significant.

The more refugees a host country has, the more assistance it is likely to receive. During those years when the refugee situation changes dramatically—usually as a result of influxes, though sometimes because of large repatriations—host countries will receive considerably more aid. The economic well-being of the host country is also an important consideration: the larger a country's GDP per capita, the less aid it is likely to be allocated once the size and severity of the refugee situation are taken into account. The significance of the urban variable is depressed somewhat when GDP per capita is included, reflecting an interaction effect between the two variables. The strength of GDP per capita is very much dependent on the inclusion or exclusion of other variables. Its independent effects are probably negligible because, but for a few oil exporters, the African countries studied here have, by and large, low GDP per capita levels by international standards.

The character of the refugee population, distinguished here in terms of urban versus rural, is a less important determinant than are the magnitude and severity of the refugee situation. To the extent that the size of the urban population affects allocation levels, those countries whose refugee populations are predominately urban get somewhat more aid. This is consistent with what we know about UNHCR response to the urban refugee problem. The surprising weakness of the urban variable can be attributed to interactions with other variables, especially GDP per capita and trade volume. More significant, however, is the fact that this model covers all years. The urban refugee problem actually became salient in the early 1970s; priorities were subsequently revised and more attention was given to those countries with smaller, but nonetheless pressing, urban refugee problems. These periodic shifts are discernible in data presented later.

Nonhumanitarian determinants prove to be more important when the measures are formulated on the basis of average interactions with the U.S. The bargaining approach is less appropriate in this regard than a persistent interests approach. Nevertheless, the nonhumanitarian variables are considerably less significant than the humanitarian ones.

The moderately significant effect on UNHCR assistance levels of U.S. bilateral aid to a country is completely obliterated when the U.N. aid variable is included. This important finding suggests that however high the correspondence between these two variables, multilateral assistance priorities are much more significant determinants of where UNHCR decides to spend its money than are America's bilateral assistance priorities.

While the UNHCR acts as the focal point for material assistance to refugees in Africa, it is not the only agency active there. As already stated, other international agencies have long been involved in material assistance, and interagency coordination has been a policy concern from the very beginning. In the late 1970s the coordination issue became more problematic and critical as the number of active agencies, especially in Thailand and Somalia, grew by leaps and bounds. Problems both of bureaucracy and of program arose as the tension between development- and relief-oriented activities became more pronounced. The significance of the U.N. aid variable reflects the multiagency character of the effort to assist refugees and satisfy long-term development needs.

An alternative interpretation points to bureaucratic politics. Countries which receive large doses of aid are presumably not only needy but also competent in influencing the bureaucracies to begin and to continue providing aid. Preliminary analyses showed that whether a country sits on the Executive Committee of UNHCR has no bearing on its receiving aid from UNHCR, after the humanitarian considerations have been taken into account. Members of the Executive Committee are presumably in a strategic position effectively to influence the agency's bureaucracy; yet it appears that, if the goal is to increase aid levels, membership does not guarantee its achievement. On the other hand, a reasonable hypothesis is that larger multilateral aid recipients are likely to get more UNHCR aid, because these countries are able to lobby effectively for complementary increases in the commitments of the various agencies involved in development and refugee assistance.

The results also show that those countries which disagree with the U.S. in the United Nations are likely to get less UNHCR aid, although the variation on this factor is not consistent enough for us to dismiss stochastic influence or chance. The proportion of American trade a country receives is a very weak determinant of UNHCR policy, perhaps because Africa as a whole, and each of the countries individually (except for oil exporters), is not a salient trade partner.

The only variable, apart from U.N. aid, with a significant effect consistent with the political model, is the measure of bilateral aid received from America. Official bilateral aid is not always distributed strictly in conformity with need; foreign policy interests can be served by stabilization programs and by general assistance, to improve the image and economic performance of a preferred regime. Similarly, aid is sometimes withheld from needy countries to promote policy changes or regime changes more consistent with donor policy interests. Yet the nonhumanitarian model would have been more definitively endorsed had the generally more critical policy interactions—military and trade relations—proven significant.

It is noteworthy that not all the effects of the nonhumanitarian variables operate in the expected direction. Those countries which tend to agree with the U.S. in the General Assembly receive significantly less aid from UNHCR once the severity and character of the refugee situation are accounted for. Similarly, countries which get either no military aid or more military aid from the U.S. and NATO tend to receive far less aid than those countries which receive larger proportions of Soviet and Warsaw Pact military aid. These results appear to contradict the argument that UNHCR priorities conform to the foreign policy interests of the major donors. More detailed consideration of these relationships will have to be taken, since they are, at least at first glance, contrary to expectations. The effects of the military variables, while negative, are not consistently significant. Nevertheless, should U.N. voting records matter at all, then agreement—consistent with both the bargaining and persistent interests approaches—could be expected to correlate positively with assistance.

Explaining UNHCR Aid in the 1970s

An important problem arises with this last formulation of the model. In calculating the averages for aid, trade, military assistance, and U.N. voting, we use data points from all the years during which a country has received UNHCR aid. On this basis, an overall score is derived for the importance of a country's interactions with the U.S. on key foreign policy dimensions. But in using information from 1981 to help explain variations in assistance levels in 1971, we are using the future to help predict the past.

This is not a wholly unreasonable strategy, for there is a high degree of stability in the relative rankings of country interactions with the U.S. over time. The simple correlations for volume of American trade from one five-year period to the next is in the .9 range. The level of U.S. aid received in the 1960s per country correlates at .94 with that received in the early 1970s. Evidently a policy shift in bilateral aid distributions occurred during the Carter administration, since the correlation between the early and late 1970s is only .36. Egypt received much higher amounts of U.S. aid in the late 1970s, as friendlier relations between the two countries helped make the Camp David agreement possible. Aid levels dropped sharply to Ethiopia and Zaire, probably reflecting the Carter administration's policy response to human rights violations there.

Military relations are also rather stable over time. Sixteen of the countries studied here experienced no changes in their primary arms sources during the period UNHCR aid was made available, as shown in Table 3.4. Sudan's greater reliance on the West, and Tanzania's on the East, were stable throughout the 1970s. Among the remaining cases, only three shifts in allegiance had important implications, especially from a geopolitical perspective, on American policy in Africa: Egypt, Ethiopia, and Somalia.

Table 3.4   Stability in Dominant Source of Military Assistance

	1963-1971	1972-1976	1977-1981
Algeria	—	0	0
Angola	—	0	0
Botswana	1	1	1
Burundi	1	1	1
Cameroon	—	—	2
Central African Republic	1	1	1
Djibouti	—	—	1
Egypt	0	0	2
Ethiopia	2	2	0
Gabon	—	2	2
Ghana	—	2	1
Kenya	2	2	2
Lesotho	1	1	1
Morocco	—	2	2
Mozambique	—	0	0
Rwanda	—	1	1
Senegal	2	2	2
Somalia	—	0	2
Sudan	0	2	2
Swaziland	—	1	1
Tanzania	1	0	0
Uganda	2	0	2
Zaire	2	2	2
Zambia	2	2	0

0 = USSR/Warsaw Pact
1 = No military transfers
2 = USA/NATO
— = No UNHCR aid

Stability in the nonhumanitarian policy areas, while a compelling consideration, ignores our assumption that policy-makers—UNHCR Secretariat officials or U.S. State Department officials theoretically bent on lobbying for particular country allocations—can forecast how compatible donor-recipient foreign policy interactions will be. To deal with this problem, three periods have been defined; data from the earlier period will be used to predict performance in the following one. This dramatically reduces the number of cases, and so statistical significance will be somewhat less rigorously judged.

The three periods were defined on a theoretically important basis. One reason suggested earlier for expecting more governmental intervention in UNHCR decision-making process is an increase in the agency's budget, especially as resources for international aid grew scarcer. The first marked increase in the level of UNHCR obligations to Africa is dated to the Sudanese repatriation program and increased sensitivity to the needs of urban refugees throughout Africa. This period coincided with economic pressures resulting from the organized rise in the price of oil. African expenditures continued to rise through the mid-1970s, although not at the unprecedented rates found in Asia which, following the unification of Vietnam, was forced to cope with emergency needs and overseas resettlement of millions of refugees from Southeast Asia. By this time, refugee affairs generally had attracted considerable attention in the U.S., not only because of the human tragedy involved but because of the sometimes negative events associated with mass resettlement there.

In the late 1970s, expenditures in Africa rose very sharply, primarily in response to the presence of hundreds of thousands of refugees in Somalia. Coincidentally, dramatic political changes and refugee crises in northeast Africa during this period made UNHCR's activities especially interesting to U.S. policy-makers for the first time. Strains upon the world economy and more widespread concern over sometimes intractable refugee situations compounded the importance of refugee policy issues. In the late 1970s, as refugees from Indochina continued to flee to the U.S., novel challenges arose with the migration of many Cubans, Haitians, and Salvadoran refugees. Legislative attention was increasingly paid to the dilemmas of refugee policy and to the amendment of existing immigration statutes.

This brief discussion is meant to provide a theoretical context to the decision to divide the overall time frame into three periods. Table 3.5 provides data on trends over the last twenty years in UNHCR expenditures, the size of the refugee population in Africa, the average levels of per capita aid, and U.S. donations to UNHCR. These data emphasize that major preconditions for increased intervention have been satisfied. Through 1971, an average of $3.6 million (in constant 1970 values) was spent at an average level of $13.40 per refugee. The material assistance made available during those years was primarily targeted for the development of viable rural settlements, once emergency needs were taken care of. The number of countries receiving UNHCR aid from 1972 on rose as aid to urban refugees, especially from southern Africa, became a higher priority. The per capita level of aid is double that of the first period.

The most dramatic changes took place after 1976. More than 60 percent of all UNHCR general operations expenditures to Africa since 1963 were spent between 1977 and 1981; much of this was concentrated during the last two

Table 3.5 Dimensions of Refugee Policy in Africa: Period Averages

	Annual expenditures (000s)	Number of refugees (000s)	Expenditures per refugee	U.S. donations (millions)	U.S. share of donations (percent)
1963–1971	$3,616.6	735.7	$13.40	$ .80	18.0
1972–1976	$5,238.8	1,079.5	$26.70	$11.67	41.2
1977–1981	$19,385.4	2,113.5	$69.60	$51.53	38.8

years. The average number of refugees doubled during the third period, and the per capita assistance level almost trebled.

Using UNHCR documentation, about 90 percent of all donations to the UNHCR voluntary funds by governments and nongovernmental organizations were tabulated. The single largest donor to UNHCR is the U.S., which has contributed an average of 30 percent of the voluntary funds since 1963. America's total contributions to UNHCR rose dramatically in the early 1970s, as did its share of all donations to UNHCR. In the last few years, the number of important donors has increased slightly, accounting for the small decline in share.

The second tier of donors consists of the European Economic Community (10.6 percent), Sweden (8.8 percent), England (7.1 percent), and Germany (7.0 percent). Scandinavia, Canada, and France donated between 4 and 5 percent, and the lowest donors are Japan (3.8 percent)—which has made large donations in the last few years—and Belgium (3.3 percent). Closer inspection reveals important changes over time in the distribution of donations and disbursements to and from the General Program and Special Operations. Between 1963 and 1971, more than three-quarters of all donations were made to the General Program. The remainder were earmarked for Special Trusts, which over the 20-year period absorbed less than 15 percent of all donations. From 1972 through 1978, more than two-thirds of all donations were made to Special Operations funds (except in 1973). Although most of this money was spent in Southeast Asia after 1975, Special Operations was the single largest source of expenditures in Africa during these years. After 1979, the General Program again became both the primary destination for donations and the source of funds in Africa, as the catch-all budget category "Multipurpose Aid" was more widely used, especially in Somalia.

At this stage of the analysis, the annual values for each humanitarian variable were again used to predict assistance during that same year. Nevertheless, the average scores for the nonhumanitarian variables from the prior period were used to test the hypothesis that the character of the foreign policy dyad influences subsequent assistance allocations.

The results indicate that humanitarian considerations are consistently the most important determinants of UNHCR priorities. Certain of the interactions with the U.S. prove to be significant determinants during the 1972 to 1976 period, providing some support for a politicization hypothesis. During the latter period, these influences should have become even more pronounced, but the results indicate quite the contrary. Humanitarian considerations remain dominant, and the influences of the trade and military assistance variables dissipate almost completely.

The formulas for allocating country budgets during these two periods differ in important respects. While the humanitarian considerations explain 52 percent of the variance in UNHCR allocations during the former period and 57 percent in the latter period, once the remaining factors are taken into account the independent effects of the humanitarian variables are substantially less significant from 1972 to 1976. This means that even among countries with comparably severe refugee situations, allocations from UN-

HCR varied considerably. Allocation decisions in the late 1970s were significantly more responsive to annual changes in the severity of any refugee situation, even though on average the extent of such change was no less in the earlier period. This might be due in part to the fact that of Africa's seven largest mass repatriation efforts, four—to Sudan (1972), Guinea-Bissau, Mozambique, and Angola (all in 1975–1976)—were mainly financed by Special Operations funds.

Countries with large urban refugee populations tended to receive much larger allocations than those with smaller or no urban refugee populations, which is to be expected given the heightened sensitivity to the problems of urban refugees during the early 1970s. At the same time, programs initially designed to provide educational opportunities and supplementary funds to urban refugees, primarily students from southern Africa, evolved into more comprehensive efforts as urban migrations intensified. While urban refugees in southern Africa continued to receive large infusions of assistance, more attention was being paid in the late 1970s to the problems in Sudan, Senegal, and Djibouti, where the urban refugee population constituted relatively smaller proportions of the total refugee population.

Another noteworthy difference concerns the cumulative and independent effects of the nonhumanitarian variables. During the earlier period, the military and trade variables had the significant, positive effects hypothesized by those who contend that the UNHCR allocation process is politicized. Among countries with comparable refugee situations, therefore, those which from 1963 to 1971 were more important trade partners tended to get disproportionately more aid. Non-alignment in terms of military assistance guaranteed the highest allocation levels, although those countries which received larger proportions of American and NATO military aid still got more UNHCR money than Soviet and Warsaw Pact allies.

The effects of the U.N. aid variable differ dramatically from one period to the next and appear to reflect aspects of the alternative approaches to foreign policy of the Nixon, Ford, and Carter administrations. From 1972 to 1976, the inclusion of the multilateral aid variable had pronounced indirect effects on the other nonhumanitarian factors. It has an independent influence that, although very weak, is likely attributable to the needs of the recipients, and is thus consistent with the humanitarian model of determinants. Yet the possible impacts of bureaucratic factors should not be dismissed lightly.

A more important finding is that U.N. assistance during this period reinforced America's conventional foreign interests. The trade and military variables become more significant and positive. Disagreement in the General Assembly had a more significant, negative effect; and the outcome of agreement in the U.N., previously likely to be less UNHCR aid, was now an even toss-up. The significance of the bilateral aid variable was also enhanced, and its negative effect might have reflected the American preference to avoid duplication in the assistance effort.

During the late 1970s, nonhumanitarian considerations should have played an increasingly important role in determining allocation priorities, since this period was characterized by successively higher UNHCR expendi-

tures, higher donations, and generally more salient foreign policy considerations. The Carter administration, however, prided itself on being responsive to humanitarian needs and sensitive to human rights abuse. Did this
policy principle end up outweighing the importance of foreign policy?

The data on the final period, which primarily covers Carter's years,
indicate that very different policy calculations were being made. It has
already been noted that humanitarian considerations here were much more
important determinants of UNHCR allocations priorities than in the earlier
period. The nonhumanitarian factors, on the other hand, were considerably
less significant and indeed had effects that contradict the expectations of the
politicized model. Unlike the earlier period, countries who were military
and trade partners of the U.S. tended to receive less UNHCR aid.

The stepwise presentation of the results allows for discussion of the
interactions among the variables. Earlier results suggest that aid during the
Kissinger years was an indirect means of promoting American foreign
policy interests in terms of balance of power and trade. In contrast,
multilateral aid was less subtly employed by the Carter administration, and
the interests served were evidently redefined.

United Nations aid has a strong partial correlation when only humanitarian determinants are in the equation; however, when the variable is included in the final step, it is not significant. Any independent effects of
multilateral aid are thus almost completely obliterated by the other nonhumanitarian variables. American bilateral aid priorities continue to have a
moderately significant, positive effect even after multilateral aid is taken into
account. This suggests that while American geopolitical and trade interests
were no longer translated into UNHCR policies, America's bilateral aid
interests were. Bilateral aid was perceived during the Carter years as a
benevolent means of upholding U.S. interests by enhancing welfare in the
Third World and thus promoting stable, sympathetic regimes.

How countries voted in the U.N. made quite a difference upon the levels
of UNHCR aid made available. Agreement depresses the significance of the
military variables and enhances those of the aid and trade variables. All
humanitarian considerations being equal, countries with closer military
links to the U.S. and NATO in the early 1970s tended to receive less aid
during the late 1970s. Agreement with the U.S. in the General Assembly,
however, tends to offset this negative effect, as it does also with regard to
those countries who were not military partners of either bloc. On the other
hand, agreement with the U.S. was likely to increase UNHCR allocations
even for those countries who were not important trade partners.

Conclusions

This essay argues for more comparative research by scholars interested in
analyzing and improving the refugee policy process. The broader questions
addressed here concern power in policy formulation. The methodological
approach exploits an existing, largely untapped data resource. In light of
Africa's distinctiveness as a continent with a history of diverse refugee
situations—and responses to them—research across countries and over time

is appropriate. The design adopted here aims to tap generalizable trends among African recipients of UNHCR aid, regardless of the size of the country authorizations, taking into account variables reflecting the expectations of two competing decision-making models. The working assumption, subject to disconfirmation, is that there are commonalities and trends; that the sympathy for the "uniqueness thesis" mentioned at the outset of this essay is misguided. Comparisons will help us to understand better the policy process and perhaps modify it so that policies can even better serve the refugees.

Diverse influences reflecting bureaucratic, national, and other special interests work against purely humanitarian motivations for public policy. This research does not prove that humanitarian factors matter and nonhumanitarian factors do not. Rather, the design adopted here allows us to identify the independent and interacting effects of both sets of variables. Thus, models purporting to describe foreign policy-making generally and refugee aid in particular can be tested and qualified.

Several conclusions can be drawn from the results presented here, as well as questions requiring further elaboration. Factors endogenous to the refugee situation are the most important determinants of UNHCR aid. Variations in the size, character, and severity of the refugee situation instigate changes in allocation priorities among states and over time. These factors taken together parsimoniously explain more than half of the variance in UNHCR aid levels.

The results prove that American foreign policy interests do influence UNHCR policy outputs, but they do so in different ways at different times. It would be a mistake to argue that UNHCR is simply a tool of American foreign policy. Aid is not dispensed as a reward or punishment based on a country's performance on key foreign policy dimensions in a given year. Rather, nonhumanitarian influences reflect themselves in terms of more persistent interests.

The relatively weak performance of the nonhumanitarian variables when all years are included indicates that the influence of America's interests is not transcendent. The foreign policy principles and priorities of the ruling administration matter. During the early 1970s, balance-of-power and trade considerations were effectively translated into UNHCR priorities. During the late 1970s, a country's standing as a military or trade partner was less critical than its bilateral aid linkages and performance in the U.N. During both periods, the nonhumanitarian factors taken together explain roughly equal portions of the variance. But they do so in sufficiently divergent ways to render inaccurate the hypothesis that, as an issue's importance increases, political intervention by major donors will determine UNHCR policy outputs.

In conclusion, subsequent elaboration of this model will need to address the following three issues, among others. Thus far only interactions with the U.S. have been included. Although the single largest donor to UNHCR, the U.S. is not the only major contributor. European interests in Africa are more established and more central to their own economic and strategic priorities than are America's. Although U.S. and European interests are often compatible, it is still possible that for particular years or countries, other donors will have independent effects on UNHCR resource allocations. This might lend support to a "power of the purse" interpretation of UNHCR decision-making.

We have also concentrated so far on explaining variations in total country allocations from the General Program. In later stages, expenditures (including Special Operations) for particular kinds of programs will be analyzed. A problem with the use of total expenditures and total refugee population is that, although all refugees in a given country are entitled to the protection of UNHCR, not all benefit directly from UNHCR assistance. Perhaps some are self-sufficient; often cooperative agreements are made with other international and voluntary agencies actively engaged in assisting refugees in Africa. Consequently, per capita levels might be depressed artificially and, while the data indicate otherwise, the refugees may be benefiting equitably from UNHCR. Information on the numbers of direct beneficiaries of specific kinds of material assistance is available, albeit incomplete.

The third, more general consideration is that, before the budget is designed and allocations are finally authorized, UNHCR policy-making process is constrained by a variety of constitutional, technical, and indeed political factors. Refugee situations that demand multilateral attention and are within UNHCR's jurisdiction are identified by the High Commissioner with the advice and consent of UNHCR administration and the Executive Committee. In practice the perceived interests of individuals or groups of states, both donor and recipient, constrain policy choices early on as the UNHCR struggles to accommodate state interests.

It is sometimes the case, then, that the numbers of people officially recognized as refugees is manipulated to minimize or intensify international attention. Budgetary decisions based on these estimates ostensibly may be consistent with more humanitarian principles. While verifiable distortions are infrequent in Africa, there have indeed been examples of, in generous terms, the rounding-off of estimates of refugee population size. These generate quiet, unofficial disturbances within the refugee policy community. In all fairness, errors in estimation are quite reasonable given the often difficult prevailing circumstances. Still, the point is that until reliable data gathering procedures are realized, there is no choice but to use official estimates. It is possible, therefore, that the evidence presented here underestimates the indirect effects of constraints on information and policy set by states in the pre-budgetary stages on later stages of the decision-making process.

Acknowledgments

The author would like to thank the Institute for the Study of World Politics for making it possible for him to conduct fieldwork in Geneva, Switzerland, during 1981 and 1982. Northwestern University's Program of African Studies has provided invaluable support throughout all stages of this research. Many individuals in Geneva and Evanston contributed as informants, discussants, and friends.

4

Refugees with No Country of Asylum: Strategies for Third-Country Resettlement

Goran Melander

The problem of refugees with no country of asylum can be illustrated by three examples. An Eritrean being interrogated by the Ethiopian police for political reasons managed to escape from his country of origin. He went directly to Italy and asked for asylum. He thought that his reasons were strong and expected no problem in being granted asylum. The Italian authorities refused him asylum, however, despite the fact that the Italian Constitution prescribes the granting of asylum to political refugees. He came from Africa; Italy still upholds geographical limitations to the 1951 Refugee Convention and the 1967 Refugee Protocol. Our refugee was not discouraged; he traveled farther north and entered Switzerland. Once again his application for asylum was rejected: a prerequisite for asylum in Switzerland is that application be made within twenty days of the escape from the country of origin, and he had now been en route for longer than that. He had to go on, and entered the Federal Republic of Germany. He went to the "Aliens Police," only to find that there was no possibility of his remaining in that country. They felt his fear of persecution was not well founded: so far he had not been persecuted, and he had voluntarily left Ethopia. His case was not even referred to federal authorities responsible for refugee status determination. He decided to seek asylum in Sweden, but made the mistake of traveling to Sweden via Denmark. The Swedish Immigration Board decided that our refugee, who had by now spent a few weeks in detention, should be returned to Denmark, the nordic state he had first entered. The Swedish authorities could invoke a provision in the Nordic Convention concerning the Waiver of Passport Control at Intra-Nordic Frontiers.

Denmark also rejected his application for asylum, invoking a bilateral agreement with Germany to return him to that country. As he realized that asylum in Germany was out of question, he continued immediately on to the Netherlands. The Dutch authorities accepted that he was a bona fide refugee, but could find no reason why the Netherlands should grant him asylum. He had, after all, escaped several months earlier from his country of origin and had passed through a number of other countries, each of which could have granted him asylum. The Netherlands could not be considered the country of first asylum, and his having been refused a residence permit in a number of countries was no reason for him to be allowed to remain there.

In Belgium his application for asylum was also rejected, since he had been en route too long. Not even in France was his application taken seriously. As Italy, according to the French authorities, should be considered the country of first asylum, he was returned to that country. Here he did not even bother to make a new application, but continued to Switzerland, and then to Germany, Austria, and Sweden. He may still be floating around Europe, constantly afraid of discovery and forced to continue his odyssey. He is a refugee in orbit, and he is not a unique case (Melander 1978). There are thousands of orbiting refugees in western Europe, each without a country of asylum.

The fate of the boat people is well known. Thousands of refugees left their country in small, overcrowded, unseaworthy boats. Eventually allowed temporary entry into countries, they were placed in camps to await transfer to another state (Wain 1981). They are also refugees with no country of asylum.

An asylum seeker from Namibia, who escaped to one of the frontline states, was immediately detained at the request of a liberation movement. An attempt was made to obtain habeas corpus, but before the High Court could give judgment, he was transferred by force to detention in another frontline state. He was freed from this country three years later, after placement had been obtained for him outside Africa. He was also a refugee without a country of asylum.

The Concept of Asylum

Before we look into the various aspects of the problem of refugees with no country of asylum, it may be useful to analyze the concept of the term "asylum." Sometimes asylum is equated with protection from being returned to the country of origin. This is the narrowest interpretation and, if correct, is applicable in all cases heretofore referred to. Asylum can also mean that a refugee be allowed to remain provisionally within a certain state. He will not be returned to his country of origin, but he will not be allowed to resettle in the second country. Sometimes this situation is referred to as temporary asylum or temporary refuge.

Sometimes a person may be formally recognized as a refugee under the 1951 U.N. Convention, but granted no form of residence permit. This is the case in Italy, for instance, where an asylum seeker can be granted refugee status and be given a Convention travel document on the clear prerequisite that he migrate to another state.

A fourth concept of asylum is that the refugee be granted a residence permit or resettlement possibilities within the country. This does not necessarily imply that he will be granted refugee status: he will merely be put on equal footing with ordinary immigrants. This seems to be the normal procedure in the U.S., Australia, and other countries accepting refugees from countries of first asylum. It should be noted that these refugees are, from a legal point of view, entitled to protection in accordance with the 1951 U.N. Convention.

A final alternative is that of asylum seekers who are formally recognized as refugees and granted residence permits or other permission to resettle in a country. To date this is the normal procedure in Western Europe and in a number of African states. The issuing of a Convention travel document is also equal to a formal recognition of Convention refugee status.

According to present refugee law, only the two last-mentioned alternatives—that the applicant should have at least been granted a residence permit or permission to resettle in a state—apply to asylum. Another problem related to refugees with no country of asylum is the concept of "right to asylum": the entitlement of an asylum seeker to asylum, and consequently the obligation of a country to grant it. The term "asylum" in international law, however, means only the right for a state to grant asylum; there is no corresponding right of an individual to be granted asylum. This traditional view is still upheld, even though the national legislation of some countries grants to individuals a right to asylum.

In Africa the situation has been improved by the inclusion in the 1969 OAU Refugee Convention of an obligation for contracting states to "use their best endeavours consistent with their respective legislation to receive refugees and to secure the settlement of those refugees who, for well-founded reasons, are unable or unwilling to return to their country of origin or nationality." This is certainly far from granting an individual right to asylum. But although such a right still belongs in the moral sphere, some progress has been made in this direction. This does not mean that an asylum seeker is totally unprotected. Since World War II the so-called principle of *non-refoulement* has developed: a prohibition against returning a person to any country, including his own, in which he fears persecution because of race, religion, or political opinion. Today this principle forms part of general international law, which means that it is binding upon states independent of their being parties to the various refugee conventions. Consequently, an asylum seeker has no right to be granted asylum, but must not be returned to a country where he fears persecution. Accordingly, if he is not granted asylum, he will find himself in a kind of legal vacuum: a refugee without a country of asylum.

Any citizen is entitled to protection by the government of his country of origin. A person who has been granted asylum is entitled to protection by the country of asylum; the office of the UNHCR functions as a kind of implementing organ in this respect. But who protects refugees with no country of asylum? The refugee problem is international in scope and character, and international cooperation, international solidarity, and sharing of burdens are necessary (Melander 1981). To fill the legal vacuum referred to above, the international community has the responsibility to protect refugees and to try to solve refugee problems.

Solutions to Refugee Problems

A refugee can be handled in one of three ways: by voluntary repatriation, by integration into the country of refuge, and by resettlement in a third country. Today the solution of voluntary repatriation is considered the most desirable. For instance, the 1969 OAU Refugee Convention contains a special article related to the problem of voluntary repatriation, and a number of resolutions have been adopted by the OAU Council of Ministers to this respect.

The choice between the other two alternatives can be problematic. It is a fact that refugee migrations to third countries have taken place to a great extent during this century, but it is difficult to find common criteria making such a solution desirable. Nonetheless, attention is drawn to the following criteria decisive for third-country resettlement.

Economic factors affecting the situation in the labor market are certainly important. At present many countries apply a kind of quota system, by which they decide the number of refugees to be received. But political considerations are certainly also important. When some 200,000 individuals left Hungary to enter Austria and Yugoslavia after the 1956 uprising, Western countries competed in accepting refugees. The Hungarian refugee problem was solved in an unusually rapid way, no doubt in protest to the Soviet intervention. Fears of Soviet intervention in Poland in December 1981 furnish another example of political considerations. As a mass influx of Polish refugees was expected, preparations were made in Sweden to accept more than 100,000 of them. Had many arrived, they would have been admitted and granted resettlement opportunities in third countries. But no such exodus occurred, and the preparations in Sweden became unnecessary. Only a few asylum seekers arrived, and their application for asylum was decided on an individual basis. A few cases were even rejected and the applicant returned to Poland.

A decisive factor for third-country migration is the willingness of the country of refuge to allow refugees to be integrated. The Italian example is illustrative. In that country, asylum seekers are admitted on the clear prerequisite that they move to another state. Only in exceptional cases is asylum granted there; other cases are transferred to third countries, mostly overseas. Another example relates to Southeast Asia, where several receiving countries have clearly stated that refugees would not be allowed resettlement. The boat people, for instance, often have even been refused entry and returned to the high seas (Wain 1981:131).

Political prejudices sometimes are a hindrance for refugee migration to a third country. For instance, some years ago UNHCR found it necessary to transport refugees from Latin America to other states, but had difficulty finding countries willing to admit them. Western European countries were most reluctant to admit refugees from Latin America, in spite of the fact that Latin American countries had accepted more than a million refugees from

Europe since the end of the war. This unwillingness was often due to the political background of the refugees: they were left-wing refugees coming from right-wing dictatorships. Recently a report was published by UNHCR about the situation for refugees in the Federal Republic of Germany. According to the report, a high-ranking civil servant connected with the refugee determination procedure stated that the Federal Republic was not willing to accept refugees holding leftist views. Assumptions regarding difficulties of adjustment are sometimes used as an excuse not to accept refugees. In some Western states it is believed that African refugees have difficulties in adjusting and consequently that immigration of African refugees should be avoided.

The influence of mass media is of great importance. The situation for the boat people can serve as an example. The flow of refugees from Vietnam had already started in 1975; the affected governments and UNHCR appealed in vain to the international community. It was not until the spring of 1979, when the world press found an interest in the serious and highly dramatic situation, that governments responded. The mass media opened the doors for refugees to enter other countries.

Conclusions

It is clear that a number of factors, which ought to be irrelevant, instead are decisive when it comes to choosing between resettlement in the country of refuge and resettlement in a third state. Too often, humanitarian considerations are not taken into account. In seeking a strategy for solving the problem of third-country resettlement, the following steps might be taken:

1. The problem of "refugees in orbit" lies in the fact that there is no generally accepted definition of the term "country of first asylum," by which it is possible to decide which country should be responsible for an asylum seeker. The problem can be solved only by the adoption of an international agreement. In this respect, a ministerial committee within the Council of Europe, CAHAR, has had on its agenda for a number of years the drafting of an agreement. So far, negotiations have resulted in nothing.
2. As pointed out, there are cases where a country cannot grant asylum when the refugee is undesirable in that country for particular reasons. In many cases he will be detained in that country until UNHCR has found another state willing to admit him, a procedure that may take years. To solve this problem a kind of "emergency quota system" should be established. UNHCR can reach an agreement, at their request, with a number of countries willing to accept difficult cases. Taking into account the low numbers of such cases—probably not more than 50 to 100 individuals each year—the acceptance of such refugees would not be a heavy burden upon any state. Such a system would mean that a country, immediately upon request of UNHCR and without looking into the merits of each case, would admit the person in question.

3. Refugee migration to third countries is often based upon an annual quota system in the receiving country. Sometimes it is decided from which country migration shall take place. For instance, Sweden has had an annual quota of 1250 refugees for years, but open only for refugees from Latin America. Restrictions should be eliminated regarding the country of origin.

4. Refugee migration to third countries should be based on facts, and humanitarian considerations should be taken into greater account. In this respect UNHCR has a great responsibility as coordinator for assistance to and protection of refugees. Only the fact that a refugee has been granted asylum in a certain state should preclude him from being resettled in a third state. Those who are in most need of being moved to another country should be accepted.

5. As stated before, refugees are the responsibility of the international community. This comprises sovereign states, each one watching the other in order to keep from doing too much when it feels that the others are doing too little. On many occasions this is due to misunderstanding and misinformation. It is of great importance that reliable and sufficient information be given regarding actions taken by governments to assist and protect refugees.

Part Two

Africa

The refugee problem in Africa began on the eve of the transition from colonial to independent Africa. Anticolonial insurgency, as well as post-independence civil strife and warfare, had generated some half a million refugees by 1964, and in 1970 the number of refugees passed the 1 million mark (Aga Khan 1971). By the end of the decade, the number of refugees and displaced persons passed four 4 million (Adepoju 1982). The current total of officially recognized refugees is close to 3 million, although the intranationally displaced population may be as high as 5 million. It is clear that Africa has a major problem of refugees and displaced populations.

Given the length of time that Africa has had a refugee problem, together with the huge numbers that exist in some areas, it is not surprising that many host states have evolved realistic and commendable programs of assistance for refugees. On the other hand, some African asylum states have done little, and refugees in those countries have essentially been left to fend for themselves. Part 2 of this volume examines some of the many dimensions of Africa's refugee problem and considers the major strategies that asylum states have adopted in dealing with their refugee influxes.

The refugees who arrive in their country of initial asylum face five sets of options. These are (a) spontaneous integration into local urban or rural communities, (b) relocation to organized settlements, (c) voluntary repatriation to their country of origin, (d) resettlement to third countries of permanent asylum, or (e) retention in holding camps until one of the other options becomes available. In Africa, all of these options are utilized, albeit with greatly differing emphasis. There are even considerable differences in the type of strategies employed in accommodating refugee influxes within single countries.

Spontaneous integration, especially among rural communities, occurs widely throughout Africa, although more often than not as a result of lack of alternate government responses rather than as a direct consequence of government policy. Such integration can be reasonably successful, as in the case of Angolans in Zambia (Hansen 1979), or can place refugees into very vulnerable and insecure situations (Chambers 1979). Little research has

43

been conducted to date among such refugees. Even less is known about the difficulties experienced by spontaneously integrating urban refugees.

The creation of refugee settlement schemes has been a major thrust in African refugee policies. Most asylum states have opted for such schemes for some time, and the experience has so far been a mixture of successes and frustrations. While in concept the strategy of getting rural refugees to become self-reliant within the ambit of organized rural settlements makes sense, in practice many schemes have been ineffective because of inadequate land or water, poor planning and administration, or lack of settler cooperation (Rogge 1981). Others have been overcapitalized, so that when international assistance is withdrawn, they rapidly grind to a halt and self-reliance remains only a dream. Throughout the 1970s, and until the Horn of Africa's refugee dilemma reached its alarming scale, most international assistance for African refugees was directed to supporting the development of organized rural settlements. More recently, most aid has been diverted to emergency assistance. Notwithstanding some of the problems encountered by this type of solution, many settlement schemes have achieved their objective of having refugees become self-reliant, and some have even been able to integrate the schemes successfully into broader national rural development strategies (Rogge 1986).

The third option—repatriation—is widely favored throughout Africa by both refugees and governments of countries of asylum. When anticolonial wars were the major cause of refugee exodus, repatriation of refugees was likely once independence was won. Also, most refugees generated by civil war have generally repatriated at the conclusion of those wars. Contemporary political developments, however, make repatriation an option that is becoming less likely. Moreover, the specter of forcible repatriation *(refoulement)* is a growing one in several areas as governments become increasingly reluctant hosts to refugees, or as the scale of refugee influx is seen to have serious detrimental impacts upon host states. While most African states are signatories of the U.N. Convention and Protocol and thus have agreed to the principal of *non-refoulement,* recent practices in at least two areas— Uganda and Djibouti—suggest that repatriation may not always be completely voluntary (Crisp 1984). Much more research is needed regarding the many dimensions of this aspect of Africa's refugee problem.

Until the passage of the U.S. Refugee Act in 1980, little or no third-country resettlement of African refugees had occurred. Unlike in Southeast Asia, where resettlement is the principal thrust of refugee policies, African refugees have been essentially seen as Africa's problem. Since 1981, a resettlement quota of 3,000 African refugees was established by the U.S.; Canada followed with a smaller quota a year later. The majority of African refugees accepted for resettlement have originated from the Horn of Africa. Although a number of the essays in this volume consider the resettlement of refugees, none focuses on African refugees, even though they are beginning to become noticeable minorities in several cities in the United States and Canada. Research is needed to determine how well African refugees adjust after resettlement, and how their problems of adjustment compare to refugees resettled from other Third World areas.

The least desirable option open to asylum states—to keep refugees in holding camps—is, unfortunately, being increasingly adopted. Refugees from Western Sahara have been in holding camps in Algeria for more than a decade, and most Ogaden Somalis continue to be maintained in holding camps where little or no prospects exist for generating even minimal levels of self-reliance. While the Palestinian experience has provided some insights into the impact of long-term camp confinement, more must be understood about the specific long-term implications of holding camp "solutions" for African refugees.

The ten essays in this section attempt to cover some of the issues introduced here. Barry Stein and Mabel Smythe look at the need for assistance to African asylum states, and whether such assistance should be only relief-oriented or whether assistance should have discreet development objectives. Stein examines the issues of "burden sharing" and "durable solutions" in the context of the second International Conference on Assistance to Refugees in Africa (ICARA II), while Smythe optimistically points to the potential for development that is inherent in the refugee crisis itself. This theme is also taken up by Hermann Schoenmeier, who argues that policy implementation should take the refugee's psychological conditions into consideration. He suggests that the apathy of refugees in camps reflects their continually being denied the opportunity to prove themselves.

Two short case studies of specific refugee situations follow. John Kabera describes Uganda's long experience with refugees from three of its neighboring states and briefly evaluates the short-term and long-term strategies that have been adopted. Alan Mabin examines, in the context of South Africa, a much-neglected aspect of involuntary migration studies, the problem of intranational displacees who now number in the thousands within South Africa.

The two essays by John Rogge and Charles Gasarasi focus upon organized rural settlements for refugees. Rogge evaluates the concept of self-sufficiency in the context of some of the rural settlements in eastern Sudan, and suggests that too many long-term commitments are planned into many schemes, making it difficult, if not impossible, for them to ever achieve full self-sufficiency. Gasarasi argues that a major contributory factor to the success of Tanzania's resettlement program has been the close cooperation and burden-sharing inherent in the tripartite agreement between the government of Tanzania, the UNHCR, and the Lutheran World Federation/ Tanganyika Christian Refugee Service.

The problem of urban refugees is a relatively recent one, yet, in a number of asylum states, urban-domiciled refugees are beginning to be as numerous, and perhaps more problematic, than their rural counterparts. Sudan has an exceptionally large urban refugee population, and the essays by Ahmed Karadawi and Eyob Goitom examine some of the dimensions of Sudan's urban refugees. Although Sudanese refugee policy is geared to maintaining its refugees in rural areas, many migrate to the major cities where their status is technically illegal. Karadawi shows that their motivations for migrating to the cities are diverse, and that there is little institutional response to their needs. Goitom evaluates the adjustment processes refugees undergo after arriving in Khartoum and demonstrates that in the face of adversity, refugees create their own systems of mutual support and communal solidarity.

The final essay focuses upon repatriation, another much-neglected aspect of refugee studies. Joshua Akol examines the problems and prospects that face repatriating refugees on their return after lengthy exiles. His case study is of southern Sudanese returning after the Addis Ababa Agreement that ended Sudan's civil war in 1972. While repatriation is frequently touted as the ideal solution to a refugee problem, Akol shows that this is not necessarily the case, and repatriates' needs for rehabilitation and resettlement are often as great as those encountered by refugees.

5

ICARA II: Burden Sharing and Durable Solutions

Barry N. Stein

The second International Conference on Assistance to Refugees in Africa (ICARA II) took place in Geneva, Switzerland, from 9 to 11 July 1984. The purpose of the Conference as set out in paragraph 5 of the December 1982 U.N. General Assembly resolution (37/197) requesting the meeting was as follows:

5(a) to throughly review the results of ICARA I held in April 1981;

5(b) to consider providing additional international assistance to refugees and returnees in Africa for relief, rehabilitation, and resettlement; and

5(c) to consider the impact imposed on the national economies of the concerned countries and to provide assistance to strengthen their social and economic infrastructure to cope with the burden of refugees and returnees.

Further, in public meetings and statements, U.N. officials and spokesmen indicated an additional purpose of ICARA II as:

(d) to mobilize political will and statesmanship to prevent future refugee problems and towards "formulating additional assistance programmes which could lead to durable solutions", particularly voluntary repatriation and, "where this is not possible, for their permanent integration in countries of asylum" [Perez de Cuellar, 1983].

ICARA II represented progress in the evolution of international assistance to refugees after the establishment of UNHCR in the early 1950s. The requests for assistance to strengthen infrastructure under paragraph 5(c) represent a form of refugee assistance not normally given to countries of asylum in the past, and a reaching out of the refugee assistance system to agencies other than UNHCR, particularly to development agencies such as the United Nations Development Program (UNDP) and the development agencies of the principal donor nations. This essay is concerned with the background and preparations for ICARA II as well as with the many issues the conference raised regarding burden sharing and durable solutions. Burden sharing is international assistance given to a heavily burdened refugee asylum country to lighten its load. Burden sharing is usually accomplished by making contributions to the cost of refugee care or by reducing the number of refugees through resettlement programs. The three classic durable solutions to refugee problems are (a) voluntary repatriation to one's country of origin, (b) local settlement in the country of first asylum, and (c) resettlement in a third country. A durable solution means helping the refugees to become self-sufficient, and enabling them to integrate and participate fully in the social and economic life of their new country or of their homeland, if they repatriate. It means more than relief in and limbo of a refugee camp, the classic non-solution.

The second ICARA was called because the first conference, in April 1981, had been only a limited success and "fell short of the expectations of African countries" (Farah 1983). ICARA I's objectives had been to (a) focus public attention on African refugees, (b) mobilize additional resources for programs, and (c) assist hosts to cope with the extra burden place on their services and facilities.

ICARA I was relatively successful in meeting its first two objectives: it focused attention on African refugees and mobilized more than $570 million, about half of what was requested, for refugee assistance. But it fell short of its third objective, since the African countries "felt that the additional assistance required to help the countries of asylum carry the heavy burden imposed on their economies by the presence of refugees and returnees received inadequate response" (Perez de Cuellar 1983). Some felt that the contributions received were not new money as a direct response to ICARA, but "was the same assistance which has been contributed regularly by some donors" (Birido 1983). That most of the money was earmarked by the donors for specific programs rather than being generally available to all host countries was also a disappointment.

ICARA I's shortfall provided a learning experience for the preparations for ICARA II. A main difficulty with the first conference, besides the basic issue of a new form (infrastructural assistance) of refugee assistance and the question of the nature and level of burden sharing, was the short period of time—from the General Assembly call in November 1980 to the conference in April 1981—to prepare for the meeting. From this lack of preparation time arose other difficulties such as a lack of guidelines or standards for proposals, incomplete or exaggerated requests for assistance, and projects that did not focus on durable solutions and the development aspects of refugee problems.

Donor governments who had provided a great deal of assistance and yet were told it fell short of expectations felt major disappointment with ICARA I. To the donors, ICARA I's requests were unrealistic and exaggerated—old, rejected development projects that had been lying on the shelf, were dusted off and given a refugee label, and were submitted for funding. Some suspected that "some African authorities . . . view refugee assistance as a target of opportunity" (Beck 1982). Other donors indicated that they were unconvinced of the need for another conference. If ICARA II were to surpass the results of the first conference, the African governments needed to win the confidence of the donor community and to convince them to give additional assistance. This required better preparation, with realistic, convincing, and detailed requests, plus indications of the requisite political will needed to reduce refugee numbers and achieve durable solutions.

A successful conference would also require consensus on the part of donors and hosts on the rationale for additional assistance. To the African countries of asylum, ICARA II was to be a burden-sharing conference to provide assistance to strengthen their social and economic infrastructure. To the donors, however, the conference promised a chance to achieve durable solutions to prevent future refugee problems and lead to the voluntary repatriation or permanent integration of refugees. Such durable solutions would ease the burden of funding care and maintenance on the international community.

Issues

Two major issues—burden sharing and durable solutions—were thus part and parcel of ICARA II and gave the conference a two-sided nature. Host and donors had different perspectives on the need and reasons for the conference, and each had different goals to be achieved at the meeting.

The General Assembly Resolution (37/197) calling for a second conference resulted primarily from the efforts of the African countries of asylum and thus reflected their views. The Resolution emphasized the "burden imposed . . . its consequences for their development and of the heavy sacrifices," but it was virtually silent on durable solutions other than voluntary repatriation. It stressed "that any additional assistance for refugee-related projects should not be at the expense of the development needs of the countries concerned." The emphasis was on having the international community assume a greater share of the burden.

On the other hand, the Secretary-General, reflecting not only the donor's point of view but also the traditional UNHCR approach as set out in Article l of the UNHCR Statute, added an emphasis on durable solutions—particularly integration into the host society—to the preparations and agenda of ICARA II. Speaking to the African host countries the Secretary-General stated: "I hope that the necessary assistance will be forthcoming from the international community to facilitate such integration . . . that the approach to be adopted for ICARA II is to be essentially geared to accelerating the search for lasting solutions."

The issues of burden sharing and durable solutions were not exclusively connected to ICARA II, but were being discussed in several forums, including meetings of the UNHCR Executive Committee and in special meetings such as the August 1983 Meeting of Experts on Refugee Aid and Development. ICARA II was important in these discussions because it set a time limit and added an action component to the talk. In July 1984 pledges were made. Whether ICARA II advanced or hampered the process of assistance remains to be seen. Before we examine these issues in greater detail, it is useful to look at some of the background and preparations for ICARA II.

Background

At present there are approximately 2 million refugees in Africa, plus perhaps another half million internally displaced persons (DPs) who are in refugee-like situations. (Under the terms of the OAU Convention Governing the Specific Aspects of Refugee Problems in Africa, Article I.2., DPs are defined as refugees. On the other hand, the U.N. Convention relating to the Status of Refugees does not define DPs as refugees.) These numbers are subject to wide fluctuations; in the mid-1970s most authorities estimated that there were 1 million African refugees, while at the time of ICARA I in 1981, the total was closer to 4 million refugees.

Whatever the actual number of refugees in Africa, they create a severe strain and burden that aggravates already serious economic difficulties in the host countries. Most of the countries of asylum in Africa, and the source countries as well, are listed as low-income, least-developed countries by the World Bank. Their ability to cope with the extra burden of refugees is thus quite limited and was one of the prime motivations for convening a second conference.

Historically, the African countries have a highly laudable tradition of providing hospitality to refugees, but this tradition developed during an era of smaller, more tractable refugee problems. In addition, high prospects of resolution of refugee problems through repatriation were often realized. Most pre–1980 African refugees resulted from independence struggles against colonial, extra-continental domination. Not only was there considerable solidarity between hosts and such refugees, there was a great expectation of ultimate victory, independence, and repatriation.

The situation changed in the late 1970s. The number of African refugees grew exponentially, and most of these refugees came from independent African states such as Chad, Ethiopia, Angola, Uganda, and Zaire. Voluntary repatriation, and other durable solutions such as local settlement, thus became more difficult and less likely to be achieved quickly. ICARA II, like ICARA I, was confronted with the problems of "massive arrivals of refugees in low-income countries where often no durable solution is at hand" (UNHCR 1983c).

To the host countries, massive numbers and no durable solutions raise the specter of an open-ended burden. In addition, some host countries have less sympathy for and solidarity with refugees fleeing from their independent neighbors than for those fleeing from imperialism. Disturbing events in Uganda and Djibouti have raised questions about the future strength of the tradition of hospitality.

The convening of two African refugees' assistance conferences within a three-year span should be viewed against a backdrop of generalized crisis in much of Africa in the 1980s, of which refugees are only a small part.

> For most African countries, and for a majority of the African popula-
> tion, the record is grim and it is no exaggeration to talk of crisis. Slow
> overall economic growth, sluggish agriculture performance coupled
> with rapid rates of population increase, and balance-of-payments and
> fiscal crises—these are dramatic indicators of economic trouble [World
> Bank 1981].

Refugee displacements are noted only briefly by the World Bank as an obstacle to growth, and far greater emphasis is placed on other, primarily economic, factors as sources of the crisis. Refugee-related development assistance is thus unlikely to have much impact on the general fragility and crisis, but without such aid the refugee burden carried by the African hosts might be unbearable. Further, this generalized economic crisis is an important factor in the desire of the African countries to explore a broadening of the concept of burden sharing to include infrastructural assistance. When economies are so fragile, the ripple impact of a sudden extra burden may be widespread and substantial.

Preparations

An ICARA II Steering Committee was established to oversee preparations. It encompassed representatives of the Secretary-General, the Organization of African Unity (OAU), UNHCR, and UNDP. Because the objective of strengthening the infrastructure of the asylum countries involved developmental activities, UNDP has been added to the Steering Committee at the invitation of the Secretary-General.

The Steering Committee was assisted by a technical team consisting of personnel from all four agencies. Between July and October 1983 the team visited fifteen of the twenty-two countries invited, to make submissions and consult with the host governments about the refugee impact on each economy. The technical team was charged to "determine, *on a priority basis*, the humanitarian, rehabilitation, and resettlement needs of the refugees and returnees, and the assistance required by the countries concerned" (Perez de Cuellar 1983, emphasis added). The team reviewed each country's submissions—which were to be reasonable, detailed, and directly related to the refugee situations—and reported to the Steering Committee. At year's end the Steering Committee issued a comprehensive report incorporating, on a priority basis, all projects.

The additional assistance being sought was divided into two categories: first, humanitarian assistance preparations for paragraph 5(b)—relief, rehabilitation and local settlement, and durable solutions—which came under UNHCR's competence and responsibility; and second, developmental assistance preparations under paragraph 5(c)—strengthening host infrastructure—which were the responsibility of UNDP and also the U.N. Office for Special Political Questions. In this preparatory period, there was more concern with the second part of the ICARA II package, the UNDP's refugee-related development assistance. At ICARA I much of the money pledged had gone to UNHCR programs. Indeed, one of the complaints regarding the first conference was that the pledges consisted mostly of old money supporting ongoing programs.

On the other hand, UNDP's role and the package of development assistance projects were included in ICARA II due to a feeling that humanitarian aid could move refugees only part-way to a new life; that development agencies should be involved so refugee assistance could be integrated into development assistance. Even so, UNDP was a reluctant, even uninterested, participant. The agency believed that its plate was already full of worthy and indispensable projects on behalf of the world's needy, and it noted that in recent years it had experienced an "unparalleled downturn" in resources, with projections of funding shortfalls of almost 30 percent in the near future. Although UNDP has a long history of working in cooperation with UNHCR on some refugee projects, its mandate does not include refugees, so such assistance requires the assent or request of a host country. Thus far, UNDP has been hesitant about putting effort into an innovative approach whose funding is uncertain.

Guidelines

UNHCR and the Under-Secretary-General for Special Political Questions issued guidelines for the development of projects for their respective areas. UNHCR's guidelines to its Field Office (UNHCR 1983a) emphasized activities aimed at achieving or consolidating durable solutions or the inclusion of "income-generating or other self-reliance activities" in those "care-and-maintenance situations for which a clearly defined durable solution is not readily apparent." Proposals were to be "imaginative and creative," while avoiding "unrealistic or impracticable" schemes that raise expectations prematurely or that exceed "the absorptive capacity of implementing bodies." About half the allocations would be directed toward achieving durable solutions. "Additional needs . . . will be submitted to ICARA II as Special Programmes" (UNHCR 1983b).

The Secretary-General's guidelines (U.N. 1983) for paragraph 5(c)—Guidelines for Country Submissions on the Impact of Refugee Problems on National Economies and Possible Development Assistance required to alleviate these Problems—focused on the need to convince donor communities of the nature and extent of the burden and to a lesser extent on the formulation of refugee-related development assistance projects. UNDP had a leading and pivotal role, in liaison with the government, to prepare submissions to prove the need for innovative burden sharing by demonstrating the impact of refugees on host economies, infrastructure, and society. The main areas of burden to be described were:

• infrastructural development—increment in capital expenditures to care for additional needs in education, hospitals, transportation, water, and environment;

- food and basic needs—direct assistance in the form of food, clothing, shelter, medicine, and other supplies;
- budgetary support—direct costs for general upkeep of refugees, capital development, and maintenance of infrastructure in refugee, areas;
- administrative and technical support—of personnel assigned exclusively to refugee activities;
- agricultural and industrial resources—allocations of land;
- employment of refugees and their impact on the labor situation;
- balance of payments—use of foreign exchange for imports for refugees offset by donor loans, credits, or grants; and
- cost of living—adverse impact of refugees on the indigenous population in areas of refugee concentration.

The guidelines also requested a "clear statement of the Government's policy regarding refugees or returnees, and particularly, where relevant, prospects for as well as obstacles to a lasting solution." Last, the guidelines requested that refugee related development projects be presented "within the framework of the National Development Plan" and "directly justified as ameliorating the problems . . . or facilitating longer-term solutions."

Early reports from the ICARA II technical team, after visits to eight countries, indicated that many host countries were unprepared or unable to design 5(c) projects. The major problem was that the host countries could not demonstrate a burden or indicate how to relieve it with infrastructural projects, even with the assistance of the technical team. It is important to recognize that these difficulties of design and proof were not a sign that no burden existed. Rather, these difficulties reflected the innovative nature of the ICARA II approach and of the information and projects that were requested. Further, the difficulties reflected weaknesses in skills, organization, and data collection in many very poor countries. The World Bank (1981) report on the economic crisis in Africa had some relevant observations.

> The ability to generate good projects . . . is essential for the efficient use of investment funds. With few exceptions, this capacity is weak in Africa . . . inability to bring together available data for technical and economic analysis . . . much more important is the sparse knowledge base. Successful project preparation often requires location-specific data generated over a fairly long period of time. Good projects cannot be developed quickly (in 3 to 9 months) by visiting teams of specialists.

The ICARA II technical team spent approximately one week in each country.

Burden Sharing

In asking the international community to assist with social and economic infrastructure costs associated with refugees, the African host countries expanded the principle of burden sharing beyond its previous meaning. In the past, burden sharing had mostly meant the taking for resettlement of "excessive" numbers of refugees from an asylum country, or contributing, in cash or kind, to the direct costs of caring for refugees. As recently as the 1979 conference on the Situation of Refugees in Africa, held in Arusha, Tanzania, this view of burden sharing was paramount. Indeed, at Arusha the emphasis had been on burden sharing by other African states rather than by the international community: "determining the particular burdens facing countries of first asylum in Africa and the extent to which such burdens could be shared within the framework of African solidarity" (UNHCR 1979). Similarly, in a follow up of the Arusha meeting, the OAU Council of Ministers urged "all OAU Member States to consider ways and means of translating the principle of *burden-sharing* into action by *inter alia*, accepting a number of refugees into their countries" (Eriksson, Melander, and Nobel 1981).

Since Arusha, in the call for ICARA I and in other forums, a broader sense of burden sharing had been advanced. Requests for infrastructural assistance now represent a concern with the indirect costs of the refugee burden that include the burden on the host's economy and administrative capacity, the diversion of scarce resources from development projects, the impact upon local populations and upon the cost of living, and other indirect burdens. Two factors motivate African countries of asylum in their request for an expansion of the principle of burden sharing. First is the fact that they are among the poorest countries in the world; thus any new burden has an impact on their fragile economies and on their development plans. The current economic crisis only exacerbates this situation. Second is a spreading awareness on the part of the African host countries that the burden and impact of refugees is not fully understood. The 1979 Arusha meeting was a turning point:

> it is estimated that well over 60% of all rural refugees are spontane- ously settled and that the assistance provided to them is often nil or negligible. . . . often interpreted to mean spontaneous integration, which in turn gives the impression that all is well . . . This belief is convenient because it absolves governments and aid-giving agencies from finding out and doing something. It creates acute conditions both for the refugees themselves and for the poorer people among their hosts [who eked] out precarious and marginal existence [UNHCR 1979].

Together these two factors create a powerful argument for more equitable assistance and burden sharing.

The African host countries have traditionally been generous in their provision of asylum, but under conditions of poverty, where they cannot meet the basic needs of their own people, they do not want their generosity to jeopardize their own societies and development efforts. The Refugee Aid and Development Report (UNHCR 1983c) concluded: "The present situa- tion of most of the world's refugees in low-income countries calls for a re- examination of existing policies, a more equitable sharing of the burden between refugee-affected countries and the international community, and new approaches to the solution of their problems."

Just as they are often unwanted in their homelands, many refugees find that in their sanctuary no one wants them or wants to be responsible for them. Many host countries view refugees as an unwanted and thankless burden. The country of asylum tries to shift responsibility for the refugees' welfare to the international community. Asylum is provided, but it is temporary and to a degree contingent on international financial and material support. The host is not responsible for the refugees, but is instead a luckless neighbor fulfilling its international responsibilities.

The view of the U.N. and the donors, on the other hand, is that the host is responsible but deserves international assistance. Refugee assistance funds are almost entirely voluntary contributions from governments of the Western democracies, given because humanitarian refugee assistance occupies a special place in the international scheme of things. This voluntary character of international refugee assistance represents a denial of responsibility and obligation to share the burden. Fortunately, reality is not quite so harsh, and generous assistance has been forthcoming, but in a framework that leaves the primary burden and responsibility on the host.

It is galling to the host governments that they must convince the donors of their need and burden through reasonable and credible requests. In addition, the host governments may be viewed with suspicion by some donors. "A particularly regrettable development has been a tendency . . . to exaggerate refugee numbers and to claim needs of expensive assistance programs where few refugees exist" (Beck 1982). To the countries of asylum this distrust smacks of an evasion of responsibility and a blame-the-victim approach. The host acutely feels the burden but cannot always detail and quantify it. In the early stages of a mass refugee influx there is often considerable international pressure on the country of asylum to respond positively and generously. This pressure, however, usually does not include commitments of international support for the duration of the problem. Many countries of asylum fear that generous assistance given at a time of emergency, drama, and tragedy may diminish in the future when the burden is less visible but just as heavy.

The donor countries do not reject the principle of expanded burden sharing, but they are concerned with two aspects of the principle: (a) additionality—refugee assistance must be additional ("not be at the expense of") to the normal development assistance given to a host country; and (b) a lack of direct connection between expanded assistance and durable solutions other than voluntary repatriation. Additionality is considered essential by the host countries and other less developed countries, who feel that in view of their extremely limited resources it is not possible for them to reallocate resources from their own people to the refugees. The countries of asylum feel it is unfair to ask them to go into debt, to share resources, or to accept less development funds in order to benefit refugees. The donors, on the other hand, feel that additionality "has little real meaning since there is only one money purse from which both activities—development and humanitarian assistance—are currently funded" (Ross 1983). The donors believe the assistance would be used better by pooling all monies into programs that seek durable solutions, within the host's National Development Plan, from the outset of a refugee situation. The donors also fear that open-ended burden sharing might make the host's burden tolerable and thus impede, or not encourage, the achievement of solutions. "Unless determined efforts are made in this direction of lasting and durable solutions, refugee programmes are in danger of becoming an end in themselves rather than a means to an end" (Farah 1983). Durable solutions, therefore, were part and parcel of ICARA II discussions on burden sharing.

Durable Solutions

The international community is deeply disturbed because "there has now been, for a long while . . . a comparative slowdown in the provision of durable solutions" (Hartling 1983) and a striking shift in the proportions of assistance monies spent on refugee relief and those spent on durable solutions. In 1970, 83 percent of UNHCR's $5.87 million General Programme budget went to durable solutions. Since then, emergency relief, care, and maintenance programs have been established for hundreds of thousands, even millions, of refugees. In 1980 the percentage spent on durable solutions declined to 33.5 percent of the budget and in 1981 to 26 percent. Improvement since then has raised the durable solution percentage to 38.6 percent for 1986. Adding to the concerns of the donors is the fact that at its 1980 peak, these percentages were for a UNHCR budget that had increased nearly a hundredfold over a decade to approximately $500 million. The overall decline in durable solutions is a problem for all continents, and the African record is better than others; in 1984 "more than half of the target submitted for Africa [was] for durable solutions" (UNHCR 1983b).

To the donors, larger refugee assistance budgets and fewer durable solutions raise the specter of an endless drain of resources, of expanded burden sharing that goes on and on with no solutions in sight. UNHCR's Director of International Protection warned at the 1983 Executive Committee meeting of the danger of an "implacable hardening of attitudes . . . and more draconian measures [because] governments and public opinion have, as they never had before, the impression that there is no end to the problem" (Moussalli 1983).

Of the three durable solutions—voluntary repatriation, local settlement, and third country resettlement—only the first two are realistic alternatives for most African refugees. Governments hold the key to achieving durable solutions, which are political solutions requiring political will and statesmanship. "If the political mechanisms do not work, the humanitarian machinery may gradually become paralyzed" (ibid.).

The African host governments have made clear their preferences regarding durable solutions; they strongly prefer voluntary repatriation and are averse to local integration. Unfortunately, the political impediments to voluntary repatriation are not easily, if ever, removed, and for most African refugee situations, particularly the larger ones, repatriation is unlikely or is far off. Many hosts, hoping for voluntary repatriation and rejecting local settlement, keep refugees in temporary care or limited self-reliance situations for long periods of time, thereby increasing assistance costs and the human toll on the refugees. President Nyerere of Tanzania offered an alternative at the 1979 Arusha conference:

It is impossible to deal with these refugees as if all that is required is temporary relief from distress. They must as quickly as possible be given a means of producing or earning their own livelihood. The only practical way of proceeding is to work as if they are likely to be permanent inhabitants of their host state. Investment to meet their needs will never be wasted in the growing African economies even if these refugees should all in the future return to the place from whence they came [UNHCR 1979].

In this view, promoting self-sufficiency rather than indefinite dependence does not necessarily imply a commitment to a solution other than voluntary repatriation.

Temporary asylum with no durable solution in sight is the lot of many refugees. Many countries of asylum, despite dim prospects of eventual repatriation, are hesitant to treat refugees as permanent inhabitants. Choosing to integrate refugees is a far more complex, vital, and difficult decision than simply weighing the costs and burden placed on the international community. Host hesitancy toward integration derives from many factors, including

- political support for the refugees' cause—particularly independence, secession, or autonomy—which would be weakened by a solution other than repatriation;
- the size of the refugee group, which in absolute or relative terms may be too large for the host to absorb;
- concern that local settlement would produce a pull factor and cause more refugees to flee to the host;
- fears of being accused of favoring refugees over needy nationals, or fears that the refugees' economic skills might lead them into competition with nationals; unwillingness or inability to make a financial contribution—by sharing development assistance from their own scarce resources, or by going into debt—for the sake of refugees;
- concerns about the refugees' ethnic, social, cultural, or political background, which might make them unacceptable to the rulers or to segments of the population;
- developmental concerns that the refugees are in the wrong place with the wrong needs and may skew development plans and priorities; and
- experience with refugee assistance for integration that establishes services and infrastructure but does not cover the long-term recurrent costs of maintenance.

When no durable solution is in sight, other alternatives for refugee assistance may be chosen. The two main possibilities are keeping the refugees in camps with care and maintenance assistance, or assisting refugees to become self-supporting through work or cultivation programs. The second alternative has two main difficulties. First, many asylum countries are concerned that refugee self-sufficiency projects may eventually become de facto integration and may lessen international pressure on the country of origin to take the steps necessary for voluntary repatriation. Refugee camps and international burden sharing are a reminder to and pressure on the world community to work toward the preferred solution.

Second, in many low-income countries of asylum, sufficient cultivable land and work opportunities are not available. In such a situation it is not possible to assist refugees without providing opportunities for some of the local population. Regarding this type of situation, the Report (UNHCR 1983c) on Refugee Aid and Development noted: "Present arrangements for international assistance are not satisfactory, however, in situations where social or economic factors make it necessary to develop programmes which, while essential to enable the refugees to become self-supporting, also benefit the local population." Without satisfactory arrangements, host hesitancy regarding either refugee self-support activities or the durable solution of local integration is to be expected.

Last, the African host countries note certain inconsistencies in the donors' view of burden sharing and their pressures to reduce costs through self-support programs or durable solutions. In the 1940s and 1950s, the European states rejected integration as a solution for many refugees who were part of a relatively light burden of only 1.5 million eastern European refugees. Instead they requested international burden sharing in the form of overseas resettlement. Indeed, ICARA II convened almost on the twenty-fifth anniversary of the beginning of World Refugee Year, which was a response to the continuing problems of only 170,000 European refugees, many of whom had been in temporary asylum since World War II or the immediate postwar period. The African hosts also note that the pressure to achieve durable solutions is uneven, depending upon the donors' political interest in the underlying dispute. A conflict that is politically salient to a major donor is likely to result in greater patience regarding durable solutions and more support to the host government (Gordenker 1983).

Conclusion

The nature of refugee problems has undergone fundamental changes since UNHCR was established in 1951. Over the years the problems have shifted from Europe to the developing countries; from struggle by colonies to achieve independence, to conflicts within and between these now-independent countries; from refugees counted in the thousands to refugee flows estimated in the millions; from conditions that could relatively easily achieve durable solutions, to situations where no durable solution is in sight; and from international assistance costs that long remained below the $5 million mark, to levels that now require a third to a half billion dollars each year. There is great variety to refugee problems, and while many new elements such as refugees in low-income countries have been added to the list, or occupy a more significant portion of it, it is useful to recall that few of the old elements, such as refugees from eastern Europe, have been subtracted. The three durable solutions have also remained the same, but the balance between them, the means of achieving solutions, and the international assistance necessary to promote durable solutions have changed and will continue to change.

ICARA II was part of the process of change and evolution in international assistance to refugees. The hosts and donors had different perspectives on the need and reasons for ICARA II, and each had different goals to be achieved there. A great deal of effort went into preparations and guidelines for project submissions, but beyond the objectives listed by the General Assembly and the Secretary-General there were almost no standards by which to measure the conference's outcome.

From the host point of view, there was a need for new money (additionality) to be used to strengthen infrastructures. The countries of asylum wanted a pledging conference—the main objective was burden sharing. The donors, on the other hand, wanted a solutions conference—to produce progress toward burden reduction through a drop in refugee numbers as a result of durable solutions.

The hosts and donors adopted views that fitted their respective needs and perspectives. Each set of views reflected new facets of old principles, but the Conference was not a contest between two sides. Hosts and donors were both "right"; each had legitimate concerns and goals. For ICARA II to have succeeded it was necessary for donors and hosts to have recognized and mutually endorsed the legitimacy of the others' goals. No one wants a repetition of the Middle Eastern model of burden sharing without a solution, nor can one expect least-developed countries to carry the whole burden of promoting durable solutions. ICARA II may well have turned out to be less important as a fund-raising meeting than as an exploration of the common ground of humanitarian principles.

6

Refugees: A Problem and Opportunity for African Economic Development

Mabel M. Smythe

At the top of the priority list of every sub-Saharan African country stands economic development. However varied their plans or ideologies, each aims toward more and better roads, communications, transport systems, health, education, capital accumulation, food production, exports, growing technology, and management of essential industries by indigenous personnel in a stable and secure economic and political environment. They may vary in prospects for achieving these objectives; they may argue over ways and means; but the vision of greater economic prosperity and self-reliance underlies the common dream of the future (Mtewa 1982).

All assume that modern vocational training in their own lands will prepare the typists, carpenters, nurses, and computer programmers of tomorrow. Africans look forward to sophisticated and effective land management, population control, and allocation of foreign exchange. Wise planning is extolled by all.

Alas, the prolonged refugee crisis is all too often the despair of the planners. Unpredictable refugee flows undo the most meticulous population projections; refugees must be housed somewhere, on land that was to have been used, perhaps, for an agricultural project or industrial installation. As refugees forage for fuel, they destroy trees and shrubs for miles around and precipitate a relapse into desertification, ruining the fragile ecology and leaving an already declining water table further reduced and sometimes fouled. Existing roads capable of carrying 10-ton vehicles break down under the weight of 30-ton trucks supplying food and construction materials to refugee camps. Even before a political decision can be taken to call in international relief agencies the newcomers must be fed and given a place to sleep. Scarce resources can sustain serious damage from short-run relief efforts; longer-term arrangements for resettlement of refugees present further complexities (Novicki 1983).

We are comfortable with the fact that agencies have been established that can and will help in these circumstances; we are aware that even when refugees from an alien culture do not understand the language of the country of asylum, African hospitality will give them succor. For the moment we need not consider the refugees' cultural dissimilarity beyond noting it as a hindrance to cooperation for economic development. Nor need we concern ourselves with the quality of talents brought by the refugees, although we can assume that the highly intelligent persons who take initiative are somewhat more likely to flee when confronted with danger than are simpler people of the soil, whose knowledge of what lies beyond the border is at best rudimentary. In any case, any large population movement necessarily includes many unskilled rural dwellers with little education, who constitute the great majority in any African country (Refugee Policy Group 1983).

Given this background, one concerned with economic development can be excused his negative initial reaction to the arrival of refugees. A logical assumption can be made that the host country will experience a hiatus in development for the time—perhaps until the uninvited guests return home and are no longer able to interfere. The world has for too long viewed refugees as symbols of unrelieved tragedy. It has for too long seen refugee situations simply as occasions for humanitarian rescue. As the Emergency Committee for African Refugees has said:

> So far, the main focus of both international and humanitarian agencies in dealing with the African refugee problem has been in the area of relief: providing shelter, food, water, and medical aid. This is as it should be. However, since the possibility of settling the refugee crisis in the near future is remote, the present refugee situation is likely to be . . . one of the major problems of Africa for a long time to come. Hence, concerned bodies and institutions should [seek] longterm solutions such as agricultural, handicraft, water development, and educational projects [Emergency Committee 1982].

A more useful reaction is to seek out the potential for economic development inherent in the crisis itself. Let us look at some opportunities provided by the crisis.

1.   Among the refugees are likely to be some persons with education, skills, even professions. With proper management their training and talents can contribute to the economy of their new environment. Whether, by astute planning, their abilities are put to use in the refugee camps or elsewhere, they can contribute to the host economy.

2.   A subtle public relations asset lies in the concern of donor countries toward poor nations which are obviously threatened in their own development by their reception of refugees. Development funding may well be easier to obtain under such circumstances. A perhaps vital flow of foreign credits may be augmented by relief funds, particularly when a portion is spent to buy locally produced goods or to hire local people.

3.   Infrastructure may be developed to provide for refugee camps and centers: water systems, roads, electrical connections, even simple air strips

may owe their existence to refugee emergencies. Fuel storage tanks in Somalia were constructed in response to a threat that food supply trucks might not be assured access to gasoline; warehouses in some camps were built after delayed food delivery threatened the lives of severely malnourished child refugees.

The emergency nature of the refugee situation provides another opportunity: flexibility. Shortcuts are developed to provide housing, to teach people to build simple structures, and to educate them for living, as refugees or otherwise. They are uniquely free to learn new skills, relatively unhampered by farming obligations or rigid cultural strictures. Never has there been so much time available to the fortunate ones whose camps have water supplies and cooking fuel.

In fact, time hangs heavy in many camps: one waits for food distribution; one waits for the water truck; one waits at the clinic. Waiting time is an asset that can often be put to good use for training in sanitation, health, and nutrition; child care; literacy and numeracy; primary school for children; and apprenticeships in construction, mechanics, simple crafts, and other skilled trades. Since political wisdom dictates that other local citizens in need of skills training should have access to the workshops and other such facilities for refugees, these can also offer an opportunity for refugees and their hosts to share a positive training experience.

How do we get from here to there? How might we transform fearful, undernourished human flotsam into energetic, capable workers and effective homemakers with high morale and a sense of purpose?

Like so many challenges, this one has its paradoxes. The very idea of being considered worthy of training is exciting to people who have all but lost hope in the struggle to reach safety. To be told that one's children can be educated, that they can be trained to earn a living in this strange new place, might for some verge on the miraculous. It is possible that the effect on morale of being told of such opportunities could transform refugee discouragement into a mood of growing hope.

We should start, then, by considering development a fundamental and essential aspect of refugee programs and refugees a fundamental and essential element in development plans, wherever refugees flee to developing countries. Whatever the basis for the refugee flow, the people concerned need to become self-sustaining. Their ability to depend upon themselves and upon each other is a vital part of both their self-respect and their effective functioning. Dependence is itself demoralizing; a program of self-improvement and other educational options can foster hope and dignity and encourage the formation of a feeling of community. Experienced workers among refugees already understand the moral advantages of being active and useful. The power to have some input into their own future could also offer hope to many.

As soon as refugees arrive and are registered, members of the group who are not too traumatized can be encouraged to help with the work to be done. There will be adolescents and/or adults who can be spared from family responsibilities to assist others with cooking or child care, to comfort the lonely, or to handle general communications. Disabled persons may be able to supervise an information corner and communicate camp announce-ments. Growing children can run errands.

Teaching refugees to form simple organizations to talk over concerns of general interest can contribute a great deal to the spirit of the camp. Such a beginning encourages an atmosphere in which group self-organization can emerge under its natural leaders. The attitude of camp authorities can also encourage self-organization efforts. There are risks, of course; leaders are not always wise and responsible, and the limits to their power must be clearly understood in advance by all concerned. Authorities must resist the temptation to handle the refugee population as if the people were passive objects, to be moved about at the whim of their leaders. Persons in this docile state might give minimal trouble, but would offer little or no initiative or personal development in return.

With the help of refugees capable of working as interpreters, teachers, clerks, health personnel, tailors, carpenters, masons, and the like, the initial registration of all may be much easier, and other urgent tasks, such as mending torn clothing, making simple baskets and other receptacles from local materials, and devising elemetary ways to make the camp site more livable, can be undertaken. Those with skills in building may be in a position to teach others while constructing crude shelters in which some of the projected activities can take place, as the camp becomes better organized and new initiatives become possible. Even before health personnel and teachers are in place, the clinic or dispensary, school, and other important service elements can be projected and discussed.

This is obviously not too different from what happens in many well-run camps. What is different is the attitude: that refugees have a life ahead of them that should focus on a positive future outlook, avoid dwelling on present calamity, and plan for important and worthwhile changes ahead.

Those changes, too, should emphasize development: provision of land for gardening, so refugees can grow fresh vegetables for themselves; setting times for instruction in a variety of learning areas related to improving living conditions; adapting to the new environment through acquisition of skills; and understanding what has been happening back home since they took flight. The development of new institutions can help refugees align their lives to these new demands and arrangements. This is consistent with the declared goal of African countries—development of human resources, al-though with considerable concern for political control of the energies thus activated.

Suppose refugees take initiative and set an example of activism for the host population. Might that situation discomfit some elements in host government circles? Might the latter not prefer to keep refugees hidden away in sparsely settled parts of the country of asylum, where they can exert minimal influence on the population, which may be less accustomed to such open expression? Would it be wiser, in any event, to have refugees less visible, especially if they set an example of activity that might not be wholly welcomed by host government officials?

Other critics suggest the possible risk that refugee status under such a plan could be too attractive, so that a decision to flee might be taken more lightly than would otherwise be the case. If it appears that the easiest way to get access to education and vocational training, as well as to achieve greater control over one's destiny, is to become a refugee, more ambitious and calculating citizens may well identify refugee status with opportunity.

It is doubtful, however, that the basic literacy, health, sanitation, and agricultural skills training, which must be the backbone of any program of rural development, would attract many of the more sophisticated urban dwellers who seek higher education. It is more likely that such refugees would continue to avoid the camps and resettlement areas, as they have in Djibouti and Khartoum. As for the majority, it would be better for the refugee experience to be less demeaning and less of a dead end for those without unusual initiative and drive.

What of the concern that it will not work, since most of the refugees are women and children, the old, the sick, and the disabled? These categories constitute the majority of rural dwellers in Africa, where 40 percent of the population may be under fifteen years of age; and women, who are responsible for the major part of food crop production in most counties, constitute close to half the remainder. The organization of refugees for greater productivity while schools educate their children could bring within reach new opportunities for better health and prosperity. If these objectives can be achieved with refugee populations, it could encourage similar development among rural populations.

What of the enormous cost of trying to rehabilitate, as well as feed and shelter, the refugees? The budget is already burdensome without the proposed new services. Besides, when repatriation and resettlement elude us, refugee camps sometimes need support for years. Do we really know that this plan would be more costly, or could it cause our budget for food and shelter to decline? The host country might then view the refugees as less of a burden, and this experiment, under the relatively controlled conditions of refugee management, might demonstrate how to help people develop their potential. Or, conversely, it might show through its mistakes what does not work, as well as what does. We might demonstrate that without massive projects, it is possible to foster development in ways that change the perceptions of the people involved and to increase the momentum of group and individual adjustment to new productive techniques.

Development must come; we can make a virtue of necessity and perhaps discover ways of achieving it more efficiently by combining our attacks on two problems: refugee crisis management and economic development. If we cannot be proud of our success in either, so far, why not gamble on the possibility that a new approach may have some useful potential to demonstrate? Representatives of the UNDP and UNHCR could consult with African national planning authorities to develop a model refugee crisis contingency plan, covering both refugees and returnees, for each country. Such a procedure, incorporated quietly and without publicity into the master development plan for each country, could (a) designate officials responsible for identifying an impending emergency, setting the plan in motion, and handling each step in a clearly prescribed procedure; (b) target specific land for camps or for clearance and cultivation by refugees or returnees; and (c) set guidelines for relations with international and other agencies likely to be called upon for assistance. Only through such careful prearrangement can proper weight be given to the development priorities and objectives of each country of asylum.

Some of the dangers and risks are obvious; manipulation of the refugee situation for financial and political advantage and exaggeration of impending need lead the list. These and other problems are inherent in the existing system. But a growing number of nations would welcome improvements in that system, with its well-known disadvantages. If UNHCR and UNDP would together provide technical assistance and incentive, giving priority to the neighbors of those countries or situations that spew forth the major refugee flows, we could embark upon a pilot effort. The first steps should be taken now. With every year of delay, more children grow older without adequate educational and vocational opportunities, and more precious time is wasted.

7

Refugee Policy: The Need to Include Psychological Aspects

Hermann W.Schoenmeier

The increasing influx of refugees and at the same time the diminishing aid from outside have turned the refugee issue into a menancing problem for the immediate host countries. Therefore W. R. Smyser, the Deputy High Commissioner for Refugees, cautioned in Berlin in 1982 that

> We have to find a way, therefore, to help refugees staying long at one place, and to help the countries that have accepted them, without jeopardizing those countries' development. We also have to try to do so in a way which promises some relief, even if not immediate, to those whose financial resources support refugee aid [DSE 1982:61].

It is becoming increasingly plain that short-term humanitarian operations will not solve the problem; what is needed are long-term planning, integrated into the country's development, and corresponding programs. The conception of such development programs should make it possible for permanent solutions to be found for the refugee problem and for self-sufficiency to be achieved on the part of the refugees. Pursuing a development policy geared to meeting refugees' basic human needs involves a number of problems.

Many refugees arrive in host countries whose economic situation is even worse than that of their home countries. Although they have perhaps saved their lives, they are no longer in a position to provide for their own economic existence but are dependent on support from national or international organizations. Especially in this situation, in which hundreds of thousands rely on international aid to meet their basic needs in countries in great economic difficulty, such as Sudan, the development policy aspect of humanitarian aid to refugees cannot be ignored. It is not possible to grant aid to refugees and refuse it to a host population that has the same or even more adverse living conditions.

Refugees cannot, for instance, be granted the right to water if this right is denied the host population among which the refugees live. In an industrialized country such as West Germany, whose daily per capita consumption of water is more than 200 liters, such a discussion would be academic. But in northeastern Sudan, 20 liters of water per refugee per day is the planning figure. This demand can be met technically and organizationally only with difficulty. Moreover, it is certainly not met by the Sudanese government for its own population in all parts of the country. If the government does not want to trigger any additional domestic tensions, at least in the so-called "refugee-affected" areas, it must first bring the refugees' water supply in line with that available for the local population, and bear in mind basic needs and the right to water as a secondary consideration.

Water as necessity illustrates particularly clearly the difficulties involved in the concept of basic human needs, although, unlike the right to education, it is biologically critical. In a political discussion of basic human needs or rights, it is not a question of the human organism's biological need for water. In the political sense of the term, it is not a question of eating, drinking, and dwelling, but rather of forms of their realization that are worthy of a human being. Social standards determine what an individual needs water for and what kind of water it has to be. The amount of water necessary for human dignity is dependent on such social standards and cannot be set arbitrarily from outside.

The demand of meeting basic human needs is a political question of attempting to grant the Third World on a large-scale basis that which is necessary for existence commensurate with human dignity. To that extent this demand is necessary and worth supporting. Yet what is vitally necessary for a certain individual cannot be determined from outside, but only by the individual and his group. No general hierarchy of human needs is valid and binding worldwide; there are as many differing hierarchies as there are peoples and cultures. At a time of ever-greater shortages of resources, if the political demand to grant rights and meet basic needs is to be met seriously, it will be necessary to turn away from the policy of determining general basic needs from the outside. At the same time it will be necessary to turn to the actual basic needs of those concerned. They themselves must articulate their ideas of life commensurate with human dignity and state their opinion as to how these ideas can be realized in a given situation.

Such a policy does not focus on organizational questions as to the composition of the World Food Rations, the number of huts to be built, or the size of the water supply network. These things are vital for refugees seeking immediate refuge. More, however, is required for a long-term perspective related to development. If refugees are to be enabled with a minimum of cost and time to care for themselves and to live in peace with the host population, this goal cannot be attained without engaging the efforts of the refugees and the host population concerned. An actual policy geared to meeting basic human needs must focus on the encounter with the human being responsible for himself. He plans for the present and the future and makes decisions he deems necessary. Of course he depends on influences from his own group or decisions made by the government, so that his scope for decision-making is frequently minimal. Nonetheless, his behavior, as that of his fellow-sufferers, is understandable only in light of their views and interpretations of reality.

The Need for Psychological Aspects in Refugee Policy

Implementing development policy geared to meeting basic human needs involves great difficulties. This is due in part to instrumental preconditions not yet fully specified. Scientific bases are lacking here that would be necessary for successful counseling on policy and project planning. In particular, the psychological aspects of strategies of basic human needs have hitherto seldom been worked out (see Lederer 1980; Stein 1981a). This lack is especially crucial to planning of programs for areas with a large share of refugees from different cultural backgrounds, as in northeastern Sudan.

Eritrean and Ethiopian refugees from greatly differing vocational backgrounds should be able to provide for their own economic existence in a few years, but possibilities existing in rural areas of northeastearn Sudan are limited. Since most of the refugees are to settle in this area, it cannot be assumed that every refugee will find work appropriate to his former experience and inclination. Rather, the refugees will be expected to make great adjustments to their change in circumstances. Nomads will have to cultivate the land, peasants will have to improve their income by working as wage-earners, students will have to abandon their dreams of modern urban life and seek reasonable alternatives in the rural sphere, and single women will have to devise strategies for supporting themselves appropriate to the Islamic environment. All of these changes are very profound and affect essential cultural values and standards.

Not all these changes can be expected to arise spontaneously or be decreed by the administration. It is of course possible to implement programs and ignore cultural realities, to react to problems and tensions by administrative means or police force, but this leads only to a heightening of confrontation.

This illustrates the necessity of integrating psychological aspects of the refugee situation into political planning. But the psychological analysis of an intercultural refugee situation needs an appropriate theoretical approach, taking into account the close interaction between culture and the individual. From different theoretical approaches, Boesch's (1975, 1976, 1980) action theory seems very promising for the analysis of an intercultural situation. Unlike other psychological theories, it attempts to view human behavior not merely as reaction to environmental stimuli or as a result of possibilities of reaction laid down in the human organism. Rather, it assumes that human action builds a bridge between the individual and the environment, leading to interaction through which the person is assimilated into the environment and in turn attempts to influence it.

The experience of the person involved provides him with feedback about his own possibilities for action (his action potential) and his ability to react suitably to differing demands made by his cultural surroundings. The diversity of these self-recognition processes is related to positive and negative evaluations of his own possibilities for action, always seen in relationship to possibilities for action of others. They thus contribute to a personal, specific feeling of self-esteem and to the forming of personal identity.

In the process of interaction between the individual and the environment, the effects of individual experience on the person's further actions

> do not depend on the outer results of acts but rather on the inner results, and that is, how the results of actions are perceived and assessed. . . . These perceptions and assessments have, though, as their precondition a "channel" affecting them, relating present stimuli to past stimuli, sorting them out and evaluating them. . . . This permanent "channel" is what we call . . . the ego [Boesch 1975:9–10].

A person's specific perception of self expressed in different areas of action over the course of time is what we call ego identity. Ego is "built up by the individual throughout his life because it fulfills positive functions in planning action; it facilitates a sense of orientation, it defines our person for others, it makes it possible for actions to be anticipated, and without this a stabilization of self-esteem . . . would be unthinkable" (Boesch 1983a:10).

This rough outline of a theoretical framework provides evidence of the significance of identity for the refugee:

> The framework of the refugee's indigenous culture, within which he has developed his action structures, differs from that of the host country. . . . The natural correspondence of models, means, goals, and compatibilities among different members of a [host] community will not apply to the refugee's action system. If we assume that the past experience of a person provides the elements for understanding the present, and that both, past and present, contribute jointly to the anticipation of goals and the means to reach them, then this natural continuity in an individual's perception of life is disrupted in the foreign culture. His everyday experience cannot be related anymore with sufficient (subjective) validity to his long-range goal anticipations; patterns of action which elsewhere were adequate . . . risk being out of place here. . . . The refugee perceives himself as straying in a behavioural maze in which he will have to find his way [ibid:28–29].

The discrepancy felt between the original culture and the host culture can thus be a major impediment to the refugee's ability to act, and that is why this question will require careful attention for solving the problem of self-sufficiency.

Such a theoretical framework also determines the way psychological aspects of the refugee situation in Sudan are approached. For political reasons, highest priority in research is awarded to those questions significant in achieving economic self-sufficiency for the refugees. From a psychological viewpoint it will be a question here of dealing with the refugees' ability to act, their action potential in the framework of the working world, and those aspects of human actions that promote this action potential.

A person's ability to act, his ability to activate his action potential again and again, to be motivated, and to seize and meet the demands made on him by his environment, require continual confirmation . Thwarting an individual's possibilities for action thus means not only denying him the experience necessary for his self-esteem, but also endangering his ability and willingness to perform in the working world. The apathy frequently observed in refugees in camps is the result of their having been continually denied the opportunity to prove themselves. It will thus also be necessary to examine to what extent the refugees' living conditions in Sudan restrict the freedom of action of a responsible person, thus encroaching on the action potential, so that speedy economic self-sufficiency is called into question.

Some Research Directions

The following catalogue of questions is neither complete nor systematical; questions are meant only to characterise the possible orientation of necessary research:

- The Eritrean and Ethiopian refugees live in Sudan either in official refugee settlements or as spontaneously settled refugees. Research could examine which refugees choose which alternative, and to what extent this decision is dependent on the possibilities for action (for instance, knowledge of Arabic or familiarity with the Sudanese way of life) or on long-term objectives (for instance, former occupation and education). The refugee's opportunities for action and his long-term goals are essential for his self-image, so are guiding parameters for the decisions made by the refugee for his stay in Sudan.
- Research could study the psychological situation of spontaneously settled refugees and that of refugees in the different forms of official settlements (wage-earning settlements or land-holding settlements) and could analyze the strategies for economic survival devised by the refugees in different places.

In this connection a series of other questions represent practical subtopics:

- Against what vocational, national, and ethnic background on the part of the refugees and in what kind of refugee settlement or spontaneous settlement are the refugees' long-term, identity-conforming objectives best met and least conducive to tensions arising between them and the Sudanese?
- In which regions or countries are official refugee settlements turned into operable social units in which the refugees articulate common interests, practice certain forms of self-help, and take advantage of vocational skills and know-how available from their fellow refugees?
- What processes of social change occur in land-holding settlements, and what are the effects of these changes on the refugees' long-term objectives and self-image? What problems arise when, for instance, nomads

are forced to settle down, or when peasants, experienced only in subsistence farming, take over modern, tractor-worked agriculture?

- Refugees have been living in the Qala en Nahal region for more than fifteen years. Research could examine the effect of such a long presence on the refugees' long-range objectives. To what extent have they set their sights on staying longer in Sudan? Which of them would be willing to adopt Sudanese citizenship if the Sudanese authorities consented to it in individual cases?

- In many cases refugees will encounter Sudanese in the working world, either as subordinates, colleagues, superiors, or as salespersons and customers. In all these cases of interaction, people meet people with different working behavior patterns determined by different cultural backgrounds. The mutual expectations of "correct" behavior vary greatly and give rise to potential conflicts. The study could also devote special attention to this set of problems.

- Research could study the psychological situation of single women, the analysis of their possibilities and difficulties, and their strategies for assuring their existence. Special attention could investigate the different position of the woman in an Islamic society as compared to an Ethiopian or Eritrean one, not only for single women but also for women in general. The study could compare social expectations in Eritrea and Ethiopia to those in Sudanese culture and determine what behavioral changes may be expected from female refugees in Sudan. Finally, the study could investigate to what extent such potential changes in behavior are still commensurate with these women's self-image and whether they bring about an identity crisis.

8

The Refugee Problem in Uganda

John B. Kabera

It is difficult to determine how serious the refugee problem was in African societies before colonial rule. But constant intertribal wars, the slave trade, famines, and other natural disasters have always forced some people to flee to safer communities. In the traditional societies of Africa, a political refugee was recognized and sheltered. Various African languages include a number of proverbs that refer to the plight of a political refugee and how he should be treated.

As a result of colonial rule, an amalgamation of tribal communities was created into states. The refugee problem that has since evolved has become greater both in volume and in area. A refugee who in earlier times would have fled a short distance now finds himself traveling hundreds of kilometers to cross his country's boundary to the safety of a neighboring state. Addressing the refugee problem in Africa in 1983, President Arap Moi of Kenya commented that: "ethnic, tribal and political persecutions are the main generators of African refugees, and the solution to the African refugee problem lies in the political will and incentive at the highest government level" (Moi 1983). The refugee problem in Africa today is a burning issue, especially since a third of the world's refugees are in Africa.

The Refugee Influx to Uganda

Uganda has had to accommodate three main groups of political refugees (Table 8.1). There have also been minor flows of refugees from South Africa, Mozambique, Zimbabwe, Angola, and Namibia.

Sudanese

The first wave of Sudanese migrated to Uganda toward the end of the nineteenth century. Emin Pasha, the governor of Equatoria in southern Sudan, led his soldiers and their families southward to avoid the violent

Table 8.1   Refugee Composition by Origin Since 1969

Year	Country of origin				Number in settle-ments	Total
	Sudan	Rwanda	Zaire	Others		
1967[a]	54.981	71,295	33,576		49,800	159,852
1972[b]	59,400	72,800	34,500	40		166,500
1981[c]		80,000	32,000	1,000	79,500	113,000
1983[d]					109,000	113,000

Sources: [a]Kabera 1982: 196.
[b]Gould 1974: 415.
[c]UNHCR 1982: 117.
[d]Uganda government, Ministry of Culture and Community Development.

consequences of Mahdist revolt of 1881. He established his headquarters at Wadlai on the west bank of the Albert Nile in Moyo district, hoping to return after the revolt. In 1891, Captain Lugard drew on this population for troops for the British East Africa Company, and eventually for British colonial rule in Uganda. Some 600 soldiers were recruited; with their families they numbered 9,000 (Dak 1974: 28). These soldiers provided the main support for Lugard's administration until some mutinied in 1897, at which time they were disbanded. Some were sent to the Kenyan coast, while those who remained in Uganda were settled in Entebbe, Hoima, and in Bombo. Many of their descendants struggled back to Sudan in 1979 after Amin, who had incorporated many of them into his forces, was removed by liberation forces from Tanzania.

A second group of Sudanese who found refuge in Uganda were labor migrants who had been entering Uganda since the 1930s. Most of them had returned annually to Sudan, but after the eruption of violence in southern Sudan in 1955 they remained in Uganda. Eventually many returned during the 1970s, together with other repatriating Sudanese refugees; the remainder returned in 1979 following the liberation war.

The largest wave of Sudanese refugees started pouring into Uganda after 1955, when the civil war in Sudan began. By the end of 1956, there were 5,000 Sudanese refugees resident in northern Uganda. The flow of this group of refugees continued through 1958 and 1960. With the resurgence of violence in southern Sudan in 1960, more refugees crossed into Uganda, and the number of asylum seekers reached its peak in 1965, when an estimated 100,000 to 150,000 crossed into Uganda.

Between 1972 and 1974, however, with the assistance of UNHCR and following negotiations between the governments of Uganda and Sudan, most of the Sudanese refugees repatriated.

Zaireans

The presence of immigrants from Zaire was first prompted by economic opportunities in Uganda during this century. They came as labor migrants;

some stayed on, and some 1,600 Zaireans were recorded in the 1931 census. These numbers increased to about 19,700 by 1948, and in 1959 nearly 24,300 Zaireans were enumerated in the census.

War and political turmoil in Zaire since 1960 has not only encouraged the permanent settlement of Zaireans in Uganda, but has also created a flow of refugees seeking asylum in Uganda. Most of these Zairean refugees subsequently returned home on their own initiative, and only a few are still remaining in Uganda (see Table 8.2).

Rwandans

Of the three major refugee groups, the Rwandans constitute the largest group and pose a delicate problem to both the Ugandan and Rwandan governments. Three main groups of Rwandans live in Uganda today. A Rwandan tribal group lives in Bufumbira county in southwestern Uganda, a county that was incorporated into Uganda early in the century. The 1931 Uganda Census reported 76,844 Rwandans, of whom only 103 were enumerated as non-nationals; the 1959 census revealed that there were already 378,656 Rwandans in Uganda, among whom 102,857 were resident in Bufumbira county. Bufumbira county is a high-density area, and many people have been emigrating from there to other areas of western and southcentral Uganda, in search of land for settlement or as labor migrants.

The second group includes Rwandan labor migrants who were attracted by wage employment on European- and Asian-owned coffee and cotton fields in Buganda and Busoga counties in southcentral Uganda. The practice

Table 8.2   Population Density in the Refugee Settlements, 1983

Settlement	District	Refugee origin	1981 population	Influx since October 1982
Onigo	Moyo	Sudan		
Agago-Acholpi	Kitgum	Sudan and Zaire		
Nakapiripirit	Moroto	Sudan and Zaire		
Kyangwali	Hoima	Rwanda	6,342	
Kyaka I	Kabarole	Rwanda	7,450	2,700
Kyaka II[a]	Kabarole	Rwanda	—	—
Rwamwanja	Kabarole	Rwanda	4,899	1,396
Kahunge	Kabarole	Rwanda	7,088	548
Ibuga	Kasese	Rwanda and Sudan	4,172	302
Oruchinga	Mbarara	Rwanda	20,975	9,956
Nakivale	Mbarara	Rwanda	28,574	12,953
Total			79,500	27,855

[a] Kyaka II opened in October 1983 to relieve pressure from Nakivale and Oruchinga.

Source: Uganda government, Ministry of Culture and Community Development.

in the early decades of this century was for these labor migrants to return home yearly, but later in the century, a large proportion of Rwandan migrants settled permanently in various areas of Buganda, Busoga, and western Uganda. The report of a 1937 investigation into conditions affecting unskilled laborers in Uganda stated that many Rwandans had brought their families and settled permanently.

The third group includes a large number of Rwandan political refugees who had flocked into Uganda during the 1959 political struggles in Rwanda, which culminated in the exile of the Umwami (king) of Rwanda. In 1962, Rwanda gained independence and was declared a republic. Both actions ended monarchical rule in Rwanda and sparked the emigration of the Batutsi ruling class, who followed their ex-king into exile in Uganda, where he was granted asylum. The liberation war of 1979 saw him leave Uganda, but large numbers of Rwandan refugees still remain in Uganda.

Strategy Formulation and Choice

The flight of refugees is characterized by suddenness of movement and human suffering. People flee across a border, often with no belongings, to become stateless in a foreign land. Governments of receiving areas are therefore confronted with the problem of providing immediate assistance. As it turns out, however, refugees stay much longer, and what seems initially to be a short-term problem can last indefinitely.

Rogge (1982:40) identifies four major strategies that could probably be adopted by asylum countries. These include (a) repatriating refugees to

Total refugee population 1983	Area in square km.	Density per km^2 1983	Remarks
	125	—	Closed
	42	—	Closed
	60	—	Closed
6,342	130	49	Operating
10,150	21	483	Operating
15,000	200	75	Operating
8,295	140	60	Operating
7,636	195	39	Operating
4,474	42	107	Operating
30,931	34	910	Operating
41,527	21	1,978	Operating
109,355			

their countries of origin at the earliest opportunity; (b) permitting the spontaneous integration of refugees into the national community; (c) retaining refugees in camps; and (d) systematically resettling refugees in self-sufficient rural settlement schemes. Of these strategies, the first is the ideal solution as long as it is a voluntary choice. The strategies devised by the Ugandan government in handling the refugees can be categorized under immediate, short-term, or long-term phases.

Immediate Strategies

Asylum and relief are the first strategies in dealing with a refugee problem. Goundaim (1970: 10) observes that asylum is the first and most fundamental of the refugee's needs, the preliminary condition for realizing all other rights. Yet the asylum strategy allows the problem of subversion. Asylum states such as Uganda have always feared that the presence of refugees undertaking subversive activity will affect relations and increase tension with neighboring states.

It is common for refugees to be sheltered in reception camps near the border of their country of origin. Due to the security risks involved in keeping large numbers of refugees close to their county of origin, and faced with the problem of not knowing how long they will stay, the government must move the refugees farther inland to resettlement areas. For example, when Rwandan refugees, having fled to neighboring states, remained in centers close to Rwanda, this proximity encouraged raids into Rwanda by extremists, which in turn kept up a general but unfulfilled expectation among refugees that they would achieve repatriation by force. As repatriation hopes faded and expectation of immediate return became remote, short-term strategies were adopted.

Short-term Strategies

Short-term strategies mainly involve resettlement and resettlement policies have so far been limited to agricultural settlement. This is due to the fact that most refugees come from a rural background. The aim of each settlement is to achieve self-sufficiency within a few years, so that further outside aid will be minimized and the refugee population will cease to drain the resources of the host nation or of the UNHCR (Gould 1974:424) Uganda, pursuing the goal of assisting refugees to attain at least minimum economic and social standards of living, set aside land in various parts of the country, mainly in western Uganda (Figure 8.1 and Table 8.2) for refugee settlements.

The refugees located on these settlements in October 1982 constituted about 30 percent of Uganda's total refugee population. The rest had been incorporated among the nationals either through marriage or through spontaneous settlements. The latter was made possible by Uganda's liberal and moderate position toward the refugee problem. One result was that other refugees also left their scheduled settlements to integrate spontaneously. This liberal attitude was eventually seen as a problem, and in 1982

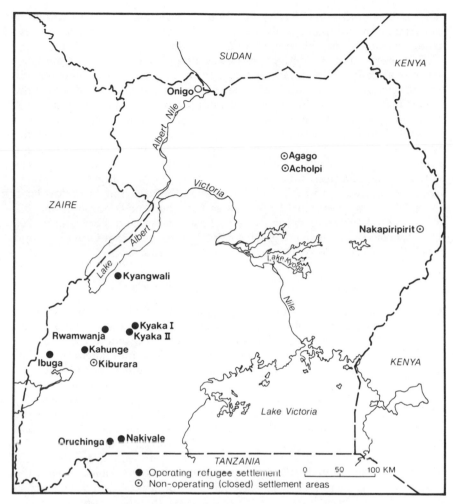

Figure 8.1 Refugee Settlement Areas in Uganda

many of the spontaneously settled refugees were forced back onto the settlement schemes (see Table 8.2).

Within each settlement scheme, basic economic amenities and infrastructure are provided, including all facilities that are normally provided for Ugandan villages. Each refugee family is allocated 10 acres of land, with the Ministry of Culture and Community Development as the implementing agency. Primary schools, health centers, bore holes, cattle dips, food stores, internal roads, veterinary services and other agricultural services, tsetse fly control, and security and administrative personnel are provided by the Ugandan government to ensure the well-being of the refugees in the settlements. Other forms of assistance, such as agricultural seeds, veterinary drugs, and some basic household requirements, are provided to individuals or groups of individuals as required. These facilities are also made available to neighboring Ugandan villagers.

The efforts made by refugees in developing hitherto sparsely populated areas is a credit to them. Many refugees in Uganda, within and outside settlements, have successfully achieved self-sufficiency. With the help of the UNHCR and UNICEF, some have been educated and now hold respectable posts in government and international organizations. Some have been integrated successfully into the rural agricultural system, engaging in the production of subsistence and cash crops and tending livestock. To some extent, refugee settlements have become growth poles in the rural areas where they are located. But a remaining problem is that refugees continue to live in these areas on a temporary basis, even though some have now been there for twenty years. Settlement areas have become congested, and the government has been generous in setting aside more land. For instance, 200 k^2 in Kyaka (Kyaka II) were given to 15,000 refugees from Oruchinga and Nakivale resettlement areas in 1983.

Long-term Strategies

UNHCR continues to regard voluntary repatriation as the optimum solution for the refugees. In Resolution 27, adopted by the Heads of States of the OAU in 1965, it was agreed that steps be taken to promote the return of refugees, with their consent, through bilateral and multilateral consultations. The OAU urgently requested countries of origin to encourage their nationals to repatriate by (a) assuring them that they would be favorably received; (b) facilitating resettlement; and (c) granting a general amnesty.

Refugees flee their countries because of fear of political persecution or the fear of being killed in war within their countries. It has been the Ugandan government's policy that when conditions that forced refugees to flee their countries of origin ameliorate, or where political amnesty is granted, refugees will be repatriated. Where such conditions have existed, as with the Sudanese refugees in 1972, successful repatriation was achieved. The majority of refugees from Zaire have also returned to their country, thereby solving an intricate problem for both Uganda and Zaire. But it is difficult to predict the future of the Rwandan refugees, for Rwanda has shown little interest in having its nationals repatriate. One reason might be that because Rwanda is a small country with a very high population density, additional population is unwelcome. Also, the Rwandans who fled the revolution in 1961 and 1962 were mainly from the royal ruling class, and the fear remains that they might return to reclaim their status.

The long-term uncertainty of the refugees' future is at the root of many of the difficulties relating to their permanent settlement. This situation is compounded by the African culture's emphasis of personal identification through ethnicity, which creates a strong cultural isolation of refugee migrants within their host communities. In the main, the refugees have kept their languages, dances, food and eating habits, and even occupations. They have learnt host languages, but the host communities have not bothered to learn the languages of the refugees; this further isolates them. The refugee is constantly reminded of his position as a refugee. Many government policies also emphasize the refugees' non-citizen status. The refugee therefore feels discriminated against, and this state of affairs undermines assimilation as a strategy for the resolution of the refugee problem.

As observed earlier, Uganda has very relaxed policies on refugee movement into and out of the settlement areas. The OAU Convention on Refugees in Africa recommended that member states issue travel documents to refugees residing within their countries, to permit them to travel outside their settlement territory. Host countries, however, fear that such action may be tantamount to granting permanent residence in the country of asylum. Still, such actions might be better than no identification at all, when the refugee resorts to using illegal means to secure the country's identity papers. Faced with these problems, the Ugandan government in 1983 embarked on a refugee identification exercise, more than twenty years after the beginning of the refugee influx. Identification papers were printed by the UNHCR, and observers from the agency oversaw the excerise.

Conclusion

This essay has attempted to evaluate the strategies the Ugandan government has so far adopted in dealing with its refugee problem. It has shown that, although repatriation has been successful with one set of refugees, this has not been the case with another. The problem is intricate and demands cooperation between the host country and the country of origin at the highest governmental level.

Uganda has been facing its own internal population and economic pressures, so that the assimilation of thousands of refugees is given low priority. Nevertheless, in the face of the failure to repatriate the refugees, because of the length of their stay and their contributions to national development, and in the light of Uganda having some still-unused land, the Ugandan government should consider the long-term strategy of granting citizenship to those refugees who wish to remain in Uganda.

9

Unemployment, Resettlement, and Refugees in South Africa

Alan Mabin

At every stage in South African history, a significant proportion of the population have been refugees of one sort or another (Marks 1980). Perhaps the earliest refugees were the San-speakers, driven into arid areas on the western side of the country by the intrusion of Nguni- and Sotho-speakers into the east coast and highveld areas several centuries earlier. Among the early white population were religious refugees from France. The period of warfare known as the Difaqane or Mfecane in the early nineteenth century pushed many people into flight from what are now northern Natal, Lesotho, and the Orange Free State. Subsequent disruptions by wars on colonial frontiers, settler occupation of land, and wars between white factions produced more refugees. Yet, as Marks has argued, the societies of southern Africa recovered with remarkable facility from these cataclysmic events. The twentieth century, and more particularly the past thirty years, has produced a displaced population more marginalized, more superfluous to their structure of work and production, and more permanently destitute than in any previous epoch of South African history. This essay is concerned with part of this population of "discarded people" (Desmond 1971).

Adepoju (1982) has pointed out that the "concept of refugees in Africa is . . . extremely broad." Political refugees, freedom fighters, women and children fleeing war and persecution, and those escaping famine and other disasters are all included. As Rogge (1981) indicates, there have also been sizable intranational (i.e., internal) displacements in countries such as Ethiopia, Uganda, and Zimbabwe. Although the concept of refugees is wide in Africa, it excludes those intranational refugees whose numbers are unrecorded but who must make up a huge proportion of the displaced persons in contemporary Africa. Tens of thousands of refugees from South Africa are accepted as such in other African countries and beyond the continent. Yet inside the country itself are many more internal refugees, accorded little recognition in any quarter (Marks 1980; Hart and Rogerson 1982). Their situation is complicated not only by the peculiar combination of forces that has produced their displacement, but also by the numerous boundaries between those Bantustans given "independence" by the South African state and the rest of the country. The reality of these different jurisdictions and their effects on people's lives cannot be ignored.

Some examples of this internal refugee phenomenon may be instructive:

- The impending removal of a group in northern Natal/Zululand precipitated their flight into Swaziland in 1979.
- Immediately before Transkei "independence" in October 1976, a Sesotho-speaking group from the Herschel district, lured by false promises of land and jobs from the Ciskei government, fled to the Queenstown district, where many still live in dire poverty (Murray 1980). In all, about 15,000 people were involved.
- Refugees have been generated by many factional disputes within the Bantustans. For example, at Maboloko, about 80 km northwest of Pretoria, disputes in 1976 and 1977 within an originally Sesotho-speaking community, isolated within the ethnic nationalism of Bophuthatswan, led to violence and twenty deaths. Exactly what became of those who fled the area is impossible to determine, whether by court records or by interviews, since the people left behind have refused to divulge any information.
- While some residents of the Winterveld, a squatter area near Pretoria which is the biggest in South Africa (population unknown, perhaps as much as half a million), have been forcibly moved from the area by Bophuthatswana authorities, others have left of their own accord as a result of the extreme harrassment suffered, particularly by non-Setswana speakers, at the hands of the police.
- The undocumented refugees of the patchwork lands of Gazankulu, Lebowa, and Venda in the northeastern Transvaal have fled the absurdities imposed on them by government-appointed chiefs—chiefs appointed to match the "ethnic" future of particular areas, regardless of the intermarriage and social unity of groups of Sepedi, Shangaan, and Venda speakers in the area (Surplus People Project 1983).

These examples are illustrative only, and come nowhere near to exhaustively describing the tragedy of South Africa's internal refugees. But they do serve to indicate the similarity of the plight of the people concerned, if not of the causes of their movement, to the plight of refugees elsewhere in Africa and in other parts of the Third World.

Although the details of each case may differ—and an analysis of the cases in detail is necessary if a full understanding of what is happening in the rural areas of South Africa is to be achieved (Murray 1980)—it is clear that some of the developing structural features of the political economy of South Africa underly the emergence of these refugees. In particular, these features are the unemployment situation in South Africa, the concentration of poverty and unemployment in the reserves or Bantustans, and the increasing responsibility of the Bantustan governments for these problems.

It will be instructive to examine the Orange Free State (OFS) and its reserves. Of the four provinces that constituted the Union of South Africa in 1910, the OFS had by far the smallest area in "native reserves." While the white republics and colonial states of the nineteenth century had been forced to reserve some land for occupation by blacks, in the OFS white farmers took up almost all the land conquered from Sesotho speakers and others, leaving only two small areas—Witzieshoek and Thabu Nchu—in the hands of certain chiefs.

Since 1969, the Witzieshoek reserve has become the Qwa Qwa Bantustan, supposedly the "homeland," with its less than 500 k^2 area, of the approximately 2 million Sesotho-speaking South Africans. The actual population of this tiny area is more than 300,000, or more than 600 per k^2 (Murray 1981). Most of these people are dependents of migrant workers whose families were forced off white-occupied farms and black-owned freehold land in the OFS (and elsewhere), as well as removed from towns in the OFS and other provinces. (Qwa Qwa abuts Lesotho and in some respects is similar to overcrowded Kangwane, which the South African government has been trying to give away to Swaziland in order to convert Siswati-speaking South Africans into foreigners.)

The only other reserve in the OFS is Thaba Nchu, which has been pieced together over the past fifty years from the fragmented remains of a freehold farming area occupied by Barolong people, who are Setswana-speaking. This historical connection led the tribal authority set up at Thaba Nchu in the 1950s to be linked with the Tswana Territorial Authority in the 1960s—the embryonic Bophuthatswana Bantustan. Before "independence" in 1977, the population of Thaba Nchu was already undergoing a rapid change: the numbers of Basotho passing into the reserve from OFS white farms and small towns changed the area from a Setswana-speaking majority to one of a Basotho majority.

There were no tribal differences between groups in the local population. Murray has chronicled the way in which pressure against the Basotho squatters at Kromdraai and elsewhere in the Thaba Nchu district intensified after the "independence" of Bophuthatswana, under Chief Minister Mangope's policy of ethnic exclusivism. But the official "home" of Sesotho-speakers—in the Qwa Qwa Bantustan—was already overcrowded beyond belief. As a result, the negotiations between the South African, Bophuthatswana, and Qwa Qwa governments for the removal of Basotho from Thaba Nchu were lengthy and resulted in a land swap between the three, in which land purchased from white farmers to the west of Thaba Nchu became a new reserve for Sesotho-speakers. As Murray describes it: "Removal of the Kromdraai squatters to the area known as Onverwacht began in late May 1979—in winter—and was completed by December of the same year. Kromdraai itself reverted to bare hillside, scrub and grazing. Only the graveyard remains."

Conditions at Onverwacht, to which not only Basotho but also Xhosa and other minorities from Thaba Nchu have moved or been moved, are indescribably bad. (Onverwacht is one of the areas where it is extremely difficult to obtain a permit to visit.) Overcrowding, unhygenic conditions, and disease are prevalent, water is scarce, and infant mortality is high. Meanwhile, "people are still pouring into Onverwacht" (ibid.) as well as into Thaba Nchu, as removals from farms and endorsements out of towns continue apace.

Unemployment at Onverwacht is extremely high. Little or no recruitment of migrant workers is proceeding, and local construction jobs provide work for very few of the 100,000 or more people who live there. It is ironic that the Sesotho name for Onverwacht is Botshabelo ("place of refuge"). Yet that is how some residents continue to see it, a refuge from the ravages of the Bophuthatswana police in nearby Thaba Nchu. Onverwacht and Qwa Qwa, while perhaps more extreme in their sheer absurdity, are actually representative of the general process of creating Bantustans. The dumping of people at such places is a process of concentrating both structural and cyclical unemployment in remote rural areas, where there is no prospect of any real relief, not even through long-distance migrant jobs, especially in current economic conditions. Whether the unemployed will be able to realize any potential for collective resistance to the system that has placed them there, remains to be seen.

Considering the disaster that is Onverwacht, one may conclude that, while apartheid and unemployment are the twin burdens of its people, there is little hope for the improvement of their conditions in the near future. They suffer because they are black, because they are poor, because they are Basotho or Xhosa or other non-Tswanas. If a group of them were to seek refugee status, in some parts of the world they would be accorded that recognition. But in southern Africa, countries do not have to have been directly subjected to apartheid government to have been reduced to dependency, poverty, and land shortage. The many hundreds of thousands and even millions who share the plight of those at Onverwacht have few places to go. Yet, even within South Africa itself, some have sought asylum. And, which is surprising, some refugees from Onverwacht have fled to Mafikeng, the capital of Bophuthatswana itself.

Mafikeng is best known for its (almost insignificant) role in the Anglo-Boer war of 1899–1902. True to its colonial origins, the old town is centered on the Imperial Reserve. But the site of Mafikeng, at the Molopo River, had for some time before been the center of these disparate groups who had settled under the authority of Chief Montshiwa after conflict with settlers of various factions. The semitraditional settlement, known as the stadt, surrounds colonial Mafikeng on two sides. To the north lies Montshiwa, the typical black township of matchbox-like houses common to most South African towns, and beyond Montshiwa lies Mmabatho, the site of huge investment in the capital of the Bantustan. The Mafikeng area has created its own refugees: for example, many in the squatter areas called Motlabeng and Dibate were forced to move from the site of newly built Mmabatho and its casino, playground of the well-heeled from across the border in Johannesburg. As one stands in Mafikeng, which lies on an almost flat plain, one can only imagine the "resettlement" camps—the local dumping grounds to which many thousands have been moved from the western Transvaal and northern Cape provinces—that lie just out of sight over the horizon.

When my research into the squatter areas of Mafikeng began, I was under the impression that the people in these areas would have come largely from "resettlements" in Bophuthatswana, such as those near Mafikeng. While some do, closer investigation of Lonely Park—the huge squatter area to the east of Mafikeng—has revealed more surprising information. Many of the Lonely Park squatters are refugees from Onverwacht in the OFS. Despite everyone being Sesotho-speakers, the tradition in the old Montshiwa country is still to welcome outsiders, so the powerful local chiefs are able to sell new arrivals (for as much as Rand 200) the right to settle on their lands. Thus far, while non-Tswanas moved to new projects like the capital city, and new claims have not received any assistance from the Bophuthetswana government, neither they nor the people from the OFS whom they have joined in Lonely Park have been forced to abandon their new homes.

The history of one family will illustrate the experience of some of the refugees at Lonely Park. Born in the northern OFS, the parents of this family were of tenant farming stock on freehold land until forced to move to labor tenancy on a white-owned farm in the 1950s. In the late 1960s, the first phase of "rationalizing" of farm labor forced them to move to Thaba Nchu, where they were able to keep a small amount of stock and grow some crops in their location—unlike later arrivals in the "resettlement camps" proper. The mid-1970s saw the family move to Kromdraai, with two sons now doing migrant work in the gold mines. In 1979 they were again forced to move, this time to Onverwacht. Their initial enthusiasm at their escape from Bophuthatswana turned to disillusionment, and in 1982, enabled by the cash income of the migrant sons, they moved as refugees to Lonely Park at Mafikeng. This flight was their fifth move as a family, each of which could have been treated as forced removal. Many other families in Lonely Park reveal similar histories, whether of a series of moves in the Western Transvaal or of repeated dumping within the OFS.

The squatters at Mafikeng are, in large part, refugees from resettlement. To say this is to argue that they are refugees from apartheid and from unemployment. They share the reasons for their flight with many others, both those in South Africa and those who have moved beyond its internationally recognized borders.

Involuntary movement in southern Africa, in which we may usefully include Kunz's (1973) category of acute (though not anticipatory) refugees, is a phenomenon that has assumed gigantic proportions in recent years. Leaving aside for the moment all those forced to move by government programs of village consolidation and land reapportionment, flight from military struggle and other strife, as well as from the implementation of apartheid policies, has delivered hundreds of thousands of UNHCR–recognized refugees across the international borders of the subcontinent. Of the countries south of Zaire and Tanzania, Angola has been the source of most of these refugees, while Mozambique, Zimbabwe, and Namibia, in that order, have occupied second position in the 1970s and 1980s (Hart and

Rogerson 1982). Perhaps the most surprising aspect of the geography of international refugee movements in southern Africa has been the relatively small numbers emanating from South Africa itself, given both the size of its population and the extent of oppression within its borders.

Several types of South African refugees may be identified. The first comprises refugees who have fled as a result of persecution, actual or potential, for their political beliefs or activities. A subgroup of political refugees is comprised of those who have left intending to join organizations such as the African National Congress (ANC) and the Pan African Congress (PAC) in the externally based struggle against the South African state (ibid.). Since 1976 the number of these refugees has neared the 20,000 mark (SAIRR 1981). This subcategory overlaps with a second category of refugee from South Africa, those who have fled the inferiority of "Bantu education." A further subcategory, related to those above and likely to become substantially larger, should the government extend military conscription beyond the whites, is the phenomenon of South African draft dodgers. Finally, there is a group of refugees who have left South Africa as a direct consequence of the implementation of Bantustan policies. While there are neither statistics nor even relatively complete information on this subject, some instances of such movements by large groups of people have been documented. One example was the flight from northern Natal or Zululand of several thousand people whose security had been threatened by their proposed forced removal and by the deposition of their chief for opposing this removal. This group fled to Swaziland and is in many respects similar to groups of rural refugees elsewhere in Africa, living close to the border of their country of origin, and posing problems of separate settlement, integration, or repatriation for their country or asylum. The situation these refugees fled and the nature of their flights are not, however, particularly different from the circumstances of the internal refugees of South Africa—the vast majority of the "refugees from resettlement."

Many of the squatters at Mafikeng are indeed refugees from resettlement. As we have seen, they have been forced in some cases to move not only once but up to five times. And their flight to places such as Lonely Park is a bid to escape the impossible conditions to which they had been subjected elsewhere: the threat of still more forced removals. The peculiarity of their situation is that they have been able, at least temporarily, to increase their security not by crossing a recognized international frontier, but by crossing the border into a geographical product of the same system that has repeatedly uprooted them: the supposedly independent Bantustan of Bophuthatswana. Like those from Zululand who fled removal and are now in Swaziland, the squatters at Mafikeng face an uncertain future. The politics of the areas in which they find themselves are volatile, and could result in almost any combination of repatriation and integration. But those in Swaziland have at least some recognition as refugees. Those at Mafikeng, like uncounted thousands of others in South Africa, have no such comfort. Under these circumstances, and given the prospect of ever-increasing flight from removals within South Africa, the accepted idea of "refugee" offers little comfort for millions of South Africans.

10

When Is Self-Sufficiency Achieved? The Case of Rural Settlements in Sudan

John R. Rogge

The principal rationale behind the creation of settlement schemes is that, once it is apparent that the refugees' sojourn will be of medium- to long-term duration, priority is placed upon reducing the burden upon host governments by fostering in the migrant population as high a level of self-sufficiency as is possible, in as short a time-frame as is practical. A secondary and less articulated aim is to integrate the latent manpower resource of the refugees into the regional economic structure of the area into which they have moved. While in many African asylum states the integration of refugee manpower into economic planning is more by accident than by design, in Sudan's case, and especially in eastern Sudan, the government's acceptance of and assistance to refugees is intimately tied to the concept that the refugees, in achieving levels of self-sufficiency, will simultaneously be an economic attribute to the region. Tanzania and Botswana are two other African states where refugee resettlement has served to bring new or underused lands into production (Rogge 1986). What differentiates Sudan's experience from others on the continent is the extent to which local rural economies have come to depend upon an abundant supply of relatively cheap and effective refugee labor. Indeed, Sudan is unique among African asylum states in terms of implementing settlement schemes where self-sufficiency is predicated upon refugees hiring out their labor rather than becoming subsistence farmers, as is usually the case in rural refugee settlements. The extent to which such "wage-earning" settlements have been successful is debatable, and there is much pressure to modify their scope to include at least some land allocation.

Before we examine in detail Sudan's refugee settlement experience, it is necessary to compare the concepts of "self-sufficiency," "self-reliance," "self-support," and "self-help," all frequently used terms relating to rural refugee settlements. Often they are used synonymously, while at other times they are used to differentiate distinct stages in the progress toward achieving full independence from external assistance. Hence it is sometimes argued that through "self-help," refugees can move to a level of "self-support," at which state they are weaned from external food handouts and eventually reach full "self-reliance," where they produce almost all their daily needs. "Self-sufficiency" is used to denote the subsequent attainment of complete independence from any form of external help, when refugees are not only self-reliant in their food production, but are able to generate all their own infrastructural needs and requirements, so that settlements are fully self-contained units. Whether such a ranking of these terms is truly valid is debatable, but implicit in such a ranking is that there are various degrees in achieving independence, and that there is no clear-cut agreement on the extent to which settlements should be completely self-contained in order to be declared fully self-sufficient.

The ability to provide daily food needs, together with the production of small surpluses to generate cash to purchase items not locally produced, is usually taken as the basis for declaring settlements as "self-sufficient." It is also argued, however, that settlements, in addition to being self-reliant in terms of food output, should generate revenue to offset the cost of local administration and of provision of basic services. Taxation of refugees by local authorities is a highly contentious issue. Refugees frequently indicate that their status is "special" and that they should not have to contribute to regional taxation. Local authorities, upon whom responsibility for settlements falls after UNHCR or other NGO support is withdrawn, expect at least the same level of tax revenue from the refugee settlements as is generated by indigenous populations. Water supplies must be maintained, roads graded, and schools and dispensaries kept up; it is therefore argued that true "self-sufficiency" is achieved only with an ability to contribute to infrastructural costs.

Another commonly expressed opinion is that "self-sufficiency" is achieved only when settlements require no external inputs of any kind. These include the provision by refugees of their own teachers, their own nurses for dispensaries, and their own administrators, and their own ability to create and maintain all infrastructural services. At this stage the settlements no longer cost the host anything and, with the exception of the land granted by the government to the settlements, they are free from any external inputs whatsoever. Such a rationale is unrealistic, however, since few if any rural communities anywhere in the world are ever able to be completely self-contained. In most rural areas, and especially in Africa, government funding for infrastructural facilities invariably exceeds income generated through taxation from the rural areas. Consequently, some measure of central government subsidy to rural regions is the norm rather than the exception, and thus must also be expected for refugee settlements. The question becomes not whether rural settlements will ever become totally independent of government aid, but whether basic subsidies for infrastructure should be the ultimate responsibility of the host government or instead be shared by the international community. This in turn introduces the issue of the long-term role and responsibility in asylum states of

UNHCR and its associated NGOs, vis-à-vis their "traditional" short-term, relief-provisioning role and responsibility.

As long as the refugees remain as resident aliens, a case can be made by host governments for receiving continuing support from the international community toward the infrastructural costs of their maintenance. Indeed, the knowledge that refugees bring in much needed foreign exchange can and does contribute to a reluctance in many parts of Africa to bestow citizenship status upon long-term refugee sojourners or their children, and in a few cases, even on their grandchildren.

To return to the question of terminology, and because there seems to be no standard nor universally accepted usage of the various terms relating to refugee support, the terms can be considered in the following contexts:

1. *Self-Help*—the most readily understood and most generally accepted of the terms. With self-help policies the refugees do as much for themselves as possible. They are encouraged to build their huts, clear their land, and develop their own services. The implementation of "self-help" policies, however, is often limited by the fact that refugees arrive in asylum in emaciated condition and are too weak to be able to do much. Or refugees may resist suggestion that they should help themselves, pointing instead to international conventions that stipulate that a government granting asylum to refugees is responsible for their well-being.

2. *Self-Support*—After refugees are settled in a rural area, priority is placed upon creating at least a minimum level of self-support in food production. World Food Program (WFP) feeding is not only costly, but can have serious repercussions on regional economies by inflating costs of foodstuffs for everyone. Also, WFP rations are not always the most nutritious, especially if only part of the designated "food basket" is available for distribution. In most cases, rural settlements should be able to clear sufficient land and plant enough crops to generate at least a basic level of self-support within a year. WFP's policy normally phases out full rations after a year, and partial rations a year or so later. In practice, however, self-support is not as readily achieved, and in many instances in Sudan and elsewhere, WFP rations have still been required after several years.

3. *Self-Reliance*—This term perhaps best describes a condition where refugees are fully self-supporting in food production, and are able as well to generate additional income from sale of surplus crops, or through providing services and selling their labor, and thus require little or no assistance in meeting their day-to-day needs. External assistance will still be necessary to keep the settlements running. For example, tractor pools may still require external help and fuel subsidies, or a water supply system will not generate adequate revenue to pay for its upkeep. Taxation and fees for service cannot fully cover costs, since refugees do not have sufficient means to pay. Many refugee settlements in eastern Sudan are in this stage. While some are progressing to full self-

sufficiency, for others progress to the final phase in their development to full self sufficiency is in fact the most difficult.

4. *Self-Sufficiency*—As suggested above, self-sufficiency cannot signify a total independence from any form of government assistance or subsidy; instead, the implication is that such assistance or subsidy be neither greater nor less than that received by local indigenous communities. In other words, refugees have achieved self-sufficiency when they are fully integrated into the rural mileau, including paying their full contribution to the tax burden. At this stage the refugees should receive levels of services equal to local populations, and indeed be accorded the rights and responsibilities of the indigenous population. If their sojourn appears to be permanent, or at least long term, refugees at this stage should cease to be refugees by being given the option of becoming nationals of their country of asylum. But while refugees have become self-sufficient in many areas in Africa, only Tanzania and Botswana have offered citizenship to their self-sufficient refugees.

Sudan's Experience

Since the Sudan has had experience with refugees for two and a half decades, it is not surprising that its policy has evolved into a series of well articulated objectives. At the 1980 Khartoum conference, these aims were spelled out in considerable detail, and while not all of the aims have been achieved, Sudan's policies are as both realistic and rational. These policies are detailed in the conference documentation (National Committee for Aid to Refugees 1980, in 4 volumes), and are briefly summarized here as follows:

1. To prepare the groundwork among refugee communities to enable them to deal with either their voluntary repatriation, should this become feasible, or alternatively facilitate their integration into Sudan, should the need for a prolonged stay arise.
2. To ensure, in the event that long-term sojourn be necessary, that integration occurs in such a manner as to create good relations between refugees and local populations.
3. To ensure that settlements created for refugees do not extend more help or care to refugees than is available to nationals living in the area, or than has been available to them previously in their country of origin. Refugees thereby enjoy the rights of other aliens residing in the country, but are not a priviledged group.
4. To operate settlement schemes for refugees in such a way as to ensure that nationals are not dispossessed from land or opportunity. Services provided by external donors to the refugee communities should at all times be made accessible to the local population.
5. To attempt to locate settlements so that they do not interfere with the balance of ethnic groups in any given area.
6. To provide refugees with a sufficient means of livelihood. Settlement schemes should have an adequate level of economic viability to allow

for margins due to crop failures or other temporary setbacks. Sufficient land and infrastructural services should be provided to satisfy not only initial population numbers, but also anticipated natural increase.

7. Settlements shall be designed to attract and retain not only people of agricultural origins, but also populations of nonagricultural backgrounds. Hence a wide range of activities must be integrated into scheme planning to permit the generation of nonagricultural incomes as well.

These points illustrate the realistic approach the government has adopted. The fact that some of these aims have not been fully met is less a reflection of the sincerity with which government has addressed the issue, than a product of the sheer scale of the problem and the very limited resources that Sudan has had available to work with.

Sudan's settlement schemes are basically of two types. First are the "land-settlements" where refugees become self-supporting by growing their basic subsistence food needs. Second are the "wage-earning settlements" where refugees achieve self-reliance by hiring out their labor. The latter group is made up of two subgroups, the rural wage-earning settlements and the peri-urban wage-earning settlements. Figures 10.1 and 10.2 show the distribution of the respective settlement types in eastern and southern Sudan.

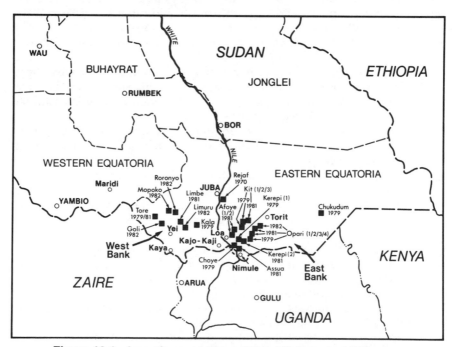

Figure 10.1   Location and Date of Establishment of Refugee Settlements (1982) in Southern Sudan

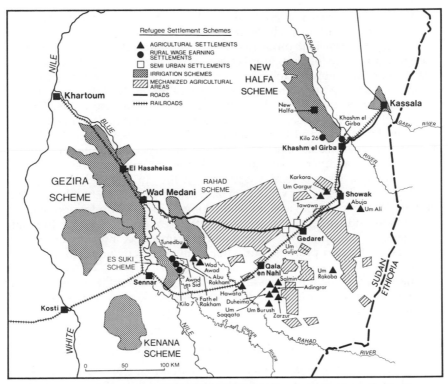

Figure 10.2 Location and Organized Settlements in Eastern Sudan in Relation to Major Sudanese Agricultural Schemes and Areas of Mechanized Agriculture

The settlement schemes have been established primarily for refugees of rural backgrounds to enable them to reestablish their traditional livelihood as quickly as possible. Refugees are allocated land holdings of between 5 and 10 feddans (1 feddan = 1.038 acres), an amount considered sufficient to generate basic subsistence food needs and to produce small surpluses for cash sales. In eastern Sudan, land is rain-fed, and where settlements are situated south of the 600 mm/year rainfall isohyet, a reasonable degree of crop security exists. Some settlements are located north of this line, however, and in such cases risk of crop failure may be as high as 30 percent (UNHCR/ILO 1982:11). Indeed, throughout the whole of eastern Sudan where refugee settlements are established, rainfall variability is high, and hence the hazard of drought is forever present (Mahdi el Tom 1974), as 1984 and 1985 devastatingly proved.

In addition to land, refugees are usually provided basic services, including piped water. But water is frequently a serious concern on several settlements, either because insufficient amounts are found or because inadequate drilling has been undertaken. At two settlements, Um Ali and Abuja, refugees must draw water from the Atbara River several kilometers away. Other infrastructural services, such as schools and clinics, are provided by scheme administrations and by a host of voluntary agencies.

One of the principal problems facing the land-settlements in eastern Sudan is availability of land. This is a complex issue, since Sudan is basically a land-abundant country. Yet in eastern Sudan, the arrival and settlement of several hundred thousand refugees has made the supply of land critical. It is also complicated by the fact that a dual land-tenure system exists. On the one hand is a large-scale, capital-intensive, mechanized farming system, while on the other hand is a small-scale, subsistence-oriented, traditional system, with a sizable livestock component. The allocation of land to refugees adds another dimension to existing competition between traditional and mechanized local landusers for the finite supply of land. A further factor affecting the viability of land settlements is the highly seasonal pattern of employment, which creates long periods of underemployment and greatly influences the chances of settlements not achieving full self-sufficiency. Consequently, settlements must introduce nonagricultural income diversification projects, but what form such activities should take is still a matter of conjecture.

The following section discusses some of the issues influencing achievement of self-sufficiency in one of the major individual settlement schemes in eastern Sudan.

The Qala en Nahal Scheme

Qala en Nahal is the oldest refugee settlement scheme in Sudan, by far the largest, and one which, in spite of frustrations and difficulties, is approaching self-reliance. It thus constitutes a model for other schemes in Sudan and elsewhere in Africa. The scheme was begun in December 1968, after the Sudanese government signed an agreement with UNHCR to resettle some 23,000 Eritrean refugees who had entered Sudan over the previous eighteen months. An allocation of 103,000 feddan of land was made, and Sudan provided the necessary manpower to establish, administer, and maintain the scheme. UNHCR funded the infrastructure, including an elaborate but critical water-supply system, at a cost of 2.5 million Sudanese pounds.

The area chosen for the scheme was a tract of largely underused land 180 miles southwest of Kassala and 30 miles south of Qala en Nahal, a small community situated on the Kassala–Khartoum railroad. It was a region of adequate-to-moderate rainfall, ranging between 600 mm at Qala en Nahal, to 850 mm at Galabat, south of the scheme on the Ethiopian border. Although soils are relatively fertile clays, the area was largely devoid of permanent settlement because of the almost total absence of permanent water. Even Shukriya tribesmen in their search for seasonal pasture avoided the area because of its infestation of biting flies. The few local Sudanese living in the area were primarily Fellata—people from western Sudan, Chad, and Nigeria who had migrated into the area after the Mahdiya, lived in abject poverty, were totally uneducated, and appeared to be generally disinterested in economic advancement. Their settlements had a tendency

to spring up and die away as their fortune waxed and waned in the area
(Barbour 1961:191).

Vegetation in the area ranges from open grasslands in the north to open
woodland-savanna in the south. Part of the area is subject to seasonal
flooding, or is unsuited to any form of cultivation because of jebels (rocky

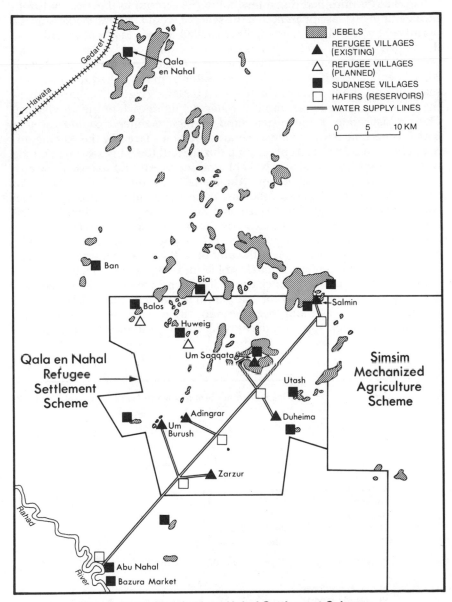

Figure 10.3   The Qala en Nahal Settlement Scheme

outcrops) or stony ground cover. In the remaining area, soils are heavy clays that, while relatively fertile, become very hard and cracked in the dry season. They also produce a prolific seasonal weed growth in the rainy season. Extensive woodland clearing has since reduced soil capability because increased run-off has caused considerable soil erosion.

Local authorities had dug a few hafirs (reservoirs) in the area, but from the beginning it was apparent that the scheme would become viable only if a permanent water-supply system was installed. Hence the "water-road" was developed: a costly and elaborate plan consisting of a 34 km pump and pipeline system capable of delivering some 45 liters per person per day for 30,000 people (UNHCR 1972). It draws water from the Rahad River in rainy seasons, and stores it in large hafirs at Abu Nahal (Figure 10.3); from there the water is pumped yearround to water points in each of the six villages. The sophistication of the system (and its high maintenance and running cost) has become one of the most serious problems faced by the scheme, for not only must pumps be kept running throughout the rainy season to fill the reservoirs, but they must also be kept working yearround to raise the water 65 meters along the pipeline from Abu Nahal to Salmin at the far end of the system. Major maintenance problems have frequently occurred, and fuel shortages or lack of spare parts are common. Moreover, it is evident that the system has nowhere near the capacity that the planner originally forecast. Consequently, water shortage is widespread, and a need exists to upgrade the system and supplement it with boreholes. It is clear that water availability, rather than the amount or quality of land, remains the ultimate determinant of whether full self-sufficiency will ever be achieved by the scheme. Refugees are required to pay for water from the system, and although initial installation costs have long been written off, revenue received from the water sales does not approach the annual running and maintenance costs of

Table 10.1   Fluctuating Population Size of Qala en Nahal Scheme, 1970–1982

	1970[a]	1971 April–June[b]	1972 March–June[b]	1973 April–June[b]	1976– early[c]
Salmin	4091				
Umm Saqqata	3629				
Duheima	1213				
Adingrar	2513				
Umm Burush	2832				
Zarzur	4000				
Total scheme	18278	17000	18130	19467	16000

[a] Official estimates.
[b] Quarterly reports.
[c] Hunting survey.

[d] M. McDonald, consultants.
[e] World Food Program.
[f] Euro-Action Accord.

the system. Some form of external subvention will always be necessary to maintain adequate water supplies for the scheme.

Cultivation on the scheme began in 1970, although most of the areas were not opened up until 1972 and 1973. By 1973, however, all six villages were cultivating at least some land. On the eve of the scheme's 1974 transfer from UNHCR to the regional local authority, the scheme appeared to be well on the road toward self-reliance for its basic needs (Rogge 1975). This was not to be, however, because serious set-backs occurred soon after its transfer to the local authority, which culminated in the scheme's virtual collapse in 1976.

The problems that befell the scheme after 1974 can be attributed primarily to the ineffectiveness and indifference of the local authorities under whose jurisdiction the scheme passed. Rural authorities in Sudan, as indeed throughout Africa, are perpetually in a financial squeeze. They are often also the end of the line for the least promising civil servants. In the case of Qala en Nahal, local government officers lacked both experience and commitment; hence very little attention was paid to the refugee settlement once UNHCR withdrew. The limited resources at the disposal of the local authority were employed in the town of Qala en Nahal or in surrounding Sudanese villages, and little or no priority was assigned to the refugees. Refugees faced major difficulties during the 1975 agricultural season. No fuel was made available to the scheme's tractor pool until mid-August, when it was already much too late to plough. Food shortages therefore arose in late 1975, and when ploughing was again delayed for the same reason in the following season, food shortage became critical. The immediate consequence was out-migration: refugees sought wage labor on mechanized farms in the area, or moved farther afield to large-scale irrigation schemes or to towns. Table 10.1 shows the consequences of the scheme's

1976–late[d]	1979[a]	1980[e]	1980[a]	1981[f]	1982[a]
3471	4400		4500	4610	6000
3276	4800		4407	3910	6000
1270	2400		2420	1750	5000
2089	3300		3367	2940	5000
1745	3600		3000	2840	6000
1438	2600		2450	2000	6000
13289	21100	21000	20144	18050	34000

breakdown, a drop in population from just under 20,000 to around 13,000. Indeed, the population may have reached an absolute low of around 7,000 to 8,000 in 1976. Verification of such data during 1976 was impossible, since neither UNHCR nor the Sudanese Commissioner for Refugees was prepared to discuss the Qala en Nahal settlement. Relations between the two agencies were strained, the low point in what has otherwise been a cordial, if not outright cooperative, relationship. A detailed survey of the scheme in 1976 by a British consultant was very critical of the manner in which the scheme had been managed, but its report was never made public, and access to this historic document is not permitted.

Not all of the blame for the scheme's stagnation during 1975–76 can be laid on the administration, however. Settler cooperation had never been enthusiastic, and several of the villages were outright resistant. A quotation from one of the scheme's quarterly reports illustrates this:

> ploughing started on 26 June in the three original villages. The refugees were very keen about cultivation this year . . . they have done a lot of hard work cleaning the land . . . with the exception of the Sawarta [sic], particularly those in the three new villages, where the majority refused the idea completely.

These attitudes prevailed through 1975 and 1976, becoming more entrenched each time the scheme's management reneged on its responsibilities. Moreover, the physical conditions of the heavy clay soils, together with the profuse weed growth, added to settler disillusionment about the viability of the agricultural economy.

Before we discuss the scheme's progress since 1976, it is useful to consider the actual land use to achieve self-sufficiency. During the 1980 agricultural season only 33 percent of the area was actually being cultivated. Moreover, almost half the cultivated area was being used by Sudanese residents on the scheme rather than by the Eritrean refugees, according to the scheme's quarterly reports: 11,000 feddans at the beginning of the 1971 season and 38,723 feddans at the start of the 1973 season. If these figures are correct, it shows the extent to which the scheme stagnated after its transfer to local authorities in 1974.

The resurgence of the scheme was stimulated by new UNHCR inputs, as well as by the need to resettle new refugees entering Sudan during the late 1970s. A major prerequisite to the reestablishment of a viable agricultural economy permitting self-reliance in food production was the reorganization and rehabilitation of the scheme's mechanized farming system. A voluntary agency undertook this task and by 1981 had achieved a reasonable degree of success: 30,000 feddans were ploughed before the rains came. In the 1982 season this progress was maintained. According to the voluntary agency that implemented this reorganization (Euro-Action/ACORD), all persons who requested ploughing were serviced during 1981, and the fees for ploughing service were paid by some 70 percent of the settlers. The remainder, consisting of the infirm, disabled, widows, and new settlers, received the service free of charge.

Adding the cost of ploughing to the other costs that farmers incur, such as seeds, labor for weeding and harvesting, and sacks and transport from field to village, and considering the relatively modest prices a sack of dura can realize in the surrounding market towns, it is questionable if self-reliance, let alone full self-sufficiency, could ever be achieved if costs of production were to rise even a small amount. Yet the tractor services operate at highly subsidized levels that are substantially above the fee per feddan paid by farmers. Consequently, although the system is capable of generating an agricultural system in which farmers are beginning to support themselves, the highly subsidized economy means that the scheme remains a long way from self-sufficiency. The question of who will, in the long term, be responsible for deficits incurred by the mechanized ploughing system has yet to be addressed effectively.

One further dimension to the problem of achieving self-sufficiency must be mentioned: its manpower resources, and especially the availability of skilled and professional manpower for servicing refugee communities. Implicit in the concept of self-sufficiency is the ability of refugee communities to provide their own administrative, educational, and medical manpower. Adequate, qualified human resources in the refugee community can doubtless fill most, if not all, administrative, educational, and medical positions on the settlement schemes. So far, however, few administrative positions, except at the lower echelons, have been filled by refugees, and this is primarily a matter of Sudanese government policy. At the same time, however, much skilled and professional refugee manpower is resident in urban Sudan, but there is clearly considerable reluctance, if not outright opposition, among such people to living in remote and environmentally hostile rural settlements. As a result the settlements remain heavily dependent upon Sudanese staff or upon manpower provided at even greater costs, albeit externally financed, by the various NGOs.

The growing volume of permanent third-country resettlement is further exacerbating this problem. While until the late 1970s there was virtually no overseas resettlement of African refugees, since the U.S. 1980 Refugee Act an increasing number of refugees are being resettled. The U.S. currently has a quota of 3,000 African refugees per annum, Canada has increased its quota from 500 to 1,000, and even Australia has introduced a small quota. While, in theory, criteria for selecting refugees for resettlement are simply that the refugees show legitimate fear of persecution and are then unable to return home, in practice the more pragmatic question of the refugee's likelihood of assimilating and becoming economically independent in North America are the issues that determine who is selected for overseas resettlement. Herein lies another problem that hinders the progress toward self-sufficiency, since invariably the very people most needed locally by scheme administrations to service the settlements are the ones most likely to be selected for third-country resettlement. Moreover, if they are already working for NGOs on the settlements, they have the additional advantage of access to information on resettlement or even counseling by well-meaning NGO staff on how best to ensure that they be accepted for resettlement. If self-sufficiency also means the ability of the refugees to service and administer themselves, thereby reducing the dependence on scarce Sudanese manpower resources, overseas resettlement must be approached in a modified manner.

Summary

When is self-sufficiency achieved? In Sudan several settlements, including some of the villages at Qala en Nahal, are certainly on the way to achieving self-sufficiency. Likewise, in southern Sudan the Zairean refugee settlement at Rejaf is fully self-sufficient and integrated into the surrounding rural milieu, as are some of the older Ugandan refugee settlements on the East Bank. But many problems remain in the settlement schemes, which make complete self-sufficiency an extremely difficult if not impossible task. This is particularly so in the case of eastern Sudan. In places such as Qala en Nahal, overcapitalization of the scheme, through its elaborate and costly water supply system, as well as through a tenure system dependent upon mechanized ploughing, makes it unlikely that sufficient revenue will ever be locally generated to fully offset infrastructural costs of the scheme. Long-term external commitments appear to be built into the scheme. Who will be ultimately responsible for these long-term commitments has yet to be determined.

A further problem is created by overseas resettlement programs. One cannot blame the educated, skilled, or professionally qualified refugee for wanting to resettle in areas of economic opportunity in North American or Europe. Conditions on the settlements are bleak, and for most educated Eritreans and Ethiopians who originate from the highlands, the environment on the settlement schemes is hostile and debilitating. Yet the fact remains that for self-sufficiency to be achieved, these same people are the ones needed by the settlements to provide the necessary leadership and human resources for development. There is no simple answer to this dilemma. One must also appreciate that on most refugee settlements, a very large component of the population consists of "vulnerable groups": people who require permanent support services and general welfare (Macauley 1983). Widows, orphans, and the disabled are an integral part of most politically generated refugee populations, and costs that they incur to settlement schemes cannot ever be written off through locally derived taxation. Hence, long-term commitments will always be required for such populations.

11

The Tripartite Approach to the Resettlement and Integration of Rural Refugees in Tanzania

Charles P. Gasarasi

Tanzania experienced its first major influx of refugees in 1961, when Rwandan refugees crossed into West Lake Province. The newly independent government of Tanganyika settled these refugees in Ngara and Karagwe Districts. Subsequently a further 3,000 Rwandan refugees who had been living in Zaire were airlifted to Tanzania following misunderstandings between them and the Zairean government, and this led to the opening up of another settlement at Mwese. These three settlements have long since been handed over by UNHCR to the Tanzania government, and a significant number of the refugees have been granted Tanzanian citizenship.

The Rwandans were not the only group of refugees who sought asylum in Tanzania. In the mid-1960s, Tanzania received a number of refugees from Malawi and Zaire. Both groups were initially settled at Pangale, but many of the Malawians found their way into various Tanzanian towns, where they either are self-employed or work in the public sector. At the same time many of the Zairean refugees voluntarily returned to Zaire following an amnesty granted to all Zaireans living outside the country.

Another source of refugees who sought asylum in Tanzania in the early 1960s was Mozambique. And in the second half of the 1960s, large influxes of Mozambiquan refugees arrived in Tanzania, necessitating the opening up of several rural settlements for them. These influxes were a direct result of the escalating liberation war in Mozambique, which was paralleled by intensified Portuguese colonial brutality and repression. The refugees settled in five rural settlements: Lundo, Muhukuru, Matekwe, Mputa, and Rutamba (Figure 11.1).

In 1975 when Portuguese colonialism was defeated and Mozambique became independent, the Mozambiquan refugees repatriated to their

Figure 11.1   Location of Refugee Settlements in Tanzania

mother country. After repatriation their former settlements were put to other uses by the government of Tanzania.

Early in the 1970s, Tanzania began to receive refugees from two other African trouble spots: Uganda and Burundi. Following the 1971 coup by Idi Amin in Uganda, many Ugandans sought asylum in Tanzania; about 5,000 of them were settled at Kigwa in Tabora Region. The Ugandans returned to their home country after the fall of Idi Amin in 1979, and the Kigwa settlement is currently inhabited by an assortment of refugees from South Africa, Kenya, and Zaire. South African refugees seeking asylum in Tanzania have increased in number as the liberation struggle gradually gains momentum and the apartheid regime increases its brutalities. The few Kenyan and Zairean refugees currently settled at Kigwa consist predominantly of radical students who are in conflict with the regimes in power in their respective countries.

The major influx of Burundi refugees into Tanzania took place between

1972 and 1974. These refugees were first temporarily settled at Pangale settlement, but later three settlements at Ulyankulu, Katumba, and Mishano were established for them. At present both the Ulyankulu and Katumba settlements have been handed over by UNHCR to the government of Tanzania, while Mishano is still growing as spontaneously settled refugees from Kigoma Region are gradually transferred there. Several thousands of spontaneously settled refugees from Burundi remain around Kigoma, and projects to integrate them within the region have been initiated.

The ways and means through which Tanzania has been able to cope with these influxes of refugees form the subject of this essay. Tanzania shouldered the burden of rehabilitating refugees alone for the first few months following the initial influx in 1961, but since then other actors have been called in to share the burden. This became necessary because of Tanzania's lack of surplus resources and because the refugee population grew to reach totals as high as 167,000.

The other actors discussed in this essay are the UNHCR and the Lutheran World Federation/Tanganyika Christian Refugee Service (LWF/TCRS). Although burden-sharing became a pan-African concern in the 1960s and became enshrined in the 1969 OAU Convention on Refugees, Tanzania has received little or no help from African countries. According to Article II, para 4 of the Convention:

> Where a Member State finds difficulty in continuing to grant asylum to refugees, such Member State may appeal directly to other Member States and through the OAU, and such other Member States shall in the spirit of African Solidarity and international cooperation take appropriate measures to lighten the burden of the Member State granting asylum.

In practice, however, this resolution has not been adhered to by most OAU members. Ten years after the OAU Convention, President Nyerere lamented the failure of the burden sharing principle, stating that:

> the 1967 Conference acknowledged the need for the refugee burden of Africa to be shared with some concept of equality among all African States. It has not happened yet . . . this meeting cannot be told anything very much about progress in sharing the burden which refugees cause for some nations [Nyerere 1979].

Despite this disappointment, Tanzania still expresses optimism for Africa's political will to collectively share the burden caused by the refugee question, considering the task quite formidable but still bearable. Tanzania's disappointment would certainly have been much greater if the burden-sharing necessity had not found its expression in the "tripartite strategy" discussed in the balance of this chapter.

The Tripartite Arrangement and Its Implementation in Tanzania

The first tripartite agreement between the government of Tanzania, UNHCR, and LWF/TCRS was signed in May 1964. This agreement was concerned with the resettlement at Mwese of 3,000 Rwandans who had been airlifted from Kivu Province in Zaire. This operation was organized by UNHCR as a result of the deteriorating political climate prevailing in Zaire, which threatened the security of Rwandan refugees living in Kivu.

Since the establishment of the Mwese settlement, other settlements have been set up and implemented under similar tripartite arrangements. These include the settlements for Mozambiquan refugees at Rutamba, with 11,500 refugees; Lundo, with 5,000 refugees; Muhukuru, with 11,500 refugees; Mputa, with 12,000 refugees; and Matekwe, with 7,000 refugees. It also includes the settlements for Burundi refugees at Ulyankulu, with 45,400 refugees; Katumba, with 48,916 refugees; and Mishamo, with 30,000 refugees.

Analysis of how the tripartite arrangement led to the rehabilitation and resettling of refugees requires an understanding of the individual characteristics of the respective partners. UNHCR is a "non-operational" U.N. agency acting within the framework of the 1951 Convention relating to the status of refugees, and directly bound by the 1951 statute. LWF/TCRS is a charitable church organization. This diversity in the characteristics of the partners makes operational contradictions inevitable phenomena, although, in most cases, concensus has prevailed.

It is unfortunate that, when considering the actors in the tripartite arrangement, one cannot include the refugees as a fourth, "corporate actor." In the actual implementation of the resettlement programs, however, the refugees cease to be mute and become an active, decisive force that determines the ultimate success or failure of the benefactors' plans. In fact, behind the occasionally divided opinion of the tripartite partners rests the unvoiced vote of the refugees themselves, and it is important to highlight the role the refugees play in the operationalization of the tripartite arrangement.

The activities undertaken by the tripartite partners in rehabilitating and resettling the refugees have been guided by government policy. Thus, in Tanzania, the broad policy of rural development has been a very useful guide. The majority of the refugees offered asylum in Tanzania have been helped to build new homes on rural refugee settlements. One of the initial contributions made by the Tanzania government toward resettlement of refugees is free land. Each refugee family is given a minimum of 10 acres for farming. The procedures for setting up refugee settlements where land is distributed to refugees has been described by Hombee (1981) thus:

> When a need for a new settlement arises the Ministry of Home Affairs communicates with the Prime Minister's office which is responsible for regional administration. The Prime Minister's office communicates with Regional Authorities where the new settlement is earmarked for establishment. Usually more than one region is approached for this purpose. In accepting or rejecting the new settlements, the Regional Authorities take into account their own long-term development plans. Once the Regional Authorities accept to establish a settlement, the appropriate District Authorities get involved, particularly in locating the site.

Since 1975, the establishment of settlements has been governed by the Ujamaa Villages Act of 1975. As a matter of policy, between 250 and 600 families form one settlement village. The social services set up in the rural refugee settlements are also guided by national policy. Thus, primary education is free and is governed by the broad policy of socialism and self-reliance; health services are free, and economic activities are guided by government policy whereby "as many economic activities as possible should be run by co-operative ventures both in towns and rural areas."

Of course, not all government policies apply to refugees in the settlements. For example, unlike for nationals, post-primary education for refugee children is not free. Refugees who are selected for secondary schools must secure a scholarship, normally from UNHCR or a voluntary agency. Furthermore, admission of refugee children to secondary schools is governed by a non-citizen quota system of 2 percent of available places. Also unlike the nationals, refugees have to acquire work permits on completion of their training, before obtaining employment from the Ministry of Manpower Development.

UNHCR's involvement has consisted mainly of providing funds for land settlement schemes, including the clearance of land, the building of access roads, the boring of wells, and the building of dwellings and community infrastructure such as primary schools, dispensaries, and community centers. The magnitude of UNHCR assistance is great. For Tanzania a $108 per capita cost of resettling refugees has been incurred. Table 11.1 summarizes UNHCR's participation in financing rural refugee settlements in Tanzania. To conceptualize the burden-sharing aspect of this UNHCR contribution,

Table 11.1   UNHCR-Sponsored Rural Settlements in Tanzania from 1963 to 1979

Settlement	Starting date and hand-over date	Average population in the period	Amount allocated by UNHCR in US $	Per capita costs in US $
Rutamba	1965–1972	9,800	541,850	52
Lundo	1966–1973	4,300	619,195	137
Muhukuru	1966–1974	11,000	924,301	84
Liputa	1970–1976	12,280	1,110,850	94
Matekwe	1969–1975	7,300	662,142	93
Karagwe	1964–1969	2,000	–	–
Muyenzi	1963–1969	6,500	–	–
Mwese	1964–1972	3,000	393,298	131
Pangale	1966–1971	920	–	–
Katumba	1973–1978	48,916	–	108
Ulyankulu	1973–1980	45,400	6,886,200	151
Kigwa	1974–1979	2,875	375,107	130
Mishamo	1978–	28,000	–	–
Total:			11,512,943	$108

Source: A.C.S. Diegues, 1981.

the expenditure should be expressed in a Tanzanian context. If Tanzania had had to raise this money on its own, it would have parted with a sum equivalent to the total investment for the period 1969–74 of the parastatal National Agriculture and Food Company. This is no small sum for a developing country like Tanzania.

As a matter of policy, UNHCR assistance to rural refugees is limited in time. It is assumed that once refugees have established a reliable base for long-term viability, the settlements will be handed over to the government to be integrated into the local administration framework.

LWF/TCRS participation in the resettlement of refugees began in the early 1960s. For the initial years following the first influx of Rwandan refugees, the government tried to cope with the situation without outside assistance. But by 1962, government assistance was complemented with some aid from UNICEF, the African Medical and Research Foundation, the British Red Cross, Oxfam, the Swedish Churches, the World Council of Churches, the Lutheran World Federation, and UNHCR. The increasing sophistication of refugee rehabilitation that resulted from the multiplicity of aid agency programs, coupled with the recognition in 1962 of the permanence of the refugee problem, necessitated a more permanent strategy to handle the refugee question.

Against this background a decision was taken in 1962 to establish the first permanent smallholder settlement project for Rwandan refugees in West Lake Region. It was also in this context that the government thought of having one single organization coordinate all assistance from voluntary agencies. Thus the government appealed to LWF, which had previous experience in refugee matters as well as a history of good relations with the government. LWF responded to the call by founding a local arm, Tanganyika Christian Refugee Service (TCRS), in January 1964. Table 11.2 summarizes the magnitude of relief shouldered by LWF over the years.

The settlement approach adopted by LWF/TCRS fits into broad national policies. Thus, when implementing a refugee settlement project, TCRS ensures that Tanzanians living in the settlement area be integrated into project benefits such as a water supply system or medical and educational facilities.

The tripartite arrangement for resettling refugees in rural areas is governed by the Refugee (Control) Act of 1965. This stipulates the nature of projects to be undertaken, the parties involved, and their respective obligations. The government of Tanzania has committed itself to providing sufficient suitable land for rural settlement on the basis of 10 acres of land per family unit. It is also understood that refugees have the same rights and terms of use of that land as do nationals living in the district where the settlement is set up.

Other government commitments include such provisions as public administration, including public safety, health, and rural development. Settlement commandants are appointed to facilitate the implementation of resettlement projects in conformity with agreed plans and government policy, and to ensure effective cooperation and liaison with concerned government departments. They also arrange for LWF/TCRS to import duty-free supplies

Table 11.2   Lutheran World Federation and Other Assistance in Cash and Kind to Refugees in Tanzania to December 1980

A. Assistance to the settlements	LWF assistance in US $	
Muyenzi and Kimuli	$ 247,009.00	
Mwese	542,068.00	
Rutamba	460,059.00	
Lundo	374,719.00	
Muhukuru	531,226.00	
Mputa	721,239.00	
Matekwe	377,782.00	
Ulyankulu	2,668,973.00	
Katumba	2,079,386.00	
Mishamo	2,420,797.00	
B. Other forms of assistance		
Christian Council of Tanzania	$	39,000.00
Medical and health services		103,555.00
Scholarship, vocational training		157,965.00
Aid to exiles and students		265,670.00
Refugee emergency		296,932.00
Rural development (other settlements)		277,825.00
Material aid		191,555.00
Supportive air services		23,000.00
Aid to liberated areas (mainly in Mozambique)		570,448.00
Donated commodities		7,550,875.00
Program implementation		1,629,084.00
Total	US	$21,529,167.00

Source: E.S.W. Nilssen, 1981.

and equipment contributed under bilateral or international arrangements or by private donors.

In establishing the rural refugee settlements, the energies of the partners in the tripartite agreement have been channeled into such activities as the establishment of the settlement headquarters, the building of access roads, the installation of water supplies, the supplying of basic requirements to refugees (such as blankets, cooking utensils, and tools), and the setting up of health, educational, and agricultural services. Some of the most recent and more elaborate settlements, like Ulyankulu, have such facilities as a post office, a bank, a police station, and branches of the National Milling Corporation and the Tobacco Authority of Tanzania.

Costs for establishing and running the settlements have varied according to the number and type of refugees involved, environmental factors, and the length of time elapsing from the inception of the settlement to its handover to government. For example, between 1964 and 1974 the cost of establishing and running the Mwese settlement (population 3,000) was $1,646,565. More populated settlements have cost considerably more, such as Ulyankulu, where population ranged from 6,287 (1972) to 60,000 (1977) and costs are estimated at $9,436,300 for the period 1972 to 1980. Likewise, Katumba's costs (population 60,000 in 1980) were $8,989,643 for the period 1973 to 1980, and Mishano's (population 37,000 in 1983), $17,869,832 for the period 1978 to 1983.

To achieve the difficult task of resettling refugees in rural settlements, the two partners in the tripartite arrangements who are permanently represented at the settlement site—the government and LWF/TCRS—have divided their labor within the general framework of the tripartite agreement. The settlement commandant is recognized as the government representative responsible for the maintenance of law and order. In this capacity, he interprets government policy and acts as a liaison officer with the district and the regional authorities. He supervises the staff who are seconded to him as well as the storage and distribution of World Food Program (WFP) commodities.

The LWF/TCRS project coordinator is responsible for expenditures incurred in the settlement and for the purchases of supplies from local suppliers. He maintains close relations with district and regional authorities, and supervises the following departments: Administration; Education; Health; Ujamaa and Co-operative; Labour Division; Roads; Water Supply; Agriculture Development; and Construction and Transport.

The Planning Factor

Since the ultimate aim of the tripartite partners is to help refugees attain a degree of self-reliance, the tripartite approach has placed emphasis on economic activities in both agricultural and nonagricultural spheres. Planning of the settlements by LWF/TCRS has followed this format:

> every year, about the end of September, the senior staff in the settlement meet with the headquarters staff to discuss plans for the coming year. They prepare work-schedules and proposals for new projects. Revision of existing projects is also discussed. Later these are presented to the tripartite partners, who discuss them further and finalize the next year's budget [Nilssen 1981].

While planning has yielded positive results, some problems have arisen. The most serious ones occurred during the initial stage of the tripartite arrangement, when none of the partners had much experience in developing rural settlements for refugees. An example that illustrates the problems resulting from poor planning was the unrealistic assignment of available land resources relative to the refugee population. At the Rutamba settlement for Mozambiquan refugees, inadequate land was made available for the permanent support of its population, and the shortage was exacerbated by malpractice in land clearing. In 1967, it was decided that 800 hectares of land should be cleared using bulldozers. But the bulldozers scraped away the topsoil, resulting in a significant depletion of the fertility of Rutamba's sandy ground.

Ulyankulu also illustrates faulty planning. There, where 60,000 Barundi refugees had been settled by 1977, it was subsequently found that the soils were unsuitable and that there was an inadequate water supply. As a result, a mass transfer sent 25,000 refugees to a new settlement at Mishamo. Even at Mishamo, the question of careful planning was raised. Hombee (1981) noted that: "the preliminary survey showed that each area earmarked for the establishment of a village had enough water. *After the villages had been established,* it was found out that only deep wells could be used for supplying water in a few villages. This resulted in increased costs."

Nilssen (1981) also found fault with the Mishamo settlement layout, suggesting that both the size of the villages and the long distances between them were too great. He wrote:

a village covers an area of about 22 sq. km, so it takes time for a field worker to cover this area. There is also a considerable distance between villages, which makes motivation and supervision very difficult. To compensate for this we have tried in Mishamo to provide the field staff, on a loan basis, with small motorcycles.

Another notorious hindrance that has impeded planning is the "ignorance factor." Because of the rapid influx of the refugees and the corresponding need for immediate action, planning teams had to rely on flimsy data bases about settlement environments and other diverse variables that affect the implementation of such projects. As a result, estimated expenditure and actual expenditure have often differed greatly.

Mishamo, the latest settlement to be established by the tripartite partners, reflects relatively high planning standards, a result of long and often agonizing trial-and-error experience by the tripartite partners. Mishamo's planning benefited from the fact that the refugees were transferees from other settlements. Ulyankulu, which was an organized settlement, and the large spontaneous settlement area in Kigoma. Their movement to Mishamo was not an emergency operation. Mishamo also benefited from the experience acquired over the years by the tripartite partners' personnel. The 715 employees of TCRS constituted an experienced team whose skills in organization had accumulated since 1977. Whenever a new settlement was established, experienced staff from former settlements were brought in to help train new staff. For example, TCRS staff came from Katumba to assist in the settlement planning and development of Mishamo.

A further factor contributing to the high standard of planning in recent refugee settlements is the participation of the refugees themselves in setting up the settlements. Prior to the establishment of Mishamo, refugee leaders from Ulyankulu, such as village chairmen, pastors, and teachers, visited the Mishamo site to gather early information about the area. After the refugees had been moved to Mishamo, 23 refugee leaders visited the Katumba settlement to observe the development work taking place there.

One of the lessons the tripartite partners have learned is to accept refugee participation in setting up settlements and in running day-to-day activities. Such participation has also reduced the information gap that refugees in earlier-established settlements once suffered from. Then, infor- mation-starved refugees welcomed any rumors and used them to fan refugee politics in the settlement, often getting into trouble with the authorities. Earlier settlements such as Muyenzi, Kimuli, and Mwese of- fered few democratic rights and little refugee participation in decision- making; orders were believed to be more expedient in an emergency situation than encouraging popular participation.

In the establishment of the most recent refugee settlements, planners have also drawn on local people's knowledge of the environment to choose sites. Mishamo is a beneficiary of this development. Nilssen (1981) illus- trates this: "The Tanzanians in Mishamo give us useful information about the area, as they have extensive knowledge about rivers, swampy areas, where there is sand, gravel, trees for timber production, etc. This helps also when one starts different economic projects which are needed for the settlement development."

The use of the accumulated knowledge of local inhabitants has thus become an important input in the employment policy of TCRS, which now tries to recruit as many people as possiblefrom the immediate settlement area.

The Resettlement Strategy

The major thrusts of the tripartite partners in developing rural settlements have been to create agricultural viability within the shortest possible time, and to set up basic socioeconomic infrastructure. Then they hand settle- ments over to the government. The length of time needed to achieve those aims has varied. At Muyenzi settlement, for example, it took about seven years (1962–69) before the settlement was handed over to the government. The factors responsible for this rather long period of dependence ranged from some refugees' unwillingness to settle permanently in Tanzania, and hence their refusal to cultivate, to such problems as crop damage by vermin and drought. Other settlements have taken as long as eight years (Muhu- kuru) and as little as five years (Katumba). On average, it has taken the tripartite partners a period of six and a half years to bring settlements to levels of independent agriculture-based existence.

A number of agricultural production methods have been tried, including the method of "block farming," which was not successful. It was introduced because Tanzania had embarked on a policy of block farming for its rural development strategy. But refugees in Rutamba responded with antago- nism to block farming, and the method was virtually abandoned except for a modest undertaking maintained by TCRS. The failure of block farms is attributed to difficulties involved in organizing labor; to the use of coercion because of refugee refusal to work together; to poor relations between farmers and technical advisors; and to inappropriate cultivation techniques.

Mechanization was also tried, both where block farming existed and on individual refugee plots. In Karagwe a tractor was donated by UNHCR in 1965 and was run and maintained by the Karagwe District Council. In 1968, however, the Karagwe District Council stopped the services of the tractor since the successes accruing from mechanization were only very modest. Mechanization was also tried in Muyenzi, where TCRS provided two tractors and agricultural implements. After the withdrawal of TCRS agriculturalists from Muyenzi, the tractors were handed over to a newly formed cooperative society, and funds were given to the society to cover running costs. Nonetheless, a lack of interest in mechanization made it impossible for the tractors to be used economically or on a large scale.

Notwithstanding this failure in some of the agricultural techniques introduced, each of the settlements gradually achieved levels of productivity at subsistence levels or higher. Refugees' contribution to the national economy is gauged by the quantity of surplus crops sold by them. After the 1975/76 harvest, Katumba settlement sold a surplus of 2,400 tons of food crops to the National Milling Corporation; and additional and considerable private trading took place within the settlement. This tonnage constituted 77 percent of Mpanda District's production in that year. Likewise, in 1976 Mputa, Ulyankulu, and Katumba settlements produced 870 tons of tobacco, or 6 percent of the total tobacco crop sold nationally to the Tobacco Authority of Tanzania. Rutamba settlement had some 20,000 cashew trees contributing to the national economy.

A wide range of other economic activities have been introduced in the settlements, such as cattle rearing, chicken raising, brick-making, charcoal-burning, carpentry, and wood carving. Furthermore, refugees with nonagricultural skills have resumed their former activities. Thus, barbers, bicycle repairers, masons, tailors, shoemakers, and petty traders are active in the settlements' economic life. In the most recent settlements of Ulyankulu and Katumba, these activities are run by multipurpose cooperative societies. An indicator of the viability of these cooperatives in Ulyankulu and Katumba has been their ability to contract out for building construction and furniture-making projects.

The tripartite partners have played a role in the introducing cattle and poultry to some of the refugee settlements. Progress of cattle raising has hampered by tsetse flies in the settlement areas, and the introduction of livestock has been determined by the clearing of woodlands. Even so, more could have been done in this regard. An earlier introduction of cattle to the Muyenzi, Karagwe, and Mwese settlements, for example, would have contributed greatly to their viability, since the Rwandans on these settlements are traditional pastoral people who are experienced in raising cattle in a wide variety of environments, including tsetse-infested ones.

TCRS established poultry units at Rutamba, Muyenzi, and Kimuli in the 1960s to distribute fertile eggs, but the project failed in all these settlements. The incubators malfunctioned, which caused hatching failures, and the refugees were generally antithetic to new breeding techniques.

The inherent manpower resource among the refugees has been a decisive force in bringing about and sustaining the viability of the rural settlements. Refugee labor has been used in all sorts of activities in the settlements, such as bush-clearing, road and building construction, and in health and education services. A number of work methods have evolved. In an attempt to effect equitable cash distribution, a system has sometimes been used where a limited number of refugees are employed for a period of time, and then replaced by other individuals. Other methods of using the manpower resource have been self-help, and work in return for remuneration in kind.

Refugee labor has also spilled over to neighboring communities. Gasarasi (1976) has shown the deployment of the Rwandan refugees around Bukoba and Karagwe Districts in the early 1960s. But Chambers (1979) has argued that a spill-over of refugee labor has a negative effect on poorer people in the host population because refugee labor drives down wages relative to costs of food, thus impoverishing those who rely partly or entirely on laboring for their livelihoods.

The endeavors of the tripartite partners to attain satisfactory levels of viability in rural refugee settlements lead to the handover of the settlements to the government. Nilssen (1981) outlined the criteria for handover as follows:

> the criterion for handover in Tanzania has usually been that the refugee settlers have reached a stage of complete self-reliance in food production, that they have some extras, basically in cash crops which will enable them to buy additional food such as salt, tea, sugar, etc. They should also be able to buy some consumer goods such as clothing, agricultural tools, household utensils, and blankets.

> . . . the second criterion is that the settlement has the necessary basic facilities, such as health services, education, water, and communication.

> . . . the third criterion is that the settlement has built up a community entity with participation in village committee activities, and that there are regular elections of council leaders, unit leaders (roads), village chairmen and committee members.

Once the time for handover has been determined by the tripartite partners, the Ministry of Home Affairs informs the Regional and District Authorities so the latter can incorporate the recurrent costs of the settlement into their budget. The Regional and District Authorities in turn are briefed by TCRS on the settlements.

Some Problems of Implementation of the Tripartite Arrangement

Since the resettlement of refugees is basically a rehabilitation exercise, it encounters the problem inherent in any such exercise. The diverse nature of the tripartite partners has led to some inevitable operational contradictions, albeit of a nonantagonistic nature. First, problems emanate from the respective partners' personal characteristics. UNHCR is a "nonoperational" organization: a funding body. It has to rely on its operational partner and the government for the efficient use of funds. UNHCR has periodically expressed dissatisfaction over the accounts for different projects, which has generated some tension. Although UNHCR accepts the rationale that infrastructural facilities for refugee settlement should also benefit the indigenous population in the neighborhood, it faces the problem of its mandate limiting assistance to refugees.

There have been times when UNHCR's interests have conflicted with those of the government. One such instance was when the government applied the Immigration Act of 1972 to the refugees working outside the settlements in West Lake Region. These refugees, who were already self-reliant, were ordered to move to the settlements, which meant being uprooted and starting a new life. Since a supply of food was required while these uprooted refugees grew their own food, UNHCR was approached for help. UNHCR's reaction to government officials was that "it was impossible to approach the international community for food assistance in such a self-inflicted situation."

Lack of mutual trust has also been cited as an indicator of conflicting interests between UNHCR and the government. As one of UNHCR's terms of reference is the legal protection of refugees, refugees have tended to approach the agency whenever they have felt, rightly or wrongly, mal-treated by the government. This has brought UNHCR and government into adversary positions.

Sometimes UNHCR and the government have differed on how certain problems in refugee settlements should be solved. For example, in the 1960s several Rwandan refugees at Mwese refused to accept refugee identity cards on the grounds that if they accepted them they would be renouncing their Rwandese nationality. The government detained several refugees and with-drew food and other assistance from the concerned refugees and their families. The action had a very negative affect on the settlement's development. UNHCR proposed that the exiled Rwandan king write a letter to those refugees advising them to accept the permits. The government rejected the idea on the principle that it did not recognize the authority of the ex-king. Thus, although UNHCR's suggestion would probably have solved the problem immdiately, Tanzania's "legal" position resulted in more protracted resistance by the refugees and certainly retarded the progress in developing the settlement.

Some observers have suggested that, since LWF/TCRS was a humanitar-ian organization, it has tended to make social considerations, such as dispensaries and schools, overshadow the economic aspects of the settle-ments. At Ulyankulu, for example, health services and education made up 30 percent of the total budget, compared to 14 percent for agriculture. Similarly, at Katumba education absorbed more than 18 percent of the total budget, health services 13 percent, and agriculture only 15 percent.

A further criticism is that LWF/TCRS has paid too much attention to building construction. The Mpanda District Development Director has pointed out the high construction cost at Katumba compared to that normally incurred in Ujamaa villages, and suggested that a 50 percent cut in costs was possible.

Constraints to the smooth implementation of the refugee settlement program under the tripartite arrangement have also been caused by both interpartner and intrapartner communication breaks. For example, in 1970 UNHCR discovered that the Office of the Second Vice President had unilaterally decided to transfer a UNHCR–donated truck from the Kimuli to the Muyenzi settlement without informing the UNHCR. Consequently, the transportation of vegetables to market failed; this led to the closure of the Kimuli communal vegetable farm. The other adverse effect caused by this transfer was the difficulty of getting supplies for the Kimuli Consumers' Co-operative. Another example: the Ngara District Council took over the primary schools at the Muyenzi settlement in January 1970, but by March the teachers had received no salaries, since the District Education Officer had no knowledge of the arrangement.

Conclusion

Tanzania's experience in rehabilitating and integrating refugees in rural settlements under the aegis of the tripartite partners is one of considerable success. Notwithstanding problems encountered on various projects, the rural settlements have attained levels of development and self-reliance comparable to that of nationals in the region. One of the factors contributing to this success is the burden-sharing inherent in the tripartite arrangement. Without the funds supplied by both UNHCR and LWF/TCRS, the government would have found it extremely difficult to cope with the subsistence needs of the refugees, let alone their development and infrastructural needs. Indeed, President Nyerere (1979) acknowledged the assistance from these agencies thus: "without their investment of capital, and their skilled and professional personnel, we would not have been able properly to meet our responsibilities to these victims of racism, colonialism, and social change in Africa."

Nevertheless, UNHCR's and LWF/TCRS's financial aid should not over-shadow the magnitude of the government's contribution, part of which cannot be evaluated in money terms. For example, the act of granting asylum to needy people is impossible to quantify. In the same light, the long-term value of the free land the refugees have been given is difficult to evaluate. Other not-always-obvious costs of government participation are administrative costs and the recurrent expenditure after settlement hand-over. For example, acccording to Hombee (1981), "the recurrent annual expenditure for running Ulyankulu settlement is 4 million shillings, while it costs the government 5 million to run Katumba."

Since the response of OAU member states to the principle of burden-sharing has not been encouraging and is not likely to improve, the tripartite approach has proved to be a viable strategy worthy of imitation in other countries. It is interesting to note that the tripartite strategy has been practiced also with success in some southern African countries such as Botswana, Swaziland, and Zambia, where the two other partners are also UNHCR and LWF.

The Sudan could benefit from a tripartite approach. There, the government and UNHCR have entered into agreement with several individual voluntary agencies for individual projects, rather than working with a single permanent implementing agency. Thus the advantage of deploying a single agency's accumulated experience is lost, and so is the harmonizing and rationalizing aspect of project planning and implementation that is accrued with experience.

This recommendation favoring a single permanent implementing agency does not preclude the possibility of involving other agencies in implement- ing settlement projects. In Tanzania the tripartite partners have signed agreements with other subimplementing agencies for running short-term projects in settlements. In the 1960s, for example, YMCA and the Danish Volunteer Team served successfully in this capacity at the Muyenzi and Kimuli settlements, respectively.

Several factors have been responsible for the relative success in rehabili- tating and integrating refugees in rural settlements in Tanzania. The avail- ability of arable land is one of these factors. President Nyerere (ibid.) has pointed to the importance of available suitable land:

> Tanzania has areas of under-utilized land on which refugees can be settled if there is an investment of capital . . . But this is unlikely to be the most productive land, and in some countries—like Djibouti or Algeria—it will be waterless desert requiring at least very heavy investment in irrigation schemes . . . And some countries have no spare land at all; Burundi and Rwanda are already overpopulated.

Since all land is the property of the state in Tanzania, it has been possible for the government to allocate land to refugees. Not all countries have land policies that allow the government to be that generous. The Swaziland government, for example, had to purchase 5,000 hectares of land to resettle refugees at Ndzevane (Khumalo 1981). Such allocation depends not only on the amount of money available for land purchase, but also on the amount of land the owners are willing to sell.

The success in implementing rural settlements in Tanzania is also a result of a well-defined policy governing the setting up of village and social infrastructure. Policies relating to education, health, cooperatives, and water supply have been functional in guiding decision-making and action. But the Refugee Control Act of 1965 has had one negative impact in that it has tended to produce authoritarian settlement commandants. In many cases the refugees on various settlements have lodged complaints about ill treatment by settlement authorities. It is therefore gratifying to note that the process of revising the act has been started.

Experience gradually acquired by the tripartite partners has been instru- mental in bringing about better results on more recently established settle- ments. The performance and levels of success of established settlements has increased, and this can undoubtedly be attributed to greater experience on the part of the implementers. Other African countries which host refugees could greatly benefit from Tanzania's experience.

Refugee status in Tanzania has not been permanent. Many of the earlier settlements have assumed a status akin to ordinary Tanzanian villages. This has happened in two ways. First, refugees who did not opt for voluntary repatriation when conditions at home changed, such as the victory of FRELIMO leading to Mozambique's political independence, were given the choice of staying, and those refugees who chose to stay integrated with

Tanzanians. Second, the status of refugees has been changed by mass naturalization. Rwandan refugees were granted naturalization in 1980. This measure brought to an end the presence of settlement commandants and marked the beginning of the total integration of these settlements into regular administrative structures of the country. It is likely that this will happen to the refugees from Burundi in the future.

12

The Problem of Urban Refugees in Sudan

Ahmed Karadawi

The term "urban refugees" is the generic name given to the category of refugees who move directly or eventually from border areas into towns. Compared to rural refugees, for whom planned settlement of whole communities is believed to be the most practical solution, urban refugees are individuals who have different cultural backgrounds, different ambitions, and who, accordingly, seek individual solutions. The continued mobility of urban refugees makes them subject to changing and mostly transient social networks. The problems of the urban refugees become more intricate because of the conflict between attitudes and expectations of the refugee and those of the host communities (Karadawi 1980).

Until 1975, the number of urban refugees in different Sudanese towns was insignificant; resources in the affected towns could tolerate such numbers. In the aftermath of disturbances that befell Ethiopia and the effects of the Ugandan influx since May 1979, Ethiopians and Ugandans (to a lesser degree) have gravitated toward Sudanese towns in the eastern and southern regions on an unprecedented scale. This essay discusses eastern Sudan, where the urban refugee influx has affected the towns of Kassala, Gedaref, Port Sudan, and Khartoum. In March 1981 the numbers of refugees in these towns was Port Sudan, approximately 55,000; Kassala, 25,000; Gedaref, 30,000; Khartoum, 33,000. An ECA report stated:

> one of the enigmas of the Sudan is the existence of vast empty spaces and overcrowded towns and cities and some rural areas. At the same time, the past and present indications have not been to fill up the empty spaces, but rather for population to move towards already congested areas and depopulating the low density areas [Gaafar and Ramchandran 1982].

Population mobility within the Sudan is caused by the fact that development efforts before and after independence have accentuated the attractiveness of certain areas. The construction of railways and highways; the developments of water transportation; the establishment of irrigated agricultural projects, new industries, and commerce and trade; and the siting of educational, cultural, and administrative centers have all focused upon Khartoum, the Gezira, and the eastern region. This has created large-scale population movement from less developed areas to these more developed or developing areas. The increasing tempo of interprovincial movement is resulting in imbalances in population growth and settlement patterns. While the mid-region, Khartoum, and Kassala provinces grew at faster rates (3 percent), Kordofan and the northern and southern regions show lower rates (1.5 percent). In other words, the eastern and central regions show tremendous growth, the north and west little growth, and the south stagnates.

The level of urbanization reflects a wide range of variation in physical and climatic conditions, as well as the uneven distribution of economic development and rates of economic growth. The urbanized centers clustered in the middle regions have a population growth rate of 7.4 percent per annum, compared to the national rate of 2.8 percent and the rural rate of 1.5 percent. Thirteen percent of Sudan's population live in five towns in the middle region, each of which has a population of more than 100,000.

Sudan's Urban Core

Khartoum

Khartoum, the capital city, has a disproportionate level of amenities and activities. It contains 73 percent of all the industrial establishments; 75 percent of the urban workforce engaged in manufacturing; and 80 percent of all banking. In a country with 6 million illiterate persons, Sudan has 54 percent of primary school–age children enrolled in school, 10 percent of eligible children in junior schools, 5 percent of eligible children in higher secondary schools, and only 2 percent of eligible persons undertaking higher education. Khartoum, on the other hand, has 90 percent of all primary school–age children at primary school and 40 percent of eligible children enrolled at the secondary level. The city contains all higher educational institutions (with the exception of the universities of Gezira and Juba). It is a parasitic town, the growth of which places a heavy burden of expenditure on national and municipal governments to build up its infrastructure. The rate of migration to Khartoum is estimated as 70 percent of the total migration to urban centers. The deficit in housing units is estimated at more than 100,000 units, and rents—which consume 40 percent of the population's income—rose more than 350 percent between 1959 and 1976. In recent years, the average income of the urban manual worker has actually decreased in real value, due to the rising rate of inflation and the continued devaluation of the Sudanese pound. Such a situation pushes workers, who provide 40 percent of the labor force in the formal sector, to move and work in the informal sector, which has been largely ignored by successive governments and thereby suffers from restrictions on licences, lack of credit facilities, and lack of technical assistance.

One of the main features of land use in Khartoum is its horizontal expansion. The concentration of urban functions in the center of the town imposes long and expensive journeys between homes and places of employment. The deficiency in public transport facilities is illustrated by extreme overcrowding, extended periods of peak traffic flow, and long waiting periods at transport stops. For people located on the outskirts of town, the inadequacy of public transport, together with the long journeys into town, can negatively affect their participation in many employment and educational opportunities.

One of the major problems of Khartoum is that its own revenue is stagnant and unreliable. Local taxes are too modest to meet its obligations, and it must depend upon funding by the central government. Yet the government's increasing economic difficulties make it difficult for the government to respond to the needs of the capital city.

Port Sudan

Port Sudan arose in 1906, and until 1937 its manpower needs were met by migrant labor from outside Sudan, as well as by migrants from other parts of the country. The 1951 census gives the number of Beja, a population not accustomed to settled life, as only 25 percent of the town's population. By 1969, however, the Beja had grown to 47 percent of the population. One of the reasons was the severe drought that hit Red Sea Province during the mid-1960s. Small groups of Bisharin and Amarar moved into the town because of the drought and were forced by authorities to live on the outskirts of town in squatter settlements *(deims)*, which have dominated Port Sudan since. Town authorities began to draw up plans in the mid-1960s to contain the problems caused by these migrations; however, their plans could not be brought to fruition because of additional influxes of Beni Amir from Eritrea.

A number of factors have contributed to a unique and intricate refugee problem in Port Sudan. Being the only seaport in Sudan and the largest town in the Red Sea Province, it has attracted migrants from both the drought-stricken areas within the province and from other parts of Sudan. Ethnic groups such as the Beni Amir and Habab straddle the international boundary between Sudan and Ethiopia. The influx of refugees has caused a recent change in attitude among the town community from unreserved sympathy for the migrants to stigmatization. The influx is believed to have created the strains on services such as housing, education, water, and health, as well as a security threat, which at times has led to physical involvement of the Ethiopean army in its pursuit of Eritrean political activists in Red Sea Province.

The first influx occurred in September 1970, when some 16,800 refugees arrived in Tokar district via Jarora and Marafit. Prevailing famine conditions in Tokar district, together with delays in the provision of relief and the failure of local authorities to keep accurate records, caused the refugees to move into the Tokar Delta and into Port Sudan, where they settled in a number of *deims* on the outskirts of the town.

Following the change of government in Ethiopia in 1974, and due to military actions in Eritrea, new waves of refugees began to arrive in Port Sudan. Police records in Tokar and Port Sudan show that 11,000 newcomers were registered between 1977 and 1978. In February 1979, a further 6,000 (mostly children) arrived, fleeing an Ethiopian army offensive against the Eritrean Peoples Liberation Front (EPLF).

Gedaref

The Gedaref region is one of the most important commercial areas in Sudan. It lies between the Rahad and Atbara rivers and has adequate rainfall and fertile, arable soil. Mechanized agriculture was introduced in the area in 1943; since then, sorghum, the staple food crop of Sudan, has been grown extensively. The demand for sorghum, both within the country and in neighboring oil-rich Arab countries, creates good markets for the area's farmers (Gaafar and Ramchandran 1982). Almost half the labor force in Gedaref town is composed of farmers, farm laborers, or traders.

In addition to a sizable influx of migrants from other parts of Sudan, Gedaref has experienced several waves of refugee migrants. Some have arrived directly from Ethiopia, while others have come from other parts of the eastern region. The concentration of refugees in Gedaref is explained by the opportunities created by the mechanized agricultural schemes as well as by a variety of agro-based enterprises that require a large contingent of unskilled labor.

The first Eritrean influx into Sudan in 1967 was initially settled around Kassala town, but was subsequently transferred to the planned rural settlement of Qala en Nahal, south of Gedaref. The proximity of this scheme resulted in many refugees moving to both Gedaref and to the Gezira scheme in search of seasonal labor. Gedaref was especially affected by the immigration of young refugees seeking employment or educational opportunities.

By 1975, a total of 23,000 refugees had crossed the middle sector of the eastern Sudanese Ethiopia border from the Eritrean town of Um Hagar. Nearly half this influx was either too young or too old to undertake anything more than minor tasks of economic value. A survey conducted in 1975 suggested that "the 1975 influx consisted, to a large extent, of urban people without farming experience for whom, therefore, other solutions than agricultural must be found" (Alla 1976). A third group of refugees came to the town in 1977: the Tigrayans, who differ from Eritreans in language, economic structure, and religion. The inflow of Tigrayan refugees has continued since and especially following the birth of the Tigrayan Peoples Liberation Front (TPLF), which caused military activity in western Tigray, the part of Ethiopia that neighbors the Gedaref region, to escalate.

Because of the size of the refugee influx to Gedaref, it was decided that the idea of sub-urban settlement be put into practice adjacent to the town.

Thus the Um Gulja and Tawawa settlements were established on the outskirts of Gedaref to enable refugees to take advantage of economic opportunities offered in the town, without causing a great deal of strain to the town's urban fabric. This policy, however, which might have worked if the numbers of refugees had remained small, has instead created a number of huge problems to both the refugees and the town, because of the increasing influx of refugees. The Tigrayan influx comprised people of both rural and urban backgrounds.

Kassala

Kassala is a provincial capital and has a very special appeal to Eritreans. As well as its proximity to the border—it is only 40 kilometers from Tessenei in Eritrea—Kassala is the spiritual capital of the Khatmiya sect that straddles the border of Sudan and Ethiopia, and which has had a great impact on both the politics and history of Eritrea and Sudan. The tomb of the Khatmiya's founder, Al Sayed Al Hassan, is in Kassala, and it was a Khatmiya, Sayed Abu Bakr al Mirghani, who organized at Keren in 1947 the first political party to strive for Eritrean independence (Karadawi 1977). As early as 1960, Kassala was among the few places where the emergent Eritrean Liberation Front (ELF) opened a branch office, and ever since then, the town has been an important host for the ELF. By the beginning of the 1980s, Kassala Province hosted some 350,000 of the eastern Sudan's refugee caseload. Also, the proximity of Kassala to the border makes it, like Port Sudan and Gedaref, an attractive destination for refugees from both rural and urban backgrounds.

"Urban Refugees": A Confusion in Definition

A common perception has developed in refugee studies in Africa that identifies urban refugees as an elaborate category of people who differ from rural refugees in terms of their background, their patterns of movement, their expectations, and their need for separate solutions. The Pan-African Conference at Arusha in 1979 identified urban refugees as young people who move to towns in their host country in search of employment or educational opportunities. The OAU's Bureau of Placement and Education of African Refugees (BPEAR) reflects this bias in its emphasis on individual rather than group solutions. Others identify the pattern of movement of urban refugees as being "anticipatory" in contrast to the "acute" or unplanned movement of rural refugees.

Nevertheless, evidence provided by the influx of refugees into Sudanese towns shows that their movement may not necessarily be individual flight of persons of urban background. In the case of Port Sudan, Gedaref, or Kassala, it is clear that rural migrants have also found their way to the towns. One can therefore identify two phases in the generation of urban refugees: (a) movement from their home area to the initial point of safety in Sudan—the refugee's involuntary migration to escape persecution; and (b) movement to a Sudanese town—a voluntary migration. Subsequent moves may include the departure of refugees for overseas resettlement to permanent countries of asylum.

The lack of definition of "urban refugees" exacerbates the problem of the lack of formal organizational structures that cater to refugees in urban areas. Refugees are in direct confrontation with local townspeople and authorities, and here the crisis of refugees is magnified. The survival of their identity and ethos is threatened, not only by the event of the flight but also by its aftermath in the urban area. The impact of urban areas upon the lives of the refugees who migrate into them has rarely been examined in studies of the refugee problem, of their needs, or of refugee programs. The section that follows discusses the array of motivations and backgrounds to be found among the "urban refugees."

Types of Urgan Refugees

The Education Seekers

Although Ethiopian communities existed in Sudanese towns before the refugee phenomenon was officially recognized in 1967, the problem of urban refugees first began to be a subject of concern in Khartoum in 1971. By that time, approximately 100 students of Ethiopian origin had arrived from Addis Ababa as a result of government suppression of the militant student movement, which had begun to oppose the government in 1965. Although the Commissioner of Refugees (COR) admitted them as refugees, UNHCR suspected the genuineness of their motivation for leaving their homeland and labeled them "education seekers." It is relevant here to note one of the shortcomings of the legal definitions of the term "refugee." While the definitions contained in the Statute of UNHCR and in the UN Convention Relating to the Status of Refugees (1951) are the same, the two documents charge different bodies with applying the definition. Under the 1951 Convention, the host country decides who shall be accorded refugee status. But according to UNHCR's Statute, it has the final say who is to be considered a refugee and therefore eligible for international protection. A consequence of this is that "recognition as a refugee by the UNHCR will not by itself either secure the admission of a refugee to a country or confer a legal status, and determination of eligibility by one country does not necessarily confer a refugee status upon the individual in other countries" (de Voe 1980). This shortcoming exposes the very serious limitations of UNHCR to define clearly its protection function vis-à-vis individual refugees, such as the "education seekers."

Rural to Urban Migrants

These are refugees who first settled in rural areas or in refugee settlements. Their migration usually begins when they are hired to work on agricultural schemes such as the Gezira. Thereafter some of them move to nearby towns; other migrants move directly to Khartoum for employment or educational opportunities. After 1976, the centralization of administrative assistance offered by the COR (especially the issuance of travel documents), as well as material assistance offered by the Refugee Counselling Service (RCS), has further encouraged refugees to move to Khartoum to seek help from these organizations for overseas migration or resettlement.

Army Deserters

This group includes military officers and soldiers who deserted from the Ethiopian army and escaped to Sudan. Although relatively smaller in number than the education seekers and the rural-urban migrants, the deserters pose considerable security and employment problems. For these reasons, the authorities in the provinces tend to send them to Khartoum.

Deserters from the Exiled Fronts

This group comprises individuals who were once fighters of Eritrean or Ethiopian political fronts opposed to the government of Ethiopia, most of whom deserted because of dissatisfaction with the internal factionalism within the Fronts. In 1978 a group of TPLF and Ethiopian Democratic Union (EDU) deserters arrived at Khartoum; the majority of deserters, however, are from the ELF and arrived in Khartoum immediately before and after it broke into two factions in April 1982.

Refugees-sur-place

This group includes Ethiopians who came to Sudan as migrant workers, but who subsequently became unable or unwilling to return home for fear or threat of persecution. They play a very important, informal role in the reception and orientation of newly arriving refugees. Because of their long residence in Sudan they tend to live in the planned residential areas rather than in the squatter areas. Newly arriving refugees locate with or near them, which explains why refugees in Khartoum seldom live in the poorer squatter settlements where Sudanese rural-urban migrants live. This informal assistance between the old-timers and the newcomers has a tendency to degenerate into an exploitative relationship, where the old-timers collect a great deal of money through counseling new arrivals.

The Activists

This group includes an array of exiled political organizations. The Eritrean groups, the ELF, PLF (People's Liberation Front), and EPLF, all have offices in Khartoum, Kassala, and Port Sudan. Each has organizations for their different membership, such as workers, women, or students. Although such organizations do not exercise total control over the refugee population, they perform an important role in providing alternative assistance to refugees, as well as being accepted as mediators between refugees and formal agencies such as COR, UNHCR, and RCS. Through their own contacts, these organizations help many young compatriots benefit from scholarships and employment opportunities offered by Saudi Arabia, Syria, Iraq, Libya, and other Gulf states. The PLF has been particularly involved in education programs and established its own schools in Port Sudan, Kassala, and Gedaref, as well as on many of the settlements. The refugee-based relief organizations such as REST (Tigrayan), ERA (Eritrean), RC/RC (Eritrean), and ORA (Oromo) are also involved in aid programs that emphasize health and sanitation, education, and income generation and training. Although young and poorly equipped, these refugee-based agencies have shown a good degree of efficiency in mobilizing refugees, gaining their trust, and helping them preserve their sense of identity. They should be encouraged and assisted by both UNHCR and the government of Sudan by extending to them legal recognition, by providing them with access to material resources, and by involving them as full partners in the whole refugee assistance structures, since to date neither RCS nor COR has proved effective in understanding and coping with the problems of refugees in the urban milieu.

The Opportunists

Clearly, many individuals migrate to Sudan to seek ways of emigrating overseas. They believe that in Sudan they can acquire the necessary travel documents, visas, and tickets, as well as receive money from relatives and friends who are already abroad. This type of movement has been encouraged by the many opportunities offered in the oil-rich Arab countries and by resettlement programs to the United States and Europe. Many refugees who go abroad correspond with their relatives and friends in the home country, and encourage them to follow their example by coming to Sudan. Many of the refugees who express a desire to return home by volunteering for the repatriation program are persons who were unsuccessful in realizing their hopes of emigrating abroad (COR 1980).

Organizational Structure for Refugee Assistance in Towns

In comparison to many host countries in Africa, the national law in Sudan—the Regulation of Asylum Act, 1974—offers the best conditions and guarantees for asylum. This act consists of fifteen articles supplemented by regulating procedures. Since it was intended to bring international principles relating to the status of refugees within the scope of Sudanese national law, the content of the act is derived—to a large extent—from the 1951 U.N. Convention and the 1969 OAU Convention Relating to the Specific Aspects of the Refugee Problem in Africa. The definition of a refugee includes the criteria of both the U.N. and OAU Conventions, with an additional clause on "unaccompanied children." In cases of mass influx, Sudan offers asylum en masse (Karadawi 1982). Employment, education, travel and identity papers are established by law as refugee rights.

The problems facing the refugees are caused by an inability of refugee organizations to coordinate their efforts in making these legal rights of practical value. The complete separation of administrative assistance provided by COR (such as the provision of identity cards, work permits, licences, and travel documents) and material assistance provided by UNHCR created a sense of uncertainty among the refugees. The apparent underestimation by UNHCR of the size of the refugee influx into the towns, as well as its insensitivity to the impact of the influx on the limited resources of the towns, has shifted the whole decision-making process from refugee-serving organizations to government authorities such as the police, the state security, and the municipal authorities. It is ironic that UNHCR is partially responsible for encouraging migration to the capital city through its decision to centralize RCS in Khartoum. By 1978, when the efficiency of RCS was suspected by UNHCR itself, the decision to evict the refugees from Khartoum was taken by the then-minister of the interior and the chairman of public security. While the role of COR was overshadowed by the minister, UNHCR's protection role proved to be worthless. Between 1978 and 1982, town authorities, police, and state security stepped up their persistent campaign against the refugee influx to towns. UNHCR neither improvised specific programs for the urban refugees nor predicted the arbitrary decisions that victimized them. After Khartoum had set the example in evicting refugees from the urban area, other towns such as Kassala, Wad Medani, and Port Sudan began to follow. COR was helpless, and as a government department trying to assist refugees, could only "row with the tide." It did manage to exempt certain refugees from the eviction orders, such as professionals, skilled workers, students, and cases under medical care. But the remainder were relocated to the rural settlements schemes.

The Refugee Counselling Service was established in 1976 in Khartoum by an agreement between COR, UNHCR, the Sudan Council of Churches, and Sudan Aid. Although these four agencies are meant to act jointly as a policy-making body, UNHCR assumed responsibility for financing and running of RCS. Since the guidelines, policy, and recruitment of staff were controlled by Geneva (the headquarters of UNHCR), COR was left completely ignorant of the role of RCS. It has no say in policy and staff matters and, accordingly, the beneficiaries of RCS have remained unknown to COR. Every move by COR to re-evaluate the performance of RCS was ignored by UNHCR. Among the suggestions for reorganization of RCS, COR suggested a decentralization of services, an introduction of group solutions targeted in refugee-affected areas, and a proposal that the role of RCS be brought to the attention of refugees through information and surveys, and that links with civic groups should be established to facilitate an exchange of information between refugees and their hosts.

This lack of coordination between organizations has created isolated programs initiated by certain agencies. While UNHCR (RCS) and COR (individual cases unit) function as two separate groups, the Sudan Council of Churches established its own counseling programs, the American resettlement program operates through the Joint Voluntary Service, and the International Red Cross runs its own tracing program. The refugees who fall through the net of these special programs tend to be exploited by the fast-growing network of passport forgers, cheap-labor employers, and greedy landlords. This imbalance in treatment of refugees is caused by the inability of the government to impose greater measures of control on voluntary agencies and the UNHCR. The absence in towns of organizations that can promote a mutual awareness of host communities and refugees, together with a lack of special programs to deal with the problem in its totality, result in both refugees and hosts creating their own misconceptions of their respective rights and obligations.

In urban areas, refugees are left to their own devices. Immediately on arrival, refugees discover the disadvantages caused by language barriers, different climatic conditions, and different cultural milieus, all of which make them vulnerable to psychological strain and living hazards. The popular conception that refugees in Africa do not feel alienated because of cultural similarities across borders becomes questionable as refugees travel farther from their home areas. The greater the distance, the more difficult it becomes for them to secure basic needs of food, housing, and even communication. One way of obtaining these needs is to rely on persons from their home country. While these are often barely able to manage for themselves, they act as reference groups for helpless newcomers. This in turn leads to congested lodgings, poor health conditions and, above all, the conspicuousness of refugee groups in the towns. In Khartoum, Port Sudan, Kassala, and Gedaref, some residential quarters have become predominantly occupied by refugees, a fact that makes townspeople look at the refugee community as an out-group. Since 1977, several complaints from local townspeople have alleged that refugees have negatively affected rents and have exacerbated pressures on public services and shortages in consumer goods.

Education and Training for Refugees

One of the serious effects of the sizable influx of refugees to the towns is the absence of educational assistance programs for urban refugees. Apart from primary schools built with UNHCR assistance in the rural settlements (where children are taught a Sudanese curriculum), no other significant educational services have been provided for refugees. While only 15 percent of refugees in rural settlements are literate, 45 percent of refugees in Port Sudan and 80 percent in Khartoum have some educational background. Some 10 percent of them had been in secondary schools (Bushra 1982). Currently, the following categories of refugee students can be identified in Sudan:

- students at primary (and post-primary) levels studying a Sudanese curricula in Arabic;
- students for whom language is a barrier and who are thus unable to resume their education in Sudanese government schools;
- students who study at self-help refugee schools built and run by the refugee community. These schools function under very poor conditions, the teachers are generally not trained, curricula are not comprehensive, and the buildings are unsuitable;
- students who study in traditional religious institutions run on local

charity support, which do not qualify students for further study or vocational training; and
- students who manage to go abroad for studies through personal contacts or through voluntary agency support.

Primary schools in the rural settlements are run by the Sudanese Ministry of Education and are staffed by its teachers using the Sudanese curricula and examinations. This policy assures comparable standards with other government schools and that refugee graduates have a chance to compete for places in junior secondary schools outside the settlements. Subjects such as Tigrinya or the history of Eritrea are given as extracurricular studies. In urban areas, refugee children can attend local schools with Sudanese children. In areas of high refugee concentration, such as Kassala, the percentage of refugee children in Sudanese schools can be as high as 50 percent. In one school it reached 80 percent (Homeida and Kabosh 1980). A report by the Ministry of Education showed that in 1981 there were 11,000 refugee children in Sudanese schools in Kassala Province.

Schools run by the refugee community provide children with awareness of their own identity. They are complementary to the existing local educational resources and cover the needs of those who do not find opportunities in official schools. They lack adequate resources.

One of the problems of secondary education is that opportunities are available only in towns. To gain access to government or private secondary schools, refugees have to move from the rural areas to the towns. RCS contributes minimally to this process. For example, in 1980 RCS assisted only 305 secondary school students, 75 at vocational training centers, and 31 at university level. Since then, UNHCR has supported a refugee secondary school in Kassala. A government proposal to establish twenty-four schools for refugee students was made to the 1980 Refugee Conference in Khartoum, and to ICARA, but neither proposal received any support.

Refugee-based agencies are more successful in providing adult education and training programs. REST's community development program in craft training, home economics, and literacy for young girls and women are useful and "offer women something to do in an otherwise long and empty day" (Bushra 1982). Small-scale artisan schemes, run on apprenticeship basis, are provided in Port Sudan and Gedaref by REST and ERA. Both organizations also run programs for women and children in Khartoum and Omdurman.

Voluntary agencies have introduced limited programs for students who have completed junior-high level, such as correspondence courses and mobile libraries, but such small-scale programs help only a very limited number of refugees, yet add to the complexity of planning for refugee education. The questions currently facing government, refugees, and agency planners are how to integrate refugee education within the Sudanese system, while simultaneously addressing the problems of:

- pressures posed on Sudanese educational institutions;
- the parents' dilemma of wishing to educate their children without risking a compromise in their identity;

- varying political viewpoints and nationist viewpoints that make concensus on uniform curricula development difficult;
- how to create a sense of commitment to their homeland through education: at the primary level to teach children to preserve their identity, while at the secondary and university levels not to create aspirations that push them away to other countries.

Employment

Refugees' right to employment is guaranteed by Article 14(b) of Sudan's Regulation of Asylum Act 1974. For rural refugees, the planned settlements have been constructed to develop traditional agricultural and pastoral economies. This strategy is intended to create levels of employment that lead to self-sufficiency. Employment for urban refugees, on the other hand, depends on available resources in the host towns. Unlike the settlements, international assistance for support of employment or income-generating programs is not available in the towns.

Urban employment is available in either the formal public sector or the informal private sector. Refugees have a better opportunity of finding jobs in the private sector, since the public sector is more competitive and selective. The huge losses of manpower in Sudan due to emigration may help qualify refugees to prove replacements. Skilled refugees, however, often opt for the same migratory pattern to the oil-rich states as do the Sudanese. The private sector also offers more income and has less restrictions, and overseas migration opportunities are many. The impoverishment of manpower shows up especially among craftsmen and tradesmen: painters, carpenters, construction workers, bricklayers, metal workers, and equipment operators are all attracted to Saudi Arabia and the Gulf. It is clear that refugees are potential replacements, but the refugees continue to be considered as peripheral to the labor market. Because of the large numbers of refugees entering towns, a process of screening urban refugees was initiated, so that identity cards and work permits could be issued.

The role of voluntary agencies in generating urban employment is negligible. There are no agency employment-generating programs in any of the towns, except for those by refugee-based organizations such as REST and ERA. Yet, they do advocate employment of refugees within existing local resources, and have pressured the government to allow refugees freedom of movement to seek work in different parts of the country. Refugee women are a particularly vulnerable group as far as employment opportunities are concerned. As Palmer (1982) stated, "little is known of women refugees' employment profile, beyond the fact that a substantial proportion take to domestic service and prostitution. A minority enter clerical and other skilled jobs."

Overseas Migration and Resettlement Programs

A permit for travel outside Sudan is one of the services most requested by urban refugees. The opportunity of gaining access to such permits creates a major pull factor for refugee migrants from rural areas. In Sudan, the

Convention Travel Document (CTD) is introduced with generous provisions for holders. The Sudanese CTD has the same validity in time and place as does a national passport. It is renewable and contains a clause allowing a refugee to return to Sudan lawfully as long as he retains the CTD. The fees paid by refugees for the CTD are one quarter the fee paid for a Sudanese national passport.

Overseas migration to work in Saudi Arabia, Libya, or the Gulf states takes place without UNHCR support. Migrants to Arab countries also include students, women and children who are united with migrants, and cases requiring medical treatment. Of the 37,000 travel documents issued by COR between 1977 and 1982, 85 percent were for travel to Arab countries. Apart from the economic prospect, one reason for this huge movement is that Eritreans have migrated to these regions since the 1940s, when the recession in Eritrea following World War II caused 20,000 Eritreans to find work in Arab countries. Added to this is the religious link of Islam: every year Moslem refugees travel as pilgrims to Saudi Arabia, and some always stay behind. Another reason is the political sympathy accorded by most Arab countries to the Eritrean political struggle, which translates, among other things, into scholarships for young refugees.

The remaining 15 percent of CTDs are issued for European countries, mostly for education or for family reunions. This percentage, however, does not reflect all the refugees who travel to Europe. Since CTDs are not recognized by several countries, many refugees use forged passports. A considerable industry in forgery of travel documents has developed, both in and outside the country. Also, since 1980, a variety of travel documents have been sent to refugees by their relatives in Europe. In many cases, refugees enter other countries illegally as stowaways or with forged documents. When they are caught, they often are forced to move from one country to another to become what UNHCR and others increasingly refer to as refugees in orbit. Eventually they may be deported and returned to Sudan. Saudi Arabia has also requested that Sudanese authorities readmit approximately 30,000 Eritreans who are in the kingdom illegally: many of these crossed the Red Sea from countries other than Sudan. Thus it can be seen that overseas migration does lessen the burden for Sudan. The COR and Sudanese embassies abroad frequently have to issue and renew refugee documents, as well as to readmit the deportees. Furthermore, there is no special provision to help refugees who are working overseas to send remittances to their relatives in Sudan. Consequently, refugees have to rely on illegal ways of transferring their money, which further exacerbates the lack of trust between them and their Sudanese hosts.

Resettlement

Resettlement to permanent countries of asylum is one of the major acceptable solutions to a refugee problem. Resettlement countries have traditionally been non-African, such as the United States, Canada, or the West European countries. The practicality of such a solution for African refugees has always been controversial. The resettlement alternative is seen to deprive the continent of the high caliber and skilled refugees who qualify for resettlement. Resettlement is selective of people, focusing on those who can adapt to the ways of life in the country of destination. The OAU's policy has always been to encourage qualified refugees to stay in Africa, but unfortunately no measures have ever been taken to help them to do so. In general, refugees prefer to go to Europe or the United States.

In the Sudan, resettlement opportunities once were processed on a very small scale by the UNHCR branch office. In 1980, a program for resettlement of African refugees to the United States was introduced. At the same time, voluntary agencies specializing in resettlement came on the scene, the Intergovernmental Committee for Migration (ICM) and the International Catholic Migration Committee (ICMC). Since then, a growing number of Ethiopian refugees have been assisted to settle in the U.S. The fact that these agencies work in isolation from COR and have little rapport with the government has made the whole program very controversial. Several meetings have been held with these agencies and with representatives of the U.S. State Department, whose Immigration and Naturalization Service (INS) decides on the eligibility of candidates. These meetings, however, have produced no changes, and the program continues to be criticized for its bias toward refugees of specific categories, and of specific nationality. The political fronts consider it an American political activity aimed at recruiting potential "counter-revolutionary" elements. Sudanese authorities criticize it as an instrument of American policy being implemented independently in a host country with its own policies for refugees. The resettlement program is highly selective of functional groups such as medical staff, who are much needed for health programs in their respective refugee communities in Sudan. It is also argued that the sums spent on such an individual approach to the refugee problem are greater than that spent on rural settlements, which assist whole groups rather than individuals. Also, the false hopes and expectations raised among the refugees by the program— most refugees then want to go to the United States—have a negative effect on the refugees, since only a small number of applicants are ever successful.

Although it is not practical to dismiss resettlement as such, one hopes that sponsors will coordinate their programs with host governments in order to guarantee equal opportunity for all refugees, regardless of their religion or nationality. Aid for resettlement should not overlap with other assistance programs, and a degree of freedom should be offered to selected refugees. There has been little or no feedback about the success experienced by refugees who have resettled in America or Europe. But if it is true that the pressure behind the 1980 U.S. Refugee Act, and the resultant resettlement quota for Africa, came from the American black constituency, one wonders on which level in the U.S. social strata the African refugees will be placed, and therefore what their future opportunities will be.

Conclusions

Legal protection of refugees requires more than articles of law and administrative instruments that regularize refugee status (such as identity cards, licences, or stay permits). Material support that assists refugees, while eliminating the pressures and fears of competition on the part of the hosts, is a very important complementary requirement.

Consolidation and upgrading of rural settlements must be set as a priority. Economically viable rural settlement will lessen the migratory movement of refugees to urban areas.

Provisions for urban refugees must be integrated into a program that brings together the efforts of UNHCR, the voluntary agencies, and the government. Such a program must be decentralized to guarantee equal treatment for refugees in the different regions.

RCS must develop an outreach program that considers the refugee problem in its totality—that is, the overall living conditions and interaction with the hosts—rather than being limited only to education and employment.

Participation of refugees, through refugee-based organizations, must be matched by encouraging civic alliances with the host's nonformal organizations, such as women's and youth associations, or trades unions and social clubs, where refugees and hosts can obtain positive exchanges by exhibiting cultural activities.

Public awareness and commitment of both refugees and hosts must be promoted by dissemination of information and research.

Monitoring of assistance programs must be devised to avoid imbalances created by resettlement and overseas migration, and their bias toward particular refugee categories.

13

Systems of Social Interaction of Refugee Adjustment Processes: The Case of Eritrean Refugees in Khartoum, Sudan

Eyob Goitom

The phenomenon of refugee migration has occurred throughout history as one of the forms of population movement and displacement. During displacement, refugees encounter new social and environmental systems. In the process, some refugee communities have successfully integrated into the host society's socioeconomic set-up, while others, keeping their sociocultural backgrounds intact, have managed to adjust only marginally. Still others live a disenfranchised existence with a low degree of adjustment to the host socioeconomic system.

In general, refugee migrants' different levels of adjustment to their new cultural (social and economic) and physical environments depend on a set of interacting variables. The dynamic process in which individuals or collectives attempt to survive in relation to the shift of a set of normative patterns of behavior is the manifestation of two interactive subsystems: the donor subsystem and the recipient subsystem. This essay will define different levels of social interaction of Eritrean refugees in the three towns that make up the city of Khartoum, Sudan.

Theoretical Conceptualization of the Refugee Systems of Interaction

The process of adjustment by refugees in the receiving place is one of social interaction within an established social system. This being a process, one must view it holistically, tracing a web of intervening, interdependent variables that facilitate or inhibit the process. Many observers have attempted a diagnosis of the refugee problem from the end result, ignoring the cause of their plight. As a result, proposals have tended to be oriented toward temporary relief assistance, as opposed to long-term solutions.

Although the necessity of meeting refugees' immediate needs cannot be denied, it does not in itself provide the conditions for a fundamental understanding and solution to this ever-growing problem. Every concerned individual and/or organization should consider these basic questions: (a) How long will it be before we stop having refugees, and when will we stop "creating" refugees? (b) How much longer will the international voluntary agencies provide the needed relief funds and materials? (c) How long will the host countries tolerate the influx of spatially, socially, and politically displaced, unwanted migrants?

One's skepticism grows when one considers the poor performance of some of the donor countries, whose contributions to international refugee "aid" agencies dwindle despite an astronomically increasing world refugee population.

If the primary objective of the international community is, as one UNHCR executive stated, "to see that those who become refugees cease to be refugees within a reasonable time" (Newland 1981:14), then a "relief" approach to global refugee problems is a dubious solution. Furthermore, it lessens the chance of gaining a basic understanding of the nature of refugee problems, an essential prerequisite to any viable solution.

An important supplement to the UN's legal definition of refugees might consider the refugee plight in light of their situation both previously in their country of origin and subsequently in their country of asylum. Describing positional shifts (psychological, social, economical, ecological, etc.) of refugee migrants, Art Hansen identifies three central concepts in refugees' social interaction: structure, process, and power. He asserts that: "social structure is the ordered relationship of social actors; process is the acting out through time . . . of psychological (one actor) and social (more than one) interaction. Power is the ability to influence actors and their actions . . . power is a function of social positions" (1982:13).

In other words, the refugee communities are properly conceptualized as consisting of groups of relatively powerless people, who have been unable to influence the events leading up to their dislocation and movement. In fact, when one considers the typologies of migrations based on the cause of dislocation from place of origin, the fundamental distinguishing factor is the refugee's large measure of stress during the process of decision-making. It would be fair to assume that all migrants make relatively "rational" decisions. Yet the time taken in the decision-making process and the atmosphere in which this process takes place vary considerably among each type of refugee migration, in relation to the strength of the stress the potential migrant receives from both social and physical environments.

The Internal Forces Involved in the Process

Investigation of historical causes for the plight of migrant refugees can become instrumental to the understanding of their adjustment mechanisms. The historical cause per se is not of as much importance to the researcher as is its degree of association with their displacement, aids in the comprehension of the adjustment process involved. Many scholars have written about the role that formal or informal clubs, associations, or organizations play in the desocialization and resocialization of rural-urban, economically initiated migrants. Such groupings, based on some sort of social and/or geographical affinity, serve to lessen the stress developed as a result of the migrants' physical and social move.

Kunz (1981), in an attempt to identify typologies of refugees, has writen a convincing theoretical paper related to the process of adjustment. He recognized two basic refugee groups, according to the refugees' attitudes toward their cause for displacement: "the reactive fate groups and the purpose groups." This essay is mainly concerned with the former group, who are essentially reacting to politically and socially intolerable forces, either perceived or real. Historically, the reactive refugee groups have been victims of national wars, national liberation movements, and violent social revolutions. This group of refugees can be seen as having a poor conceptualization of the forces leading to their decision to flee. Furthermore, they have a strong, common, ideological belief that not only strengthens their cohesion as a group, but also perpetuates a sense of impulse and incentive to form into an action group working toward an end to their plight. Whether due to the guilt-consciousness that Kunz refers to as "historic responsibility," or to the sense of "comradeship" to siblings, relatives, or the whole community, or to the indignant reaction to refugee life and the conviction that they have been unjustly treated, most refugees have a tendency to coalesce as an active group for a shared cause. This often helps to create and strengthen, aside from political motivations, a close-knit social niche in which the refugees continue with their own culture and also explore the new culture of the receiving society. If one considers it as an interaction of two social worlds, the phenomenon can be conceptualized as a process of continuity and change.

Since such groupings are political in nature, their interaction is reinforced by the existence of a politically motivated formal organization. This organization would work not only politically and/or militarily toward the publicization and recognition on international levels of the plight of these refugees, but would also strive to mobilize its people and gain their support. Social organizations of different forms and levels of complexity have always been part of human systems of interaction, and one can hypothesize that the nature and complexity of social organizations with which the refugees are associated could be an important parameter of the adjustment process of refugees.

The study of the social relationships of refugees cannot be limited to formally institutionalized sociopolitical organizations serving as a strategy or approach to the social networks in which they interact. Although almost all refugees rely on formal associations or organizations, we cannot assume that all refugees actually join the formal associations. This could either be a manifestation of the individual objective priorities (i.e., short-term versus long-term objectives) or a matter of individual negligence. Whatever the cause, individuals revert to what is usually referred to as "informal" group relationships (Fischer 1976) as a means of social interaction. All human relationships can be described as functional, but the distinguishing characteristic of informal associations is that relationships are personal whenever interactions and intimacy are not based on rigid forms of written rights and obligations. Additional major characteristics may include scale of operation, depth of influence, sharpness of boundaries, and degree of group discipline observation.

Viewed from the perspective of the refugees, informal social networks are cemented by friendship, kinship, geographical propinquity, and other short-term functional interests. In contrast, formal associations are based on relationships that are more or less initiated by long-term ideological beliefs and objectives. This does not undermine the fact that ideological compatibility among the community members at large would facilitate a permissible atmosphere for the development of informal relationships.

Because informal refugee interaction systems are based on limited spatial and social power relationships, it is difficult and somewhat naive to develop concrete categories for them. In general, however, they tend to fall within overlapping groups in terms of membership and services, such as the realm of family and kinship affinity, peer group and friendship ties, occupational or other special interest groups, coffee-house intellectual groupings, and the neighborhood, as a "natural" base for social interaction (ibid.). Together they perform a number of interrelated functions in the community as a whole, in the form of material and emotional support and recreational purposes. In addition, these systems serve to generate a field of information for the refugees, which is a key component in their process of adjustment to the receiving societal system.

Within the general theme of refugee social adjustment, these internal forces reinforce and are reinforced by the refugees' emotional links with their past. Of particular importance are family ties in the place of origin, awareness and strength of their sense of nationalism, and other social, psychological, and physical factors that date back to their social and territorial origins. This is further compounded by the sheer numbers of the refugee population at one particular place in time. The significance of the size of a particular population merging into alien socioeconomic networks is related to the frequency of simple day-to-day interaction as well as to the practicing of inherent social, cultural, and religious beliefs. Although these are extremely difficult to measure quantitatively, they can act as useful parameters of individual or group social interaction networks.

Most migrants, because of the change in the systems of social interaction and economic environment, are exposed to a new process of socialization that Hansen (1982), in his case study of Angolan refugees in Zambia, refers to as "(re)socialization." This is actually a process that demands learning the host society's social roles, values, and norms, new sociopolitical institutions, and new knowledge and skills applicable to the host country's economic structure. Although the process is highly dependent on the socioeconomic and physical proximity of both the sending and receiving societies, the migrants' background is particularly influential in the process. Background education, the type and level of skills, and the degree to which past status, learned skills (informal and formal), and experiences are transferable to the new environment will all serve either to inhibit or to facilitate the adjustment process.

The Possible External Forces Involved in the Process of Interaction

These variables, which we will term for convenience "internal" forces (i.e., forces directly related to the refugee communities themselves), form only one side of the refugee adjustment mechanism in this interactive and reactive process. In any social interaction, and more so in such victimized communities, the behavioral response of the migrants is determined not only by their inner actions, but also by the actions that act upon them. In other words, on one hand the migrants' social behavior is a factor of their mechanical response to an already established system; on the other hand, how the established system and society influence, shape, and incorporate the behavioral reorganization of these migrants in the host society must be examined.

One aspect of social adjustment is the establishment of confidence in one's own self-image. Self-image is a manifestation of one's position, as an individual or as part of a group, in a given social structure. Self-image can, in fact, be measured only as reflected by another social body. The refugee's self-image within an established social system is highly influenced by the role he plays in the host society. Not only physical events, but also the host community and government's perceptions and attitudes of the refugee's role in the socioeconomic development of the host country have a detrimental effect on the development of refugee self-image and identification with the host society. Thus the crucial question arises as to whether one perceives the relationship as donor-client dependency or, conversely, whether one considers refugees to be playing a contributary role in the receiving society.

In theory, the issue narrows down to the consideration given to forces at work in the host country, which are external to the refugee population in their process of movement and adjustment. In any category of migration, be it forced or voluntary, sociocultural and spatial proximity have played a predominant role in the decision-making process, and in the process of adjustment in the host country. Refugees, however, are victims of forced decisions. In most cases physical proximity, associated with the difficulty involved in moving, is taken into consideration in the decision to move. And the degree of sympathy, political and/or humanitarian, that the host society displays toward these political migrants has a preeminent influence in the process. As Kunz (1981:46) has reiterated, when making decisions "the refugees are seldom aware of these [the sociocultural compatibility between background and host societies] crucially important factors." Sociocultural and economic affinity of both places certainly play an important role in the processes of accommodation, adaptation, integration, and assimilation. Although these forces are internally related and definitely influence each other, the host society's reaction to the refugees responds to the existing economic environment: to the employment situation and to the provision of such public services as health, transportation, or housing in the host country.

The government's role in the process of adjustment is reflected not only in its "open-door policy" regarding entry of refugee migrants, but also in its integration of the refugees into its society and economy through refugee employment, education, trade and occupational training opportunities, and the provision of different types of documents, such as passes, identification documents, permits, passports, or citizenship. In general, state power is used to incorporate the refugee population into the national socioeconomic structure.

In short, refugee adjustment mechanisms can be summarized as a process of interplay between internal and external forces at work in the refugee systems of interaction. Moreover, the weakness or strength of the level of adjustment can be inferred from the compatibility of these forces. In a situation where the internal and external forces are of a higher compatibility, we would, in theory, expect a higher degree of adjustment. In a situation where the external forces are favorable for the process of adjustment but the internal forces are negatively weighted, the consequence might be mutual distrust between the two societies, probably culminating in conflict, with the refugees resisting imposition. Furthermore, should internal forces of motivation for adjustment be restrained by external forces (that is, perceptions, attitudes, and policy considerations), this might cause the refugees' widespread psychological frustration, resulting in their withdrawal from participation in the wider society. It is hard to say what the exact strength of the different forces and variables would be in these processes, but this relational approach would provide a better and more realistic understanding to refugee systems of interaction and hence to the form and nature of their adjustment mechanism.

The Eritrean Refugees in Khartoum: Socioeconomic Exposures and Interaction

For various reasons, accurate and systematically organized quantitative data required for a detailed study of the issues outlined in the previous theoretical section of this chapter do not exist for the Eritrean refugees in Sudan. The problem becomes even more acute because of the extreme mobility of urban refugees residing in Khartoum. Hence, more research is needed to structure the typologies of the Eritrean refugees in general, and the urban refugees in particular. This essay's attempts to elucidate the urban Eritrean refugees' systems of interaction in the process of adjustment is based primarily on data generated by participant-observation. This long-established social research technique becomes even more informative and penetrating in a situation where the observer occupies the same role or status as the population he is observing.

Participant observation was supplemented by group discussions and a sample questionnaire. The group discussions were conducted in the places of refugee daytime concentration, which developed with time into informally functional meeting places. The questionnaire surveyed 320 refugees and investigated the social and economic situations of the refugees both at place of origin and of destination. It is not possible to state the percentage of the refugee population represented by the sample, because the authorities do not know the exact number of refugees in the Khartoum urban area. Furthermore, the sample survey failed to capture many of the variables that should have been included. For example, sensitive questions related to political, religious, and national affiliations were not included in the questionnaire. Thus, data from the survey should be taken only as indicators rather than "absolute" conditions.

Historically, the Sudan hosted Eritrean migrants long before the contemporary refugee influx into the country (Smock 1982). These earlier migrations can be traced back to, among other things, the extensive common border that both countries share; a colonial heritage of artificial boundary demarkation, which resulted in the division of single ethnic groupings into separate political territories (in this case the Rashaida, the Beni Amer, and the Hadendawa); and the economic needs of both societies.

Earlier migrations of Eritreans included seasonal movement of nomadic populations in the western lowlands, who crossed into Sudan along the Gash-Settit rivers in search of grazing and water. Another movement from Eritrea to Sudan was circular labor migration, which probably began with the development of mechanized agricultural schemes in Sudan. Although most such migrants were unskilled agricultural laborers from rural backgrounds, some migrated to Sudan's urban centers, where they engaged in the so-called "informal sector" economy of petty-commodity production and distribution (Forbes 1981; Gerry 1974).

The refugee influx is a direct consequence of political instability in the region and the development of the revolution for national liberation of Eritrea that has been going on for almost half a century. With each periodic stage of the revolution, there was a distinct population displacement effect in both spatial and social terms (Table 13.1).

Three stages in the displacement of Eritrean refugees are proposed in Table 13.1. The primary stage of the revolution, which goes back to the

---

Table 13.1   A Model of the Processes of Stress and Displacement Effects Among the Eritrean Refugees

Stages	Nature of struggle	Displacement effect
1. Primary period (1940s–1961)	Political agitation	"Elite" urbanites
2. Transition period (1961–1973)	Sporadic armed confrontation	Mixed, but strong in localized rural areas
3. Maturity period (1973–)	Massive involvement — intensive armed struggle — mass mobilization	Mixed, with strong urban effect

British occupation of Eritrea, focused exclusively on urban centers where the activists were nationalists who grew up during Italian and British colonial rule. The displacement effect of this period manifested itself among these elite urbanites. During the transitional stage, armed conflict was limited and political mobilization was localized to only a few regions of the countryside, as was the concomitant dislocation of population. In 1967, the first mass influx of Eritrean refugees to Sudan occurred. Predominantly of nomadic and/or peasant backgrounds, these refugees settled in rural areas to become self-supporting agriculturalists (Smock 1982).

The third stage, the period of maturity, is characterized by intensive and extensive military confrontation and political mass mobilization—a definite shift away from defensive to offensive and counteroffensive actions by the liberation movements. In this period liberation forces pointed their guns at the urban centers where most Ethiopian soldiers were concentrated. Consequently, the cities and towns became centers of confrontation, while rural areas formed the nucleus of "development" and defense. Under these circumstances the urban population was pressured to move out, and displacement has affected urban residents of all walks of life. It is this population of urbanites who found their way to Khartoum.

The nature and pattern of the refugee influx has changed continually with the changing fortunes of the war. At present, Eritrean refugees form as much as 20 percent of Africa's refugees. Since 1974, however, in a period of intensification and diffusion of revolutionary military activity and political mobilization, there has been a far greater flow to the urban centers of Sudan, and particularly to Khartoum.

The Socioeconomic Structure of the
Eritrean Refugee Community in Khartoum

It is the general policy of Sudan that all refugees be settled on designated rural settlement schemes. To this effect restrictions are imposed on the movement of refugees within Sudan in general, and to Khartoum in particular. All refugee travelers are required to show identification cards and travel passes at police checkpoints.

Despite these restrictions, a high rate of refugee concentration has developed in Khartoum. The intensity of flow into Khartoum can be explained by a number of interacting variables, such as past residential experience (in terms of rural-urban differentials), the availability of services and employment, the immediate objectives of the refugees, and the perceived unattractiveness to the refugees of the rural camps. Indications are that the majority of Eritrean refugees in Khartoum are of urban origin. According to this writer's case study, refugees of urban origin form about 98 percent of the sample, with almost half originating from Asmara, the capital of Eritrea. Seventy-five percent of these refugees plan to go abroad; the rural refugee settlement schemes hold little attraction for these urban refugees.

The refugees' socioeconomic background is relevant to an understanding of the process of refugee adjustment. Socioeconomic variables such as sex, age, marital status, occupation and trade, and education reveal little on their own unless they are related to the society's perception of the roles of each group. Although age-sex selectivity might be expected to diminish with the strength of the dislocation stress factor, the case study in Khartoum shows that young adults (aged 15 to 30) form the majority of the sample population (85.7 percent), while those over 40 constitute only 1.2 percent. The sample also indicated that males constitute about 72.2 percent of the population. This differential displacement of the sexes is basically a manifestation of Eritrean society's attitude toward and treatment of women. Women tend to have limited exposure and experience outside the family territory, and a higher degree of restriction is imposed on them by parents and society. Female enrollment in schools is low, and as a result women are treated as dependent members of the family with limited responsibility outside of domestic chores.

This limited exposure has unquestionably had a detrimental effect on Eritrean refugee women's adjustment to the host country's social system. With few occupational experiences or skills, Eritrean women form the most vulnerable refugee group in Khartoum. Their occupations are limited to domestic servant and, even worse, prostitution. The marginalization of this particular group is further aggravated by Sudanese society's attitude toward women in general, and to Eritrean women in particular.

Marital status of urban refugees in Khartoum is primarily single, as indicated by 80.9 percent of the survey sample. Many married refugees tend to migrate as singles, leaving their families behind. The predominantly single status is no surprise, considering that the majority of refugees are between the ages of 15 and 25. In addition, the economic and political instability does not create a favorable atmosphere for marriage. It is difficult to measure the impact of marital status on adjustment; however, marital status does seem to affect the degree of flexibility, and the unstable and unpredictable environment demands a high degree of flexibility from the refugees.

A further major determinant in the process of adaptation is the refugees' occupational background. Although they fall into the active and productive age category, their incorporation into the economic system largely depends upon their having the appropriate know-how as required by the host's socioeconomic structure. In addition, the state's readiness to invest in this particular human resource and the existing economy's ability to absorb the additional labor should be questioned. The two communities, being of similar levels of socioeconomic development, have a high degree of skill and occupational transferability. Nonetheless, the receiving economy may not have the demand for this labor, and the migrants may not possess the needed skills for this system.

The past occupational structure of the urban refugees suggests that the majority, 45 percent of the sample, are senior and junior secondary school students who have acquired no special skills. Another major category is the professionals, who constitute 20 percent of the sample. This group includes builders, tailors, drivers, mechanics, teachers, nurses, doctors, engineers, agriculturalists, accountants, and other skilled and semiskilled intellectuals.

Clearly they are a marketable labor resource within Sudan's level of economic development.

The most vulnerable group is the unskilled refugees—farmers, nomads, daily laborers, and domestic servants—who constitute 12 percent of the sample. When students are included in this latter category, the proportion of unemployable population increases to 58 percent.

The final group of refugees is made up of merchants (7 percent), including people owning transport vehicles, wholesalers, retailers, and import-export agencies. Despite this group's entrepreneurial experience, the majority of them fail to participate to capacity within the system and are forced to join the ranks of the working class. This is partly attributable to lack of capital, to inability to meet the local competition, or to the Sudanese government, which denies them the necessary permits and licenses.

The economic adjustment of refugees is best reflected by their present occupational structure. More than half of the sample survey is unemployed. About 38 percent of those employed occupy marginal jobs, including domestic service (17 percent), daily laborers including those who work in the "informal" sector (13 percent), and receptionists and bartenders. Although students form almost half the sample population, less than 1 percent were currently enrolled in any educational institution. This is due to a variety of factors, including language barriers at the high school level, limited high schools offering classes in English, inadequate funds, lack of appropriate certificates, and a lack of interest in schooling on the part of the refugees.

Although the Eritrean refugees in Khartoum are willing to take on any job at low wages, the moribund nature of Sudan's economy provides only limited employment opportunities. High unemployment rates among nationals causes the government to enforce strict work permit regulations for qualified refugees, who cannot be employed without the knowledge and approval of the Sudanese Labor Office. It is the responsibility of this office to determine, before a refugee's work permit is approved, that no Sudanese applicant could fill the position.

With the steady decline of the Sudanese economy, resentment toward urban refugees began to be expressed by both the public and government. Refugees cause strains on the resources of the nation, and particularly exacerbate problems of daily living, housing, and transportation in the capital. Government leaders emphasize that refugees be concentrated on the rural settlement schemes.

One of the adjustment reflexes that refugees adopt as a result of the economic situation is shared living. A measure of the density of single-room dwellings among the refugees indicated that 36 percent of the sample reside with a group of 4 to 6 people, 28 percent reside with a group of 7 to 9 people, and another 17 percent dwell with a group of 10 to 12 people.

Adjustment is not limited to residential dependence, and material cooperation among refugees in Khartoum extends to day-to-day survival. The case study revealed that 24 percent of the sample is dependent for their support on relatives or friends living in Khartoum, while another 30 percent totally depend on, or supplement their low incomes from, remittance from relatives or friends working abroad.

One of the major problems of the refugees is low levels of skill. The majority are unskilled or semiskilled and have not completed high school. Migrants can integrate into the economic milieu of a host society either by attaining new skills or by up-grading already-acquired skills; socially this helps refugees gain a new understanding and appreciation of the host society's sociopolitical system. Educational enrollment of refugees in Khartoum is insignificant. UNHCR and the Sudanese High Commissioner for Refugees, in collaboration with various humanitarian organizations, coordinate the funds for refugees who managed to find school places. Yet there appears to be an emphasis on university education. The survival-of-the-fittest policy of concerned authorities fails to consider the majority of the population whose needs are for more basic education. Nonetheless, the refugees' low incentive for learning also contributes to this phenomenon.

The refugee community has attempted to organize an elementary school for young children. Sudan Council of Churches helped by providing books, and a local private school provided space. But UNHCR's response was minimal, and the government's reaction was negative, since the program did not fit in with the Sudanese school curriculum. As a result, the school did not succeed, but the attempt illustrates the desperate need for schools. Moreover, there is a need for schooling based on the curriculum used in Eritrean schools, where emphasis is placed on Eritrean history, geography, and languages. As in any minority community, the Eritrean refugees in Khartoum are determined to keep their national identity.

Systems of the Refugees' Social Interaction

In general, formal or informal group interaction among Eritrean refugees in Khartoum serves to facilitate the flow of information, provide material assistance, and stabilize morale and psychological factors. The formal group interaction of the Eritrean refugees is primarily represented by the national liberation movement, which symbolizes the root cause of their displacement. The objective is to mobilize and politicize the Eritrean people under the common motto of "national independence."

As in any other political grouping, a control system observes group discipline and cohesiveness. Every member is obliged to fulfill certain duties and obligations. This gives refugees a sense of participation and a feeling of oneness with the liberation movement, and helps to develop a sense of comradeship among themselves and with their fighting brothers and sisters.

This comradeship, and continuous information via the liberation movement about the war, keeps the organized and unorganized refugees in contact with the process of nation building, and helps boost their cause of nationalism. In addition to the formal refugee organizations' capacity to maintain and build an Eritrean identity, they morally and psychologically help to give a value to a destitute refugee existence and a feeling of hope for the future. This is due not only to a common ideological understanding of the problem, but also to the organization's ability to put the general Eritrean problem and the specific problem of refugees into a global perspective.

The formal organizations are not limited only to fulfilling long-range political motives, but they also serve other intermediate and immediate needs of the refugees. Being place-specific, they act as a base of initial contact with other refugees. In fact, they are centers for the start of informal group interaction. In addition, they are sources of information, such as on employment and educational openings. Since they were recognized by Sudanese authorities as official representatives of the Eritrean people (at least until 1980), the political organizations attempt to solve individual refugee problems through guidance and consultation, liaise with Sudanese authorities in cases of misunderstanding, represent refugees in legal or police cases, and assist refugees to acquire papers demanded by government officials, companies, or other organizations.

Informal social interaction is manifested in the day-to-day groupings of the refugees. Although such groupings might have religious, regional, and political overtones, they function on the basis of friendship, regardless of the degree of intimacy. Most of these interactions are project-oriented. In addition to providing the information needed to acquire a particular paper, this network of refugee groups knows how to penetrate the bureaucratic red tape involved with government or non-government refugee offices.

Certain places of refugee interaction (that is, nonresidential use of space) include eating and drinking places that range from small tea-shops to international hotels and restaurants. These places serve both friendly and business relationships, among the refugees themselves and with outside communities. The other major category of refugees' places of social interaction is the different government and nongovernment documentary offices. These include the offices of the Sudanese Ministry of Interior, various UNHCR offices, and foreign embassies. Most refugees go to these places to obtain travel or certification papers; the "informative" groups primarily carry on their work around these places, and the places also serve as meeting places for friends. Additional meeting places include parks, libraries, and churches, which are places for friendly interaction and socializing.

As centers of physical contact, such places form the nucleus of informal refugee interaction. Because of the size of the Eritrean refugee population in Khartoum, such relationships tend to occur often. Involvement in such interactions bring refugees in direct contact with the practical workings of the system. In fact, such places and forms of interaction are the main source of information on who is around or on the nature of the socioeconomic background of the host society.

The tendency of the refugees to band together, and the fact that the Eritrean refugees concentrate in specific places in large numbers, seems to have had some backwash effect on the Sudanese perception of the refugees. The refugee concentration in such places alienates them as a specific group and identifies them as a group who mix little with the community.

Conclusion

For the Eritrean refugees in Khartoum, their structural disadvantage will continue to foster a belief that the refugee state of existence is temporary. Because the majority of the refugees have migrated as single individuals, the emotional links with their home place will persist. This emotional feeling is symbolized in their link with the liberation movement, and hence encourages a close identification with their historical cause of forced dislocation.

It is a known fact that people exposed to external or internal dangers (sociopolitical and economic) tend to show a high degree of community solidarity on many levels. The refugees' level of survival is based on changing strategies, a mechanism demanding a continuous information flow. The more numerous a refugee's sources of information, the higher his chances of adjustment within the host system. This fact and the need for survival have always perpetuated a sense of mutual dependence within refugee communities.

Mutual dependence is the source of social interaction. As illustrated by the urban Eritrean refugees in Khartoum, their economic, political, and social environment and that of the host community make manifold forms of social interaction mandatory. The formal and informal types of social interaction have served the refugees as important sources of information for survival. Although it is difficult to identify the forms, intensity, cohesiveness, and other characteristics of these informal groupings and the degree of their articulation, they play an important role, along with formal associations, in the day-to-day practical life of the refugee population.

14

Southern Sudanese Refugees: Their Repatriation and Resettlement After the Addis Ababa Agreement

Joshua O. Akol

In recent years, the problem of refugees in general and in Africa in particular has drawn the attention of scholars in many disciplines. Most of their analyses have focused on the causes of refugee migrations, on legal dimensions of the refugee problem, and on refugee resettlement and their adjustment in new environments (Betts 1980; Brooks and El-Ayouty 1970; Hamrell 1967; Holborn 1975; Kibreab 1985; and Rogge 1985a). Little attention has been paid to the repatriation of refugees and their subsequent rehabilitation.

In the context of Southern Sudan, which has experienced one of the largest repatriations on the African continent, some research has focused on the origin of the refugee problem and the flight of refugees during the civil war (Beshir 1968; Salih 1971; and Sommer 1968), but none has dealt with the socioeconomic transformation the refugees underwent during their displacement. The process and problems of rehabilitating refugees following their return should be better understood, since many of the continent's current refugees may well be repatriated at some point in the future.

This essay will (a) describe the repatriation of Southern Sudanese refugees after the civil war to show the magnitude and nature of problems encountered by the Repatriation and Resettlement Commission, and (b) discuss the rehabilitation process of the various categories of refugees after their return to their homeland.

The Repatriation Process

The peace agreement between North and South was signed in Addis Ababa on February 27, 1972. It brought to an end the bitter war that the Assistant

143

Secretary-General of the Organization of African Unity (OAU) had referred to as "the largest fratricidal war waged on the African continent in the last two decades" (UNHCR 1973a).

After the agreement there was an urgent need to create conditions in the South that would facilitate the return of both the refugees from neighboring countries as well as those who had been displaced within the South. Yet local resources were inadequate to meet the needs of returning refugees and displaced population, and thus the government was dependent upon contributions from the international community. To generate, distribute, and prioritize the aid received, the government established three agencies: the Special Fund Committee (Presidential Order No. 43), the Resettlement Commission (Presidential Order No. 44), and the Repatriation Commission (Presidential Order No. 45).

The Special Fund Committee, which had its headquarters in Khartoum, was to "meet the expenses of repatriation, resettlement, relief and rehabilitation of Sudanese refugees of the Southern Region" (Government of Sudan 1972a). The Committee was to provide refugees with cash and aid in kind. The Resettlement Commission's terms of reference were:

> the resettlement, relief and rehabilitation of Sudanese refugees from the Southern Region now residing abroad, and all expatriates and other Sudanese of the Southern Region who have abandoned their homes in the Southern Region and are now residing in other areas and towns within that region or outside it [ibid.].

In discharging these functions, the commission was to have due regard to the special circumstances of the different categories of refugees that existed in the South:

- refugees from countries neighboring the Southern Region of Sudan;
- persons who had abandoned their original homes and were residing in the towns of the Southern Region and elsewhere;
- persons who took refuge in "the bush"; and,
- invalids and other persons incapacitated as a result of military operations, and orphaned children.

The responsibilities of the Repatriation Commission were:

1. to register the number of Sudanese refugees in the different countries, specify their identities, professions, trades, ages and original homes;
2. to prepare a timetable for the repatriation of such refugees from camps where they were staying, in accordance with the resettlement and transportation plan laid down by the Resettlement, Relief and Rehabilitation Commission;
3. to establish emergency camps inside Sudan for refugees who would not abide by the timetable or those who wished to return immediately to Sudan even before the resettlement plan was put into effect;
4. to provide refugees in emergency camps with food, medicine, and work implements to facilitate the maintenance of adequate living conditions

and assist them in contributing to national reconstruction until they were resettled; and
5. to constitute subcommittees inside and outside Sudan in order to discharge, on its behalf, any task within the framework of the functions of the Commission as set forth in the Order.

The commission established branch offices both inside and outside Sudan. Within Sudan, subcommissions were established in each of the three provincial capitals—Juba, Malakal, and Wau. A fourth office was located in Khartoum to process refugees returning from abroad as well as displaced persons who had taken refuge in the North. Outside Sudan, subcommissions were established in the four neighboring countries that harbored most of the Sudanese refugees—Central African Republic, Ethiopia, Uganda, and Zaire.

The anticipated influx of refugees required contingency planning for their orderly repatriation and reception. To facilitate this, the commission established resettlement camps in various parts of the South (Figure 14.1). Most were located in what has now become Eastern and Western Equatoria Provinces, and to which the majority of the refugees from Central African Republic, Uganda, and Zaire repatriated. Four types of resettlement camps

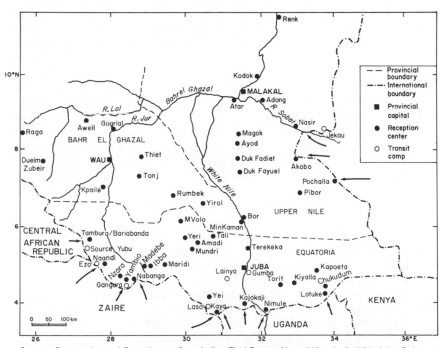

Source : Repatriation and Resettlement Commission, Final Report, May 1972 – April 1974, Juba, Sudan

Figure 14.1   Location of Resettlement Camps for Returnees in Southern Sudan, 1972–1973

were established: transit, reception, distribution, and leper camps (Repatriation and Resettlement Commission 1974). As their names suggest, these
camps were designed to perform specific functions for the refugees. Their
organization and the type of assistance they offered varied, and their
location depended on the functions they were to perform.

The Southern Sudanese Refugees after the War

The impact of the civil war in Southern Sudan was enormous in terms of
population displacement. Of a total population of about 4 million, more
than 25 percent were displaced during the war (Mills 1977). Even so, the
differences in the definition of refugees adopted by various concerned
agencies contributed to diverse, if not contradictory, data on the South's
refugee population. For example, at the Relief and Resettlement Conference
of February 1972, the government suggested a total 327,000 persons were in
need of relief assistance, while UNHCR proposed a figure of 680,000 in May
of that year (Government of Sudan 1972a; UNECOSOC 1974). Yet by the
end of its operation in April 1974, the Repatriation and Resettlement
Commission reported that it had resettled more than 1 million refugees
(Repatriation and Resettlement Commission 1974). Also, Mills (1982) reports that estimates on the number of Southern Sudanese refugees ranged
from 2 to 2.5 million. Even today, the accuracy of the number of Southerners
displaced during the civil war remains in doubt. Despite the lack of
concensus on the number of refugees, the official figure reported by the
Repatriation and Resettlement Commission will be used in this study.

The External Refugees

Of the total number of displacees, the external refugees in Central African
Republic, Ethiopia, Kenya, Uganda and Zaire were estimated at 219,400
(Repatriation and Resettlement Commission 1974). Their burden was une-
venly distributed among the asylum countries. For example, Uganda and
Zaire hosted about 70 percent of this total, causing serious strain on
socioeconomic services in the areas where the refugees were heavily concentrated (UNHCR 1975a).

    Apart from the uneven distribution of refugees among host countries,
there were also considerable differences in their manner of settlement. Table
14.1 shows that 50.2 percent of refugees settled spontaneously among local
populations, while the balance lived in organized rural settlements. The
largest group of spontaneous settlers was in Uganda (63.5 percent), Zaire
(55.2 percent), and Ethiopia (42.9 percent).

    Host governments usually discourage spontaneous settlement of refu-
gees for two reasons. First, it is costly to distribute relief assistance among a
widely dispersed population. Second, since dispersed refugees tend to be
less under the direct control of government authorities, the asylum state
fears that they may engage in political activities against their home government which, in turn, would cause political tensions between the asylum
state and the refugees' country of origin (Rogge 1982).

Table 14.1   Distribution of Southern Sudanese Refugees by Country of Asylum and
Nature of Settlement, 1972

Country of Asylum	Total refugees		Spontaneous settlers		On rural settlement schemes		
	Number	%	Number	%	Settlement	Number	%
Uganda	86,000	39.2	54,600	63.5	Nakapiripirit	11,600	36.5
					Agago	9,600	
					Onigo	8,500	
					Ibuga	1,700	
Zaire	67,000	30.5	37,000	55.2	Aba	15,000	44.8
					Amadi	10,000	
					Nugadi	5,000	
Ethiopia	35,000	16.0	15,000	42.9	Gambela	20,000	57.1
Central African Republic	30,900	14.1	3,000	9.7	M'Boki	27,900	90.3
Kenya	500	0.2	500	100.0	No rural settlement schemes	—	—
Total	219,400	100.0	110,100	50.2		109,300	49.8

Source: Repatriation and Resettlement Commission, *Final Report*, Juba, 1974.

In the areas where spontaneous settlement occurs, two factors should be taken into account. First, political boundaries cut across ethnic territories, and many refugee migrations, although crossing a political boundary, nevertheless remain within the same ethnic territory. Consequently, the ethnic associations between the host population and refugees tend to encourage such settlement. Second, the frequent failure of host governments to take immediate action upon the refugees' arrival by default allows the refugees to seek their own solutions through spontaneous integration among local populations.

In contrast to spontaneous settlement solutions, organized rural settlements were relatively effective in regrouping refugees in specified areas where a variety of services and infrastructural facilities could be provided. In Central African Republic, for example, 90.3 percent of the refugees were settled at the M'boki rural settlement (UNHCR 1969), while in Ethiopia, 57 percent were settled at Gambella. In Uganda and Zaire, however, only 36.5 percent and 44.8 percent, respectively, lived on organized rural settlements.

As the repatriation of refugees progressed, the commission was optimistic that its task would be completed within the prescribed period of 18 months (May 1972 to October 1973). Nevertheless, only about 45,000 refugees repatriated during 1972. Many refugees remained uncertain about the government's intentions and as a result adopted a "wait and see" attitude. When the commission finally completed its work in April 1974, it had repatriated a total of 158,292 refugees from the targeted 219,400 persons. Of the remaining 61,108 (27.9 percent) who were not repatriated by the commission, 13,153 remained in Uganda and Zaire for purely personal and economic reasons. The balance remained unaccounted for, but it is commonly accepted that they returned independently and were thus not registered by the commission.

The Internal Refugees

In addition to the refugees who fled to neighboring countries, the war generated a large internal population displacement. These are referred to as internal refugees, and consisted of three subgroups: (a) those who took refuge in the "bush" within the South; (b) those who escaped to towns in the South; and (c) those who sought refuge in the North.

Following the civil war, the Repatriation and Resettlement commission found it much more difficult to determine the precise number of internal displacees, primarily because only those in need of relief assistance reported to reception centers. Nevertheless, it is commonly accepted that of the 1 million registered refugees, about 800,000 were internal displacees (Government of the Southern Region of Sudan 1974). As was the case with the external refugees, the pace at which the internal displacees returned during 1972 was slow. For example, by the end of that year, the commission estimated that only 320,000 refugees had returned to their homes (Government of the Southern Region of Sudan 1973). Only after an intensive government campaign among the refugees and their leaders were the apprehensions and fears prevailing among the refugees overcome.

The Response of the Refugees to Voluntary Repatriation

The problems encountered by the Repatriation and Resettlement Commission varied from one country to another. While in some areas the repatria-

---

Table 14.2   Sequence of Repatriation of Southern Sudanese Refugees, May 1972–June

Country of asylum	Total number of refugees	Number repatriated from		
		May–Dec. 1972	Jan.–Oct. 1973	Nov. 1973– June 1974
Uganda	86,000	17,570	37,193	4,531
Zaire	67,000	8,808	38,259	47
Ethiopia	35,000	7,400	16,084	—
Central African Republic	30,900	10.830	17,070	—
Kenya	500	—	500	—

Source: Repatriation and Resettlement Commission, *Final Report*, Juba, 1974.

tion process was completed within a short time, in others it was a protracted operation (Table 14.2).

The manner in which refugees had settled during their exile was reflected in the repatriation process. Unlike spontaneously settled refugees who had dispersed widely and were thus not easily regrouped for repatriation, those on rural settlement schemes were readily mobilized and repatriated with minimal problems. In Central African Republic, 90 percent of refugees were concentrated in a single settlement at M'boki. Also, the location of some settlements along main transportation routes or their proximity to border areas facilitated the repatriation process. The latter was the case at Gambella in southwest Ethiopia, where "many refugees preferred to cross the border on foot with their cattle" (UNECOSOC 1974).

In Uganda and Zaire the large proportion of spontaneously settled populations created many problems in the repatriation process. For example, in Uganda, the commission, with the cooperation of the Ugandan government, had to set up thirteen holding camps to congregate the refugees for processing. Such additional expenditures resulted in the cost of the Ugandan repatriation exercise accounting for about 30 percent of the total budget, compared to only 0.4 percent for the repatriation from Ethiopia. Moreover, the Ugandan repatriation extended over a two-year period, compared to only six months for the repatriation from Central African Republic.

Since many African countries are both source areas of refugees and asylum states, sporadic conflicts have periodically erupted as exiles cross back to their country of origin to undertake guerrilla activities or operate as freedom fighters. Tensions are thereby created between governments of asylum states and those of countries of refugee origin. In the case of Southern Sudan, Zairean refugees had long been spontaneously settled in border areas, and the Zairean government was apprehensive that an opening of the Sudan–Zaire border might facilitate and encourage Zairean refugees to infiltrate back to Zaire to engage in guerrilla activities. Consequently, this apprehension delayed the opening of the border and thereby

1974

UNHCR-assisted repatriation	Self-repatriation	Total repatriated May 1972–June 1974	Number left behind
52,294	15,306	74,600	11,400
47,114	18,133	65,247	1,753
23,484	11,516	35,000	–
27,900	3,000	30,900	–
500	–	500	–

retarded the repatriation process of Southern Sudanese from Zaire. Moreover, when the border did finally open, repatriation was limited to one crossing point at Aba.

An important factor that influenced the desire to repatriate was the level of socioeconomic development the refugees had achieved while in exile vis-à-vis prevailing conditions awaiting them in their home country. For example, many refugees had become self-sufficient and perhaps even affluent, and were thus reluctant to return to a war-devastated economy. As a result some 11,400 refugees decided to remain in Uganda after the war. On the other hand, refugees who had been living in conditions of poverty, or those who had not developed any economic or psychological attachments to their area of exile, were more readily prepared to return home.

Well-established social relations, based on common ethnicity between refugees and their host population, may also have contributed to some refugees' lack of interest to repatriate. Southern Sudanese ethnic groups straddling the border include the Anuak and Nuer, who are also located in southwestern Ethiopia; the Acholi and Madi, who are also in northern Uganda; the Kakwa, who are also in northwestern Uganda and northeastern Zaire; and the Zande, who are also in northern Zaire and eastern Central African Republic. It is not surprising, therefore, that many southerners found refuge across the border among their ethnic kin or acquaintances. Such ethnic linkages encouraged spontaneous settlement by the refugees and especially in Uganda and Zaire, where many became so well established that they decided to remain even after repatriation became possible.

The Impact of Repatriation on Former Host Countries

Although host governments in Africa have borne the heavy burden of refugees for many years, they have nevertheless benefited from numerous rural development projects established by the various international agencies for refugees. It is estimated that between 1964 and 1972, UNHCR spent over US$8 million in establishing and maintaining rural settlement schemes for southerners in Central African Republic, Ethiopia, Uganda, and Zaire (UNHCR 1973a). With repatriation during 1972 and 1973, financial allocations by UNHCR to host countries terminated; this clearly had a negative economic impact in the areas of refugee settlement.

On the other hand, after repatriation socioeconomic infrastructure was left for local rural communities. In general, the refugee settlement schemes had been established in sparsely populated and previously underdeveloped areas. At M'boki settlement in the southeast of Central Africa Republic, for example, large acreages of cultivable land, an array of buildings, and health and educational facilities were left to benefit local populations. The former refugee settlement also provided a nucleus around which subsequent development of the region could be organized.

A similar transfer of facilities to local populations was made at the Gambella settlement in Ethiopia and at the Amadi and Nugadi rural settlements in Zaire. In Uganda, the government inherited social and economic facilities left at the Agago, Nakapiripirit, and Onigo rural settlements. The Nakapiripirit settlement has since become the headquarters of the South Karamoja District, and the Onigo settlement became a government community center (UNHCR 1974). In this sense it is sometimes argued that long-term benefits to host governments may offset some of the short-term problems caused by an influx of refugees.

Rehabilitation and Resettlement of Returnees

The rehabilitation and resettlement program followed the initial repatriation and relief program. The Resettlement Commission's policy was to resettle all returnees with minimal stress and to permit them to resume a normal life as quickly as possible. The resettlement program was designed to meet the needs of the various categories of returnees, and its implementation involved material assistance of food and agricultural tools to farmers; the reinstatement of government officials and employees in their original or equivalent positions; the employment in white-collar jobs of persons who had acquired the necessary qualifications and skills while in exile; and the integration of the "Anyanya" forces into the national army, police and prison service, or in other government departments.

On the basis of previous occupations, experience, or qualifications, six categories of returnees resettled by the commission can be identified (see Figure 14.2). The main features of the rehabilitation and resettlement process varied among the categories.

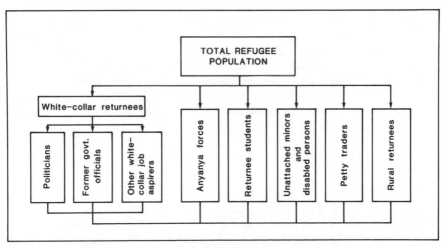

Source : Repatriation and Resettlement Commission, Final Report, May 1972 – April 1974, Juba, Sudan.

Figure 14.2   Types of Returnees Resettled by the Resettlement Commission

The White-Collar Returnees

This category of returnees consisted of two subgroups. First were the politicians, some of whom had taken part in the Addis Ababa peace negotiations. Many of these returnees were subsequently appointed as ministers in the regional government, while others obtained high-ranking positions in the civil service. Second were former government officials and employees and other white-collar job aspirants who had acquired qualifications or experience while in exile. This group was absorbed into various regional ministries and departments. Each returnee was reviewed by the Regional Ministry of Public Service, and when found acceptable was reinstated into a public service position.

Once reinstated, many officials began to transfer to other ministries in the regional government. Such transfers were in response to better working conditions prevailing in some ministries, or to personal or political reasons. The result was that severe shortages of qualified personnel developed in some departments, while others were staffed with persons lacking qualifications or experience.

The "Anyanya" Forces

The success of the Addis Ababa Agreement depended much upon a satisfactory accommodation of the "Anyanya" guerrilla forces. For this reason, the position of the armed forces in the South had considerable significance in the settlement of the southern problem. Of the ten-day negotiation in Addis Ababa aimed at reaching a formula on security in the South, discussions on the size and composition of the future army took up five days (Alier 1976). It was agreed that the armed forces in the Southern Region would be composed of 12,000 officers and men, of whom 6,000 were to be from the ex-"Anyanya" forces (Government of Sudan 1972). The size of the "Anyanya" force had been estimated by the regional government at 25,000, of whom another 4,000 were to be absorbed into the police and prison service. The balance, estimated at more than 14,000 persons, were to be employed in various government departments. But because many "Anyanya" did not have the discipline and training associated with regular army life, they experienced difficulties in coping with their new assignments. For many, the shift of regimentation was too abrupt, and as a result some were dismissed by their units in the source of integration.

Returnee Students

Students constituted one of the major categories of returnees who needed placement. The overall impact of the war on education in the South had been catastrophic. For almost two decades, most schools had been closed, and consequently the majority of children, both inside and outside the country, after the Addis Ababa Agreement created an enormous pressure upon the limited existing educational facilities. For example, in Equatoria Province, which had the majority of returnee students, a system of shifts was adopted wherever possible to counteract shortages of space and teachers (Government of the Southern Region of Sudan 1974). Under the shift system, two schools operated on the same premises but at different times, one operating in the morning and the other starting in the afternoon.

The regional government, recognizing the wide range in ages of the potential student population and the fact that few schools existed, gave priority for primary school enrollment to children eight years and older who had not had educational opportunities either inside or outside Sudan during the civil war. Consequently, during the immediate years following the Addis Ababa Agreement, the student population included a high proportion of mature students.

A further problem generated by the war was that of the language. The returnee students who had been in exile or in "Anyanya" bush schools had used either French or English as a medium of instruction, but on their return they were required to make the transition to Arabic. Not only was this a problem of language, but also of script. The regional government attempted to deal with this problem by establishing some exclusive schools or additional classrooms in existing schools where the medium of instruction remained English.

Unattached Minors and Disabled Persons

The social problems generated by the civil war in the South were enormous. An estimated 2,300 unattached minors lived in Aweil, Juba, Malakal and Wau in 1975, and the number of the physically handicapped in the South was estimated at around 100,000 persons (Government of the Southern Region of Sudan 1977). The government's immediate response was to establish the Department of Social Welfare with the mandate to:

• improve psychosocio-economic conditions of destitute families;
• rehabilitate vagrant and unattached minors and psycho-socially handicapped;
• provide care for orphaned, abandoned, and pre-school infants and children; and,
• train personnel to achieve these objectives (ibid.).

In the resettlement process, the department's policy was to encourage the orphans' closest relatives to take responsibility for them. While there are no specific records, it is generally agreed that this approach was successful. The government also established orphanages and rehabilitation homes for unattached minors whose parents were not found or whose closest relatives had declined to care for them.

Petty Traders and Small Businessmen

A program of loans to petty traders and small businessmen was initiated by the Resettlement Commission to revive small businesses that had been destroyed or dislocated during the civil war.

Those who benefited most from the loans were the progressive businessmen who had strong urban connections. Loans were conditional upon potential recipients putting up security and being guaranteed by government personnel known to the loan authorities. Such conditions were met only by individuals who had strong backing within the regional government. As a result, the loans program's economic impact upon the average small businessman was negligible, which reinforced the already widening gap between the progressive businessmen and the rest of the traders. The program was discontinued after the first year because of lack of funds.

Rural Returnees

This group of returnees consisted of subsistence farmers who had been forced to abandon their homes during the civil war. They constituted the majority of the more than 1 million displaced population resettled after the conflict. Conscious of the high expectations of many returnees, the regional government outlined a program for their immediate employment in various government departments. The jobs thus created were to be only temporary until other, more permanent opportunities could be generated. Planned developments, such as a Jute mill at Tonj and sugar refineries at Mongalla and Melut, were expected to become fully operational and to serve as major sources of employment. This anticipated industrial growth did not materialize, however, and consequently the government was forced to lay off many who had been temporarily employed during 1972 to 1974. Estimates put 83 percent of the 26,000 returnees in this category.

Although the government made substantial savings from the layoffs, they generated bitterness and resentment among those affected. Interpretation of government policy differed from one group to another; to the ex-"Anyanya" who were laid off it represented a breach of the Addis Ababa Agreement. Others rejected the government's economic explanations for the layoffs, arguing that the international community had contributed generously to the South's redevelopment, including the provision of employment for returning population, and the government was reneging on its responsibilities and promises.

The Impact of Refugees' Return on Their Home Environment

It is useful to examine whether the internal refugees' experiences during exile affected them differently after their return than did the experiences of the external refugees. A basic question is whether displacees who found refuge outside Sudan in alien environments experienced greater levels of change to their lifestyles after the war than did those who remained within Sudan.

Although causes of displacement may be similar, displacees react in different ways to uprooting and thus experience varying degrees of psychological and socioeconomic adjustment to new environments. Depending on levels of adjustment achieved by displacees while in exile, the uprooting may have a positive or negative impact on socioeconomic performance following repatriation.

A study of Yei and Maridi Districts has shown that the nature of population displacement during the war played a major role in determining levels of displacees' current economic performance (Akol 1986). Refugees who were displaced outside their ethnic territories have experienced a wider range of change to their socioeconomic conditions since they returned than did those who remained within the same socio-economic space.

Throughout Africa, refugee migrations across borders have often resulted in people moving into areas of different levels of socioeconomic development. In general, when refugees migrate from less to more developed areas, their socioeconomic conditions improve. Consequently, diffusion of new ideas and farming techniques to the displacees' home country may occur when such refugees subsequently repatriate. For example, the Mozambiquans who repatriated from organized rural settlements in southern Tanzania transferred new ideas into the much less developed areas of northern Mozambique to which they returned.

Terrill's study of the Acholi in Torit District suggests that the Acholi had been transformed after they returned from exile. The various changes in attitudes to society and economy during the war were so great that they "could not be reversed or simply annulled" after their return. According to him, "the Acholi repatriates and returnees brought with them the perceptions, attitudes, values, ideals, needs and, in some cases skills, trades and savings variously moulded, developed and accumulated during the period of asylum in a wide range of locations and socioeconomic conditions" (Terrill 1983).

Terrill also observed that following repatriation there was a distinction in social and economic aspirations between the returnees from Uganda and other Acholi. In particular, the returnees from Uganda tended to be more aggressive toward life, and more responsive to the work of foreign development teams in the area. Thus, even within a single ethnic group, traditional experiences, outlook, and behavior that characterized the prewar society had been replaced by a diversity of often-conflicting economic and social values.

Implications of Sudanese Experience

Since the beginning of the 1960s, the number of Africa's refugees has continually increased, and thus the potential for further repatriation exercises remains great. A number of lessons can be learned from countries that have repatriated, either successfully or unsuccessfully, refugees from neighboring states. From the range of problems faced by Sudan during its repatriation and resettlement process, the following conclusions become apparent:

1. Personnel involved in refugee work should be properly selected. In Southern Sudan, ill-equipped political appointees and inexperienced civil servants were seconded to the resettlement offices. Their lack of vision about the magnitude of the resettlement process frequently resulted in conflicts between refugees and the staff.

2. Unrealistic propaganda by government agents charged with wooing refugees home was detrimental to the repatriation process in Southern Sudan. Refugees in exile were given favorable impressions of events in Sudan, but on their return found that the facilities or positions promised them did not exist. This caused much resentment among returnees, and some even returned to Uganda or Zaire.

3. Language can become a factor in the reintegration process of returnee students. In Southern Sudan, returnee students who had studied in French in Central African Republic and Zaire or in English in Ethiopia and Uganda had difficulty adjusting to school systems taught in Arabic. The magnitude of this problem was recognized only after their return.

4. Rural development plans for reintegrating returnees must take into account the socioeconomic systems to which the target population became adjusted while in exile. In Southern Sudan, no attempt was made to draw on the wide range of experiences and skills displacees had acquired while in exile.

Conclusions and Recommendations

The repatriation of southerners after the civil war provided problems of considerable magnitude, which were dealt with by the Repatriation and Resettlement Commission with varying degrees of success. The prevailing social, economic, and political conditions in the immediate postwar period played an important role in determining the rates of voluntary repatriation following the end of the war. Further, the rate and duration of repatriation varied significantly from one host country to another. Displacees who repatriated immediately following the civil war tended to be those who were least well adjusted in their places of exile, while those who had adapted and had become economically integrated in their asylum areas were in no hurry to repatriate. The heavy burden of support of Southern Sudanese refugees borne by Central African Republic, Ethiopia, Uganda, and Zaire for almost two decades resulted in some long-term benefits, since they subsequently inherited the rural development projects that had been established by international agencies for refugees.

Displacees who migrated outside their social and economic levels, and thus were exposed to different farming systems, experienced greater economic transformation after the war than did their compatriots who remained within the same social and economic space. We can infer that repatriating refugees in other parts of Africa may have greater potential for successful resettlement at home if, during their exile, they became self-reliant on organized rural settlement or had settled spontaneously among more economically developed rural communities. Conversely, refugees who spent extended periods in wholly dependent camps can expect to experience greater levels of difficulty in reintegrating in their home areas after repatriation.

When other studies of refugee repatriation are developed, two areas important to research need further investigation.

1. In Africa, where voluntary repatriation is much more common than permanent resettlement to third countries, the process of reintegration of displacees into their home societies needs to be better understood. Social scientists have yet to examine how spatial displacement affects displacees' subsequent readaptation to their home environment after they return.

2. Although most of Africa's refugee migrations involve only relatively short distances, the movements are not necessarily confined within either the same physical environments or ethnic territories. The question of the extent to which the displacees' new environments, both physical and cultural, help bring about changes in their economic activities, communal attitudes, and ethnic relationships after they return home has yet to receive serious attention from researchers.

Part Three

Central America

Of all the world's refugee-generating areas, Latin America has probably received the least attention from either the media or the academic community. Yet South and Central America, as well as some of the Caribbean states, have been adding to world refugee numbers for much of the postwar era. The revolution in Cuba resulted in close to a million Cubans migrating to the United States. Political turmoil in Argentina has created periodic refugee movements, and the 1973 overthrow of President Allende in Chile resulted in a worldwide dispersion of Chilean refugees to places as disparate as Canada and Mozambique. The more recent problem of Haitian refugees, especially those arriving by boat in the southern United States, has added substantially to the debate about the definitions of refugee and to the growing awareness of the concept of "economic refugees." But the principal refugee-generating arenas are found in Central America, where most of the contemporary refugees in Latin America are currently located.

Although UNHCR acknowledges that upward of 1 million people have been displaced during the past decade in Central America, only around 120,000 had benefited directly from the protection and assistance of the agency by mid-1986 (Barton 1986). Nowhere else around the world does such a wide discrepancy exist.

The current problem in Central America involves three groups of refugees: Guatemalans, Nicaraguans, and Salvadorans. They are distributed throughout all the countries of the region, although Mexico and Honduras support the majority of them. Although there has been some third-country resettlement to the United States and Canada (and allegedly much illegal migration into the U.S.), and some limited periodic repatriation, the majority of refugees are being maintained in numerous refugee holding camps or have spontaneously integrated among urban and rural communities.

In Nicaragua, for example, Salvadoran and Guatemalan refugees remain relatively inconspicuous since most are considered integrated into the social fabric of the host society. Salvadoran and Nicaraguan refugees in Costa Rica have also been integrated spontaneously, although two transit camps were established and a rural settlement is being developed since the escalation of new arrivals in 1985. In Honduras and Mexico, most refugees are maintained in holding camps, most of which are settlements providing only the minimum needs for survival. The development of agricultural settlements, where refugees are provided with the prospects of achieving self-reliance, has yet to approach anything near the level of Africa's response to its rural refugees.

The three essays in this section will introduce some of the problems facing Central America's refugees and their host countries. Elizabeth Ferris focuses on Mexico's refugee policy and the manner in which that government is reconciling contradictory pressures in coping with its growing stream of refugees into Mexico. Although Mexico is not a signatory of the U.N. Convention and Protocol on refugees and thus does not recognize the Central Americans as "refugees," it has provided them with at least some of the support and guarantees that recognition of their status would imply. Mexico, however, wants to discourage potential refugees from seeking refuge in Mexico: by making life for refugees difficult it is hoped that other destinations will be sought. The concept of "humane deterrence" is not unique to Southeast Asia.

Bruce Harris and Miguel Ugalde focus on Guatemalan refugees in the Mexican state of Chiapas, which has been especially inundated with refugees. Harris and Ugalde critically examine Mexico's policy toward Guatemalan refugees, and its concentration of all refugee assistance under the authority of a single agency—the Comision Mexicana de Ayuda a los Refugiados (COMAR).

An issue that is often ignored in the study of refugees is the impact of an influx of refugees upon the local population into which the refugees are thrust. John Everitt examines this problem in the context of Belize, where immigrants in general, and "Latin" refugees in particular, are threatening to upset the delicate social and cultural balance of this small country's population.

15

Dilemmas of Third World Refugee Policies: Mexico and the Central American Refugees

Elizabeth G. Ferris

An estimated 97 to 98 percent of the world's 13 to 16 million refugees are currently living in the Third World (Keely 1981). Yet scholars have paid relatively little attention to the particularly painful policy choices facing Third World governments in formulating policies toward refugees. Mexico's experiences with the Central American refugees serve as a case study of the way in which one Third World government is reconciling contradictory pressures in coping with an unanticipated stream of refugees.

The violence in Central America today is producing a new type of Latin American refugee; the earlier cases of political leaders individually singled out for governmental persecution have been replaced by mass movements of hundreds of thousands of peasants who are fleeing the generalized violence in the countryside. El Salvador and Guatemala have produced an estimated 2 million refugees, most of whom remain in their countries as displaced people. An estimated 600,000 Central American refugees have reached the United States in search of safety. Since they are not recognized as political refugees and since political asylum has been extended to only a handful of individuals, the Central Americans in the U.S. live under constant threat of deportation. Perhaps 30,000 Salvadorans are currently in camps in Honduras, where they are watched with distrust and hostility by security forces sympathetic to the Salvadoran government's counterinsurgency campaigns. Another 10,000 Salvadorans have fled to neighboring Guatemala, where they face a precarious existence. Less than 10,000 Guatemalans are in Belize and other Central American nations.

Approximately 250,000 Central American refugees are living in Mexico today, more than in any other country in the region. International observers see Mexico as a crucial case for the future of the Central American refugees in the region. Viewed as a progressive government sympathizing with revolutionary forces in Central America, the Mexican government's precedents in coping with this current flood of refugees are vitally important to those seeking more humane treatment of Central America's displaced millions.

Refugees in Mexico

Central American refugees currently in Mexico fall into three distinct groups, each posing a different set of problems for the government.

1. *Salvadorans and Guatemalans in transit to the U.S.* Approximately 50,000 Central Americans are using Mexico as a pathway to the U.S. Although least problematical to the Mexican government because they make the fewest demands for services, these refugees raise the thorny issue of cooperation with U.S. immigration officials in deporting the refugees back to Central America.

2. *Salvadorans and Guatemalans living primarily in Mexican cities.* Probably 100,000 Central American refugees live throughout Mexico with varying degrees of legal recognition, but only a handful (perhaps 500) have been granted political asylum. The refugees in this group come primarily from Salvadoran and Guatemalan cities and small towns. Many are young men who have come (alone) to Mexico out of fear of being pressed either into military duty or into the guerrilla forces back home. Officials in Mexican relief organizations report that many in this group will probably settle in Mexico.

3. *Guatemalan peasants living in camps along the border.* The approximately 100,000 Guatemalan peasants in Mexico's southern provinces are very different from the refugees who have traveled to the cities. Overwhelmingly rural and from indigenous groups (95 percent speak indigenous languages), these peasants arrive with their families and occasionally their whole communities, to seek temporary protection from the violence back home. They generally arrive destitute and malnourished, and frequently wounded or sick as well. Officially, 40,000 refugees are registered and live within forty camps and two "officially designated" zones, but most observers estimate that an additional 60,000 refugees live in the area. This is the most problematical of the three groups for the Mexican government. The refugees depend almost completely on the Mexican government (and the nongovernmental organizations that work through the government) for food, housing, and services. Conditions in the camps expose the government to criticism from both domestic and foreign sources. Moreover, the refugees are a constant source of tension for Mexico's already troubled relations with Guatemala. Numerous military incidents have occurred along the border, and Mexicans as well as refugees have been killed by Guatemalan security forces in pursuit of presumed guerrillas crossing the border into Mexico.

Mexican Policies Toward the Refugees

As is the case of many Third World (and indeed First World) governments, Mexican policies toward the refugees have been formulated on an ad hoc, stop-gap basis. The tide of refugees caught Mexico unprepared for such massive numbers of migrants; consequently, Mexican policies have concentrated on reacting to the immediate problem and not on planning long-term policies. Mexican policies toward the refugees may be summarized as follows: (a) Mexico does not recognize the Central American immigrants as political refugees; (b) nonetheless, Mexico allows those fleeing the violence in Central America to remain within its territory; (c) Mexico does not encourage refugees to come and, in fact, discourages future refugee migrations by making living conditions for the refugees precarious; and (d) overall, Mexico wants to keep a low profile toward the refugees and discourages publicity about either the refugees or the government's policies toward the refugees.

Mexico is not a signatory to the U.N. Conventions on refugees, nor does it recognize refugee status within its immigration laws. Indeed, the Mexican government argues that Mexican domestic legislation offers sufficient protection for refugees and that there is no need to ratify additional international agreements on the subject. It does not seem likely that Mexico will ratify the U.N. conventions in the near future. As one Mexican official stated, "It would have been easier to do so five years ago. Now with a quarter of a million Central American refugees already here and more wanting to come, it's just about impossible." So Mexican policy continues in a state of ambivalence, with the government refusing to recognize Central Americans as refugees while giving them the guarantees such recognition of status would imply.

At the same time, the Mexican government is under considerable pressure to formulate policies toward the Central Americans streaming across its borders consistent with Mexican traditions of political asylum and with its foreign policy heritage. Consequently, Mexico tacitly accepts the Central American refugees and allows them to live within its territory. Along its southern border, the Mexican government has established camps that are administered through its agency, the Comision Mexicana de Ayuda a Refugiados (COMAR). COMAR was established in 1980 to coordinate Mexican policies toward refugees, to administer the camps, and generally to serve as an advocate for refugees within the Mexican bureaucracy. Nongovernmental organizations such as Oxfam, Catholic Relief Services, the Mexican Friends Service Committee, and various European organizations, as well as UNHCR, have been active in providing funds and services within the camps. Yet the government maintains control over the camps, and the activities of nongovernmental organizations are much more limited than in other Central American nations.

Mexico discourages further refugee migrations by making life difficult for refugees. The government provides only minimal services in camps and virtually no services in urban areas. Hunger, disease, and infant mortality rates are high within the camps—even in comparison with existing high rates in Guatemalan and Mexican rural areas. Provision of essential services is particularly inadequate in the small outlying camps. Mexican officials point out, however, that there is much poverty and hunger among Mexicans, particularly in the southern state of Chiapas where most of the camps are located. To provide more for refugees might cause resentment on the part of local populations who are not as well served.

Moreover, the Central American refugees have virtually no legal protection. Except for the few who are given political asylum, the refugees live in constant insecurity. The Mexican government deports between 600 and 1000 illegal Central American immigrants weekly, and there is no way of determining which are refugees and which are "economic" migrants. In addition, there are occasional mass deportations of Guatemalans from the camps. These appear, however, to derive more from spontaneous decisions made by particular officials within the bureaucracy than from official policy. Since the vast majority of Central Americans living in Mexico are doing so without legal recognition by the government, such deportations cause widespread fear and uncertainty.

Finally, the Mexican government seeks to downplay the whole issue of refugees. The refugees are politically controversial, and the government seeks to avoid controversy. "Rightist" Mexicans see the refugees as communist guerrillas spreading revolution in the country, while the "left" uses the presence of the refugees to urge more radical foreign policy stances by the government. Officials in the government clearly perceive that publicizing the situation will only make matters more difficult for the regime.

Many contradictory pressures on the Mexican government have led to this particular mix of policies toward the refugees. Some are unique to the Mexican historical experience, while others are common in many Third World countries. In formulating its refugee policies, the Mexican government has responded to the pressures of living up to Mexico's heritage of generous political asylum, maintaining consistency with Mexico's progressive foreign policy image, and working within the constraints imposed by Mexico's current political and economic difficulties. The results of these contradictory pressures have been the ad hoc, inconsistent, barely welcoming refugee policies described above.

Mexican policy-makers, like leaders of other host nations, were unprepared for the influx of Central American refugees. While proud of its tradition of extending refuge to the persecuted, Mexico has never before had to commit significant amounts of scarce resources to the implementation of its refugee policy. Previous political exiles from Spain, Chile, and Argentina had largely come from the intelligentsia and professional classes. After an initial period of aid and governmental support, such exiles were able to become integrated (to varying degrees) into the community. In contrast, the Central Americans currently coming to Mexico represent precisely that group of laborers of which Mexico has an alarming surplus—unskilled or poorly skilled workers. While Mexico welcomed Latin America's professionals with open arms, policies toward poor *camposinos* have been much more ambivalent, giving rise to charges that Mexico has a two-class refugee policy. These charges are particularly painful for Mexico because of its desire for a progressive foreign policy image. The refugees create complications to this progressive policy, and the deportation of Central American refugees is contradictory to its progressive image. It is inconsistent for Mexico to condemn the repressive Salvadoran regime while deporting the refugees—the very victims of that regression. It is also inconsistent, and Mexican officials are acutely aware of that inconsistency, for Mexico to deport Central Americans, or to treat them in a less than compassionate fashion, while protesting the expulsion and maltreatment of undocumented Mexican workers in the United States.

In recent years, the Mexican system has faced severe economic difficulties triggered by declining oil prices. In 1982, the government announced that it was simply unable to pay its $85 billion debt run up during the oil-rich years. The renegotiation of the debt required severe austerity measures on the part of the government. Public expenditures were slashed, with resultant increases in unemployment; food and gasoline subsidies were reduced, leading to harsher conditions for Mexico's poor; and the number of businesses declaring bankruptcy reached an all-time high, producing lower levels of private investment. Moreover, according to most economists, economic conditions will become even worse in the future. The Consejo Coordinador Empresarial estimated in 1983 that 50 percent of all companies would have to fire at least part of their workforce during that year.

The political consequences of the economic crisis have been severe. Public criticism has expanded beyond specific individuals and regimes to include attacks on the political system as a whole. The economic and political climates place constraints on the de la Madrid regime's ability to formulate policies toward the refugees. Economically, the resources are simply not available to provide for refugees; politically, the administration must be very cautious in finding a moderate position regarding the refugees.

Conclusions

The contradictory pressures on the government—a need to maintain Third World revolutionary solidarity and to act in the best tradition of Mexico's heritage of asylum versus the concrete political and economic necessity of limiting the number of visibility of refugees—have led to the ad hoc, somewhat inconsistent policies toward the refugees discussed in this chapter. Mexico's unique foreign policy tradition and history of liberal political asylum have set it apart from other Third World nations with different cultural and historical experiences. But the economics and political pressures mandating a more restrictive refugee policy are commonly found throughout the Third World. Limited economic resources and difficulties in maintaining political stability, rather than the ideologies and intentions of governments, are the principal determinants of refugee policy in the Third World.

The pressure on the Mexican government from all sides will undoubtedly increase in the years ahead. As the violence in Central America escalates, the number of refugees from that violence will surely increase. Faced with a growing number of refugees needing shelter, the Mexican government will find itself in an increasingly difficult position. As the economic situation creates lower living standards for the population, the political and the economic costs of providing for the refugees will also grow. Yet the Mexican government will simultaneously experience increasing pressure to maintain support for revolutionary regimes abroad and to live up to its progressive traditions. Such imperatives would mandate a more open policy toward its Central American refugees. The long-term political risks to Mexico of not making the right decision are very high.

The policies that de la Madrid is following toward Central American refugees are full of contradictions. Mexico does not recognize refugee status but has a governmental commission to aid refugees. Camps are built for some Central American refugees; others are routinely deported back to violence. Some governmental officials emphasize Mexico's heritage of asylum, and promise that all victims of the violence will be allowed to stay in Mexico; others openly discuss the need for mass deportations. The government proudly publicizes its foreign policies toward Central America, and the newspapers are full of stories of diplomatic initiatives to resolve the crises, while stories of refugees become harder to find. These contradictions will undoubtedly deepen as the political and economic pressures that create them increase. For the moment, refugees are relatively safe in Mexico, at least in comparison with the other host countries, but the trend is clearly in the direction of more restrictive policies toward the refugees. It is, of course, the refugees—persecuted in Central America, discouraged in Mexico, deported from other countries—who are the victims of such policies.

16

The Guatemalan Refugee Situation in Chiapas, Mexico

Bruce Harris and
Miguel Ugalde

In May 1981, a group of 470 scared and emaciated Indians crossed the 550-mile international border from Guatemala into the southernmost Mexican state of Chiapas. This group was not part of the annual migrant workforce that regularly crosses into Mexico looking for work on the coffee farms of Chiapas. It was a group composed mostly of Indian refugees fleeing the repressive government of General Romeo Lucas Garcia, who took power in rigged national elections in 1978.

According to UNHCR, by 1983 the number of refugees in Mexico had grown to more than 120,000 people, half of them children under the age of fifteen. Roman Catholic and Protestant relief organizations believe that some 100,000 Guatemalans live in the largely inhospitable, dense jungle of the Mexican border region in thirty-one makeshift refugee camps. They live in squalid conditions with no housing, no sanitation, and only river water for drinking. In one camp 118 children died of sickness and starvation between December 1982 and February 1983.

The Mexican Ministry of the Interior estimates that there are only 10,000 Guatemalan refugees in Mexico. This very low and unrealistic figure reflects the delicate position in which the Mexican government finds itself. The growing violence in Guatemala poses increasingly serious diplomatic and moral quandries for Mexico which, despite traditional sympathy for revolutionary movements of Central America, is equally anxious to avoid problems along its southern border.

The Situation in Guatemala—A Background

In 1954, the regime of General Jacobo Arbenz Guznan was overthrown by anti-communist forces aided by the Central Intelligence Agency. On November 13th, 1960, an unsuccessful military coup resulted in a second period of guerrilla warfare that lasted seven years and cost the lives of thousands of Guatemalans. After the elections in 1978, General Romeo Lucas Garcia took power. His almost dictatorial military position brought about a wave of terror and political killings. Reports have suggested that the extreme right-wing death squads were directed from the Presidential Palace.

The leftist guerrillas reacted to this wave of terror with their own strikes against the Guatemalan army and security forces. Caught in the middle of this terror was the civilian population. In 1980, President Carter cut off U.S. foreign aid to Guatemala after Amnesty International reported tens of thousands of deaths caused by Guatemalan government death squads.

While the terror initially took place in the major cities of Guatemala, government forces increasingly undertook "pacification" programs in rural areas, trying to eradicate the guerrillas' base of support. The left-wing forces have traditionally found support among the indigenous rural population of the western highlands (altiplano) of Guatemala—an area containing 60 percent Indian people out of a population of 7 million. Right-wing death squads and *ejercito* set about killing the Indians as they "cleansed" the countryside of leftist guerrillas. As a consequence, in the spring of 1981, the first group of refugees left the northern Peten province and headed for the relative safety of Mexico.

On March 23, 1982, a military coup took place and a three-man junta was set up, headed by retired General Efrain Rios Montt. International hope arose that Rios Montt—a self-proclaimed born-again Christian—might stem the political violence. That hope was short-lived, however, and the activities of the death squads continued. Rios Montt was afraid that the rural Indian population was giving greater support to the guerrillas, and stepped up the "pacification" program. After his June 1982 declaration of a state of seige, he sent army reinforcements to the departments of Quiche, Solola, San Marcos, and Huehuetenango, where rebels were believed to be ensconsed. He then introduced a policy of guns and beans—those who sided with the government were fed; those who did not, were shot. Rural residents were thus forced to choose sides—neutrality was not accepted. The flow of predominantly Indian refugees into Mexico rose dramatically, with hundreds of wounded and emaciated Guatemalans arriving each week. This massive migration took Mexican authorities by surprise.

In July 1982, Rios Montt dissolved the three-man junta, named himself president and, under the state of seige imposed earlier, suspended civil liberties, including freedom of expression. Amnesty International reported that 2,600 Indians and peasants, many of them women and children, were massacred in the first five months of Rios Montt's government. The violence continued, to a lesser extent in the urban areas but increasingly so in the rural highlands. As a result, waves of refugees hiked through the thick jungles to Mexico. Many died on the way. In March 1983, the state of seige in Guatemala was lifted. The pacification program continues, however, and the number of Guatemalan refugees in Mexico is, by some reports, now close to 120,000.

Mexico and the Guatemalan Refugees

The situation regarding Guatemalan refugees in Mexico is a very delicate one for the Mexican government, for several reasons.

Mexico's International Image

Traditionally Mexico has been a haven for political and intellectual exiles, but it was totally unprepared for the influx of mostly illiterate Guatemalan peasants. A move by the Mexican government in May and again in July of 1981 tarnished Mexico's proud "haven" image. The government of Jose Lopez Portillo deported all but 46 of 1,900 Guatemalan peasants and Indians who had fled to Mexico from the Guatemalan province of Peten. The move provoked strong protests from leftist and human rights groups in Mexico. The Lopez Portillo government insisted that the group had returned to Guatemala "voluntarily," adding that Mexico would maintain its open borders to all political refugees in need. Press reports at the time, however, said that the refugees had been given the choice of leaving on their own or of being forced out. The regional office of UNHCR in Costa Rica was "greatly concerned" about the deportations. By the deportation Mexico had violated its agreement and signature of the San Jose Pact of the Organization of American States, which states that refugees should not be deported when such an act would put their lives in danger.

Mexican Foreign Policy

In 1980, Mexico began to seek political leadership in Central America and the Caribbean to offset the historical influence of both the U.S. and Cuba over the troubled region. It started to exert influence on its neighbors, using the tools of oil, aid (although the country's financial state has necessiated diminished aid) and, perhaps most important of all, the cultural persuasion of a shared history, in which Mexico has always been preeminent. A yet-unmentioned reason for Mexico's regional leadership in Central America may be its fear that political unrest and economic crisis might convert Central America and the Caribbean into a focus of East-West tensions.

Mexico's foreign policy in the region has been irritating to the U.S., which has tended to view itself as the sole "overseer" in this area. A real thorn in the side of the U.S. has been Mexico's relations with Cuba: close political ties with Cuba have always been used to symbolize Mexico's independence from the U.S. A major geopolitical worry for the U.S. is the effect that revolutions in Central America might have on Mexico's own political stability. A Hudson Institute study (Mengers 1980) somberly predicts that, if Mexican foreign policy helps bring about a series of victories for the extremist left in Central America and the Caribbean, serious turbulence in Mexico will then follow.

The Mexican Foreign Ministry seems embarrassed by the apparent inconsistency in its sharp criticism of El Salvador's rightist regime and its silence on human rights violations in Guatemala. But the Interior and Defense ministries argue that events in Guatemala have too many domestic repercussions to be handled as an exclusively diplomatic issue. The Defense Ministry has long maintained cordial relationships with the Guatemalan army; to the dismay of liberal Mexican politicians, it even invited Guatemala's former Defense Minister Oscar Mejia Victores to observe the Independence Day parade in Mexico City in September 1982, despite Mejia Victores having become head of state a month earlier by overthrowing Rios Montt.

The Mexican Military and the Refugees

A speech by Senator G. Martinez Corbala, a member of Mexico's Foreign Policy Commission, sums up the de la Madrid administration's feelings toward the increasingly volatile frontier between Guatemala and Mexico. He stated that

> it is not to our advantage to militarize the border area. Doing so would require a fundamental change in the spirit of our foreign policy, exchanging international law for military power. If Mexico militarizes the Guatemalan border, they will have the pretext to concentrate their troops there. This could lead to an artificial conflict. An artificial conflict would be sufficient justification for the U.S. government to arm Guatemala; the arms would be used against popular movements.

Despite Martinez Corbala's speech, many would question whether Mexico is, in fact, trying to keep the border region, where the thirty-one refugee camps are located, a nonmilitarized zone. While officially the border area is not a militarized zone, there is an obvious presence of the Mexican military in the state of Chiapas, and military camps have been installed in Tenosique and Palenque to cover the frontier zone.

Guatemala and Mexico share a long, undefended frontier of mountainous rain forest, through which the Indians of both countries move without much detection. To the alarm of the Mexican government, in August 1982 Guatemalan troops entered Mexico and fired at workers involved in jungle clearing along the border under the terms of the two countries' International Commission on Limits and Waters. There had been numerous unpublicized border incidents, according to workers in the camps, but the Mexican government's decision in September to protest formally the August incident reflected their concern that the situation in Guatemala had been deteriorating since the launching of its governnment's anti-guerrilla offensive.

An escalation in the seriousness of these incursions occurred later in September 1982, when more than a hundred armed Guatemalans, some in military uniform and others in peasant clothes, seized control of the Mexican border hamlet of San Pedro Neuro, where several hundred Guatemalans had taken refuge. According to local leaders, the Guatemalans spent the night inside Mexican territory and took six Guatemalan refugees with them when they left the next morning. Later the military unit kidnapped two Mexicans and two Guatemalans in Benito Juarez, a Mexican border village in the foothills of the Tacana volcano. A further incident occurred in January 1983, when from 80 to 100 armed men in peasant clothing crossed from Guatemala into Chiapas, killing four Guatemalan refugees and wounding a fifth, whom they abducted to Guatemala.

Mexico's new president, de la Madrid, appeared eager to show his concern for the refugees and his determination to stand up to Guatemala's military government. After a meeting with UNHCR's Paul Hartling, Mexico promised to guarantee the security of refugees and also to maintain its traditional policy of providing asylum to refugees and political exiles.

True to Mexican politics, however, several other ministries had differing opinions. Mexican Interior Minister Manuel Bartlett announced a new, very conciliatory attitude toward the Guatemalan government and armed forces. He said that Mexico would neither reinforce its southern border with additional troops nor move refugee camps away from the frontier area, for the latter could be viewed as a gesture of hostility. The incursions into Mexico by Guatemalan forces are continuing and, despite words from Mexico City to the contrary, the militarization of the border appears to be increasing.

Mexican Government Aid for the Refugees

The problem in dealing with Guatemalan refugees in Mexico, aside from the political issues, is one of deciding whom to make responsible for the situation. In a "normal" refugee crisis, UNHCR greatly assists and often totally coordinates refugee camps in the host country. In Mexico the situation is different. Mexico has never signed the 1951 Geneva Convention on Refugees; under Mexican law, as a result, UNHCR is unable to assist physically in the refugee situation in Chiapas. But UNHCR does pick up most of the costs and spent about $6 million in Mexico in 1983, a 250 percent increase from 1982.

When in 1982 the government was faced with the enormity of the Guatemalan refugee problem, they created the Comision Mexicana de Ayuda a los Refugiados (COMAR) and gave it responsibility for the thirty-one refugee camps along the border. This is the only agency officially able to assist the refugees; despite offers from many international voluntary agencies, Mexico has insisted that all aid, including that of U.N. agencies, be channeled through this commission. Many nongovernmental agencies will not do this. A major problem with the organizational structure implemented by the Mexican government is the extreme inefficiency and lack of coordination of COMAR.

After the expulsion of Guatemalan refugees in July 1981, the coordinator of COMAR, Gabino Fraga, resigned in protest of the decision. This resignation illustrates the continuing disagreements within the Mexican government over its refugee policy. A further incident also illustrates the ubiquitous lack of coordination among Mexican government agencies. In October 1982, almost 2,000 Guatemalan refugees were forcibly evicted from Rancho Tejas, one of the thirty-one refugee camps along the Guatemalan border. According to the COMAR coordinator, the eviction was carried out by local authorities in contravention of policy: a dispersion of refugees without known motive. Later reports showed the eviction to be the work of the head of the Immigration Department in the Chiapas border region, a man frequently accused of collaborating with Guatemalan military authorities and local conservative landowners, to the detriment of the refugees.

By late 1982, under pressure from UNHCR, the Mexican government began to issue 90-day visas allowing refugees to stay in Chiapas camps, and refugees with family links to Mexicans were encouraged to legalize their status. But Mexico, anxious to discourage refugees from staying indefinitely or increasing in number, provides them with minimal assistance. Arrivals in Mexico are given some medicine, food, and plastic sheets with which to cover improvised shacks. According to the Immigration Department, "everything we give them is to emphasize that their stay in Mexico is temporary, and obviously we prefer to see them farther away from the border."

Roman Catholic nuns and priests in Chiapas were the first to aid the refugees, and they continue to do so. The Roman Catholic church has also recently charged that Mexican farmers have exploited Guatemalan Indians who seek refuge in southern Mexico but find only poor living conditions, cheap wages, starvation, and disease. The government is unhappy about the involvement of the Roman Catholic liberals in the refugee problem, fearing that this could lead to greater social activism by poor Mexican peasants in Chiapas.

Hence COMAR is faced with internal and intragovernmental conflict, as well as with the logistical problem of daily having to fly more than 10 tons of basic foodstuffs (corn, beans, rice) into the camps to feed the estimated 100,000 refugees. There are no roads to the majority of the camps, but a few are accessible by boat along the Lacatun River, which flows into the densest jungle areas.

Guatemala and the Mexican Refugee Camps

The government of Guatemala continues to consider refugee camps in Chiapas to be full of either guerrillas or at least people sympathetic to the leftist cause. They feel that arms are flowing from Cuba and the Soviet bloc through Mexico to the guerrillas. The refugees vehemently dispute this and say that they are innocent victims caught in a civil war. It would seem that the Mexican government currently believes the refugees, for it is allowing them to remain crammed into the camps.

More recently, Guatemala has begun a campaign to persuade refugees in Mexico to return home, saying that the violence that made them flee over the last years has abated. In a series of letters and diplomatic visits, it has sought the help of Mexico, the International Committee of the Red Cross, and UNHCR. But UNHCR officials continue to fear for the safety of any Guatemalan Indians repatriated against their will. Despite Guatamelan proclamations that the countryside is "pacified," many Indian families continue to cross into Mexico with stories of brutal atrocities.

The Mexican government is placed in a very difficult situation. While they deny that the refugee camps threaten Guatemala, there is a growing concern (illustrated by the Mexican military buildup) that through its own goodwill Mexico may be drawn into Central America's political violence. Guatemala claims that the war is over and refugees can go home. But by refusing to encourage the refugees to return, Mexico is in effect condemning Guatemala's policies. This creates a growing level of friction between the two countries. With increasing social unrest within Mexico, a worsening of the internal economic situation, and increasing external pressures on Mexico from Guatemala regarding the "terrorist" refugee camps, the administration is being placed in an increasingly tight corner.

17

Small in Number, but Great in Impact: The Refugee Migrations of Belize

John C. Everitt

Migrations in Central America have become a topic of considerable debate and study in the past few years both because of the increasing number of people involved and because of the increasing number of countries concerned with these movement networks (Lippman and Diaz-Briquets 1981:8–11). Underlying these discussions about migration is the very real fact that migration "can profoundly alter a community or an entire country within a short time" (Weeks 1981:149), and can be "an essential component of economic development" (Jackson 1979:1).

The effects of migration are significant in Belize, where recent movements of a variety of migrant groups are currently altering, and may have the potential of "profoundly" altering, the ethnic structure of the country, and where immigration has long been cited as a necessary factor in the economic development of the nation. In this essay, three major questions are posed. First, how has emigration, and particularly recent emigration, affected Belize, and why has this taken place? Second, what major flows of migration have gone into Belize, and what are the reasons for these movements? Third, what are the effects of these migratory patterns on the human and cultural geography of Belize?

The Study Area

Belize is located on the mainland of Central America, although it has many cultural and demographic ties with the Caribbean. The country has been dominated since the middle of the seventeenth century by a British or British-derived culture, and the present Creole population of Belize is in large part the result of intermarriage between early British occupants and their African slaves.

The colony was also subject to landward influences; in particular it was settled by Spanish/Mestizo and native Mayan groups. In the mid-nineteenth century these groups formed a most important addition to the population of the country when they fled from what is now Mexico during and after the Caste War of Yucatan, which broke out in 1847 (Dobson 1973:249–50). These groups thus constituted one of the earliest and most significant refugee migrations to Belize (Buhler, n.d.).

In addition there have been influxes of other minority groups. Until recently, the most significant immigrant groups had been the Garifuna or Black Caribs, who first arrived in the early 1800s and were themselves refugees (Solien 1971:140; Taylor 1951), and the East Indians, who settled in the middle of the nineteenth century (Everitt 1970:311–13). Many other smaller subcultures have also entered Belize—including even some Confederate refugees after the American Civil War in the 1860s—but not in significant numbers.

Thus the population of Belize has long been one of "social diversity" (Lowenthal 1961:786), having had its origins in immigration in general and often with refugee movements in particular (Bolland 1977:3; Thompson 1972:4). The actual numbers in each of the subcultural groups is difficult to determine, however, in part because, since 1970 at least, "ranking members of government have wanted to avoid any reference to potentially divisive racial distinctions" (Collins n.d.:32). The census did not attempt a racial or ethnic breakdown between 1946 and 1980, and the difficulty of estimation is illustrated by two recent approximations of the Creole population, both based upon the 1970 census. Dobson (1973:256) asserts that "Creoles form almost 60 percent of the total population," whereas Buhler (in *Brukdown* 10 [1978]:15) believes that this group constitutes only 30.8 percent of the total.

Although Belize is slightly larger in area than El Salvador, its population (144,857 in 1980) is considerably smaller than that of its Middle American neighbors, and the population density is quite low—slightly more than 6.2 persons per k². Consequently, it can easily be affected by numbers of immigrants that would hardly be noticed elsewhere. In 1950 the foreign-born element of the Belizean population amounted to only 8 percent (Bolland 1977:4), and some of this proportion was made up of incoming Mennonite groups (Everitt 1983). Since this time, however, both emigration and immigration have taken place at a significant level, and the ethnic demographic landscape has been considerably altered.

Emigration from Belize

Since its foundation as a British settlement, there has always been a fairly fluid movement of people into and out of Belize, but few of these migrations have had a significant influence upon the ethnic structure of the country, and none has had such an impact since the mid-nineteenth century. Recently, however, this pattern has changed, with a relatively massive movement of Belizeans to the U.S. in search of better employment opportunities, a result of a long-distance acculturation process that has drawn Belizeans to the promised land of North America (Everitt 1982).

Although official data are lacking, it is estimated that at least 1 percent of the present Belizean population is eligible for U.S. citizenship, having been born in the U.S. to temporary emigrants to that country or having since changed citizenship. This number is, however, just the tip of the emigrant iceberg, as there are probably between 35,000 and 50,000 Belizeans in the U.S. at present, at least two-thirds of whom are "out of status" (illegal).

Perhaps more important than the numbers involved in this migration is its ethnic makeup. The vast majority of the emigrants are Creoles or Garifuna—the black portion of the population of Belize. Relatively few Mestizos or Maya move north, and few of the other subcultures emigrate, outside of some dissatisfied Mennonites (Everitt 1983). The reasons for this ethnic pattern are complex, but two main ones can be cited.

First, the black population lives mostly in what have become the least developed parts of the country—the coastal settlements and their hinterlands—including the former capital Belize City and the regional administrative center of Dangriga. The members of this group move in response to push factors as well as pull factors, with joblessness, overcrowded cities, and unemployment often being crucial in the decision-making processes of the migrants; consequently they may be considered "economic" refugees. In some cases Belizean families even try to send a child to the U.S., both to better the lot of their offspring and to gain economic support from the child (Stavrakis and Marshall 1978:A-31).

The process is likely to continue in the foreseeable future, as "development" in Belize is unlikely to be fast enough to stop the movement; and in addition the emigration of these economic refugees may be viewed as a development strategy in itself. The latter suggestion sees out-migration from the developing world to the United States "as a means of limiting unemployment, maximizing foreign-currency earnings, and providing an outlet for dissidence" (Teitelbaum 1983:13).

Second, the urban black population (most of the Creoles and Garifuna live in towns and cities) is the subculture that has been the most influenced by the impact of North American culture over the past twenty years.

The effects of these migrations can be seen easily in the population data. While the population of Belize rose by nearly 21 percent from 1970 to 1980, that of Belize City (the Creole "capital") rose by only 2 percent, and that of Dangriga (the "capital" of the Garifuna) dropped by nearly 5 percent. The rural portions of Belize District and Stann Creek District, where Creoles and Garifuna also predominate, showed increases in numbers that were well below the national average. Some of these changes reflect internal migrations, but most of the variation is a reflection of the international movement.

Immigration to Belize

Belize has long encouraged policies of immigration (Dobson 1973:177–78; Holdridge 1940), especially when the British government perceived it to be underpopulated. Indeed, both the Evans Commission and the Downie report argued that Belize "needed" immigration—from the Caribbean—"to provide an economic basis for the social, technical, and financial commitments that are obligatory for an independent country" (Downie 1959; Evans 1948; Fox 1962:15–16; see also Blood 1950 and Crosbie and Furley 1967:57–58). Although the country has particularly welcomed "immigrants who are in a position to establish themselves without assistance of the Government" (*Labour and Immigration in Belize* 1977:8), it has also seen itself as a traditional haven for refugees running from persecution and injustice (*The New Belize* 11, no.12 [1981]:5). For just as long a period, however, there has been a fear within the country of the immigration of uncontrolled numbers of people from a variety of ethnic groups (Dobson 1973:329–30). These fears surfaced most recently with the movement of Guatemalans and Salvadorans into Belize, and with the touted immigration of Indo-Chinese refugees into the country (*The New Belize* 11, no.1 [1981]:10).

The Guatemalan immigrants are of two streams, one consisting of traditional Kekchi Maya Indians and the other of Mopan Maya and Mestizo peoples. The 5,000 Kekchi mostly live in Toledo District, although in the past five years they have been migrating in small numbers to western Stann Creek District and the eastern parts of the Cayo District. In some cases they have begun to interact and intermarry with the Mopan Maya in the western areas of Belize (Howard 1975). The Kekchi originally migrated from the Vera Paz region of Guatemala and remained almost unnoticed as they settled in the remote southern areas of Belize (Dobson 1973:253; Waddell 1961:38). Their latest settlement has been more significant. It has involved several hundred families and has been encouraged by the government. The migration of Kekchi currently involves some ten families a year. The authorities have encouraged the settlement of the Mayan Indians, as it increases the agricultural base of the country, as well as solidifying the Belizean claim on disputed territory (with Guatemala) in the southern regions. A settled agricultural landscape of Belizean-oriented people is viewed as being an excellent claim to support political ownership in the south of Belize. Because the Kekchi are productive, are still largely geographically isolated, and have taken neither economic resources nor territory used by other Belizeans, they have aroused little antipathy in the country. Also, since the migration has taken place over a long period of time, the recent increase in their numbers and territory has not even been noticed by many Belizeans.

The Guatemalan migrations into Cayo District from the Peten region have been handled with considerable secrecy by the government, and have met with adverse reaction on the part of the populace—particularly by the non-Hispanic Creoles and Garifuna. These Mopan Maya and Mestizo immigrants are preponderantly Spanish-speaking—and more significant, non-English-speaking. The majority of Belizean Maya Indians and Mestizos have a reasonable command of English, as it and Spanish are taught in school. Often the Guatemalans have come back and forth across the border for many years. They tend to blend in with the local population and have family on both sides of the border. In addition, there has been a recent increase in the influx of Guatemalans in the form of refugees, who are supported by UNHCR.

Aside from this recent immigration, most of the Guatemalans "have work permits and are usually sponsored by employers in Belize. Many, after five years residence here, are in the process of acquiring Belizean citizenship, and still more have children who, by nature of being born here, are also Belizeans" (*Brukdown* no.1 [1982]:9). The exact number of these immigrants cannot be ascertained; some critics claim that there are several thousand, while the official government position is that there are "very few." What is certain is that the extent of the Guatemalan immigration is not being publicly recognized because of the potential political and ethnic problems that it might cause.

For most of these Guatemalan immigrants the migration does not appear to be the result of violence or strife-related problems in Guatemala, although as previously mentioned, the number of "Convention" (UNHCR–supported) refugees entering Belize out of fear for their lives appears to have increased recently. Mostly, the reasons for the migrations are similar to those commonly found in Middle America: economic opportunity, better education, and upward mobility for the migrants' children—that is, a result of structural factors that differ between the two countries' cultures and economies (Lippman and Diaz-Briquets 1981:9–11). These groups may both be considered as economic refugees in the same sense as might be the Creoles and Garifuna migrating to North America. They may also be viewed as part of a continual and even inevitable process of movement that "has been taking place all over the English-speaking Caribbean close to the mainland . . . and will not stop" (Davidson 1983). Their significance in Belize has simply been accentuated by the emigration of many members of the black subcultures.

The Salvadoran migrants began to move into Belize in the late 1970s. These early entrants were largely middle-class people who invested in Belizean land and agro-business, perhaps as a hedge against future problems in their own country. Some of these people still live in Belize, "but many have moved on to the U.S., Canada, or even back to El Salvador" (*Brukdown* 1 [1982]:7).

As the civil war in El Salvador increased in scale, a different type of migrant—the refugee peasant—arrived in Belize, often illegally, after a more than 600-kilometer journey across Honduras and Guatemala. The reasons for their arrival are many and varied, and the refugees probably represent all parts of the political spectrum. It does appear, however, that "they are mainly small farmers etching out a subsistence way of life" (*The New Belize* 11, no. 12 [1981]:4).

The Belizean government initially received a modest amount ($70,000) of emergency aid in 1980 from UNHCR to help support the Salvadorans (*The New Belize* 10, no. 9 [1980]:2). In 1981, the government announced a plan in concert with UNHCR for the eventual settlement of 200 families (made up of Salvadorans and some Belizean families as an aid to integration) in the Belize River valley in Cayo District (*The New Belize* 11, no. 12 [1981]:4). The settlement known as the "Valley of Peace," is being assisted by the Mennonite Central Committee and by the nearby Mennonite colony at Spanish Lookout, and is funded by a grant of $10,000 from UNHCR. The government of Belize "donated some 15,000 acres of fertile land just north of the Belize River, about 20 kilometers from the capital, Belmopan" (Asomani 1982:22).

Thus, as with the Guatemalan immigrants, these settlers will be living in the interior of the country in the traditionally Hispanic-oriented areas and away from the home areas of the black population. Estimates of the numbers involved with this Salvadoran migration range from the official government figure of 2,500 (*Brukdown* 1 [1982]:28) to that of a UNHCR estimate of 7,000 (Cabib 1982:12). Regardless of the exact figure, however, it seems that many of the Salvadorans are also in Belize to stay, probably on a permanent basis, in contrast to the settlements in other Central American countries.

Although the situation for the Salvadorans in Belize initially seemed positive, more recent reports indicate a degree of tension in Belize between the government and the UNHCR officials. Some refugees have apparently been expelled for a short time, and the entry of new refugees has been curtailed. As a consequence, Guatemalans and Salvadorans badly in need of protection have been left without a haven, and those already in the country have not been helped to the degree previously expected. This apparent reversal of policy is undoubtedly a government response to the opposition party's criticism that the immigration of Hispanics prejudices the traditional Belizean racial situation and is changing the identity of the country.

Analysis and Conclusions

Although, as Grigg (1980:76–77) makes clear, overseas migration is unlikely to solve problems of rural congestion in the Third World, international migration may have helped to relieve population problems in parts of the Caribbean and could help to relieve urban congestion in Belize City, where the population problem is probably at its worst. More particularly for Belize, however, the major significance of the aforementioned migrations may be cultural, since they are affecting the ethnic balance of the country. Belize used to be mainly black (and principally Creole) in ethnic composition, and these groups formed up to 60 percent of the population until recent times. It is clear that this balance has altered quite radically in recent years; there may now be more Hispanics than any other group, in additional to a large proportion of Mayan Indians. These changes are causing a considerable amount of tension and controversy in Belize.

The major anguish is felt by the Creole and Garifuna, who believe that the country is slowly "Latinizing" through "a combination of immigration by Mestizos and Indians from the Republics and dark-skinned Belizeans moving to North America" (*Brukdown* 1 [1982]:28). The blacks share a concern for their future in Belize, should the process continue. The government does not acknowledge this problem for two reasons. First, they do not acknowlege that more than 3,000 immigrants of Hispanic background have recently entered the country. Second, they say that this population could be balanced by an equal number of black refugees from Haiti immigration into

Belize (ibid.), under a proposal that involved the settling of 600 Haitian families (or about 2500 persons) along with Belizeans—following the "Valley of Peace" model in the Moho River area of Toledo District (*The New Belize* 12, no. 7 [1982]:10).

The Intergovernmental Committee for Migration, a heavily government-subsidized private U.S. group, has been administering the Haitian settlement plan. But this plan has not yet advanced past the study stage, although it might become a reality in the future if it can surmount a number of serious obstacles, including its significant cost, its lack of popularity within some sectors of the U.S., and more particularly its unpopularity with Belizeans. Within Belize, it has been suggested that this proposal is simply a way of placating or at least distracting the black population, or is a method of reducing the fears for the future of this segment of the populace.

The effects of these changes in ethnic population structure can increasingly be seen in the Belizean landscape. Outside the traditional urban strongholds of the black population, the countryside is becoming more settled than ever before, and this settlement process is dominated by the Hispanic elements of the population. Although most Belizeans still speak English, the mother tongue of an increasing proportion of the population is Spanish or one of the Maya tongues.

The government's policies now appear to be twofold with regard to immigration. The first part is that all newcomers must be fully integrated into Belizean society. Unfortunately, because of the numbers presently involved, this may prove to be a lengthy and difficult process, particularly as Belize is a developing country with few surplus resources. It is also likely to be, to some degree, a futile process, as the resulting cultural mix will inevitably be different from that existing at present and also quite different from that of twenty or thirty years ago, which is the situation that many blacks would like reinstated. Thus acculturation might well occur, but the result for Belizeans will not be the same as it would have been without the immigration.

The second part of the policy is that any organized immigration must be as ethnically balanced as possible to prevent further change in the contemporary racial and cultural structure. But, again, this condition will be difficult to fulfill, for even if black immigrants (and perhaps particularly French-speaking Haitians) enter Belize, they will be culturally different from the present subcultures and will double the number of foreign immigrants. The second policy might indeed increase the probability that the first would fail.

For Belize there seems to be no easy solution to the problem, and at present it is impossible to say whether the government's policies and the present migration patterns will be beneficial or detrimental for the country. In the long run, however, it is possible that all the immigrant groups will be viewed as economic assets to their new homeland, and thus the main hope for Belize may be a more accommodating position on the part of the black population. If so, we may see a new ethnic balance in Belize and find that the immigration flows that led to this new balance are then, in retrospect, viewed as positive additions to a developing country.

Acknowledgments

The author would like to thank those who helped him with his fieldwork in Belize and the Brandon University Research Committee (Grant Number 2652) which made this fieldwork possible. He would also like to thank the Geography Departments at the University of California, Los Angeles, and California State University at Fullerton, which made available the facilities for writing this essay. Stewart Krohn of *Brukdown* Magazine inspired the title of this paper.

Part Four

Western Asia

The two largest refugee-generating areas in the Third World are the Middle East and Afghanistan. The former is also the most protracted of all of the world's refugee crises. The displacement of Palestinians began even before the creation of Israel in 1948 and the first Arab-Israeli war that followed. Since then, the size of the Palestinian refugee population has grown both as a consequence of further military confrontations in the region and from high rates of natural increase. It has increased from around 726,000 in 1949 (Buerig 1971) to more than 2 million, of which 775,000 are in Jordan. The problem of Palestinian refugees has been with us for so long that it is almost taken for granted. The prospect for a lasting and durable solution, acceptable to all parties, is no closer today than it was in the late 1940s. Nevertheless, the frustrations and anger of the Palestinians are regularly brought home to us through the acts of wanton violence bred by the hopelessness of the situation.

One reason why Palestinian refugees frequently appear to be "forgotten" in reviews of world refugee problems is because they do not fall under the mandate of UNHCR and thus are never included in any of the agencies' documentation. When the Palestinian refugee crisis first erupted, the geographical limitation (to Europe) of UNHCR's mandate resulted in a separate agency being created. The United Nations Relief and Works Agency for Palestinian Refugees (UNRWA) has had responsibility for all assistance to Palestinian refugees since 1948.

When one examines the Palestinian refugee problem, a number of issues emerge that should be related to other refugee arenas in the Third World. One of these is the consequences of long-term camp confinement of refugees. Although many Palestinians have left the refugee camp to resettle overseas or to become "permanent" migrant laborers in the Middle East and elsewhere, those who remain in camps are testimony to the despair that the non-solution of permanent refugee camps engenders, as well as to the political fanaticism that can thereby be fomented. Yet several other potential "Palestinian" situations are looming elsewhere in the world, where holding camps initially set up to dispense relief and provide temporary refuge become long-term non-solutions. The Sahraoui have lingered in Algerian holding camps for more than a decade, the Ogaden Somali remain in such

183

camps, the Hmong have now been in Thai camps for more than a decade, and many of the Afghan refugees are destined to long-term camp existence.

A related issue is that of the long-term political implications of such refugee communities beginning to create a state within the host country. The crisis in Jordan in the 1970s illustrates the extreme situation that can develop, resulting almost in a state of civil war. While Jordan adopted radical measures to regain control over Palestinians within its borders, Palestinians in Lebanon remain one of the powerful factions engaged in that country's lingering internecine war. The danger of other refugee concentrations evolving into a state-within-a-state situation cannot be discounted in such areas as the North West Frontier Province in Pakistan or along the Thai-Kampuchean border.

The essay in this volume by Musa Samha that deals with the Palestinian refugee problem describes the scale of the problem in one of the host-countries—Jordan. It traces the growth of the refugee population since 1948 and shows that many Palestinian refugees have in fact been refugees more than once: initially fleeing to the West Bank, only to be uprooted again in 1967 to flee to Jordan or elsewhere.

The Afghan refugee crisis erupted almost immediately after the Soviet occupation of Afghanistan, and by mid-1979 UNHCR had become actively involved in Pakistan. Since then, the number of refugees has surged to 2.5 million in Pakistan and up to 1.9 million in Iran. This translates into 25 to 30 percent of Afghanistan's population being in exile in neighboring states. Moreover, of the total in Pakistan, close to 80 percent are concentrated in the North West Frontier Province, creating there the heaviest refugee concentrations anywhere in the world. Pakistan's response (as well as Iran's) has been generous and ungrudging, despite the numbers and prevailing developmental problems in the areas of influx. It is understandable that problems are arising as a consequence of increasing competition between refugees and locals for space, essential commodities, and jobs. The intense pressure upon land resources created by the refugees' arrival is also having severe environmental impacts on regions with a precarious ecological balance.

Two essays consider the Afghan refugees in Pakistan. Dan Greenway examines the options faced by Pakistan in having to find long term-solutions to the refugee problem. In addition to the long-term camp confinement and the risk of the creation of a nation-within-a-nation, Pakistan faces the additional security risk arising from the role that many of the refugees play in the internal guerrilla war in Afghanistan. Such factors, plus an array of social and economic problems, lead Greenway to be pessimistic about the long-term option of local settlement and integration.

Hanne Christensen takes a somewhat more optimistic position, focusing upon the resourcefulness of refugees even under the most adverse conditions. Her essay is especially valuable because it adopts a comparative approach by contrasting the situation in Somalia to that in Pakistan. In both cases, Christensen concludes, individuals are quick to adopt initiatives and ideas that help them reestablish their previous life styles despite the constraints of their predicament. Much can be learned from such a comparative approach to refugee studies.

18

Camp Refugees in Jordan's East Bank: Distribution and Problems

Musa Samha

The problem of the Palestinian refugees resident in camps in Jordan is unresolved, despite the fact that they have been homeless for thirty-five years. The refugees continue to suffer, and the numbers dwelling in the camps, resulting primarily from the two movements in 1948 and 1967, continue to grow.

Researchers dealing with the Palestinian refugees problem in Jordan face shortage and inaccuracies in data regarding the size and movements of the refugee populations, for the following reasons:

1. Jordan is the only Arab country that has granted Palestinian refugees the option of citizenship. While some have taken up this option, an additional quarter-million refugees live in camps in Jordan who have not opted for Jordanian citizenship.
2. The natural increase during the long period of refuge, the fact that there were major movements in 1948 and 1967, and the high mobility among the refugees are all factors that make it difficult for the responsible authority—the United Nations Relief and Works Agency for Palestinian Refugees (UNRWA)—to provide accurate estimates of the refugee numbers.
3. The instability of the refugees within their camps and their tendency to concentrate in cities (half a million are dwelling outside the Jordanian camps) further complicate the compilation of data on their numbers.

For these reasons this documentary statement is confined mainly to the camp populations, and has relied mainly upon UNRWA data and data from the Joint Ministerial Committee for Displaced Persons (JMCDP).

The Growth of Refugees and Their Distribution

The precise number of Palestinian refugees who were exiled in 1948 is still unknown. After 1967, the problem of numbers became more complex since it was impossible to distinguish between refugees who had fled for the second time and those who sought refuge for the first time. Thus researchers do not agree on the exact number of refugees and their distribution throughout the Arab countries. UNRWA data are used here as the basic source, since the Agency is responsible for the refugees, but even UNRWA warns that its records do not contain wholly accurate data.

In 1949, a U.N. economic mission estimated the number of Palestinian refugees at 726,000, distributed as follows: West Bank—280,000; Gaza Strip—190,000; Lebanon—100,000; Syria—75,000; Jordan—70,000; Egypt—7,000; and Iraq—4,000 (Buehrig 1971).

By 1950, the number of refugees aided by UNRWA and various other voluntary agencies was estimated at 957,000 (ibid.); by 1952, the number was estimated by UNRWA at 850,276, distributed as follows: West Bank—363,689; Gaza Strip—201,173; East Bank—101,981; Lebanon—100,642; Syria—82,781.

The camp population was estimated at 307,301, or 36.1 percent of the total refugees (Hagopian and Zahlan 1974:35). But not all Palestinians expelled in 1948 are included in UNRWA data: excluded were those considered as self-supporting refugees. As Buehrig (1971) noted:

> the question of the refugees was further confused because the educated among them and those possessing urban skills were not dependent on relief, at least not for long, and presumably many of them were never included on the relief rolls of either the voluntary agencies or of UNRWA. Educated and skilled were later estimated by UNRWA to have constituted some twenty percent of the exodus in 1948.

The number of the Palestinian refugees increased to 1,344,576 just before the June War in 1967. This figure reflects many additions and subtractions made during the seventeen years between 1950 and 1967. Most of the increment was due to natural increase, while losses were due to death, emigration, and false registration.

When the tragedy of 1948 was repeated with the 1967 June War, a new wave of refugees was produced. UNRWA estimated that 175,000 of the refugees registered with the agency fled for a second time (that is, those who were refugees as a result of the events of 1948 had fled again in 1967). Of these, 17,500 left the occupied area in Syria, while 7,000 left Gaza for Egypt. It is apparent, however, that the majority of those fleeing for a second time came from Jordan's West Bank, while some 45,000 Gaza-registered refugees left Gaza, most of whom were admitted by Jordan to the East Bank (ibid.:41). UNRWA estimated the number of new refugees fleeing for the first time at 350,000, of which 100,000 fled from the occupied area in Syria, while others left Sinai for Egypt. The balance fled the West Bank to Jordan's East Bank. The above estimates suggest that the total number of second-time and first-time refugees fleeing as a result of 1967 war was 570,000.

According to UNRWA figures, these numbers had grown to 1.5 million by 1971 and to 1.9 million by 1983. During the same time, people in the camp populations increased from 643,333 to 731,495; the distribution of the registered Palestinian refugees in the camps is shown in Table 18.1.

The Palestinian Refugees in Jordan's East Bank

In his kinetic models of the movement of refugees, Kunz (1973:131) noted that "some refugees pass through the border of their homeland either under military pressure or as a result of sudden movements without having apparent desire to become citizens of another state, and only after some period spent in countries of asylum become settlers in a country willing to offer them hospitality." Although the Palestinian refugee movement may be included in the above pattern, one may add that after thirty-five years of exile 759,160 refugees still remain in Jordan, of whom 237,477 remain in the camps. The Middle East continues, therefore, to be one of the major areas in the world containing nonsettled refugees (David 1969). Rogge (1977:191), in discussing solutions to the problems of refugees, mentions that "camps are costly, even as a short term solution, and the social and political conse-quences of long-term camp confinement in the absence of other solutions are nowhere better illustrated than [by] the Palestinian refugees." Jordan, which has received the largest share of Palestinian refugees of all Arab host countries, in 1983 was sheltering 38.9 percent of the total Palestinian refugees, or 32.5 percent of the total Palestinian camp population in the Arab countries.

After the events of 1948, only two parts of Palestine remained within Arab control: the West Bank of Jordan and the Gaza Strip. The former became the home of 369,689 refugees. About 100,981 refugees settled on the East Bank, where they were later unified with their West Bank compatriots when the Hashemite kingdom of Jordan was created. Thus the total number of refugees in Jordan in 1952 (West and East Bank) was estimated at 464,670.

The number rose to 475,000 in 1959, when they accounted for 36 percent of Jordan's population (El Badry 1965), and increased further to 631,000 by 1961. Jordan is alone among the Arab host countries in granting citizenship to all Palestinian refugees who desire it. Employment opportunities thus became available to such refugees; some benefited from their decision to acquire Jordanian citizenship by becoming migrant laborers to the oil-producing countries in the Gulf and Saudi Arabia.

As a result of the 1967 war, Jordan had no choice but to accept the largest number of the new wave of refugees. The West Bank exodus has been the most publicized of the out-movements sparked by the events of 1967 (Harris 1978). The war produced further confusion over the volume of refugees as well as over the definition of who is a "refugee." In this connection, two points should be noted. (a) Following the 1967 war, a clear distinction was made in Jordan between those who were refugees for the second time, i.e., refugees from 1948 who had lived on the West Bank or the Gaza Strip and who moved to the East Bank as a result of the 1967 war, and those coming from the West Bank and the Gaza Strip who were refugees for the first time.

Table 18.1　Distribution of Registered Palestinian Refugees and of Camp Refugees, 1971 and 1983

| | Total registered refugees | | | | Number of camps | Number of persons living in camps | | | |
| | 1971 (June) | | 1983 (March) | | | 1971 (June) | | 1983 (March) | |
	Number	%	Number	%		Number	%	Number	%
East Bank (Jordan)	551,612	36.3	759,160	38.9	10	223,282	34.7	237,477	32.5
West Bank (Occupied)	278,255	18.5	344,449	17.6	20	71,850	11.2	88,839	12.1
Gaza (Occupied)	324,567	21.5	380,863	19.5	8	205,734	32.0	209,704	28.7
Lebanon	184,043	12.2	243,761	12.5	15	95,372	14.8	125,605	17.1
Syria	168,163	11.2	224,851	11.5	10	47,095	7.3	69,870	9.6
Grand total	1,506,640	100.0	1,953,084	100.0	63	643,333	100.0	731,495	100.0

Source: UNRWA.

Table 18.2　Distribution of the Palestinian Refugees in Jordan (East Bank), 1983

| Area | Total | | Original refugees | | Former West Bank residents | | Former Gaza residents | | Living in camps | |
	Number	%	Number	%	Number	%	Number	%	Number	%
Amman	531,756	70.0	292,725	69.3	202,160	70.4	36,871	74.5	115,455	48.6
Irbid	119,676	15.8	93,329	22.1	23,821	8.3	2,526	5.1	33,529	14.1
Balqa	107,728	14.2	36,428	8.6	61,205	21.3	10,095	20.4	88,493	37.3
Grand total	754,160	100.0	422,482	100.0	287,186	100.0	49,492	100.0	237,477	100.0

Source: UNRWA.

The latter were recognized by the Jordanian government as "displaced persons." (b) UNRWA did not take financial responsibility for these "displaced persons" from the 1967 war; the Jordanian government did.

Considering the above points and based upon reports of the JMCDP, the total number of refugees fleeing to the East Bank as a result of the 1967 war and subsequent aggression was 385,277, made up of the following groups:

- 41,293 displaced persons from the West Bank,
- 40,000 second-time refugees from the eastern Jordan valley,
- 85,572 second-time refugees from the West Bank who came under UNRWA care,
- 24,600 second-time refugees from the Gaza Strip who came under UNRWA care, and
- 194,000 displaced persons from the West Bank and the Gaza Strip who came under JMCDP care.

Most second-time refugees were sheltered in the emergency UNRWA camps, and by 1983 the camp population accounted for 43 percent of the total registered refugees in the East Bank. Their distribution is summarized in Table 18.2, which shows the heavy concentration in the Amman area, where 48.6 percent of the camp population are resident.

The Distribution of Refugee Camps in Jordan

Following 1948, most refugees settled in West Bank emergency camps, confidently expecting to return to their homeland within a few weeks; even those arriving on the East Bank shared this feeling. By 1952, however, the political situation had not improved. Refugees were not permitted to return home, so some started to move from the camps to towns, and especially to towns in the East Bank. This situation was repeated following the 1967 war when most refugees were sheltered in camps in the eastern Jordan valley; but this time the refugees were forced to move to the eastern uplands because of Israeli aggression on the East Bank camps, and especially after the complete destruction of the largest Jordan valley camp at Al Karameh (Samha 1979). To avoid the problem of urban refugees after the June War, the Jordanian government decided to build six emergency camps in the uplands (Figure 18.1; Table 18.3).

Problems Faced by Refugees in Jordanian Camps

UNRWA is responsible for the supervision of the refugee camps and provides such benefits as housing, general services, health, and extra meals for children. The internal structure of the camps has been described by Yughi (1973) as follows:

> housing units in the camps are crowded together in compact lines with no more than one meter separating one from the other. Some of them are enclosed by a crudely constructed wall of tin sheeting, sack cloth, brick or cement blocks to ensure a minimum of privacy. The

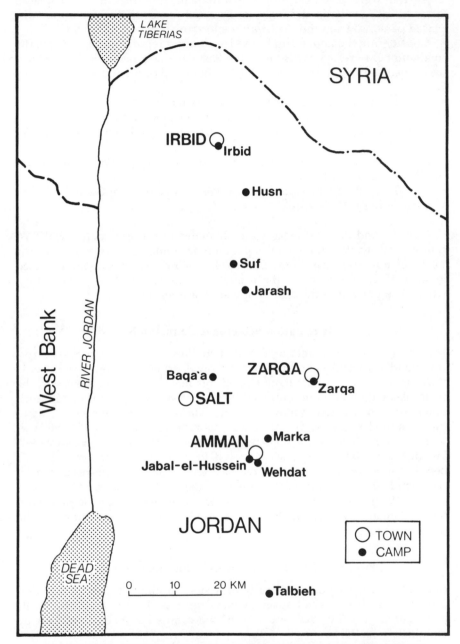

Figure 18.1   Distribution of Refugee Camps in Jordan (East Bank)

Table 18.3   Population of Camps in Jordan at Time of Refuge and in 1983

Camp	Population at time of refuge	Population in March 1983
1948 refugees		
Jabal Hussien	8,000	27,301
Amman New Camp (Wehdat)	5,000	36,474
Zarka	8,000	14,143
Irbid Camp	4,000	17,444
1967 refugees		
Baqa'a	26,000	63,375
Jarash	11,500	15,175
Souf	8,000	9,943
Huson	12,500	16,085
Marka	15,000	30,677
Talbieh	5,000	6,860
Total	103,000	237,477

Source: UNRWA.

Table 18.4   Health Indicators in the Emergency Camps in Jordan, 1976

Camps	Population	Clinics	Doctors	Nurses	Midwives	Sanitation
Baqa'a	52,869	1	5	11	6	115
Marka	26,008	1	3	9	4	60
Talbieh	6,171	1	1	2	—	21
Huson	13,348	1	1	7	3	41
Souf	9,184	1	1	6	3	28
Jarash	13,794	1	1	6	3	36
Total	124,074	6	12	41	19	301

Source: JMCDP, Annual Report, 1976.

Table 18.5   School Enrollment Among Displacees, Refugees, and Indigenous Population, 1975–1976

Population	Authority	Students	Schools	Teachers	Student/ teacher ratio
Displacees	JMCDP	25,875	43	652	40:1
Refugees	UNRWA	156,505	180	2,848	55:1
Indigenous	Government	572,162	1,951	18,854	32:1

Source: UNRWA, Education Division, 1976, and Department of Statistics, 1976.

roads leading to these houses are muddy in winter with streams of dirty water running down the middle due to lack of a proper underground sewage system. . . . since most of the roads are not paved and because there is much rain in winter, the streets in the camps become mud fields . . . drains are mostly inadequate . . . many camps have no proper electricity networks.

We cannot expect, however, that such settlements be developed on an objective economic basis. Unemployment remains high, and only a few refugees in the camps are employed by UNRWA. Most are forced to look beyond the camp for any type of work they can find, usually abandoning previously acquired skills and experience. Many refugees leave the camps altogether to work in the Arabian peninsula.

In collaboration with UNRWA, JMCDP offers medical facilities to the camp refugees. Table 18.4 shows that there are only twelve doctors for all the refugee camps, servicing 124,074 refugees, a ratio of one doctor per 10,340 refugees. This compares with 744 doctors for the East Bank's 1.9 million refugees, or a ratio of one doctor per 2,624 persons. The situation actually declined between 1976 and 1982, when the number of sanitation workers in the camps fell from 301 to 169, and the doctor-to-refugee ratio fell to one doctor per 11,756 refugees.

Table 18.5 shows that the student-to-teacher ratio among the displacees and refugees is much higher than that for the indigeneous population. Hagopian and Zahlan (1974:64) indicated that while there were 600,000 students in primary and secondary education, UNRWA was educating only slightly more than half of these students, while the rest were being educated in government schools. They also found that the drop-out rate in schools supervised by UNRWA was much higher than that in government schools, and suggested that this was due to the prevailing social conditions in the camps.

Conclusion

It is clear that there is an acute shortage of reliable data on refugees in Jordan, and this dearth of data is a major constraint to research and analysis on the refugees' socioeconomic conditions. Although there has been an increase in UNRWA's budget allocation for education and health since the beginning of the decade, neither education nor health standards seems to have improved. This is in part due to rapid population growth in the camps. The main task of UNRWA continues to be economic development for the refugees. But the refugees' overall socioeconomic problems will not improve until politicians of the countries throughout the Middle East, including Israel, find a solution to the Palestinian refugee problem.

19

Prospects for the Resettlement of Afghan Refugees in Pakistan: A Cultural-Geographical Assessment

Dan Greenway

An estimated 2.5 million Afghan refugees are currently receiving asylum in Pakistan. Most live in camps referred to officially as Refugee Tented Villages, along the Afghan border from Chagai (Baluchestan) in the south to Chitral in the north. Heavy concentrations are found near the cities of Peshawar, Mardan, Kohat, and Dera Ismail Khan; perhaps a third of the refugees are located in the Tribal Areas. During 1983 approximately 36,000 refugees were moved to the Punjab near Isa Khel on the west bank of the Indus River, and there are plans to relocate an additional 300,000 refugees to the Punjab under a phased program (FBIS 1983a:Fl).

The magnitude of the refugee problem in Pakistan is impressive. For example, it is estimated that the populations of Kohat, Dera Ismail Khan, Mardan, and Abbottobad districts, along with that of Mohmand Agency, have increased by as much as 20 percent because of the refugee settlements. North Waziristan and Bajaur Agencies and Chagai and Pishin Districts may have grown between 70 and 100 percent, and the population of the Kurram Agency could be more than double the pre-refugee level. As might be expected, the cost of maintaining these refugees is high. Pakistan spends more than $1.2 million a day to provide the Afghans with food, clothing, and shelter. Half of this amount comes from the Aid-to-Pakistan Consortium, which acts primarily through UNHCR and the World Food Program (ibid.). Without this assistance the government of Pakistan would be unable to maintain the refugees.

Beyond the Afghanistan border the situation that precipitated the refugee flight is still operative. The war continues and appears to have escalated since 1983. The Soviet military is still present in force, a significant percentage of the Afghan population remains opposed to the Karmal government, and neither a military nor a negotiated settlement appears imminent. While these political conditions prevail, the refugee situation in Pakistan will continue and likely grow worse. This essay considers the Pakistani options for dealing with the refugees.

The Questions

In any refugee situation, the possible outcomes are limited to (a) continued asylum, (b) repatriation (voluntary or forced), (c) resettlement to a third country, or (d) resettlement within the community of asylum. Of these options, voluntary repatriation is by far the most favored, since it represents most nearly a return to normal conditions. But because of the assumption that the situation in Afghanistan will remain constant, the probability of repatriation of refugees from Pakistan seems very low. A May 13, 1983, editorial in *The Muslim* stated that "it is only when its [the Soviet Union's] troops withdraw from Afghanistan and a more representative government takes over in Kabul that the voluntary repatriation of the refugees to their homes can be made possible" (ibid.).

Resettlement to a third country can also be an acceptable and workable alternative in refugee situations. Several factors presently mitigate against this option for Afghan refugees. First, there seems to be a "glut" on the refugee resettlement market, due, in large part, to an "overproduction" of refugees in Southeast Asia. State Department figures show that, despite the resettlement of 1.3 million refugees between 1975 and 1981, the Indochina refugee camp population remained at 211,500 in 1983, down only 30,000 from the previous year's total (U.S. Department of State 1983, 1984). Second, the worldwide recession and associated unemployment problems have made the acceptance of refugees for resettlement less attractive and more difficult for many countries than in the past. The fact that total Indochinese refugee resettlement for March 1983 was down to just over half the March 1982 level is fairly convincing evidence that the resettlement flood has passed its crest. Finally, no Western developed nation has a direct involvement in the Afghan War. Unlike the situation in Vietnam, which created a large pool of civilians and former military personnel who became subject to persecution because of their association with the U.S. war effort, in Afghanistan there is no conscience to ease, no debt to pay, and no real pressure to accept the refugees if they should opt for third-country resettlement. Thus the probability of large-scale third-country resettlement of Afghan refugees is likely to remain low.

Continued asylum is therefore the most probable outcome, at least in the short run, but the disadvantages of this alternative are acute. The costs to the host country and to the world community of providing continuing assistance to the refugees, as well as the deprivations of camp life, make this the least attractive option for all concerned. In fact, it is no real solution at all.

A final possibility, that of resettling the Afghan refugees within Pakistan, has both advantages and disadvantages, but should be considered carefully.

The Argument

The utility of resettling Afghan refugees within Pakistan can be analyzed from a number of different perspectives. For example, even though long range Soviet policy objectives in Afghanistan are not clear, the resettlement of refugees in Pakistan might be to the Soviets' advantage. Not only would such a solution continuously deny the Islamic National Insurgency valuable local support by depopulating large areas in the Afghan countryside, it could also mean that the refugee population would be distributed across Pakistan, thereby weakening the Mujahedin strongholds along the border and making resupply of both men and material more difficult. Further, if their families were relocated permanently in Pakistan, the young men who routinely cross the border to fight in Afghanistan might be less inclined to do so. For the refugees, on the other hand, local resettlement would mean that their chances of returning to their homeland in the foreseeable future would be sharply reduced, an outcome they would presumably view unfavorably. But because the policy decision to change Pakistan from a country of asylum to one of local resettlement rests with the government, and because the consequences of such a change would have the greatest impact within Pakistan, the Pakistani perspective has been adopted for this analysis.

It seems likely that several benefits would accrue to the Pakistani government if, failing any other solution, it decided to resettle Afghan refugees within its borders. First, such a decision would be seen as a humanitarian gesture of the first order. While neither the war in Afghanistan nor the plight of the refugees in Pakistan receives adequate daily news coverage, the world is nonetheless acutely aware of the problems and hardships associated with any refugee situation. A decision by the government of Pakistan to assume the obligations and risks associated with resettling the refugees, especially if the process went smoothly, would speak well for both the Zia government's concern for human rights and for its efficiency. The development might also set a precedent for intraregional refugee resettlement, which, if adopted in other regions, could mean that refugees currently in camps awaiting permanent solutions and any future refugees might be spared some of the trauma associated with beginning a new life in an alien culture.

This decision would also be consistent with one of the "Pillars of Islam" (charity) and be a demonstration to the world of Muslim solidarity, an ideal that is important to President Zia. Moreover, the Zia government has publicly pledged to accommodate the refugees if they were ultimately unable to return home (Jung 1983).

Finally, if the refugees could be settled along the border they might once again become pawns in the "Great Games of the Tribes" once played by the British when they occupied the region. The rules would be different and the stakes would be higher, and perhaps Pushtun militarism would be less effective. If the Soviet effort prevails in Afghanistan, however, a tribal buffer along the borders would be of great strategic value to Pakistan.

Several factors are working against a Pakistani decision to resettle refugees. First are social issues. If the government decides to admit refugees, it must resettle them in areas where host populations will accept the new arrivals with minimum social unrest. Throughout the country there are Pakistani Pushtuns who are well adjusted to living away from their traditional homes and social organizations, and are accepted by the majority ethnic groups. Their numbers are small, however, when compared to the present refugee population, and their absorption was a gradual process that minimized the shock to migrant and to host alike. Resettling 2.5 million refugees would almost certainly be a much more traumatic experience.

More specifically, the chances of settling a significant number of refugees in the Tribal Areas are very low. Because of the importance of familial ties in their social organizations, the tribes can assimilate new groups or individuals only with great difficulty. By tradition and custom, the refugees would probably not be allowed to buy or own land in these areas. According to Ahmed (1980), any local tribesman selling land to an outsider would be permanently alienated from his tribe or subdivision, and thus would be unlikely to enter into such an arrangement. The Pushtunwali imperatives of *milmastia* (charity) and *nanawati* (asylum) apparently do not apply in the case of permanent arrangements. Consequently, the refugees would be closed out of the economy. In the remaining "settled" and "merged" areas of North West Frontier Province (NWFP), the chances of successful resettlement may be greater. In general, the settled tribes have strayed from "the way of the Pushtun" and have ceased to be tribal in any political sense. Nevertheless, group and geographical loyalties remain very strong, and there would be no guarantee of successful integration, even though from a cultural point of view the resettlement of Pushtuns among Pushtuns would appear to be the least traumatic alternative (ibid.).

Similar resistance to resettlement should be expected in the provinces of Punjab and Sind, where communal animosity is strong. It is unlikely that large numbers of Afghans could be settled along the Indus valley without protest. The refugees who have already been moved to the Punjab, for instance, are camped near Isa Khel on the west bank of the river in traditional Pushtun territory. To this writer's knowledge, no refugees have been quartered in traditional Punjabi or Sindhi territory. This is not to say that these issues would be intractable barriers to resettling Afghan refugees in Pakistan. Nevertheless, social issues and communal prejudices are important considerations in any attempt at refugee settlement, and are problems that the government would have to deal with carefully.

Apart from social issues, serious economic concerns in Pakistan would complicate refugee resettlement. First among these in this agrarian-based economy is a shortage of agricultural land. Recent figures show that Pakistan has only 3.7 acres of cropland per agricultural worker (Government of Pakistan 1982:4; Nyrop 1974:295). More than half the farms are 5 acres or less in size, and only 2 percent exceed 50 acres (Nyrop 1974:298). Of the 50 million acres under cultivation in Pakistan, two-thirds are in Punjab along the Indus River (one of the most densely settled areas of the world); 20 percent are in Sind; and only 10 percent are found in the NWFP, where the resettlement of refugees makes the greatest sense from a cultural standpoint (ibid.:296). Climate, soil, and relief combine to restrict the amount of available arable land in the NWFP, all of which has long since been developed by the indigenous population. Some estimates suggest that, with additional irrigation, a further 30 million acres could be available for agriculture in Pakistan. But even if such estimates are correct and the necessary irrigation works were installed, the average holding per agricultural worker among the rural Pakistani population would increase only to less than 6 acres. The shortage of land has made landlessness, underemployment, and unemployment in rural areas one of the most serious problems facing Pakistan. No matter how the government decided to slice the pie, very little suitable land would be available for redistribution to the refugees. As a result, it seems unlikely that many Afghans could be resettled as farmers without causing even greater economic and political problems for the government.

Despite recent rapid industrial growth, this sector of the economy is unlikely to meet Pakistan's future employment needs for Pakistanis, let alone for Afghan refugees. Industry plays a relatively modest role in the economy, producing only 25 percent of the GDP and employing only 20 percent of the labor force. Hence, the annual increase in jobs is less than the annual increase in the labor pool, which is estimated at 2.9 percent per year (World Bank 1982). In addition, by adopting automated technology, Pakistan has set out on a course designed to reduce rather than increase the demand for labor. As a consequence, Pakistan is presently one of the world's leading labor exporters. The 1981–1982 Pakistan Year Book estimated that nearly 2 million Pakistanis worked overseas, and at that time the government planned to export an additional 200,000–250,000 workers. This policy was expected to continue so that by 1986 there would be 3 million Pakistanis working abroad (Akhtar 1981:303). Pakistan is is clearly unable to absorb its own population growth into the industrial sector, let alone additional Afghan refugees.

Finally, rampant population growth intensifies all these factors. Between 1972 and 1981 the population of Pakistan increased by 18.5 million at an average annual growth rate of approximately 3 percent. The Population Reference Bureau (1982) estimates that the population will reach 142.7 million by 2000, and perhaps 198 million by 2020. In a poor country struggling to develop its resources and dependent to a substantial degree on foreign assistance, rapid population growth is one of the greatest deterrents to progress. Both the profits of the national economy and assistance from foreign governments are rapidly consumed to meet the daily needs of an expanding population, thereby drastically reducing the available resources for capital formation and economic growth. Adding the refugees to Pakistan's population would further accelerate population growth. For example, if one adds in an estimated annual natural increase of 2.4 percent for the refugees, the projected population for Pakistan in the year 2000 becomes 146.5 million. Thus, the long-term implications of Pakistan accepting the Afghan refugees affects Pakistan's demographic crisis and, indirectly, its struggle for economic development.

The Assessment

Each of the above factors translates into a political or an economic reality for the government of Pakistan and for President Zia in particular. The issues discussed in this essay are elements in a problem that will determine whether permanent resettlement in Pakistan is a viable option for the Afghan refugee situation. While Zia's sincerity and concern for Muslim solidarity as well as his compassion for the refugees may be genuine, he is a nationalist rather than an internationalist. Overwhelmingly, Pakistan's greatest problem is being caught in a web of poverty exarcerbated by rapid population growth and an underdeveloped economy. The government understands its problems and recognizes the steps that must be taken to resolve them. To break this web, Pakistan requires capital to expand its economy and to create the necessary conditions to complete its demographic transition. What Pakistan does not need is more unskilled labor and the liability of an additional 2.5 million uneducated subsistence farmers draining off precious capital.

It seems likely that if conditions in Afghanistan do not improve, Pakistan will be unable to support the refugees without large and continual doses of international aid. If for any reason international assistance for refugees decreases, if declining economic indicators increase pressure on the government, or if social unrest develops as a reaction to the presence of refugees, Zia may be forced to examine other alternatives. At this point his options would be limited to internationalizing the Afghans by resettling them in third countries, or to withdrawing Pakistani hospitality and attempting to force them back into Afghanistan.

20

Spontaneous Development Efforts by Rural Refugees in Somalia and Pakistan

Hanne Christensen

In January 1983, the United Nations Research Institute for Social Development (UNRISD) launched a major comparative sociological research project on the effectiveness of relief to refugees and refugee integration in the Third World. The research described here forms part of the broader study.

When globally applied, the term "refugees" embraces persons who have fled the country of which they are citizens, in fear of persecution for reasons of race, religion, nationality, or political opinion, and who must be unable or unwilling to return to that country. The same criteria apply to persons who, lacking nationality, are living outside the countries of their former habitual residence "Refugeeism" is not a modern phenomenon: it is as old as the wars and conflicts from which it originated, and has evolved as such wars have broken out now in one region, now in another. Current refugee scenarios are developing predominantly in the Third World.

In Africa and Asia, the two continents accommodating the greatest number of world refugees today, Somalia and Pakistan host some of the largest concentrations. According to official government estimates in mid-1982, Somalia was sheltering some 700,000 refugees and Pakistan about 2.7 million (UNHCR 1982). The overwhelming majority originated from rural areas in their home countries (Ethiopia and Afghanistan) and are currently accommodated in the countryside of their host countries.

In both host countries the refugees live in camps or camplike mass accommodation. Crowds of refugee families are housed in areas just a few kilometers in width and length, with no large-scale local economic activities to support them. The refugees are sustained by international aid programs under which donated food and other essentials are distributed regularly.

Somalia

Refugees started arriving in Somalia from Ethiopia in 1977. The first wave came in 1977–78, followed by a second in 1979–80. During the period 1978 to

1981, forty-four camps were established. By late 1981, thirty-three of the camps had been closed to newcomers, whereas eleven were purely transitory, for temporary accommodation of new arrivals. Since early 1982, the latter have been in the process of being shut down. Existing camps are situated in the regions of Lower Shebelle, Gedo, Hiran, and North West, with the heaviest concentration in Gedo and Hiran regions. These inter-riverine areas are the potential granary of Somalia.

From 1978 up to 1982, the Somalia government viewed the refugees' presence as a purely temporary phenomenon that would be solved by eventual repatriation. Thus, throughout that period no integration measures were considered. Since 1982, however, income-generating activities have been launched for a small selection of the camp population, and pilot agricultural schemes have been organized to supply families with cash and fresh food. In early 1983, the government decided to integrate refugees who wished to stay, and to repatriate those who wanted to return to their home country.

In late 1981, an exploratory survey was carried out in one refugee camp in each of the Gedo, North West and Hiran regions. The survey, which covered fifty households per camp, was combined with interviews of some of the camp staff and with personal observations. It revealed the conditions described below.

Food rations (maize, wheat flour, milk powder, edible oil, beans, and tea) were dispatched to the camps every ten days for a population of 500,000 refugees. All food seemed to come through to the camp level. The official estimated population, however, appeared at least 25 percent too high. Further, the sample population of 150 households appeared in fact not to consume all donated food. A general and distinctive surplus of food therefore seemed available in the camps at the time of the enquiry.

The refugee camp population, however, appeared highly stratified in terms of access to food. Three categories were distinguished: Category A—a group of 10 to 15 percent—had five to ten bags piled up in the homestead; Category B—some 70 percent—had one to three bags stockpiled; while Category C—10 to 15 percent—had no food available at all. The food in stock in the homesteads visited consisted primarily of maize, and to a lesser extent milk powder. Category A was composed of section leaders, deputies or subsection leaders, that is, persons who were formally in charge of food distribution among the refugees. Category B had no specific characteristics, while category C was made up of households that typically contained disadvantaged groups, such as single fathers with children, grandparents with grandchildren, or infirm adults either alone or with children. In this category, the children's physical appearance indicated malnutrition. Food availability as described here was not affected by the timing of food distribution. Even immediately following distribution, some of the households lacked food stocks.

Categories A and B seemed to sell maize directly to local traders or at markets in adjacent areas. Category A appeared to sell one or two sacks of maize every second month, whereas B seemed to do so only twice a year. The money obtained was mainly spent on sugar. A few households in Category A used part of it to purchase livestock.

Both A and B also exchanged maize for fresh food. An organized food exchange system was in operation between refugees and local people. The amount exchanged by the households in categories A and B seemed to correspond on average to the maize rations of one person. Some 4 to 6 kilos of maize were traded for about 300 grams of goat's meat, for 2 to 3 liters of fresh milk, or for a small piece of cheese of 200 to 300 grams. The food exchanges tended to be institutionalized. The refugees had regular contact with two or three local livestock-raising families, and food was reportedly exchanged approximately twice a month. The refugees were thus able to obtain food items that had previously made up a major part of their diet in the Ogaden. The locals gained access to maize, which they used for porridge.

A small group of refugees kept livestock, but only two households in the sample had one to two head of cattle or other animals. Such livestock production clearly had little impact on the camp food situation. The general impression gathered from respondents in the camps suggested that former nomads among the refugees aimed, little by little, to build up a herd of animals in order to be able eventually to resume a nomadic life outside the camps.

The exchange of surplus food appeared to be a reasonable action. It improved diets slightly and brought variety to the menu by adding meat and cheese. Last, it provided access to items of great cultural importance to the refugees.

The food exchange system also had a social impact. It linked the refugee population and the local people in a relationship of mutual benefit, and thus prevented refugee camps from becoming segregated areas. Moreover, it precluded antagonism between the highly subsidized non-food-producing refugee groups and the little or nonsubsidized, food-producing groups residing in the same localities.

The sample roughly comprised the following: children below 15 years of age—60 percent; adult females—25 percent; and adult males—15 percent. Given a situation of dependence on external food supply, females took care of the systematic running and maintenance of the household, while males engaged in the production of household utensils.

The women took care of children and collected water and firewood. (The latter was an especially tiresome job, because progressive desertification forced women to walk 6 to 8 kilometers to gather fuel.) They collected, exchanged, processed and prepared food, cleaned the compound, washed clothes, constructed and maintained homesteads, and made mats, bags, bowls or dishes from fibrous plants. The men made wooden utensils, such as the mortar and pestle for stamping maize, combs, spoons, and stools, as well as doors and cans for oil and ashes out of scrap drums. Young children assisted their mothers in the domestic chores, collected firewood or water, and looked after small siblings or cousins. Both girls and boys made themselves useful. But when parents had a choice, the boys would be sent off to school, while the girls would be kept at home for domestic training.

Apart from the daily workload, each household in the nonmarginal categories engaged to some extent in income-generating activities, which were divided into female and male spheres. The women used their capacity solely for physical work, collecting a surplus of firewood for sale to teashops or to local people in the neighborhood. They undertook these income-generating activities at intervals when actual needs so demanded. In general they seemed to earn 150 to 200 Somali Shillings per year (12.3 Sh.So. = 1 $U.S.). Cash was used to buy a variety of items, in the following order of priority: fresh milk, meat, sugar, cheese, vegetables, clothes, stationery, and books for school children. Men were less frequent money-earners, but their activities were relatively more profitable. When sufficient stocks had been piled up, they appeared to sell large quantities of food to local traders or at markets in adjacent area. One 50-kilo sack of maize sold for 40–50 Sh.So. Two to six sacks were sold annually (about 90–270 Sh.So.). Some men also obtained casual employment in the camp once or twice a month. Finally, the camp facilities, such as feeding centers, schools and clinics, offered salaried employment to a small number of skilled or semiskilled refugees.

Thus, the resources of the refugee communities were created by the camp setting. The refugees bartered the plentiful distributed food for fresh food or exchanged it for cash in order to reestablish their previous highly valued diet, and to meet basic needs such as clothing and teaching materials for the children's education. Second, they invested some cash income in animals or merchandise, so as to be able to resume former livelihoods. Exploitation of the camp environment provided another source of material gain—firewood and water to sell to local people.

The data from Somalia, although tentative, indicate that refugees generally appeared to be highly active, turning standardized relief into meaningful livelihood resources. They seemed to improve camp life and to be full of initiative and ideas about how to use available resources to reestablish their previous life styles after starting from scratch (Christensen 1982).

Pakistan

Since 1978, there has been a mass exodus from Afghanistan to Iran and especially to Pakistan, where the refugees are granted asylum and official refugee status. At the end of 1979, and in the summers of 1980 and 1981, respectively, Pakistani government authorities recorded some 400,000, 932,000, and 2 million refugees. By mid-1982, government figures reflected the registration of some 2.7 million refugees in Pakistan. About 2.09 million, or more than three-quarters, had been listed in the North West Frontier Province, and some 0.6 million, or just under one-quarter, in Baluchistan. The refugees are accommodated in about 330 camplike villages in these two provinces. The villages are freely accessible, and the refugees are at liberty to enter and leave as they wish.

The Pakistani government considers the installation of refugees as temporary. Large-scale food production activities have not yet been launched to support refugee communities, but extensive income-generating activities employing the refugees' traditional artisan and handicraft skills are now about to be introduced to help sustain the refugee communities.

Food is provided for village refugees who present a family identity card registered in recognized villages. Food baskets made up with donated food include a ration of cereals (wheat flour), dried milk, edible oil, sugar, and tea. Identical rations are given to each member of the population—adults and children, male and female. Such rations provide a daily diet of about 2,200 calories per capita, with protein components amounting to some 69 grams per recipient per day.

A preliminary survey carried out in August and September 1982 in three villages in Baluchistan, among a total sample of 150 households (50 per village), disclosed the following tentative characteristics. First, donated wheat supplies appeared plentiful on the whole, whereas there was a general unavailability of donated milk powder and cooking oil at the household level. Second, the refugee population seemed highly stratified in terms of access to food. Certain refugee leaders (maliks), who were observed to be involved in direct distribution of food to refugees, appeared to hold elite positions since they had large quantities of wheat flour stockpiled in private store rooms. A minority of 10 percent had only limited access to donated food, and were merely able to purchase needed quantities of supplements to compensate fully for the reduced level of donated rations. All in this group had only a fragile relationship with the leaders of their areas, and had few chances of by-passing them with food claims addressed to local government authorities.

Within this context of a somewhat insufficient food supply, the refugees were obviously trying to supplement donated food, mainly with purchased commodities, some fairly small-scale animal production, and a little vegetable gardening or food barter. The results of these efforts improved their total food position.

All sampled households earned income in various ways. Some had found short-term, irregular, unskilled employment in local shops in the districts or elsewhere in Baluchistan. Others provided local farmers with seasonal labor for the harvest. A small number reportedly collected firewood for sale, and a few animal owners sold some goats or sheep and surplus wool to local people and to wealthy fellow refugees. A proportion found skilled or semiskilled employment such as brick-making, construction work, or canal-digging for local people or for other refugees.

The householders and older boys were the main and most frequent earners, but women and girls supplemented the family income with handicrafts. They made clothing and fezes, did various types of braiding and beadwork, and wove rugs. All items were regularly sold in the neighborhood by the men. The refugees' income was spent primarily on food, sugar, sweets, and clothing, and secondarily on luxury goods such as radios and tape recorders.

Markets with various types of stores (bazaars) and tea-shops were established by the refugees in or between villages. These markets served two functions: they supplied the refugee communities with fresh food and essentials for daily use, and made available recreation facilities for the men.

The refugees had institutionalized forms of work organization. Kinfolk and neighbors would form a team to accomplish certain tasks. Groups of women often assisted one another in weaving or processing wool, with each woman carrying out her specific function. Bread was baked by two women, with one preparing the dough and the other heating up the oven. Men formed gangs for brick-making. During the temporary migration of males for employment away from home, essential domestic duties were reassigned to remaining relatives and friends.

The refugees appeared to possess outstanding skills, a flair for appropriate technology, and training potential for handicrafts and trades. They showed a remarkable willingness to use their skills and resources to earn a livelihood, given a situation of free provision of food and essential commodities. While the refugees remained dependent on external aid, in the process of building up an independent means of livelihood they had already initiated a self-reliance process, and their social situation showed considerable potential for the achievement of efficient self-provisioning (Christensen 1983).

Commentary

At the time the surveys were undertaken, both refugee populations were living under temporary conditions in camps in their countries of reception. Relief aid was distributed regularly, but neither government had established long-term policy measures to deal with the refugee presence. Exploratory surveys showed, however, that the sample households had themselves spontaneously initiated a process of change within the relief situation.

Refugees in these two countries had in fact considerably improved their relief conditions by developing their own economic self-help systems. In Somalia a barter and trade-off system evolved; in Pakistan trading and workforce economic activities had come into being.

The assistance provided by the international community was one source of livelihood and was undoubtedly an important factor in ensuring the survival and meeting basic needs of the refugees. But it was not the only one. As the surveys clearly revealed, the refugees were not solely and passively relying on support from the outside world; they were actively and energetically supplementing it with efforts to obtain more secure sources of livelihood and to achieve satisfactory living conditions.

The surveys showed that the relief aid was not being distributed to populations which, lacking social organization, were having to start from scratch. It was, rather, being incorporated into social systems where the rules applied and the institutions created were carried over from former life styles. Relief was managed according to the principles of the prevailing social order of the refugee communities in exile. As described above, access to relief assistance had already become stratified. It was thus demonstrated that it is not the relief aid as such that ensures survival and improves living conditions among refugees, but rather the connection between the external aid and management thereof by the recipient communities. Especially significant is their potential for and resourcefulness in utilizing relief supplies for things other than mere survival, and their capability for creating supplementary sources of livelihood and by responding to the workforce needs and opportunities existing in the host communities.

It further became apparent that observed self-help development efforts were embarked upon well before the host governments had made long-term plans for the future of the refugees. Consequently it cannot be said that favorable official government attitudes had exerted any influence on the refugees' development of their own socioeconomic systems. The newcomers were slowly establishing themselves in exile and building up means of livelihood to provide themselves with meaningful living conditions before the host government had reached a decision whether to incorporate the refugees into their own populations and include them in prevailing economic development schemes.

Moreover, the reported food barter systems, food production, and income-generating activities, as well as the establishment of markets and trading operations, provide a continuing process of change and adaptation steadily evolving toward independence from external support. These changes had almost certainly begun to take place at the time of arrival in the host country and may be termed "development efforts." They are rooted in a consensus concerning a fixed target to be reached and the process leading toward it. In these cases the target is the refugees' perception of the needs to be met to obtain what represents for them a meaningful livelihood. Their methods for achieving their goal, and the time involved, constitute the process.

A development effort is a normative concept. This concept comprises a point or a set of points on a certain scale of values, such as the targets to be reached under circumstances in which it is possible to compare a given state of affairs with a preferred one. Broader applied development efforts, at the national level, refer to multifaceted process changes with political, social, and economic connotations, to changes in structures, institutions, and growth and output of a given society (Baster 1972). In this context the self-help efforts of the refugees described above operate at the microlevel representing development from below, namely, changes initiated by and geared to the need for improvement in the situation of the participants in the society concerned. The action taken toward autonomy was neither directed nor managed by the national authorities and/or the international aid administration. Instead it appeared as a process that involved almost the entire sample refugee population in the two countries and seemed, first and foremost, to be related to a desire to reestablish habitual life styles and levels of living previously enjoyed in the home countries.

When long-term installation policies are to be developed by the national governments and the international community, three options are open to them. They may (a) take into account and systematize the activities already being carried out by refugees; (b) encourage certain efforts that are in harmony with prevailing national planning and discourage others that are not; or (c) launch an alternative and diverging set of development measures. As the literature on the impact of development projects on the living conditions of rural people shows, however, a policy launched without taking into consideration the spontaneous efforts, goals, and rationale of the people affected runs the risk of being resented by them and consequently obstructed by a series of counterproductive initiatives and activities, to the disadvantage of all concerned.

Part Five

South Asia

The Indian subcontinent is not a region commonly associated with refugees, yet some of the displacements of population in the area rank among the world's largest. Also, a number of potential refugee-generating conflicts currently exist in the area, and considerable internal displacement is also occurring.

Two of the largest population displacements in the post-World War II era occurred in South Asia: the forced population transfers between India and Pakistan following independence in 1947, and the exodus of Bangladeshis to India during Bangladesh's war for independence from Pakistan to 1970. The former saw between 14 and 16 million people uprooted (Beijer 1969), while the latter conflict created 10 million refugees. Neither India nor Pakistan received much international assistance in coping with their population transfers; the displacees were never recognized as refugees by the international community. UNHCR was active, however, in assisting Bangladeshi refugees in India, both in terms of their temporary support in Indian refugee camps, and with their subsequent repatriation following Bangladesh's independence.

Another oft-forgotten refugee crisis in the region was the absorbtion by India of much of the Tibetan exodus in the wake of China's annexation of Tibet in 1952. Most of these refugees remain in India to this day and have generally become integrated into Indian society. Bangladesh has also had to cope with a refugee influx since its independence, the Burmese minorities who entered Bangladesh in the late 1970s as a result of persecution in Burma. Currently, the ethnic conflict in Sri Lanka is responsible for generating a major refugee problem. Sri Lankan Tamils have flooded into southern India—in mid-1986 they numbered 130,000. They have also become one of Western Europe's principal group of asylum seekers, and in the summer of 1986 some 150 Tamil "boat people" arrived in Canada to claim asylum. The conflict has also created a major internal displacement within Sri Lanka.

Intranational displacement of population is a serious problem in Bangladesh, albeit most of its internal involuntary migration is caused by natural hazards rather than by political events. Some 1 million Bangladeshi peasants are displaced each year by the migration of channels of the major rivers that flow through the country and erode away large tracts of land. To date, there has been little or no substantive documentation of this phenomenon. The landlessness that this creates, together with pressures for new lands generated by the country's expanding population, is leading to a rapid "colonization" by Bangladeshis of lands in the Chittagong Hill Tracts, which displaces the tribal people in these areas. In the first half of 1986, 7,000 to 12,000 hill tribe refugees sought refuge in India, and there is growing fear that the Shanti Bahini insurgency in the Hill Tracts will escalate and lead to further population displacement.

The problem of intranational displacees, as well as displacees resulting from India's partition, on the one hand, and of the break-up of Pakistan, on the other, is a dimension of the region's migration experience that is little understood or publicized. The 1947 partitioning of India divided Bengal between India and East Pakistan, and the essay by A. F. M. Kamaluddin traces the plight of Bengali minorities in India's northeastern state of Assam who have been subjected to much persecution, as well as pressure to return to Bangladesh. Although not refugees in the legal sense, their displacement continues to be a contentious issue between the governments of India and Bangladesh, and the specter of their forcible repatriation to Bangladesh cannot be discounted.

Although most West Pakistanis left Bangladesh after its independence, and while all Bangladeshi refugees in India repatriated, to this day a completely unresolved refugee dilemma remains—the Biharis in Bangladesh. Chowdhury Haque examines this problem: "refugees" unrecognized by the international community, unacceptable to Bangladesh, and unwanted by India (from where they originate) or Pakistan (under whose aegis they arrived in what is now Bangladesh). In the meantime they remain in a state of hopelessness and despair, living in abject poverty in some of Dhaka's worst shanty-towns.

The third essay in this section is a short documentation by Maudood Elahi on the background to the Rohingya refugees from Burma who fled to Bangladesh. He examines their current status and concludes that although they have repatriated, the risk of renewed flight remains as long as Burmese authorities disregard the human rights of their minority ethnic groups.

21

The Problem of Non-Locals in Assam

A. F. M. Kamaluddin

Assam, Indian's oil state in the northeast, extends over an area of 78,523 km² and is inhabited by 19.2 million people. The population density exceeds 250 people per km². On its western frontier lies Bangladesh (100 million and a density of more than 600 per km²) and the Indian state of West Bengal (55 million and a density of more than 600 per km²). Together, these regions contain more than 150 million Bengali-speaking people—the third-largest linguistic group in Asia after the Chinese and the Hindi. Since 1979, there have been successive movements by Assamese against illegal infiltration of "foreigners" into their territory, as large-scale immigration has given rise to strong fears and discontentment among Assamese over the increasing control of their internal affairs by non-locals. The roots of this discontent can be traced far back into the past, but in recent years troubles have rendered the state virtually ungovernable.

The huge influx of migrants has had unsettling repercussions for Assam. As migrants now account for 45 percent of the electorate, the locals fear they may soon loose administrative and legislative control over their native land. Considerable social diversity also makes intercommunity tensions a threatening issue. A general misunderstanding has been generated through differences in religion (Hindu vs. Muslim), language (Assamese vs. Bengali), ethnicity (tribal vs. non-tribal), and even in terms of settlement (tribal-Assamese vs. migrants). An economic depression is aggravated by Assams's provincial status. Despite the fact that Assam produces half of India's oil, their oil is refined in Bihar state. Although Assam supplies half of the nation's tea, most is marketed through Calcutta. Within Assam, the best of the fertile valley soil is cropped by "foreign" peasants. Such issues had raised intersocietal anomosities to dangerous levels by 1983. In a regional context, the welfare of Bengali and Nepalese migrants has become a matter of great concern to Kathmandu, Dhaka, and Calcutta. Furthermore, there are perhaps as many as 4 million Indians in Nepal and large Indian communities in Bangladesh. Thus any outbreak of violence against the

migrants in Assam is a potential political threat to the stability of relationships between India, Nepal, and Bangladesh.

Historical Background of Ethnic Composition and
Territorial Organization

The original people of Assam are of Mongoloid stock, but Indo-Iranians
migrating from the west gradually attained numerical superiority. The
presently dominant ethnic group, known as the "Ahoms," migrated to
Assam in the thirteenth century from Thailand and subsequently converted
from Buddhism to Hinduism. By the sixteenth century, Hindu "Vaishnava-
ism" became the dominant religion of the whole Brahmaputra valley.

Assam resisted successive attempted Moghul invasions and maintained
independence almost until the time of British domination. Burmese invasion of the fertile intervale in 1817 was most destructive, and totally
disrupted the Assamese way of living. The British evicted the Burmese in
1826, and Assam was incorporated into the Bengal presidency in 1838. Since
then, Bengali influence has dominated the Assam scene. In 1874, Assam
was awarded separate entity from Bengal, and thereafter was controlled
administratively by a chief commissioner from Shillong, the state capital.
The Muslim-dominated district of Sylhet was included within the new
province. Bengal, the most populous province of British India, was parti-
tioned in 1905 to include Assam in its eastern territory; thus arose the new
province of Eastern Bengal and Assam where Muslims formed the majority
of the population. West Bengal, in contrast, remained predominantly
Hindu. Due to strong resentment between Assamese and Bengali Hindus,
yet in total disregard of Muslim sentiment, the British annulled this partition of Bengal in 1912, and Assam once again became a separate province in
the Brahmaputra valley, keeping within its newly set-up boundaries the
districts of Cachas (West Bengali Hindu district) and Sylhet (Eastern Bengali
Muslim district). In 1947, most of Sylhet was annexed to East Pakistan
(Bangladesh), and subsequent political development within Assam resulted
in the creation of four new states—Nagaland, Meghalays, Arunchal Pradesh, and Mizorram (Figure 21.1).

These processes of territorial amalgamation and division have led to
substantial population movement within the region. Specifically, it led to
movement from the populous zones of Bengal to the thickly populated areas
of the Brahmaputra valley and dense forest belts of Assam. These movements remain the primary cause of widespread ethnic, cultural, and linguistic diversities within Assam. "Foreign" control of Assam, to most Assamese
the most crucial problem confronting their society today, does not appear to
have arisen through outside political activity. Underutilization of vast
potential resources by the Assamese themselves seems to have provoked
"foreign" interest in the province.

Land Economy and Growing Discontent

Although migration into Assam started as an unrestrained and spontaneous
population movement after the incorporation of Assam into the Bengal

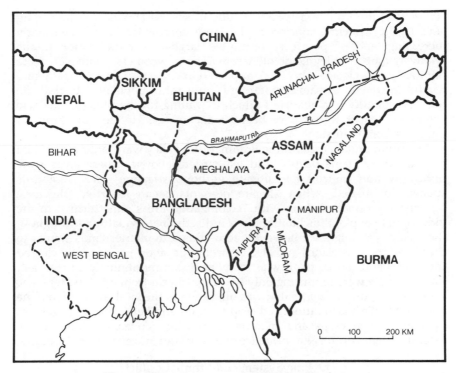

Figure 21.1   Assam and Adjoining Regions

presidency in 1838, it continued even after the annulment of the 1912 partition of Bengal after which Assam became a separate state from India. From 1905 to 1912 Eastern Bengal and Assam constituted one province; Bengali Muslims were allowed unrestricted movement anywhere in Assam. Hindu Bengalis from Cachar were also searching for better job opportunities, particularly administrative jobs in expanding urban areas.

Since good fertile land was readily available to Assamese, they were not drawn by the British tea-planters' offers of work as pickers on their plantations. Instead, the planters initially drew labor from the tribal communities of Southern Bihar, and Muslim Bengali peasants later received active encouragement from both the British and the Assamese landlords to migrate to Assam as agricultural laborers. By 1891, one-quarter of the population of the Brahmaputra valley was estimated to have originated outside the region.

The major influx of migrants occurred after 1900, when Bengali Muslims started to flow into the Assam valley. The majority originated from Mymensingh, the largest and very densely populated district of East Bengal, which lies immediately south of Assam. By 1911, 120,000 migrants had settled in Assam, of which 64 percent were from Mymensingh, and in 1921 migrants constituted nearly 20 percent of the population of Soalpara District and 14 percent of Nowgong District.

The continuing outflow of immigrants from East Bengal into Assam

(Table 21.1) until the mid-1940s was due to several factors. The prevailing land tenure system characterized by large landowners and a constantly increasing landless peasantry prompted large-scale outmigration to the relatively empty valley lands of Assam. The newcomers, moreover, were not totally unwelcome when they appeared in Assamese terrain, as Premier Saadullah stated, "Assam is suffering from want of population to cultivate the vast quantity of arable land which is waiting for the plough." He also suggested that it would have been "most unwise" to stop the flows of migrants from Bengal.

The submountain areas of the Brahmaputra valley were largely inhabited by hill tribes, plains people, and tea-garden laborers. These areas were unhealthy and difficult to cultivate without irrigation, and were thus sparsely populated. When Muslim peasants began to arrive, the local bureaucracy provided them with "colonization areas" unattractive to the indigenous people, thus limiting their indiscriminate squatting throughout the valley. The migrants, however, accustomed to inferior lands similar to these riverine wastelands and also to strenuous labor, permanently cleared the forests and started to grow as many as five crops annually. In contrast, the Assamese were producing only two crops a year from much better soils. Jute was introduced, a crop that was unknown to the local landowners. The Bengali Muslims also introduced crop rotation and better soil management by using green crops and manure. Thus the Bengali Muslims slowly extended their control and influence over the land and society in Assam.

The Line System and Ethnic Conflict

The reaction against the influx of non-locals into Assam was initially provoked by the Line Systems, which segregated the Bengali-Muslim migrants from the Assamese and tribal population. It was a means of guiding and controlling those from Mymensingh, for the "purpose of avoiding social conflicts and tension" (Dev and Lahiri 1978).

The Line System, first introduced into the district of Nowgong in 1920,

Table 21.1 Population Change in Assam, 1911 to 1941

	1911		1921	
	Total	Percent Muslims	Total population	Percent Muslims
Goalpara	600,643	35.22	762,523	41.51
Kamrup	667,828	9.68	762,671	14.64
Darrang	377,314	5.38	477,935	7.64
Nowgong	303,596	5.17	397,921	17.74
Sibsagar	690,299	4.31	823,197	4.25
Lakhimpur	468,989	2.86	588,295	2.63
Total	3,108,669	11.41	3,812,542	15.36

Source: Census of India, Vol. 3, Assam, 1941.

classified villages into four categories: (a) villages exclusively for indigenous people; (b) villages reserved for Bengali migrants; (c) villages divided by lines between Assamese and migrants; and (d) mixed villages for free settlement. It was eventually adopted in districts elsewhere in the valley. Nevertheless, the lines drawn were often arbitrary and evoked bitter resentment among Muslim settlers, who claimed that the government was more concerned about providing adequate land for tiger, rhino, and buffalo than providing adequate land to landless immigrants.

The Line System was against the spirit and principle of the Government of India Act,[1] and in the absense of any central legislation against interprovincial migration, was in fact highly illegal. In 1943, a "grow more food" program was introduced, which liberalized the Line System considerably.[2] It led to the withdrawal of restrictions on immigrant settlement, and nearly 53,000 acres of new land were soon settled by immigrants. This settlement of Bengali Muslim peasants was possible because of the existence of 6.03 million acres of uncultivated land. Thus the relaxation of the Line System not only resulted in more widespread squatting by older immigrants in restricted and reserve lands, but also caused considerable influxes of land-hungry immigrants.

The Congress government, formed in 1946, was determined to remove all trespassers from reserve lands or hitherto prohibited areas, and served summary eviction notices to "new encroachers." Immigrants who had settled on land for more than twelve years before April 1, 1937, were exempted from the eviction notices. In reality, however, all immigrants settled beyond the arbitrary line under the Assam Line System were evicted, their homes were demolished, and their crops were burned (Mujahid 1947). The eviction policy, considered by the Muslim peasants to be a Hinduization policy, soon had serious political repercussions. Muslims turned increasingly militant in their attempts to achieve the abolition of the Line System, on the one hand, and the establishment of Pakistan, on the other.

1931		1941	
Total population	Percent Muslims	Total population	Percent Muslims
882,748	43.92	1,014,285	46.23
926,746	25.95	1,264,200	29.07
584,817	11.54	736,791	16.42
562,581	31.60	710,800	35.19
933,326	4.70	1,074,741	48.17
724,582	3.58	894,842	4.98
4,614,800	20.44	5,695,659	31.07

The Movement of Assamization

What Assam had experienced in the pre-partition years was possibly an extension of the communal conflict that prevailed throughout India. Yet the Bengali culture disturbed the Assamese most. The economic clash was mostly at the white-collar level, where urban Bengali Hindus could seize control. The Assam Line System had been initiated at the insistance of the Bengali Hindu bureaucrats; this group was also instrumental in manipulating the political situation that led to the eviction of bona fide Muslim immigrants. The Assamese gained a real hold on the politics and administration of their own state only after the partition of India in 1947. Thereafter, however, they embarked upon a program of "Assamization."

The focal point of Assamization was the principle of ethnicity. Widespread unrest occurred among the hill tribes after the mid-1950s, and especially in 1962, when Assamese was proscribed as the official language of the entire state. Furthermore, the All Assam Students Union insisted that any special treatment given to the tribal people would only bring divisive forces into Assamese society. The Assamese failed to anticipate the reaction of the tribal people, who were very sensitive to the issue of language and preservation of their special identity.

The tribesmen regarded themselves as the earliest settlers of Assam and did not differentiate between Assamese and the later immigrants; all were seen as foreigners on their lands. These sentiments, and the resultant conflicts, eventually led to the creation of several separate states within the Indian Union: first Nagaland in 1963, followed by the others after 1973 (see Figure 21.1).

The Assamese began to see the Bengali Hindus as their immediate rivals in the administrative control of their state. With the proclamation of Assamese as the state language, and with drives to reestablish local culture as well as to improve job prospects for the Assamese middle class, tensions between the Assamese and Bengali Hindus increased.

In cases of confrontation between Assamese and Bengali Hindus, Muslim peasants and tea-pickers from Bihar tended to support the Assamese; they feared possible eviction from their land and deportation to East Pakistan. The Bengali Hindus and the Bengali Muslims had old scores to settle; the Muslims remembered the distress and suffering when the Bengali Hindus controlled the affairs of state. In contrast to the Bengali Hindus, the Bengali Muslims declared Assamese to be their language and supported the Assamese-dominated Congress Party in state elections. In 1972, anti-Bengali sentiments flared up throughout the Brahmaputra valley, resulting in violent clashes between Assamese and Bengali Hindus, while the Muslims sided with the Assamese.

The weakening of relations between Assamese and Bengali Muslims came about during the 1970s and was based upon a combination of ethnic, linguistic, and political factors. These can be summarized as follows:

- The Assamese began to consider the substantial increase of non-locals in the electoral rolls as representing Muslim emigrés from Bangladesh.
- The split of the Indian Congress had weakened the population's confi-

dence in the party's ability to regain power and provide stability, which intensified mutual distrust between the different communities.
* Some Bengali Muslims had switched to the political left, introducing new idealogical beliefs among the migrants.
* Many legitimate demands of Bengali Muslims had been consistently overlooked by Assamese landlords.
* The political parties opposed to the Congress actively contributed to the deteriorating relationship between the two broad communities so as to deprive Congress of potential migrant votes.

The present Assamese movement appears to be concentrated primarily against the Bengali Muslims, who account for about 17 percent of the population. Urban Assamese launched a movement in 1979, demanding that electoral rolls be screened to eliminate illegal migrants. They proposed 1961 as the cut-off date for such revisions, with migrants who had arrived later to be eliminated from the rolls. More recently, Assamese have agitated for the total disenfranchisment and deportation of nearly 5 million Bengalis to Bangladesh, even though there has been no migration of Bengali Muslims to Assam since Bangladesh was created in 1971.

The Recent Violence in Assam

In the course of the 1983 conflict between locals and non-locals, more than 5,000 people, mostly women and children, were slaughtered in one of the ugliest incidents of communal violence ever to take place on the continent. It is difficult to determine the ultimate responsibility for these massacres. The tribal people felt insecure toward the Assamese, who, like the Bengali migrants, were regarded as people who had usurped their lands and forced them deeper into the reserve forest areas. Although the Assamese demand that the encroachers be evicted, no alternative settlement land has been provided. The massacre of Assamese by Budo tribesman at Gophur in 1983 was basically due to tribal sentiment.

In the carnage that took place at Nellia, Bengali Muslims were victims of brutal attacks by tribal and non-tribal groups, while Assamese police were passive onlookers. Although since resettled in their forest villages, the survivors of the Nellia and other massacres find themselves as hostages of their misfortune. They can move about their own villages, but their freedom does not extend more than a few hundred feet beyond it. Nor can they visit the weekly market without escort, and Assamese continue to threaten them in their fields and steal their cattle.

Those migrants who managed to escape the violence in Assam fled in all directions. Tribal refugees now live in camps along the border of Arunachal Prudesh State; Bengali Hindus have found temporary refuge at Dangi Camp in West Bengal, where there are now 25,000 refugees. A large number of Bengali Hindu refugees also escaped to Tripura State. Finally, hundreds of thousands of Bengali Muslims, some of whom had settled in Assam 50 to 75 years earlier, have fled to Bangladesh. Numerous refugee settlements currently exist all along the northern border of Bangladesh.

Tragically, the refugees from Assam, be they Hindu, Muslim, or tribal, are unwelcome everywhere on the subcontinent. Moreover, Assamization continues, and while there was a lull in the violence after the 1983 outbreaks, agitation appears once more to be on the rise as further demands for the detection and deportation of "foreigners" arise. The central government's efforts to negotiate with the Assamese have been frustrated by the question of a cut-off year to be used in determining the legitimacy of the immigrants.

The political stituation in Assam continues to be troubled, and relations between Assamese and Bengali Muslims remain tense. Regardless of further developments, the Assamese will likely be reduced to a minority status within their own state. It is ironic that the Bengali Muslims, the only group among the migrants who have assimilated to a degree and have integrated linguistically with the Assamese, have been driven into intolerable living conditions. But because of their numbers, as well as their general poverty, they remain a group that is unlikely to be able to leave Assam to settle in Bangladesh or elsewhere.

Notes

1.   Section 298 of the Government of India Act, 1953, states: "No subject of His Majesty domiciled in India shall on grounds only of religion, place of birth, descent, colour or any of them be ineligible for office under the Crown in India or be prohibited on any such grounds from acquiring, holding or disposing of property or carrying on any occupation, trade, business or profession in British India."

2.   The "Grow More Food Campaign" provided a great opportunity to keep the Line System in abeyance and make settlement of lands with the immigrants at an unprecedented pace. This could be done by inducing immigrant cultivators to substitute rice for jute crops, by more widespread utilization of current fallow land, or by settlement of new land by immigrants primarily for cultivation of food crops, particularly all varieties of paddy. The last method was found to be more suitable, and thus Colonisation Officers in Kamrup, Nowgong and Darrang were required to devote much time to the settlement of new lands with Mymensinghias wherever possible (Dev and Lahire 1978).

22

Non-Bengali Refugees in Bangladesh: Patterns, Policies, and Consequences

Chowdhury E. Haque

The involuntary migration of Muslim and Hindu refugees following the partition of India in 1947 is considered to be one of the largest migratory streams in the twentieth century (Keller 1975:17). Estimates by various sources claim that 8 to 9 million Hindus were expelled from Pakistan and 6 to 7 million Muslims from India during the first decade of the separation of the subcontinent (Beijer 1969:20; Visaria 1969). This turnover in population and socioeconomic structures of Bangladesh (formerly East Bengal and later East Pakistan) has had a number of far-reaching implications for political, social, economic, and cultural processes in the territory. Because of the different nature and background in ethnicity, language, habitation, and especially in the overall cultural and ideological spheres of these refugees in comparison to local Bengali Muslims, the assimilation and integration of the refugees became a complex process in the political arena of Pakistan during the years 1947 to 1971. In the 1970s and early 1980s, the plight and predicament of the non-Bengali minority group have emerged as one of the serious obstacles to the socioeconomic development of Bangladesh.

This essay attempts to determine the causes of the refugee migration to what now constitutes Bangladesh territory, and critically to analyze the policy strategies taken by the government of Pakistan from 1947 to 1971 in the light of their consequences. Therefore, attention will be focused on the period during which Bangladesh constituted the eastern wing of Pakistan. The problem of millions of political refugees cannot be understood without sufficient understanding of the roles of politics, religion, culture, and language in the political and economic relations among the countries of the subcontinent and the wider context of the origins of Hindu-Muslim politics in the region.

Roots of the Problem: The Partition of India

The Hindu-Muslim communal rivalry began in India as early as the seventh and eight centuries of the Christian Era, when Arab sailors and traders first brought Islam to the Makran coast of Beluchistan and the lower Indus valley. The effective introduction of Islam into India came in the eleventh century with successive Turko-Afghan invasions, as well as following the conquest of India by Mughals from Chinese Turkestan in the sixteenth century. It is interesting to note that religious tolerance was great during the Mughal rule over India, the height of which occurred during Akbar's regime (A.D. 1556–1605). In this context, Gankovsky and Gordon-Polonskaya (1964:6) succinctly point out that:

> Neither did differences of religion impede India's economic, political and historical integration, a process that began in the precolonial period. There was religious tolerance, as a rule, in the feudal Indian empires of the Muslim rulers and in the States of Hindu rajahs. . . . In some parts of India differences in religion coincided with class and social differences . . . The merchants, money-lenders and the bulk of the population . . . were mostly Hindu, while many peasants and artisans embraced Islam.

The colonial invasion by Europeans and their rule over India for 300 years did not radically change the geographical map of the subcontinent, but had profound influence in the ideological and sociopolitical spheres. The creation of new class structures along religious lines weakened the internal solidarity of the masses and thereby facilitated prolongation of colonial rule and exploitation. The emergence of Indian nationalism, resulting largely from the implementation of a formal and elementary education system and the emergence of predominantly Hindu capitalists, was attended by an accelerating conflict between India and Britain, on the one hand, and among Indian groups fragmented along religious lines, on the other. The British "divide and rule" policy gradually redirected the national movement for independence. British authorities encouraged the Muslim communal movement to challenge openly the Congress or Hindu proclamation for independence of a united India (ibid.:17). This surfaced when the Indian Council Act of 1909 instituted separate electorates for Hindus and Muslims, thus formalizing the policy of separating the religious communities.

Incidents of communal riots increased alarmingly during the next three decades whenever either of the two major national political parties attempted to counter programs put forward by the opposing party. The Indian Statutory Commission (1930:27) recorded that more than 5,000 people suffered harm during the 1923–27 "civil disobedience" of the Congress, with 450 losing their lives. The Lucknow session of the Muslim League in 1937 adopted a new constitution based on the "two-nation theory," which established the frame for dividing India on a religious basis. One of the remarkable aspects of the distribution of Muslims in India prior to the partition was their concentration in Punjab and Bengal, two contiguous regions, in which Muslims formed more than 50 percent of the population. The frequent communal rages, riots, and persecutions implicitly encouraged by the extremist political institutions, such as the Muslim League, Jamat-e-Islami, or Hindu Mahashava, virtually ensured the division in the interest of their respective adherents and, underlying this, in the interest of the respective capitalist-landlord classes. Communal riots broke out with renewed vigor in 1946, in anticipation of an uncontrollable situation that would compel the British ruling class to consent to the scheme of independence and partition. The first severe outbreak occurred in Bengal in August 1946: the carnage later known as the "Great Calcutta Killing." Both Hindus and Muslims suffered equally in the four days of mass killing, in which the death toll was estimated to have been about 15,000 (Lumby 1954:120; Tuker 1950). In the district of Noakhali in East Bengal, an estimated 200 Hindus were persecuted and 5,000 were made homeless. Bihar and the United Province were involved shortly afterward; the estimated deaths there were 5,000 to 8,000, of whom the majority were Muslims (Symonds 1951:69).

In the face of the rapidly deteriorating situation, British Prime Minister Clement Attlee, who had announced Britain's intention to quit India by June 1948, instead implemented it as early as August 14, 1947. Although the Muslim League initially insisted on separation on the basis of provincial majorities of religious groups, in the face of opposition from the Congress agreement was made that the Punjab and Bengal be divided. Ali (1970:28–29) concluded that:

> British policy, combined with Hindu and Muslim bigotry and an extremely shortsighted attitude on the part of the Hindu bourgeoisie, ensured that moves towards separatism would increase. Though the class interests of both the Muslim and Hindu bourgeoisies were identical, the competitive struggle between the different groups became confused with religious and caste differences. The struggle for two states thus reflected the uneven and combined development of two national bourgeoisies.

Aftermath of Partition: Refugee Migration to East Bengal

The policy and process of India's partition were accompanied by vociferous agitation for a mass exodus of Hindus and Sikhs from Pakistan, and of Muslims from India. In the provinces of Punjab and Bengal, the two dominant nationalities were objectively divided by the religious approach to partition. Gankovsky and Gordon-Polonskaya (1964:96) observed that:

> No sooner were the festive inaugural speeches concluded at the Constituent Assembly of the newly founded Islamic state, than reports streamed in of wholesale massacres, demolished town blocks, and gutted villages. Entire streets were destroyed in Lahore, Rawalpindi, Amritsar, and other Punjab cities. There were riots and killings in Delhi, the United Provinces and Bihar, and in the States of Rajputana and Hydrabad. Something like half a million people were killed in the Punjab alone. The woulded and those who lost hearth and home added up to over 12 million.

Following the partition, apart from persecutions, the Muslim minorities were singled out as a separatist group by the policies of governments at various levels in India, and described as "anti-national" (Sakir 1972:11). The Muslims in India met with deliberate discrimination (Habibullah 1968:17), as did the Hindus in Pakistan, especially in the economic sphere. The discrimination against Muslims in matters of employment, in grants of licences, permits, contracts, and admission of various institutions, had virtually brought them to the verge of economic ruin (Kaul 1961:45), and resulted in a mass exodus to East Bengal.

Although it is difficult to estimate the dimension and proportion of refugees in linguistic groups, it is possible to determine some gross estimates from the official statistics. As Whitaker (1972:7) reports, a total of some 8 million Muslim refugees moved from India to Pakistan, of whom 1.3 million entered East Bengal. Nearly 1 million are estimated to have emigrated just from Bihar and its neighborhood. Yet these estimates have been considered excessive by some analysts. Visaria (1969), using official statistics of the subcontinent, estimates that 0.7 million immigrated to Bangladesh territory from India during 1947–51. Khan (1974) also supported this figure. The Census of Pakistan of 1951 enumerated 699,079 refugees (called *Muhajirs* in Pakistan) in Bangladesh. According to this census, about 95.9 percent of the refugees immigrated to Bangladesh from the eastern states of India (namely, Bihar, West Bengal, Assam, Orissa, Nagaland, Manipur, Tripura, and Sikkim), followed by 3.3 percent from the northern zone (Punjab, Rajsthan, Uttar Pradesh, Delhi, and Himachal Pradesh), and 0.8 percent from other states (Government of Pakistan 1951). The influx of Muslim fugitives from India continued long after the partition, swelling considerably during the 1950 communal riots in and around Calcutta, the 1960 upheaval in Assam against Bengali-speaking people, and the anti-Muslim outbreaks in Maddya Pradesh and Uttar Pradesh in 1961 and in West Bengal and Assam in 1962 and 1964–65. A study by the ILO (1959:113) reports that at least 0.5 million Muslims moved to East Bengal between 1951 and 1956. The 1961 Census of Pakistan counted 800,247 persons who stated their mother tongue as other than Bengali. The two largest groups were the "Biharis," speaking Urdu and Hindi (451,473), and those speaking Assam-Burmese tongues (136,475). The Census recorded 627,389 "Pakistanis born in the Pakistan–India subcontinent beyond the limits of the Census of Pakistan," of which 434,081 were born in eastern India. The inference can be drawn from these enumerated figures that the majority of the non-Bengali settlers in Bangladesh was Urdu-Hindi-speaking "Muhajirs."

Figure 22.1 shows the patterns of distribution of non-Bengali refugees by place of origin in 1951. It is interesting to note that the regional distribution of non-Bengali refugees was markedly concentrated in some selected districts, namely Kushtia, Rangpur, Dacca, Rajshahi, Dinajpur, and Mymensingh. As mentioned above, the majority of the refugees migrated from the non-Bengali eastern states of India. The localization curve clearly indicates the comparative pictures between Bengali and non-Bengali population distributions in 1951 (Figure 22.2). The considerable extent of concentration of the non-Bengali refugees is well reflected in the index of concentration of

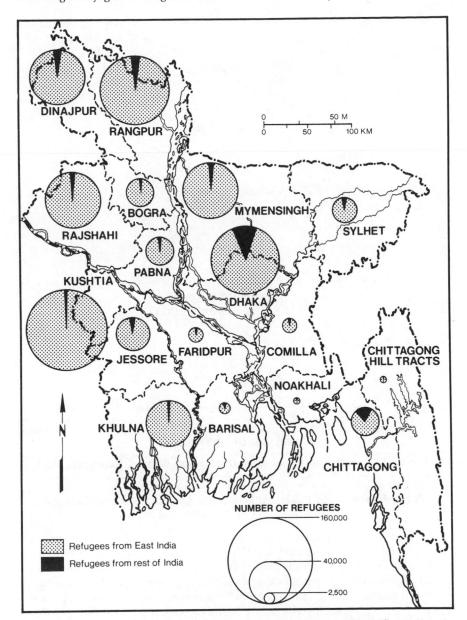

Figure 22.1 Distribution of Refugees (by Place of Origin), 1951

0.50, whereas it was only 0.22 for the Bengali population. This unevenness in the distribution of refugees limited the scope for their sociocultural assimilation with the Bengali masses in the country of asylum; it also caused the peasantry of Bangladesh to view the concentration in certain enclaves with suspicion.

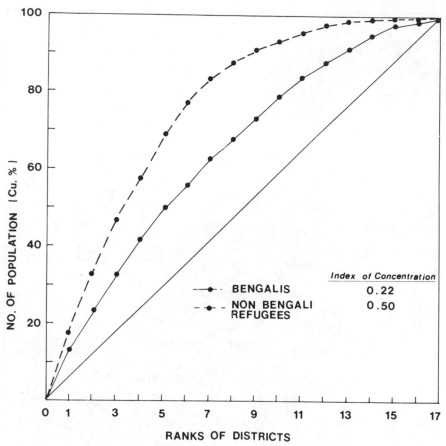

Figure 22.2   Distribution of Bengali and Non-Bengali Refugees, 1951

Policy Strategies of Pakistan: Economic Assimilation and Cultural Alienation of the *Muhajirs*

In addition to causing the common deprivation of the Bengal peasantry by the colonial ruling class and the Hindu landlords after the Permanent Settlement (1793), the success of the British rulers in dividing Bengali society on a religious basis gave political and economic power to the Urdu-speaking Indian capitalist, and to land-based nobles of West Punjab. The preponderance of non-Bengalis in the administrative set-up of East Bengal (later declared as East Pakistan), which resulted from the central government's conscious policy of favoring Urdu-Hindi-speaking persons at the expense of local people, was deeply resented by Bengalis. This grievance was reflected even as early as 1948, when an East Bengali member of the Pakistan Constituent Assembly complained that the province was being treated as a "colony" of West Pakistan (Sathyamurty 1979:226). Within three years of partition, *muhajirs* were provided not only with the domiciled citizenship of

Pakistan, but also with a privileged or equivalent employment share in each sector of the economy. The 1951 census registered a 30.1 percent participation rate of refugees in East Pakistan, whereas the respective figure for the remaining Bengali and other people was only 30.2 percent (Government of Pakistan 1951). In certain private ownership sectors and in public sector employment, priority and privilege were specifically given to *muhajirs* by open public policy measures, for instance in the railways, post and telegraph, armed forces, private industries, trade and commerce, etc. In the East Bengal Railway alone, 39,500 employees were absorbed. More than 50 percent of these workers had worked under different systems and had come from various parts of India which are different from Bangladesh both physiographically and socioculturally (Kamaluddin 1980:4). The effect of this policy of unconditional privilege for the non-Bengali *muhajirs* was that the central leaders of the Pakistan Muslim League, with the help of the local non-Bengali and land-based aristocrat class, created a new comprador class from the Urdu-speaking political refugees in Bangladesh. The major advantages of the policy for the ruling class were (a) that these refugees were alien to the Bengali culture and tradition and thus were more emotionally inclined toward the West Pakistani ruling class; (b) that the new comprador bureaucratic, merchant, and trading class was more reliable and most likely to favor the transfer of economic surplus to the west wing from the east wing of Pakistan; and (c) that these new "domiciled citizens" were necessary for the subjugation, both political and economical, of emerging Bengali nationalism.

The process of comparative advantage in economic sectors provided by public policy is well reflected in the 1951 Census enumeration (Tables 22.1 and 22.2). The 1951 Census showed that only 15 percent of the Bengalis were engaged in non-agricultural activities, whereas about 50 percent of the non-Bengalis were engaged in this sector (Table 22.1). In every sector of industrial and commercial activities, non-Bengali refugees were represented in greater proportion than were local Bengalis, especially in manufacturing, commerce, transport, and government services. Similarly, in occupational distribution, in all sectors of both blue- and white-collar jobs, the proportional dominance of *muhajirs* was clearly evident (Table 22.2). In this connection, Whitaker (1972:8) observed that:

> They [*muhajirs*] found jobs such as small traders, civil service officials and clerks, doctors, and skilled workers on the railways and in the mills. Some of them were useful to the Pakistani administrators of Bengal, who gave them posts in much the same way as Asian minorities were used by European colonists in Africa.

A number of additional public policy measures were taken to meet the colonial motives of West Pakistan rulers. These included the building of large-scale estate housing facilities and the granting to them of major subsidies, for example the Mohammadpur and Mirpur housing estates of Dhaka, Halishahar and the Wireless Colonies of Chittagong, and Khalishpur Colony of Khulna. It also included bank credit facilities for industrial and commercial investment at nominal interest rates, and permits and

Table 22.1   Distribution of Bengali and Non-Bengali Population by Industry, 1951

Industrial sector	Bengalis		Non-Bengalis	
	Number	%	Number	%
Agriculture, Forestry, and Fishery	10,811,301	85.24	104,430	51.63
Mining	2,522	0.02	55	0.03
Manufacturing	481,277	3.79	17,411	8.61
Construction, Electricity, Gas and Water	136,634	1.08	7,689	3.80
Transport, Storage, and Communication	182,140	1.44	20,170	9.97
Commerce	477,510	3.76	25,044	12.38
Government service	168,340	1.33	10,775	5.33
Personal and community services	424,020	3.34	16,682	8.25
Total	12,683,744	100.00	202,256	100.00

Source: Calculated from Government of Pakistan, *Census of Pakistan, 1951*, Vol. 5 (Karachi: Ministry of Home and Kashmir Affairs).

licences for local and international trade. As part of long-term strategy, Urdu schools were established in different parts of the province, and provision was made for allowing study in Urdu in Bengali schools.

The imposition of the purposeful educational, cultural, and economic policies of the West Pakistani ruling class on the Bengali people did not end with suspicion or grievances; the outrage emerged as a mass movement against the semicolonial rule by West Pakistan with whom, except for religion, Bengalis had no identical characteristics. The movement began in 1952 with the Language Movement and concluded through successive nationalist movements in the 1971 War of Independence.

Emergence of Bangladesh and the Non-Bengali Refugee Crisis Once Again

Following the independence of Bangladesh in December 1971, the non-Bengalis who had identified themselves with the Pakistani cause and were thus opposed to Bengali nationalism opted to resettle in Pakistan. While West Pakistani civilians were evacuated to India along with the defeated army, the non-Bengali *Biharis* were left behind by Pakistan to face the accumulated rage of the Bengalis. As a result, the non-Bengalis had no alternative other than to wait in camps for repatriation. Keesing's Publications (1973) reported two occasions where large number of non-Bengalis were killed even in the camps by Bengali mobs:

Table 22.2   Distribution of Bengali and Non-Bengali Population by Occupation, 1951

Occupation	Bengalis		Non-Bengalis	
	Number	%	Number	%
Technical and professional	117,922	0.93	3,206	1.59
Administrative and managerial	12,632	0.10	1,543	0.76
Clerical and office workers	180,566	1.42	12,724	6.29
Sales workers	474,402	3.74	28,152	13.92
Farmer and fishermen	10,806,869	85.20	103,708	51.28
Skilled operatives	583,859	4.60	25,649	12.68
Unskilled laborers	292,351	2.31	15.624	7.72
Service workers	212,619	1.68	11,597	5.73
Others	2,524	0.02	53	0.03
Total	12,683,744	100.00	202,256	100.00

Source: Calculated from Government of Pakistan, *Census of Pakistan, 1951*, Vol. 5 (Karachi: Ministry of Home and Kashmir Affairs, 1951).

After a Bengali corpse had been discovered just outside a jute millworker's camp near Khulna, groups of former guerrillas armed with knives raided the camp on March 10, 1972, and were reported to have killed about 1,000 Biharis. A similar incident occurred on April 18 in the Dacca suburb of Mirpur, after a pit of skeletons had been discovered nearby. . . . When busloads of Biharis who had been visiting relations in prison returned to the camp they were attacked by a mob, who were reported to have murdered over 200 of them.

The number of non-Bengali refugees remaining in Bangladesh after independence cannot be determined accurately, since there are no official data. But a mission led by David Ennals (a former minister in the British government) reported in 1972 that more than 700,000 non-Bengalis were living in enclaves, about 278,500 of them on the outskirts of Dhaka (Whitaker 1972). In March 1973 Prime Minister Sheikh Mujib of Bangladesh stated that of the 700,000 non-Bengali community, 410,000 "non-locals" were asked to make a choice regarding their future nationality, and 150,000 opted for Bangladesh and 260,000 for Pakistan. Yet Pakistan has continually refused to admit these refugees.

Pakistan initially indicated that it would accept only West Pakistanis who had been stranded in Bangladesh in 1971, along with 40,000 others who were formally employed by the Pakistan government or who had strong family links with Pakistan. Under the New Delhi Agreement, however, Pakistan subsequently agreed to accept "a substantial number" of non-Bengalis from Bangladesh and to hold discussions with Bangladesh on how many others it should admit. The repatriation began in September 1973 and was completed by the following June. UNHCR announced in July 1974 that a total of 108,750 non-Bengalis had repatriated to Pakistan directly from Bangladesh, and a further 10,870 via Nepal. This meant that some 120,000 non-Bengalis, who had opted for resettlement to Pakistan, still remained stranded in camps and enclaves in Bangladesh cities and towns.

Today, the physical and sociopsychological conditions of non-Bengali refugees in the temporary camps are grim and extremely depressing. In two enclaves on the outskirts of Dhaka, at Mirpur and Mohammadpur, more than 20,000 refugees live at densities of ten people or more to a tent. The camps contain a large number of widows and infants; half the population is under the age of fifteen. Short-term problems in the camps are not confined to food and health, but include the questions of shelter, water (nearly 10,000 people queue for one fresh-water tap), sanitation, and security. Each camp is an open and stinking sewer. Camp residents do not dare to "set foot outside the narrow confines of the camp for fear of death or attack" (Keesing's Publications 1973). The extent of depression is reflected in a statement recently given by a refugee to a foreign visitor: "What is to become of us? Pakistan will not take us, India will not have us, and we will be either liquidated or starved to death here."

Conclusions

The Muslim non-Bengali *muhajirs* in Bangladesh have gone through one of the most complex and unfortunate ordeals among the histories of world refugee communities. They were uprooted from India for their minority religious identity. In their country of asylum (Pakistan) they were given undue privileges and used as an instrument for regional exploitation. This was facilitated by their distinct differences in cultural, linguistic, and ethnic characteristics from the local Bengali population. Subsequently, they again became victims when their role against the majority was challenged, and were subjugated after their masters left. Even after 35 years of residence, they had remained as a completely unassimilated cultural community among Bengali society.

Given the current grim situation of the non-Bengali refugees in Bangladesh, Pakistan should be persuaded to receive at least those refugees who have opted for Pakistan. Similarly, India should allow the unification of Muslim *Biharis* with their kin in the northern states of India; this could be achieved by ensuring effective protection by the state. Further, reconciliatory statements by the government of Bangladesh are clearly not sufficient to change and redirect the refugees' willingness to pledge allegiance to the state of Bangladesh. A return by the government to the refugees of their houses, industries, and other assets might be a significant step in this direction. Establishment and development of special educational and social institutions would also effectively aid the refugee integration into the Bengali society.

23

The Rohingya Refugees in Bangladesh: Historical Perspectives and Consequences

K. Maudood Elahi

In historical demography and in branches of population studies dealing with population movements, the significance of large-scale expulsion of human population for political, religious, ethnic, and related reasons by a dominant group has largely been ignored. Even the expulsion of a minority group for any of the above reasons can rightly be considered as a case of political persecution. The political changes that have taken place in the South Asian subcontinent during the present century have triggered widespread population exchanges and movements: a result of these migrations is that long-term consequences have ensued for both the expelling and receiving countries (Elahi and Sultana 1980). In fact, the South Asian region has experienced several waves of refugee movement from historic times to the present decade. One of the recent refugee situations involved the Rohingya Muslims from the Arakan province in Burma, who have sought shelter in Bangladesh. This essay will review the historical perspectives of and consequences for the Rohingya refugees.

Burma and the Rohingya Muslims in Arakan

Burma is a land of valleys and mountains lying on the western periphery of the Southeast Asian peninsula. Covering about 262,000 square miles and with a population of about 36 million, Burma shares a 172-mile border with Bangladesh (Figure 23.l). In most senses, Burma is really part of what is generally called the "Indo-China complex" since it has more affinities with that region than with neighboring South Asian countries. During British colonial rule, however, it was part of British India for administrative convenience. When India gained independence, Burma also became an

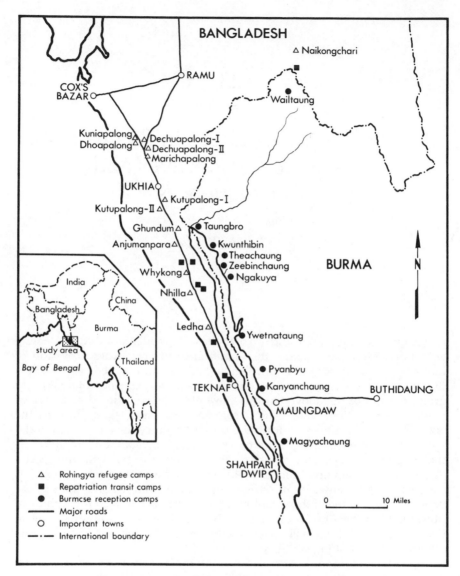

Figure 23.1   Rohingya Refugees in Bangladesh

independent sovereign state. The country came under the rule of the Anti-Fascist People's League, an enthusiastic and heterogeneous party, faced with governing a pluralist society comprising different ethnic, linguistic, and religious groups, such as the Burmans, Shans, Kachins, Karens, Mons, Magh, and others. Some 80 percent of the population is Buddhist, but three other religions—Christianity, Islam, and Hinduism—have sizable followings. Tribal dissensions, particularly in the north, arose immediately after independence. In short, the immediate post-independence era recorded a series of rebellions launched by communist groups and by various non-Burmese tribes, including the Karens, the Shans, and the Kachins. Given this situation, the army became fearful of secessionist movements in the non-Burmese regions, and overthrew the ruling party to install a revolutionary administration under General Ne Win in early 1962. After a brief period of near total isolation from the outside world, Ne Win's government adopted a socialist constitution in 1974.

The pluralism of Burmese population and society owes its origin to the geography, history, and culture of this transitional zone between South and Southeast Asia. The Arakan region in western Burma, the home of the Rohingya, is part of this transitional zone lying adjacent to the Bangladesh border. The Rohingya are a racially mixed but predominantly Burmese ethnic group, and are Muslims by religion. Pioneer Muslim settlers came to the Arakan region in the seventh century A.D. when Arab and Yemani traders first visited the seaport of Akayab and were accompanied by Muslims preachers. Many of them were attracted by the relatively easy and good life of the local inhabitants, and consequently settled in Arakan and its adjoining coastal areas as far north as in Chittagong (now in Bangladesh) and Tippera (now in India). Gradually, a mixed Muslim-Burmese society and culture developed and flourished. By the fifteenth century, in response to the expansion of the Mughal empire on the Indian subcontinent, other Muslims, mostly from lower Bengal, also migrated to the Arakan region. During this period, the king of Arakan had close diplomatic relation with Bengal, and until the middle of the eighteenth century the Arakan Muslims maintained close cultural affinity to Muslims outside Arakan. Arakan continued its independent status until it was incorporated by the British in 1885, and later, despite local opposition, was merged with Burma on its independence in 1948. Today, the Arakan Muslims have become known as the Rohingyas, while the non-Muslims of the area, most of whom are Buddhists, but are otherwise of the same ethnic stock as the Rohingyas, have become known as the *Magh*. Despite the political changes that have affected the Arakan region, major Muslim settlements continued to develop. In many places Muslims form more than 50 percent of the total population.

The Genesis of Religious and Political Persecution of the Rohingya Refugees

The Arakan Muslims have become a target of religious and political persecution in a systematic manner only during the present century. Arakan is an important province of Burma, but because it has long been a Muslim-populated area, it has developed a distinct culture dating back for over 1300 years. The relative isolation of the Arakan region from the Buddhist Burmese mainland has perpetuated and strengthened its distinctiveness in terms of identity and culture.

There is evidence that religio-political conflicts between the Arakan Muslims and the Maghs and other Burmese coming from eastern and northern Burma began in the latter part of the seventeenth century. In 1785, the king of Burma invaded and occupied Arakan, leading to large-scale persecution of Arakan Muslims. Soon after the annexation of Burma by the British in 1885, signs of tribal and ethnic strife once more resurfaced. When rural rebellion broke out in 1931, Burma, together with the Arakan region, was separated from India and was subsequently given internal self-government in 1937. In the years following this political arrangement, however, a series of interreligious and interethnic conflicts arose, particularly in the Arakan region, where sporadic violence against the Muslims erupted.

Burma was occupied by the Japanese for a brief period during World War II; following the defeat of the Japanese army, a huge quantity of arms was left behind. These eventually flowed into the hands of various rebel factions, including the Maghs and other Burmese hill tribes who cherished a deep dislike for the Rohingyas. A number of commissions and inquiry committees were appointed: in 1947 alone, four commissions were set up by the government of Burma, but all failed to find a solution to the problems of interreligious and interethnic strife in Arakan. Soon after independence, the Rohingyas demanded autonomous status within the Union of Burma, but these aspirations were designated as being akin to a separatist movement. In 1970, a joint representation was made to the government by Arakanese Rohingyas and Maghs for autonomous status of their region, and while it was granted to the Maghs in 1974, it was denied to the Arakan Rohingyas. For the latter, widespread persecution resulted. The extent of this persecution throughout this period is summarized in Table 23.1.

Table 23.1   Persecution of the Rohingyas in Arakan, 1942–1976

Nature of persecution	Approximate number of people affected	Areal extent/remarks
Destruction of settlements	692	Rohingya settlements
Indiscriminate use of explosives	500,000	Rohingya areas
Massacre	100,000	In 1942 alone
	20,000 to 30,000	Between 1942 and 1976
Severe attacks/wounding and torture	5,000	Rohingya areas
Rape (reported)	1,500	Rohingya areas
Murder/assassination	5,000	With marked mutiliation
Abduction	3,000	Rohingya and other Muslims
Destruction of mosques and religious schools	600	
Destruction of holy books and documents	200,000	
Confiscation of religious property	2,000 (acres)	
Removal from government jobs	10,000	
Kidnapping (disappeared mostly after arrests)	20,000	"Left the country," according to the Burmese government

Source: Documents of the Rohingya Patriotic Front as quoted in Bichitra 1978.

Muslim persecution in Arakan reached its climax in February 1978, when it was perpetrated by the Burmese army under the code name of "Nagamin Operation." The purpose of this operation was to determine the nationality of Arakan Muslims as a prelude to a forthcoming national census. The army determined nationality by identifying smallpox vaccination marks on people's arms. Those with vaccinations were regarded as non-nationals, since vaccinations had been administered during the years of the British rule in parts of Arakan and the adjoining areas of what is now Bangladesh. Eventually, the Burmese army arrested some 400 Rohingya women as suspect aliens. Protest to this action led to further arrests and oppressions of the Rohingyas. Throughout March 1978, thousands of Rohingyas were arrested and tortured and their villages burnt. As a result of this persecution thousands of Rohingyas fled across the Naaf River into Bangladesh. Between April and July 1978, more than 200,000 Rohingyas entered the Teknaf, Ukhia, and Cox's Bazar areas in Bangladesh (Table 23.2, and see Figure 23.1).

Present Status of the Rohingya Refugees

The exodus of the Rohingyas in 1978 was precipitated by a census of the Arakan region. Although legally citizens of Burma, the Rohingyas have periodically been apprehended as illegal migrants (Rizvi 1978) and have been subject to a policy of discrimination by the Burmese government. Regulations restrict their movements within the country and the granting of citizenship to them. They are also restricted from entry into government services and from trade and commerce. Thus the Rohingyas felt impelled to leave their homeland and to take refuge across the Naff River in Bangladesh.

Table 23.2   Rohingya Refugees from Burma in Bangladesh Camps, 1978

Camps	Number registered
Dechuapalong I	23,150
Dechuapalong II	26,797
Dhoapalong	13,774
Kutupalong I	10,018
Kutupalong II	15,220
Anjumanpara	13,816
Whykong	14,522
Nhilla	26,193
Ledha	20,395
Ghundum	7,317
Naikongchari	21,674
Kuniapalong	8,459
Marichapalong	21,200
Total	222,535

Source: Bangladesh Red Cross Society, 1978, as quoted in Kamaluddin 1980.

This refugees influx has resulted in considerable pressure on the Bangladesh economy, as well as straining the relations between the two neighboring countries. But in July 1978, Bangladesh and Burma reached an agreement on repatriating those refugees who could produce evidence of prior legal residence in Burma. By late 1979, all but 10,000 of the refugees had repatriated to Burma, and some $7 million of UNHCR assistance was made available to the Burmese government to rehabilitate the returning refugees in the Arakan province (Azam 1983). While this return is frequently cited as an example of successful repatriation, the continuing discrimination against the Rohingyas must be considered.

The return of these refugees led to the drafting of a new citizenship law in Burma that created two classes of citizens: members of indigeneous Burmese ethnic groups, and "naturalized" citizens—mainly people of Pakistani, Bengali, or Chinese origins, who number about 3.5 million of Burma's total population of 36 million. The law excluded "naturalized" citizens from joining the military or participating in elective government office, and also prohibited them from certain key economic activities. The assignment to the Rohingyas and other Burmese Muslims of "naturalized" citizenship status does not indicate a bright future for them. The measure is not only repressive but also highly discriminatory, and is in clear violation of the U.N. Declaration on Human Rights. The potential for further disregard of human rights by the Burmese government against the Rohingyas and other minority groups in Arakan is bound to perpetuate a persecution syndrome, and the concerned populations are likely once more to flee to asylum in the neighboring country.

Part Six

Southeast Asia

For most people, the refugee problem in Southeast Asia is synonymous with "Indochinese refugees." The region, however, has experienced several other refugee movements during the post-World War II era. Also, Indochina generated sizable population displacements long before the end of the Vietnam War brought the region's refugees to media attention. This lack of general awareness of pre–Vietnam War displacements in Southeast Asia is largely due to the fact that none of the earlier movements gained international recognition as a "refugee migration." Indeed, the displacements were mostly intranational. Indonesia has probably witnessed the largest intranational involuntary migrations in the region, at least until the post–Vietnam War displacements within Vietnam and Kampuchea. The latter two countries have experienced massive internal redistribution of their respective populations as a consequence of their radical social, economic, and political transformations since 1975. Little documentation or analysis of these displacements has yet appeared in the literature.

Apart from the current residual Indochinese refugee populations in the region, two other significant areas of refugee dispersal should be noted: the exodus (since the mid-1970s) of some 90,000 Muslim Filipino to the Malaysian state of Sabah, and the influx since 1984 of refugees from Iryan Jaya to Papua New Guinea. Yet the principal refugee problem of the region continues to be that of the Indochinese, whose rate of arrival in first countries of asylum continues steadily, so that the total remaining in the region is not being reduced to any great extent. Indeed, between 1984 and 1985 there was an overall reduction of 15 percent in the rate of third-country resettlement, and this trend is clearly continuing. Moreover, 75 percent of all departures from the region were being resettled in three principal receiving countries: the U.S., Canada, and France. This is a dramatic reversal from the generous acceptance levels of refugees by most Western countries at the height of the crisis in the early 1980s (Rogge 1985). Thailand continues to be the Southeast Asian first-asylum country bearing the brunt of the Indochinese exodus, with some 82 percent of the remaining refugees contained in Thai camps. But in addition to approximately 130,000 refugees, Thailand accommodates close to a quarter-million Kampucheans who have been "temporarily" housed in camps along the border following the 1984-1985 Vietnamese offensive against Khmer resistance forces.

Among the Third World's refugee-generating areas, Southeast Asia stands out for its almost total dependence upon third-country resettlement as the only acceptable durable solution for Indochinese refugees. From the beginning of the post-Vietnam War refugee exodus, the ASEAN states made it known that they will provide only temporary asylum pending resettlement. A number of states, particularly Thailand and Malaysia, emphasized this point by refusing to allow boat-people to land until Western governments committed themselves to the principle of resettlement. The consequence has been the absorption of more than 1 million Indochinese in the West. In addition, some quarter-million Sino-Vietnamese have been successfully absorbed by China. Yet a concern is growing, especially in Thailand, that a "residual" Indochinese refugee population will be left within the region, made up in large part of refugees deemed unacceptable for permanent resettlement in the West.

Notwithstanding this emphasis on resettlement, some local integration of specific refugee groups within the region has taken place, and some, albeit very modest, repatriation. Malaysia has absorbed by far the greatest proportion of the region's refugees. In Sabah, much of the Filipino refugee population has been integrated into the local labor force and economic milieu. Malaysia has also permitted some Indochinese to settle locally, namely several thousand Cham—a Muslim ethnic group from Kampuchea. In the earlier stages of the Vietnamese exodus, some refugees were permitted to settle locally in Hong Kong; however, this policy changed dramatically after the number of boat people arriving in Hong Kong surged, and instead the colony adopted its humane-deterrence policy. Even Thailand has permitted a few Indochinese to settle, but only those who can substantiate an historic claim to Thai citizenship.

The eight essays in Part Six deal with three aspects of the region's refugee problem: the refugee experience within the region; the problem of intranational displacement; and the resettlement of Indochinese to Western industrialized states. Graeme Hugo's first essay describes the scale of the post–Vietnam War exodus and summarizes the problems experienced by first-asylum countries and the policies that they adopted toward refugees. In the first of two country profiles, Sothi Rachagan contrasts the Malay response to Filipino refugees in Sabah with response to Vietnamese in the Malay Peninsula. He points out that in Malaysia all refugees are considered as illegal aliens, but that quite different policies have emerged with respect to the Muslim Filipinos vis-à-vis the non-Muslim, and predominantly Sino-Vietnamese. The second regional study by Netnapis Nakavachara and John Rogge focuses upon Thailand's long history of refugee influx, and whose approach was forced to become hostile by the sheer scale of the post-1975 influx. With declining resettlement rates, Thailand is especially fearful of being left with a large residual refugee population.

The second essay by Graeme Hugo examines the often-ignored subject of internal population displacement. Specifically, Hugo describes the scale, causes, and consequences of intranational refugees in Indonesia and the Philippines.

The remaining four essays focus upon the resettlement of Indochinese refugees in the West. Michael Lanphier contrasts the resettlement programs in the U.S., Canada, and France. His paper is one of the first to approach this topic on an international comparative basis. Jaqueline Desbarats describes a secondary movement frequently taking place as refugees leave their initial points of settlement to concentrate in areas where their needs for community can be realized. Doreen Indra, in her review of the Canadian experience with Indochinese resettlement, suggests that one of the impacts of the high degree of dependence upon private sponsorship in Canada's resettlement programs has resulted in a dispersal of refugees throughout Canada, and she describes the scale and nature of research into the resettlement process in Canada.

The final essay of this volume examines the socioeconomic adjustment of Indochinese refugees in Canada. Based upon a detailed study of Indochinese refugees in Ottawa, Toronto, and eastern Ontario, as well as on a longitudinal government study, Gertrud Neuwirth describes the handicaps refugees encounter in their attempts to integrate into the labor market. She shows that refugees, hampered by lack of adequate language and job skill training, remain concentrated in low-paying jobs and locked into the bottom rungs of the occupational ladder.

24

Postwar Refugee Migration in Southeast Asia: Patterns, Problems, and Policies

Graeme Hugo

Most recent migration research in Southeast Asia is based either explicitly or implicitly on the premise that population movement is a fundamentally voluntary process. Partly due to an inappropriate transfer of concepts and models developed in contemporary Euro-American society, there has been an overstressing of voluntary choice in population movement and not enough emphasis upon less voluntary and more-or-less forced migrations. Migrations impelled by religious, ethnic, and political conflicts, persecutions, tyranny, and war have occurred on a massive scale in several Southeast Asian countries since World War II.

The migrants, whose flight has taken them across an international boundary, are officially classified as "refugees" and have deservedly become a focus of attention of a few researchers and international agencies. A disproportionately large share of this attention, however, has been directed toward those who eventually resettle in countries outside Southeast Asia, while those remaining in the region have been little studied. Moreover, as with much migration research, there is a general neglect of the impact of such population movements on the areas from which refugees leave. The purpose of this essay is to review some of the major patterns of refugee migrations out of and within Southeast Asian countries, and to assess some of the social and economic consequences of these migrations.

In 1981 UNHCR indicated that 2.16 million of the world's 12.6 million refugees were located in Asia. Of these some 657,600 were located in the arc of countries from Burma to Hong Kong referred to as Southeast Asia (Keely 1981:33). Such figures give little indication of the impact of refugee movements on those countries, especially during the past decade. Before we examine the major refugee movements, two general points about Southeast Asian refugee movements should be made. First, only the Philippines is a signatory of the 1951 U.N. Convention on Refugees and the 1967 Protocol, and is thus the only state in the region bound to its recommendations. Second, unlike the situation in Africa, no Southeast Asian country is willing to accept significant numbers of refugees on anything other than a temporary asylum basis.

Refugees in Vietnam

The refugee problem in Southeast Asia has been dominated since the reunification of Vietnam in 1975 by outflows from Indochina. Between 1975 and 1983, some 775,000 Vietnamese refugees landed in neighboring countries. Yet as Billard (1983a) points out, "it is possible to count [only] those who finally arrived . . . no one will ever know how many were lost at sea. The wrecks and human remnants washed ashore on the beaches of Southeast Asian countries give only a faint idea of the extent of the tragedy." In any case, at least 1.5 percent of Vietnam's total population has left the country since the beginning of 1975. Over the same period the outflow from Laos and Kampuchea has totaled 518,315, or more than 5 percent of their total combined national populations. Almost all of these 1.3 million refugees found refuge initially in an Asian country of first asylum. Figure 24.1 shows that the majority have since resettled in a third country of permanent asylum outside Southeast Asia. By March 1983, 839,853 Indochinese refugees had been settled in third countries, of whom 504,493 were Vietnamese boat people. Another 260,000 Vietnamese had permanently settled in China by 1978. Nevertheless, some 190,000 Indochinese refugees remain in camps in other Southeast Asian countries, and of these only 22 percent are Vietnamese, with the remainder being Laotians and Kampucheans. Figure 24.1 shows that the major country of settlement has been the U.S., which accounts for 59 percent of those settled since 1975 and, together with France (10.5 percent), Canada (10.2 percent), and Australia (8.9 percent), accounts for nearly 90 percent of all third-country resettlement. Most of the remaining 10 percent have been resettled in other West European countries.

The enormity and complexity of the recent Vietnamese refugee movements have diverted attention from the fact that it is really a further phase of refugee movements from Vietnam, following the two preceding decades of more-or-less continuous warfare and massive population displacement. Thus, it is useful to review briefly the earlier displacements.

During 1954–55, when Vietnam was being divided at the 17th parallel, some 900,000 "ideological refugees" left the North for the South, and 90,000 went the other way (Olson 1979b). In the subsequent two decades, huge flows of refugees continued to migrate to and from North and South Vietnam. It has ben estimated that about half the population (some 10 million persons) in the South was displaced between 1954 and 1975. In the North most of the displacement was from the area immediately north of the demilitarized zone, where some 2 million people had to leave their villages after being made homeless by bombing. Turley (1976:622) reports that more than 1 million people were moved between 1960 and 1975 out of the northern delta and plains into the hills. There was also a prolonged evacuation of northern cities during the air war.

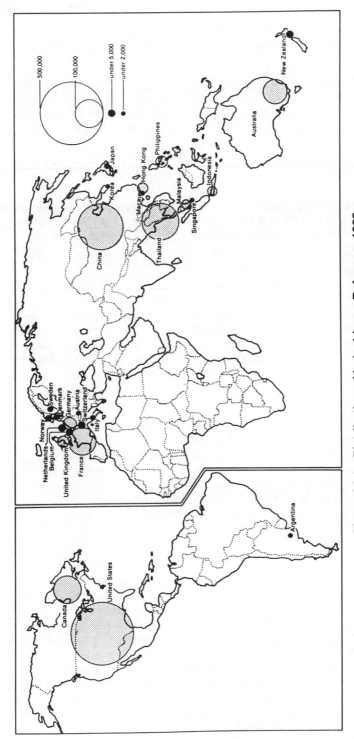

Figure 24.1 Distribution of Indochinese Refugees, 1983

Table 24.1   A Model of Refugee Migration Associated with Revolutionary Warfare

Stage of revolutionary warfare	Refugee population
I Subversive activity is a potential threat or subversive incidents occur in an organized pattern, but no major outbreak of violence.	Small, homogeneous, consisting of large landholders, officials, or important supporters of legal government
II Insurgent movement gains sufficient local or external support to initiate organized guerrilla warfare.	As stress becomes greater the number increases, but still a socially distinct group
III Insurgency becomes primarily a war between organized forces of the insurgents and those of established authority.	When stress levels reach their peak, there is a high rate of refugee generation and virtually no social selectivity.

Source: Adopted from Rambo 1968.

Rambo (1968) conducted a detailed field study of the causes and characteristics of civilian population displacement in the South and produced a model of refugee migration created by three stages of revolutionary warfare. This model is summarized in Table 24.1. Further, he suggested the following hypotheses regarding the characteristics of refugee migrants:

- literate persons move earlier than illiterate;
- large landholders move earlier than small landholders and those with no land move earlier than landholders;
- those with relatives within the legal government move earlier than those without such connections;
- persons with skills move earlier;
- younger people move earlier than older; and
- minority religious groups move earlier.

The bulk of migration in the South was to cities, resulting in an increase in urban population from 20 percent in 1954 to 50 percent in 1975. This pattern of rapid urbanization is shown in Table 24.2. Goodwan and Franks (1975) studied the dynamics of migration to Saigon from 1964 to 1972. More than two-thirds of their sample of migrants moved to Saigon (now Ho Chi Minh City) for war-related reasons or to join their families. Goodwan and Franks found little correlation between migrants' intentions to stay in Saigon and their reason for migrating there in the first place: "once a migrant came to the city, his or her tenure was determined by experience there rather than by changes in the elements which originally led to migration." Although the largest single group of refugees remained in Saigon, the proportion of forced migrants that made up city populations was greatest in middle-sized cities such as Danang Qui Nhon and Cam

Ranh, which became major refugee reception centers near areas of heavy fighting (Turley 1976: 620).

In addition to urbanization, there were refugee movements between rural areas. These flows reached a crescendo in the final months of the war, when hundreds of thousands of refugees fled before advancing North Vietnamese forces. A field study (Que, Rambo, and Murlin 1976) of these refugee movements found that, among 70 households interviewed, a predominance of people were of North Vietnamese origin, of religious minorities (Catholics), of urban dwellers, and of nonfarming groups. Most had moved of their own volition and cited fear of the National Liberation Front and North Vietnamese forces as the cause of their migration. A second important motive was fear of being caught up in the fighting.

Following reunification, a new set of movements began. First, the problem of the swollen southern cities was tackled; Turley (1976) suggested that first priority was given to resettling the 3 million people who had been forced to evacuate their home areas because of the U.S.–South Vietnamese military strategy. Some 18,700 people were resettled within the first month after the war, another 40,000 by the end of the second month, 227,000 by October 1975, and 600,000 by August 1976. This is producing what Turley calls an "urban transformation," and suggests that the program was marked by rapid institutionalization of resettlement procedures. The explicit goal of reducing Saigon"s population by at least 1.5 million has frequently been mentioned (ibid.). An ambitious program of redistributing the population was mounted, and in mid-1975 the new authorities estimated that of the 10 million displaced persons in the South, some 5 million would have to be resettled in the countryside. Of these, some 2 million would return to their home villages, and the remainder be resettled to the New Economic Zones. There is also an ambitious program to redistribute some 2.1 million people from the northern delta provinces and from the central highlands (Chanda 1977). It has also been suggested that the authorities' encouragement of particular urban-based groups to flee to other countries is also part of a population redistribution strategy aimed at reducing the size of the urban population.

The flight of refugees that accompanied the advance of North Vietnamese forces during 1975 was followed after the war by a steady flow of clandestine refugee emigrations. In 1978 the outflow from Vietnam changed dramatically after some 30,000 private businesses in Cholon, the Chinese business quarter of Ho Chi Minh City, were closed by government action; subsequently, in a move to eliminate cash hoarding, the Vietnamese currency was changed. The effects were immediate: "convinced that a harsh life of agricultural labor awaits them in Vietnam's new economic zones, thousands of ethnic Chinese from Cholon have fled the country in small fishing boats, destined for what they hope will be a brief stay in refugee camps before resettlement in Western countries" (Weintraub 1978). It is clear that this flight of ethnic Chinese was not clandestine. Das and Sacerdoti (1978) reported in late 1978 that "there can now be little doubt that Hanoi's encouragement of the current refugee exodus from Vietnam is both calculated and widespread. Scores of interviews with recent refugee arrivals on

Malaysia's east coast reveal details of how quasi-legal organizations operate with the connivance of Vietnamese government officials to facilitate refugee departures." They reported that US$2,000 per person in gold or hard currency bought ethnic Chinese passage on boats out of Vietnam. (At this time, the vast majority, around 85 percent, of Vietnamese refugees were ethnic Chinese.) During the same time there was also a large flow of ethnic Chinese from North Vietnam into southern China. UNHCR estimates that by 1983 some 263,000 Vietnamese had sought refuge in China, most of these unskilled, and the majority settled on State Farms (Obrecht 1983). This refugee flow represents the majority of the North's estimated 300,000 ethnic Chinese, and prompted one contemporary observer (Weintraub 1978) to remark, "it is unlikely that a similar percentage could quit the south, but the extent of the northern exodus suggests that Vietnam's leaders view the Chinese in their midst as something less than a precious national resource."

In the period since reunification, the number of refugees leaving Vietnam has fluctuated widely, as Table 24.3 shows. The outflow of boat people in 1978, however, was only a harbinger of the greater crisis of 1979: "in a single month more than 60,000 tried to find asylum in Thailand, Malaysia, Hong Kong, Indonesia, Macau, and even the Philippines and Japan by braving high seas, pirates and death" (Davico 1983). This placed enormous strains on countries of first asylum and UNHCR, and has led to placement of increasing restrictions upon arriving refugees. A consequence was the initiation of the "Orderly Departure Programme" (ODP) by UNHCR and the Vietnamese authorities. Initially this program developed bottlenecks because of competing priorities on lists of potential migrants compiled by Vietnamese authorities and those compiled by host countries. In 1979 only 2,000 Vietnamese left under the scheme. The program eventually became more effective, and in 1982 a total of 12,918 left Vietnam; one out of five

Table 24.2   Patterns of Urbanization in South Vietnam, 1960–1970

Size of City	1960	
	Number	Population
1 million or larger	(a) Saigon metropolitan area	2,296,000
	(b) Saigon prefecture	1,400,000
500,000–999,999	0	—
300,000–499,999	0	—
100,000–299,999	2	207,000
20,000–99,999	15	582,000
Total urban		3,085,000 (22%)
Total rural		10,987,000 (78%)
Total population		14,072,000

Source: Goodman and Franks 1975.

leaving in that year did so under the auspices of ODP. By 1983, 50,345 people had left Vietnam under the ODP scheme.

Refugees in Laos

A thorough study of refugees in Laos has been completed by Olson (1978, 1979b). This landlocked nation has been subjected to more-or-less continuous conflict throughout the postwar period, especially between Vietnamese-backed Pathet Lao forces and the American-backed Royal Lao Government army. Olson (1979b) suggests that by 1959 there were some 40,000 refugees within Laos in the government-controlled area in the northwest of the country. Up to 1960, this movement was of families "who felt threatened because of their economic or political positions in the territories held by the Pathet Lao." Many of these refugees were entrepreneurs of Vietnamese, Chinese, or Indian origin. During the 1960s the ferocity of fighting caused whole villages to flee the firing zones, and by 1963 the number of refugees was estimated at 125,000. These numbers continued to increase as more and more territory was lost to the Pathet Lao; by 1969 there were 210,000, and by 1970 there were more than 260,000. Most refugees moved toward the Mekong River—the border with Thailand. After the 1974 cease fire, refugees began either to return to their home areas or to relocate permanently elsewhere (ibid.). Finally in 1975, the large-scale movements into Thailand began.

Nearly 300,000 Laotian refugees have crossed the Mekong into Thailand since 1975. The first major wave was in late 1975, when some 44,000 hill tribe people arrived. Thereafter a further 7,000 to 10,000 hill tribe refugees arrived annually, and the flow picked up momentum in 1979 so that, by the end of that year, 61,474 hill tribe refugees were settled in six camps in

Number	1970 Population	Percent change 1960–1970
1	3,320,000	45
1	1,761,000	26
0	—	—
1	385,000	—
6	842,000	307
28	1,559,000	161
	6,060,000 (35%)	
	11,273,000 (65%)	
	17,333,000	

Table 24.3   Refugee Flows into Southeast Asian Countries from Vietnam, Laos, and
             Kampuchea, 1975-1983

	Vietnam[a]		Kampuchea and Laos[b]	
Year	Number	Percent change from previous year	Number	Percent change from previous year
1975-76[c]	5,619		112,045	
1977	15,657	+179	29,780	- 73
1978[d]	88,712	+467	62,839	+111
1979	205,448	+132	188,114	+199
1980	75,833	- 63	92,318	- 51
1981	74,754	- 1	24,882	- 73
1982[c]	43,825	- 41	5,185	- 79
1983	28,043	- 36	9,280	+ 79
Total	537,891		524,443	

[a]These data include only the so-called boat people traveling by sea from Vietnam to Southeast Asian destinations. They exclude a few thousand "land people" comprising refugees
who made their way across Kampuchea into Thailand and Vietnamese army deserters who
fled into Thailand from their Kampuchea-based units. In mid-1982 between 2,000 and
3,000 such refugees were in Thailand (McBeth 1982b, p. 48).
[b]These figures include only refugees fleeing into Thailand and are officially registered. They
exclude refugees from Kampuchea settling in Vietnam, numbering about 21,000 in late
1983. They also exclude the thousands of refugees (mainly Laotians) who have illegally
settled in Thailand "after slipping unnoticed across the Mekong" (McBeth 1982b, p. 48).
[c]Excluding 130,000 Vietnamese who arrived in the US before reunification.
[d]Excluding 260,000 Vietnamese who arrived in China.
[e]In 1982 and 1983 data there were no registrations from Kampuchea since, under the
Thai "Humane Deterrence" policy, no new refugees were accepted, although some may
have settled illegally on the Thai side of the border.
Source: UNHCR.

northeastern Thailand. The numbers of lowland Lao (ethnically very similar
to northern Thais) refugees entering Thailand was relatively small until
1978, when their numbers increased from 10,000 to 30,000, and by the end
of 1979 there were nearly 70,000.

In addition to the outflow of refugees to Thailand, Laos has been a
recipient of refugees from neighboring countries. Some 10,000 Cambodians
fled across the border into Laos following the Khmer Rouge's takeover in
Phnom Penh in 1975 (McBeth 1983a). Unlike the refugees who moved into
Thailand, these migrants were not concentrated in camps but were allowed
to settle in southern Laos. An agreement was recently reached between the
two governments to repatriate the refugees.

Refugees in Kampuchea

Unlike its Indochinese neighbors of Laos and Vietnam, Kampuchea's first
two decades after World War II were not characterized by conflict and

devastation. During the 1970s, however, Kampuchea suffered upheaval, hardship, and horror. Meng-Try (1981) has summarized the demographic impact of the civil war, the subsequent revolution, and the Vietnamese invasion as "excess mortality from war, from massacres and executions, and from famine; by forced migrations and flight of refugees, and by greatly reduced birth rates." No country in the contemporary era has experienced greater forced migrations of its people.

The 1970s began for Cambodia with the forced relocation of its large, local ethnic Vietnamese population into resettlement camps, following a similar strategy to that of the Brigg's Plan in Malaysia. The explanation given for the resettlement was concern for the safety of the ethnic Vietnamese and that they might have been assisting Vietnamese communist invaders. Eventually South Vietnam and Cambodia agreed on the repatriation of about half of the ethnic Vietnamese population, which was achieved by air and sea lift in the summer of 1970 (Kunz 1973). During the early 1970s a massive displacement from the countryside resulted from the Vietnamese invasion, the U.S. bombing of Cambodia, and the growing civil war. The cities, especially the capital of Phnom Penh, grew rapidly from the influx of more than 2 million refugees. When the Lon Nol regime fell in 1975 and the Khmer Rouge seized control, the latter immediately evacuated virtually the entire population of the swollen cities. Meng-Try (1981) quotes a Khmer Rouge official thus: "we have removed from the capital and all other cities 4,237,856 people, of whom some 2,000,000 were townspeople by origin (including 400,000 Chinese, of whom 170,000 were naturalized Khmers of mixed origin): the remainder consisted of refugee peasants." Phnom Penh became a virtual ghost city overnight. As Meng-Try points out, "this massive and brutal evacuation, effected without advanced planning, resulted in enormous suffering." The evacuees were put to work in the countryside.

The flight of Cambodians to Thailand at this time is discussed elsewhere in this volume. In 1978 there were also 50,000 Kampuchean refugees in Vietnam (ibid.), as well as some 200,000 ethnic Vietnamese who had repatriated after the Khmer Rouge victory in 1975. All told, between 1975 and 1978 there was an estimated net out-migration of 450,000 persons to neighboring countries.

The onset of famine in 1979, as well as the repression perpetrated by the Samrin regime, has ensured that population displacements have continued. Although precise numbers are not known, Meng-Try (1981) suggests that some 900,000 moved either into Thailand or close to the border, where they could benefit from food assistance provided by international organizations. Planned settlement of Vietnamese civilians in Kampuchea began in 1979, and Meng-Try (ibid.) estimates that at the end of that year they numbered between 200,000 and 300,000.

The UNHCR data show no new registrations of refugees from Kampuchea in Thailand in 1982 and 1983, since under the "humane deterrence" policy initiated in early 1982, new refugees could not be accepted for third-country resettlement. Undoubtedly there has been illegal movement into the Thai side of the border, but it is clear that Thai policy reduced the flow of refugees across the border until the 1984–85 border offensive once more resulted in a flood of refugees into Thailand. As a result, there has been a build-up of refugees in camps along the Thai side of the border. By early 1985, the U. N. Border Relief Organization (UNBRO) estimated that some 250,000 Khmer displacees were in the border camps.

Refugees in Malaysia

A wide range of conflict-induced refugee movements has affected Malaysia in the postwar period. First were significant internal movements associated with the "Emergency" (1948–60), when the Malayan Communist Party (MCP) attempted to establish an independent "People's Democratic Republic" in Malaya. The main base of support for the MCP was among the Chinese. Initially a policy of detention and deportation was implemented, followed between 1949 and 1952 with the imprisonment of some 40,000 squatter families. Some 24,000 Chinese and 2,000 Indians and Indonesians were also deported (Sandhu 1964); it soon became apparent that this response was unworkable because of the huge numbers involved and because China refused to accept the deportees. Thus the "Briggs Plan" proposed: (a) *Relocation:* the transfer of dispersed rural settlers (whether squatters or legitimate settlers) to prepared fortified sites known as New Villages; and (b) *Regroupment:* the transfer of dispersed mine and estate laborers, their families, and dwellings to a fortified point of concentration.

A total of 573,000 persons were transferred to New Villages during the emergency, of which 300,000 were squatters and 86 percent were Chinese. Most of this transfer was achieved by the end of 1952. It is estimated that 650,000 persons were regrouped: 71.5 percent on estates, 21.5 percent at mines, and the rest in factories, sawmills, etc. (Sandhu 1964). Of this regrouped population, 45 percent were Chinese, 32 percent were Malays, and 18 percent were Indians. With the creation of all these new settlements, the settlement pattern of the Malay peninsula was permanently changed. The program also added 216 urban centers, so that between 1947 and 1957 the urban population increased from 26.5 to 42.5 percent.

Malaysia, together with Thailand, has borne the brunt of the refugee exodus from Indochina. In late 1978 Vietnamese refugees into Malaysia (Figure 24.2) peaked with some 45,000 refugees. Malaysia's resources were put under great strain, and considerable local resentment developed toward the refugees, especially on the east coast of the peninsula where most of the refugee camps were located. The Malaysian government was the first in the region to declare the boat people as "illegal immigrants" rather than refugees and to push refugee boats back out to sea. The two main refugee camps on the east coast were on the islands of Pulau Pidong and Pulau Besar. The former housed some 25,000 refugees by late 1978. Refugees were crowded together, and the limited supply of food was kept from becoming critical only by a thriving black market. There were a growing fear of disease and an all-pervading atmosphere of uncertainty in the camp; "the beehive activity of Pulau Bidong is only a temporary antidote against despair, not a symbol of hope" (Das and Sacerdoti 1978).

Malaysia has been adamant about refusing entry to the predominantly

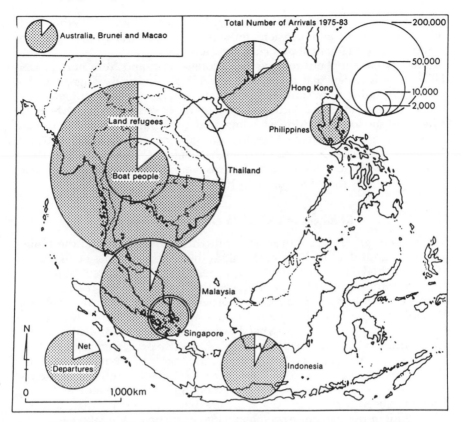

Figure 24.2   Net Migration of Indochinese Refugees, 1975–1983

ethnic Chinese refugees from Vietnam and has emphasized its policy of third-country resettlement. At the peak of refugee influx, boat people suspected of being "economic refugees" were prevented from landing in Malaysia and were forced to seek asylum elsewhere. It has been estimated, for example, that 80 percent of boat people arriving in Indonesia had previously attempted to land in Malaysia. By mid-1983 some 95 percent of Indochinese arrivals in Malaysia had been resettled in a third country, and only 10,112 refugees remained in the camps. While the number of boat people arriving in Malaysia in recent years has declined, Malaysian officials are still concerned about the rate of third-country acceptances, as well as about new waves of refugees occurring (Das 1983).

Unlike the boat people, Muslim refugees from the Philippines, Kampuchea, and Burma have been allowed to settle in Malaysia. Undoubtedly this difference in policy is influenced by the fact that the Vietnamese refugees are predominantly ethnic Chinese, and that any large-scale settlement of them in Malaysia would therefore change the politically sensitive balance there between Malays and Chinese. This whole issue of ethnicity and refugees is clearly an important one in Southeast Asia, where ethnic-based conflict is a significant cause of many refugee migrations, and ethnicity is obviously one of the dimensions influencing whether or not refugees are accepted for settlement at particular destinations.

Little is known about refugee migrations within and from Burma. UN-HCR has suggested that there are some 187,000 internal refugees in that country resulting from continuing conflicts between government and communist insurgents in the north and from ethnic-based conflicts between hill tribes and the lowland Burmese-dominated government. In addition there have been refugee movements across Burma's borders, such as the 100,000 Muslim refugees who crossed into Bangladesh in 1978 (Olson 1979a). These Rohingya (native-born) Burmese Muslims were driven out of Arakan state; the majority repatriated to Burma in 1979.

Refugees in Indonesia and the Philippines

The majority of refugee movements influencing Indonesia and the Philippines in recent decades have been within the nation. Yet these two nations have also played an important role in resettling Vietnamese refugees to third countries, and both have Refugee Processing Centers (RPCs) where training programs for refugees are provided before they are resettled. Because refugee boats had been landing at islands scattered throughout both archipelagoes, there was a need to relocate and concentrate them at the RPCs. Indonesia's and Philippines' RPCs have also processed refugees from other countries of first asylum, mainly Malaysia and Thailand. Nearly a third of refugees processed on Indonesia's RPC on Galang Island were not direct arrivals in Indonesia. The treatment given to refugees at Galang Island has been so successful that it has created some resentment among the local resident population. Awanohara (1983) explains: "the refugees have a higher standard of living than many Indonesians living in nearby areas, some say. They point out that the refugees are guaranteed food, water, medical and other welfare facilities, education, and on top of that resettlement in rich countries." In the Philippines, Vietnamese refugees have been concentrated in camps on Palawan Island, in a camp on the outskirts of Manila, or in an RPC on Bataan.

Refugees in Hong Kong, Macao, and Singapore

Hong Kong has long been a destination for refugees or illegal immigrants from China, although numbers have varied widely over time depending upon conditions in China and levels of surveillance on both sides of the border. A gentleman's agreement between Hong Kong and China in 1973 provided for only 50 legal migrants to Hong Kong a day; by 1979, however, the estimated daily arrivals of illegal migrants were around 1,000 (Bonavia 1979). Between 1978 and 1982 some 530,000 immigrants from China settled in Hong Kong, which resulted in the population of the crowded island (population density of 4,712 people per km^2) growing by 10 percent despite a considerable fall in local fertility rates.

Since 1975 Hong Kong has also become one of the major destinations of boat people from Vietnam. The peak of boat people arrivals was in 1979. In recent years Hong Kong has had the highest caseload of boat people among first-asylum countries. It has had the lowest ratio of departures to arrivals for boat people: by mid-1983, for example, only 84 percent of all arrivals since 1975 had been resettled in a third country. This has clearly been a concern to Hong Kong authorities, and since mid-1982 they have adopted a dissuasive measure, locking-up Vietnamese boat people in so-called "closed camps" as soon as they arrive. This amounts to virtual imprisonment, since the inmates are unable to leave the camps and are subject to strict discipline (Billard 1983b). These measures, however, have not appeared to change drastically the rate of arrivals of boat people in Hong Kong.

Macao has offered temporary refuge for some 7,000 Vietnamese refugees, 90 percent of whom are ethnic Chinese; most of them have been resettled in third countries. In addition, some 9,000 so-called "fake boat people" are Vietnamese who had fled to China in 1978 and subsequently migrated to Macao, where they claimed they had crossed the South China Sea directly from Vietnam. Most of these have since been forcibly repatriated to state farms in China's southern provinces (Obrecht 1983b).

Singapore has been little influenced by refugees. It adopted a strict policy of not allowing refugees to land without a guarantee that a third country would accept them. Hence, as Figure 24.2 shows, practically all the 25,5l3 boat people who arrived in Singapore between 1975 and 1983 have been resettled.

Conclusions

Forced migrations in Southeast Asia have been a neglected area of research among social scientists. This is partly explained by limited secondary data regarding such movement and by the obvious difficulties in studying refugee migrations at first hand. Yet since 1945, Southeast Asian circumstances have created a wide variety and varying scales of involuntary population movements. The policies developed to cope with the major international refugee movements initiated by conflicts within Southeast Asia are enumerated in Table 24.4. The refugee problem has clearly been dominated by the post–1975 outflow from Vietnam, Kampuchea, and Laos, which in the subsequent eight years amounted to nearly a 3 percent loss to the population of those countries. This movement has been somewhat selective in that people of Chinese ethnicity as well as urban dwellers and urban occupations have predominated. Thus, in the countries of origin the impact of these refugee movements has been to reduce significantly the size of local Chinese and urban bourgeois populations. This has given rise to speculation that to some degree these refugee movements have been part of a politically and ideologically based program of population redistribution and change.

There is a pressing need for more detailed studies of the impacts of these refugee movements and of the various policies initiated to cope with them. Conventional migration data collection strategies are often insufficient for this purpose, and more innovative, flexible, and appropriate strategies need

Table 24.4   Refugee Policies in Southeast Asian Asylum States

Country	Refugee group	Short-term asylum
Vietnam	Kampucheans (mainly Chinese)	UNHCR camps and Khmer Pagodas in Ho Chi Minh City
	Vietnamese from Kampuchea	
Malaysia	Filipino, Muslims in Sabah	Allowed to stay indefinitely
	Vietnamese	Under UNHCR auspices mainly in east coast camps. But considers many as illegal migrants rather than refugees, and some not allowed to land
	Kampucheans (small numbers)	Under UNHCR auspices
	Muslim refugees from Burma (small numbers)	Allowed to stay indefinitely
Thailand	Kampucheans	Some granted asylum in UNHCR camps, but many classified as "displaced persons," not refugees
	Laotians	Some granted asylum
	Vietnamese	Some granted asylum
Laos	Thailand (small numbers)	Accepted
	Kampuchea	Accepted
Indonesia and Philippines	Vietnamese	Under UNHCR auspices
Hong Kong	Chinese	Accepted
	Vietnamese	Under UNHCR auspices but since 1982 placed in prison-like closed camps to deter further refugees
Macau	Vietnamese	Boat people accepted under UNHCR auspices
Singapore	Vietnamese	Not accepted unless prior guarantee of acceptance by third country

	Long-term Policies	
Settlement	Repatriation	Third-country resettlement
Not accepted	Some repatriation following overthrow of Khmer Rouge	Included in Orderly Departure Program
Accepted for resettlement	Some repatriation since Vietnamese occupation of Kampuchea	
Accepted for settlement	Much coming and going between southern Philippines and Sabah	
Not accepted	—	Under UNHCR auspices
Some being accepted	—	Under UNHCR auspices
Some being accepted	—	—
Not accepted	Large-scale involuntary repatriation and some voluntary repatriation	After 1982 under "humane deterrence" policy barring third-country resettlement to new refugees. But seeking third-country resettlement for all previous refugees
Not accepted officially, but some illegal settlements	UNHCR voluntary repatriation scheme and some informal repatriation	Some difficulties because hill tribe peoples not anxious to be resettled in Third Countries. "Humane Deterrence" policy since 1982
Not accepted	—	"Humane Deterrence" policy since 1982. Third-country resettlement
Accepted	Voluntary repatriation	—
Accepted	Agreement between Lao and Kampuchean governments for repatriation	
Not accepted	No programs	Under UNHCR auspices has a Refugee Processing Centre for refugees from Malaysia and Thailand en route to third-country resettlement
Limited numbers accepted, but much illegal migration	No programs	—
People not able to be resettled in third country placed in open camps and allowed to seek work	No programs	Under UNHCR auspices
Not accepted	Vietnamese refugees coming via China repatriated to China	Under UNHCR auspices
Not accepted	—	Only accept refugees guaranteed third-country resettlement

to be develped. In Southeast Asia, a wide variety of repatriation, resettlement, and deterrence policies and programs has been initiated, so that a thorough assessment of the wider social and economic consequences both to the refugees and to the countries of asylum would be very beneficial to the often hard-pressed policy-makers and program officials. In recent years the outflow of Indochinese refugees has been somewhat reduced, but levels of third-country acceptance have also decreased, which causes considerable concern to the countries of first asylum. There are no guarantees that international refugee flows will cease in the region, and it is important to consolidate the hard-learned lessons of the last decade so that this knowledge can be used to ameliorate the suffering of future refugee movements.

25

Refugees and Illegal Immigrants: The Malaysian Experience with Filipino and Vietnamese Refugees

S. Sothi Rachagan

Throughout recorded history people have sought refugee status during troubled periods. Since state frontiers were not clearly defined or jealously guarded, the movement from one country to another did not prove problematic. The right to asylum was commonly recognized and honored, and waves of refugees did not create a refugee problem. Today two world wars, modern dictatorial regimes, the growth of modern nationalism, and increasingly strict immigration laws have changed the scope, variety of causes, and difficulty of solutions of current refugee tides compared to those of earlier centuries.

Malaysia is not a signatory to any of the international conventions or treaties pertaining to refugees. Entry into Malaysia is governed by the Immigration Act of 1959/1963 (revised in 1975). The act appears in seven parts. Part II of the act deals with admission into and departure from Malaysia, and the provisions envisage three categories of persons: (a) citizens who are entitled to entry; (b) fifteen classes of persons prohibited entry; and (c) all other persons who are entitled to entry only with a valid permit or pass. In no part of the principal act or subsidiary legislation are refugees mentioned. In addition, the principal act allows for the minister (of home affairs) to exempt any person or class of persons from having to obtain an entry permit or pass. Similarly, the Immigration (Prohibition of Entry) Order of 1963, although making no explicit mention of refugees, refers to the powers of the minister under Section 55 of the principal act and excludes from the category of prohibited persons "any person permitted by the Minister to enter the Federation on special compassionate grounds."

The position of asylum seekers within Malaysian Immigration Law is that they are prohibited entry unless able to prove that they belong to one of the above-mentioned eligible categories. Nothing short of ministerial intervention prevents persons seeking asylum from being treated as illegal immigrants. Indeed, the position of refugees in countries not signatories to any international instrument pertaining to refugees, and which have these provisions incorporated into municipal law, is much the same. A refugee, like any other category of asylum seeker, can and often does find himself classified as an illegal immigrant.

Malaysia is in the unique position of having received asylum seekers from five different countries: Philippines, Vietnam, Kampuchea, Burma, and Thailand. Beginning in the late 1960s and continuing into the 1970s, Muslims from southern Philippines came to the East Malaysian state of Sabah. Two major movements took place, in 1972 and in 1974. The 1977 Census of displaced Filipinos recorded about 71,000 such persons, although the actual number at that time was estimated at 100,000 to 200,000, constituting approximately 10 to 20 percent of the total population of Sabah. The Vietnamese arrivals came in two major waves—the first immediately following the end of the Vietnam War, and the second beginning in 1978. They are still continuing to arrive, although in much smaller numbers. More than 250,000 have passed through Malaysia, and about 8,000 are still awaiting entry to third countries. Toward the beginning of 1981, about 500 Muslims from Thailand crossed the border into northern peninsular Malaya, simultaneous to the arrival of some 200 to 300 Muslims of Burmese origin. The Thai and Burmese arrivals have all since returned to their homelands. In the past few years Malaysia has also admitted two groups of 2,000 to 3,000 Kampuchean Muslims who had previously sought asylum in Thailand.

The responses of the Malaysian government to each of these groups has differed. The Filipinos, labeled "displaced persons" and "refugees," received identification cards, found occupations, and are rapidly assimilating into Sabah society. The Vietnamese have been classified "illegal immigrants" and were confined to special camps until their departure to third countries. At one stage, they were provided with rations and towed out to sea in the boats in which they had arrived. The Thai and Burmese were provided temporary asylum. The Cambodians were classified as refugees and accepted for permanent settlement in Malaysia. This essay examines and attempts to explain the Malaysian response to the Filipino and the Vietnamese arrivals—the two largest groups involved—and then considers the need for some international agreement applicable to these mass exoduses.

The Filipino Muslims in Sabah

The struggles of the Muslim Filipino against their Spanish and American colonizers has been extensively documented (Gowing 1977; Majul 1978; Tan 1968, 1977) The roots of the present conflict involving the Marcos government and the Muslim separatist groups in Mindanao lie in these earlier experiences and, in particular, in American-initiated efforts to exploit Mindanao. After the battle of Bud Bagsak in 1913 ended large-scale Muslim resistance to American imperialism, American designs for Mindanao, the

"Land of Promise," were quickly unveiled (Gleek 1974). A program of systematic settlement of the island was proposed, and the migration of land-hungry Christian Filipinos to the south was encouraged (Tan 1977:79).

Close on their heels came American and Japanese business interests, including rubber, pineapple, and abaca plantations. The vast Koranadel and Allah valleys in Cotabato Province were swamped with migrants, many on government-sponsored resettlement programs; this "provided the opening wedge for the massive and systematic exploitation of the vast natural resources of Mindanao" (Silva 1979:48). In the 1950s and 1960s prospectors, multinational industrialists, loggers, and local and national elites dispossessed Muslims, tribal Filipinos living in Mindanao's uplands, and even Christian migrant peasants of their lands through title frauds, tedious application procedures, and costly legal processes (Tan 1977:113).

Christian migration from Luzon and the Visayas into Mindanao before and after independence meant that the Muslim Filipino gradually became a minority in his traditional areas. Today, only four southern provinces have Muslim majorities. More disturbing to the Muslim Filipino is the fact that official government estimates place the number of Muslims at about 2 million, or less than 5 percent of the total population. Muslim sources, however, alleging "statistical genocide" and dismissing these figures as "colonial statistics," claim up to 5 million Muslim Filipinos (George 1980:225; O'Shaughnessy 1975).

The Kamlum uprising of 1951 on Jolo Island, the restriction of traditional free trade between Sulu and Borneo, the resettlement of Hukbalahap prisoners in Mindanao under the Economic Development Corps (EDCOR) program, the actions of the Philippine constabulary and army units, and the general neglect of the Muslim areas in government development programs all contributed to the feeling among Muslim Filipinos that they were on the verge of being physically overwhelmed by exploitative outsiders, both Filipinos and foreigners.

Clashes occurred in the late 1960s between the Ilagas (Rats), described as a "Christian" gang led by the notorious Kumander "Toothpick," and rival Muslim gangs called the "Barracudas" and "Blackshirts." Muslim Filipino resentment and anger peaked with the massacre of 28 Muslim army recruits on Corregidor Island in March 1968. In May of that year the Mindanao Independence Movement (MIM) was organized and secession was discussed (Noble 1976:409–10). By the end of 1971 the violence had claimed 800 lives, and there were 100,000 refugees (Gowing 1977:195).

The "Mindanao War" was one of the main reasons given by President Marcos for his imposition of martial law throughout the Philippines on September 1972. The Martial Law Proclamation held that because of:

> disorder resulting from armed clashes, killings, massacres, arsons, rapes, pillages, destruction of whole villages and towns, and the inevitable cessation of agricultural and industrial operations, all of which have been brought about by the violence inflicted by the Christians, the Muslims, the "Ilagas," the "Barracudas," and the Mindanao Independence Movement against each other and against

our government troops, a great many parts of the islands of Mindanao and Sulu are virtually in a state of actual war. . . . The violent disorder in Mindanao and Sulu has to date resulted in the killing of over 1,000 civilians and about 2,000 armed Muslims and Christians, not to mention the more than five hundred thousand of injured, displaced and homeless persons as well as the great number of casualties among our government troops, and the paralyzation of the economy of Mindanao and Sulu.

The first major armed clash in the south after the imposition of martial law was in October 1972 when, just days before the deadline for surrender of firearms, rebel Muslims calling themselves the "Mindanao Revolutionary Council for Independence" attacked Marawi City. Within a few months, fighting on Jolo Islands and in Zamboanga and Lanao, and carefully coordinated attacks by Muslim rebels in many municipalities in Cotabato Province, took place. These were countered by government use of force, which signaled the start of a new stage in the centuries-old struggle of Muslim Filipinos against what they perceived as "foreign" aggression. Now emerged the loosely knit organization known as the Moro National Liberation Front (MNLF), under whose umbrella gathered adherents of differing backgrounds and motivations, including personal, local, and provincial loyalties (Noble 1976:412). The MNLF Central Committee set broad policy outlines and managed an effective international campaign to gain worldwide recognition, support, and assistance. The fighting continues today.

In consequence of the fighting, two major waves of evacuees came to Sabah. The first, which crested in 1972, coincided with the declaration of martial law; the second, which peaked in 1974, coincided with the destruction of Jolo. But the actual number of Filipinos who entered Sabah is unclear. Although the 1970 Census recorded 20,367 Filipinos, most of these were economic migrants whose presence in Sabah predated the current conflict in the southern Philippines. This group does not cite the conflict as the primary reason for their presence in Sabah. The 1980 Census enumerates the Filipinos along with the indigenous groups in Sabah. Further, while the very large numbers of evacuees in 1972 were required to register upon arrival, following the official declaration by the Sabah government in October 1974 that their entry would be stopped, no further record of their numbers was maintained. The evacuees, nonetheless, continued to arrive.

In January 1977 the government of Sabah attempted to rectify this situation by launching a campaign to register all Filipino evacuees in Sabah. Instead of sending officers to the homes of the evacuees to record their numbers, the government merely urged the evacuees to present themselves at various central points. The accuracy of the figures compiled is suspect; furthermore, many evacuees, especially those who did not hold valid passes, did not register for fear of being repatriated to the Philippines. The January 1977 report of 71,000 evacuees in Sabah represents the minimum number. Estimates of their actual numbers vary from 100,000 (*The Star,* March 24, 1980) to 200,000 (personal communication, Ignatius Malanjun, President of Party Pasuk, Sabah).

Found mainly in the coastal urban centers, more than a third of the Filipinos are in Semporna, where they constitute more than 50 percent of the local population (Table 25.1). Another quarter of the Filipinos are in Sandakan. The others are confined to Kota Kinabalu, Lahad Datu, Tawau, and Kudat. These six urban centers and their environs contain almost 99 percent of the Filipino arrivals.

The initial arrivals were aided by the Sabah Social Welfare Services Department, which assisted in the distribution of food and provided health services whenever funds were available. The department's services were thought essentially *ad hoc.* In December 1976, the then-newly elected Berjaya State government set up a Department of Displaced Persons under the chief minister's supervision. At present, the department is headed by a director, assisted by a deputy director and a small clerical staff.

Several reasons may help to explain why both the Sabah and the Malaysian governments accommodated such large numbers of Filipinos. It has been said that the Malaysian government assisted the MNLF partly out of sympathy for the Muslim cause and partly because of Philippine's claim to Sabah (Noble 1976:409–10). The *Straits Times* of March 11, 1974, for instance, reported that

> The Philippines has informed Malaysia it has captured in Mindanao Filipino Muslims who claimed they were trained in Malaysia to fight in the south for secession from the Manila government . . . The sources claimed the Malaysians were extending support to the rebels to pressure the Philippine government to drop its claim on Sabah.

More tenable are two considerations that to date have not been given due weight in assessments of the motives of the Sabah and Malaysian governments. The first relates to the inclinations and role of Tun Mustapha, the chief minister of Sabah from 1968 to 1976. Tun Mustapha claims paternal lineage from the sultans of Sulu, through whom the Philippine government derived its legal claim to Sabah. Although the Sulus in Sabah constitute only

---

Table 25.1   Distribution of Displaced Filipinos in Sabah, 1977

Location	Number	Percent of total displaced Filipinos
Semporna	25,800	36.4
Sandakan	17,700	25.0
Kota Kinabalu	10,000	14.2
Lahad Datu	8,500	12.0
Tawau	6,500	9.2
Kudat	2,000	2.9
Elsewhere	500	0.3
Total	71,000	100.0

Source: Sabah, Survey of Filipino Displaced Persons, 1977.

5 percent of Sabah's Muslim population, like Mustapha himself nearly half the original Executive Committee in Sabah were Sulus. From the formation of Malaysia in 1963 until 1968, Sabah politics saw the population align itself into three groups: the indigenous Muslim population led by Tun Mustapha; the non-Muslim, largely Kadazan indigenous population; and the Chinese. By 1968 Mustapha's party, with federal support, had effectively overwhelmed its opposition. Mustapha displayed his commitment to spreading Islam among the non-Muslim peoples of Sabah, and embarked on a flurry of religious activity including the wholesale Islamization of the people of Sabah, regardless of their ethnic origin or of their professed faith. By 1972 some 50,000 persons had been converted, and by 1974 there were 93,000 converts. Indeed, Tun Mustapha himself claimed credit for increasing the percentage of Muslims in Sabah from 38.7 to 53 percent during his time in office.

Critics have charged that, under Mustapha, conversion to Islam was a prerequisite for success in almost any venture in Sabah. Tun Mustapha's supporters were accused of permitting only the practice of Islam in Sabah, using deceit and threats in converting animists bumiputras, utilizing government officials to disseminate Islam, expelling Christian priests and missionaries from the state, discriminating against government servants who were Christians, and even detaining Christians under Emergency Law (Jilil 1979:97). Priests who had been served expulsion orders and who had failed to leave Sabah had been detained. The departing bishop of Sabah alleged gross religious persecution. Tun Mustapha denied these allegations but throughout the rest of his time in office, religious persecution in Sabah was given extensive coverage in the international press. With the formation of Berjaya in 1975 and a more free press in Sabah, the issue received coverage in even the local press, and was a principal campaign issue in the Christian areas during the April 1976 elections, which Mustapha lost to Berjaya.

By declaring Islam the official religion of Sabah in 1973, Mustapha had disregarded one of the cardinal principles of the agreement for which Sabah politicians had sought guarantees at the time of Malaysia's formation in 1963. The first of these principles was: "while there was no objection to Islam being the national religion of Malaysia, there should be no State Religion in North Borneo, and the provisions relating to Islam in the present Constitution of Malaya should not apply to North Borneo." The Malaysian Constitution consequently specified that, though Islam would be the official religion for the entire federation, the Malayan constitutional provisions restricting the propagation of non-Muslim religions among Muslims were not to apply to Sabah and Sarawak. The Constitution further provided that, whenever the federal government gave financial aid to Muslim religious or educational institutions, a proportionate sum of tax money was to be returned to the Sabah and Sarawak governments.

By declaring Islam the official state religion of Sabah, Mustapha, theoretically at least, committed Sabah to practicing the teachings of the Holy Koran. Welcoming the Muslim Filipino evacuees from the fighting in the southern Philippines was thus a tangible declaration of submission to the words of God. Sabah and the Muslim areas of southern Philippines now constituted part of *daral-Islam* (Islamic territory), the defense of which is enjoined by the Holy Koran.

The second powerful factor determining the Sabah government's accommodative policy toward the Filipino arrivals was the severe labor problems the state was then facing. Sabah has a relatively small economy, and most of its development has been in directions offering mainly unskilled employment—timber production, estates, settlement schemes, construction, etc. By 1970, however, the education system was turning out an ever increasing stream of young people oriented toward white-collar jobs. The problem posed by this predisposition was compounded by the fact that in the early 1970s the economy of the state was, because of a rudimentary transportation system, not a single economy but a collection of enclaves centered around various population centers, each having minimal contacts with the others.

The shortage of labor was particularly acute in the estates and timber camps. In the estates the shortage had in part been met by migrant workers from the other Malaysian states, brought into Sabah on two-year contracts by the efforts of the Malaysian Migration Fund Board. The board, launched in 1966, had by the end of 1970 brought in more than 5,000 workers, plus their dependents. But despite the higher wages and the chances of entering land schemes, the majority of the workers went home upon completion of their contracts. By the early 1970s the scheme was fading away. The nearly 2,000 workers brought in in 1970 alone dwindled to 720 who arrived in 1971 and to 455 in 1972.

Despite the efforts of the Malaysian Migration Fund Board, the number of persons employed by estates with more than twenty workers fell from 13,295 at the beginning of 1966 to 11,577 at the end of 1970. In the rubber estates, the number dropped from 7,337 to only 4,703 in the same period. Particularly hard-hit were the smallholders who, unlike the larger estates, had been unable to take advantage of the scheme because of the high standard-of-living accommodation and wages required by the Labour Department and the Malaysian Migration Fund Board. Data are not available on the average acreage of rubber trees left untapped on rubber smallholdings where the problem was more severe.

The problem in the rubber industry reflected the situation in other economic sectors, and planners of the Second Malaysia Plan for Sabah, noting the state's chronic labor shortages at all levels, concluded:

> unless employers can manage to raise wages to a more attractive level, which, unless commodity prices rise substantially, seems unlikely in view of their high costs, estates will find it difficult to have sufficient workers without a large immigration of foreign workers who are prepared to work for lower wages. In spite of its unceasing efforts, the Malaysian Migration Fund Board has not solved the problem, though it has certainly prevented it from getting completely out of hand.

Official thinking was that not only could Sabah accommodate immigrants, it could not do without them. The arrival of the Filipino Muslims was therefore seen as the long-awaited solution to Sabah's labor problems. In November 1979, the Malaysian minister of home affairs declared that Sabah's labor force in the internal and remote areas had been considerably increased by the Filipino refugees (*New Straits Times,* November 20, 1979).

Although the causes and immense cost in lives of the conflict in the southern Philippines have been much discussed, as has been the concomitant social and economic dislocation, most accounts have concentrated on the immediate problems of the conflict at the expense of long-term implications for Mindanao, the Philippines, and Malaysia, as well as for the rest of the world.

For Sabah the presence of large numbers of Filipinos, even while satisfying the critical labor needs of the state, presents immense social and political implications. The Filipinos now constitute perhaps the second-largest community in Sabah, and their numbers tend to raise the percentage of Muslims in the state. The predominantly non-Muslim Kadazans, who consider themselves the "definitive people" of Sabah, feár that the influx of Filipino Muslims jeopardizes their tenuous claim to supremacy in Sabah.

The 1976 and 1981 election campaigns in Sabah indicate that the presence of the Filipinos is a divisive issue. The Kadazans are not alone in their fear. The Chinese, who are among the principal beneficiaries of the cheap labor of the Filipinos, have also been responsive to the alarm raised by the politicians. When, as is soon likely, the Filipinos cease being merely a source of cheap labor and by social and economic mobility become competitors, prejudice and unrest are likely among the local population. Even now, despite official denials, the Filipinos are held responsible for the alleged increase in crime rates (*New Straits Times,* ibid.). Clearly, the Malaysian body politic will continue to be plagued by the Filipino Muslim conflict and by the displaced persons who have arrived in Sabah.

The Vietnamese

The fall of Saigon to the Vietcong in April 1975 marked the beginning of a new era in the international flow of Vietnamese refugees. In the years that followed, no less than 1 million refugees—both ethnic Vietnamese and Chinese—poured out of Vietnam. At the 1979 U.N. ministerial-level Conference on Indochinese Refugees and Displaced Persons in Geneva, China claimed that she had accepted up to 250,000 Chinese Vietnamese. Most of the remainder took to the seas, and those who survived found their way largely to the ASEAN countries.

The first Vietnamese arrived in Malaysia in May 1975; by the middle of 1979 arrivals totaled more than 100,000 (see Table 25.2). Initial response to these arrivals was one of deep concern and compassion. The refugees were placed in camps in Trengganu, Kelantan, and Pahang on the mainland, and in Pulau Besar and Pulau Bidong. Under the auspices of the Red Crescent and in coordination with UNHCR, the refugees were provided for, and their admission into the country at this stage was not conditional on any guarantees for their eventual settlement elsewhere. The refugees enjoyed a certain freedom of movement.

Table 25.2   Vietnamese Boat People in Malaysia: Arrivals and Departures, 1975-1983

	Arrivals	Departures
1975	1,539	1,081
1976	1,793	356
1977	8,259	2,798
1978	59,183	15,956
1979	54,453	67,338
1980	18,274	40,014
1981	22,991	25,661
1982	14,853	16,654
1983 (until Aug. 8)	8,245	5,363

Source: UNHCR.

But the new government grew apprehensive as refugee numbers passed the 5,000 mark, and by November 1977 it adopted a new tough posture. The refugees were classified as "illegal immigrants"; the provisions of the Immigration Act prohibited their entry in Malaysia. The refugee camps were classified as restricted areas, the movement of those refugees outside these camps was curbed, and contact between the local populace and the refugees was prohibited. From November 1977 on, with increasing frequency, arriving Vietnamese refugee boats considered seaworthy were restocked with fuel and food supplies and towed back out to sea.

The new policy was a consequence of a number of developments both at home and abroad. The principal cause of the refusal to accommodate the refugees is explained by the numbers. More than two years after the communist takeover of Vietnam, the refugees were still coming, with no indication that the tide would abate. Malaysia feared a "residual problem," as departures of refugees to third countries was minuscule compared to the scale of arrivals (see Table 25.2). Worse, selection procedures of the third countries assured that the more trained and skilled among the refugees were chosen, leaving behind what Malaysian Home Affairs Minister Ghazali Shafie unkindly referred to as the "scum."

The large numbers of refugees placed a heavy demand on social services within the country. Antagonism in the relatively backward state of Trengganu culminated in the stoning of Vietnamese boats by villagers, who felt that the Vietnamese were accorded benefits that they themselves were denied. Malaysian Education Minister Musa Hitam explained that "the poor people in the East Coast feel the Vietnamese refugees have been taken care of much better than they themselves. The hospitals there are literally full of Vietnamese sick people and children at the expense of the local population" (*The New Straits Times*, November 29, 1978).

Local hostility increased during the fall of 1978 when, as a result of the influx, residents experienced difficulty in obtaining such essential items as matches, canned products, and bread. Traders preferred to deal at black market rates with the refugees or in bulk with the organizations catering for them, contributing to even greater inflation.

With the Vietnamese came a flood of gold and American dollars. But local banks were reluctant to buy American currency, fearing it to be counterfeit. The government ordered all refugee gold to be deposited with Bank Negara until the refugees departed for third countries. Nonetheless, dealings in gold and American dollars on the black market occurred. Perhaps of greater concern to Malaysia, whose stringent sanctions include the death penalty for the possession of firearms, were the weapons found among incoming Vietnamese. In Trengganu itself 526 guns, 14 grenades, and 51,000 rounds of ammunition were seized from the refugees between 1975 and 1978; during 1978, police seized 13 weapons and 103 rounds of ammunition from the Vietnamese boats anchored off Pahang.

In Malaysia, with the specter of communism ever present, the arrival of large numbers of principally ethnic Chinese refugees proved politically sensitive. Malay-based organizations and political parties urged the government to stem the refugee tide, and by December 1978 the parliamentary secretary to the Malaysian prime minister found it necessary to criticize "certain political parties for using the Vietnamese refugee issue to split Malay unity." He held that "the National Front has been accused of strategically inviting these refugees to the East Coast so that they will outnumber the Malay population" (*The New Straits Times*, December 28, 1978). Parliamentarians urged the government to take stiff measures.

To the other partners of ASEAN, the boat people problem was clearly not of the magnitude that it was to Malaysia. But in the latter half of 1978, the refugee exodus became a more critical problem. The Western media reported the existence of well-organized syndicates profiting from the flow of refugees. An Associated Press report in November 1978 stated:

> scores of Vietnamese families who fled to the US when Saigon collapsed in 1975 have started paying middlemen to arrange passage for relatives out of Vietnam. The exile grapevine has passed around phone numbers for contacts in Los Angeles who prove to be Vietnamese of Chinese ancestry. They accept names and addresses of relatives in Ho Chi Minh city selected for passage, along with the promise of US $ 2,000 for each person, payment in advance. . . . When the checks clear, the names are passed on to Hong Kong, where Chinese who have lived in Vietnam take over . . . they have access not only to ships but also to ethnic Chinese who are still in Ho Chi Minh City . . . these Chinese not only pay off the Ho Chi Minh City officials, but arrange for small fishing boats to pick the passengers up and rendezvous with larger craft at sea. . . . They sail across the South China Sea to Malaysia, where they have landed [*The New Straits Times*, November 20, 1978].

The arrival of the *Hai Hong* in Malaysian waters and the *Tung An* in Manila Bay, each with more than 2,000 refugees, lent credibility to these reports. This was no longer a haphazard flow of desperate refugees fearing reprisals at home, but permanent emigrants who found the political and socioeconomic climate in Communist Vietnam unacceptable and consequently bought their way out themselves or through relatives overseas. Organized syndicates obviously operated in collusion with Vietnamese officials. The departure points were often in public places, and the emigrants were assisted into increasingly larger boats by Vietnamese government officials and soldiers. That such public acts could take place without the sanction of the increasingly all-encompassing communist machinery is unlikely.

Malaysian officials saw the increase in refugees in part as an attempt by Vietnam to maintain control of its population in the face of the particularly severe economic problems of 1978 and 1979. Vietnam, it was believed, was pushing people out both to overcome a shortage of food and to divest itself of an urban middle class that the communists felt to be an implacable enemy. Furthermore, in view of the Sino-Vietnamese conflict, Hanoi appeared to be determined to rid itself of its Chinese minority. Taxing these departees and organizing the traffic, it was estimated, earned Hanoi approximately US $115 million for the year preceding June 1979—about 2.5 percent of its total estimated gross national product.

More sinister than these internal factors for Hanoi's participation in the refugee traffic was what some observers perceived to be Vietnam's plan to throw Southeast Asia off balance, with a view to eventual domination. This theory, consistently held by Singapore and occasionally sounded by its other ASEAN partners, began to be more common among ASEAN officials toward the end of 1978. Vietnam's intentions aside, the refugee tide was causing considerable destabilization in Southeast Asia.

The immediate cause for a joint ASEAN effort came from developments within the organization itself. Malaysia, faced with an ever-increasing number of refugees and with growing protests from politicians, began to turn away the refugees, who threatened to inundate the shores of its ASEAN partners, in particular Indonesia. In the face of Indonesian sensitivities, Malaysian Home Affairs Minister Ghazali Shafie held: "If one ASEAN country drives away the illegal immigrants another will get them. I am most determined that the boat people should not be the cause of acrimony amongst ASEAN and that ASEAN must approach this subject together to find a permanent solution" (*The New Straits Times*, December 8, 1978).

In mid-November 1978 Malaysian Foreign Minister Tengku Ahmad Rithaudeen discussed the Vietnamese refugee problem with his ASEAN counterparts when they were in Brussels for the European Economic Community–ASEAN dialogue. Initial progress was slow; a month later there was still no consensus among the ASEAN partners. Said Indonesian Foreign Minister Mochtar Kusumatmaadja: "We are still deliberating through the consensus process. It's slow, but it works" (ibid., December 10, 1978).

In January 1979 a special meeting of ASEAN foreign ministers on Indochina Refugees was held in Bangkok. The communiqué issued after the meeting restated the problem, sought greater international aid and refugee intake into third countries, and called upon Vietnam to tackle the problem at source. Despite Ghazali Shafie's statement of January 17th that the ASEAN foreign ministers had decided on a common approach to the problem, the Indonesian foreign minister revealed a month later that no overture had yet been made to Vietnam on the refugee issue, since talks between ASEAN members were still in a preparatory stage. He further revealed that discussions would be taken up with the UNHCR only after consensus on the refugee problem had been reached among ASEAN members.

In the meantime, following what had already been aired in Kuala Lumpur, Malaysia proposed at the Geneva Conference on Refugees in December 1978 that a processing center be established on a Pacific island. Despite initial skepticism among conference members as to its viability, the Indonesian and Philippine governments each offered an island for such a center, and in March 1979 conditions were issued for the establishment of such an island by Indonesia and the Philippines. These conditions were that a firm commitment be granted by third countries that no residual problem would result, and that the cost of development, maintenance, and administration of the center, as well as of logistic requirements including transportation and transfer of the refugees to the proposed site from the ASEAN countries, would not be borne by the host country. The host country would retain sovereignty, control of administrative and security matters, and the right to limit the number of refugees at the center according to the responses from third countries.

In May a 24-nation ASEAN conference met in Jakarta to discuss the proposed center, in particular the suitability of Galang Island in Indonesia's Riau Province south of Singapore. The Indonesians insisted on stringent conditions for the center: it would be open only to refugees already approved for eventual resettlement in third countries, and would accommodate a maximum of 10,000 people. Constituted that way, it could have been nothing more than a holding center for what was then a week's outflow from Vietnam, which was clearly far short of Malaysian and Thai expectations. Malaysia and Thailand at least obtained agreement that "consideration would be given to the ASEAN countries of first refuge most severely affected by the refugee problem."

The most significant aspect of the 1979 conference was that ASEAN had invited Vietnam to attend, in an attempt to draw Hanoi into a discussion of the problem. The Vietnamese delegation was extended every courtesy and the other delegates were urged not to confront Vietnam. It was clearly an attempt by ASEAN to begin and maintain a dialogue with Vietnam and to persuade Vietnam not to push its entire Chinese minority of about 1.5 million into fishing boats and out to sea. Despite the overtures, Vietnam was not in a relenting mood. Confronted by no complaints by conference delegates, the Vietnamese offered bland sympathy and the hope that the day would soon come "when the difficulties and privations of the first days have been eliminated and the responsibility and patriotism have awakened so that there will be no more reason for these Vietnamese to leave the country" (*The New Straits Times*, May 21, 1979). Furthermore, the Vietnamese delegation announced its willingness to let an estimated 600,000 aspiring emigrants leave—clearly more a threat than a statement of liberal immigration policy.

The proposed island processing center advanced only to the stage of a feasibility study. The boat refugees poured into ASEAN countries at the greatest pace ever. Within the first two weeks of May 1979, 9,000 reached Malaysia, almost 7,000 arrived in Indonesia, and 1,000 found their way to Thailand. In June both Malaysia and Indonesia announced tougher measures. Indonesia's "Operation Lightning," with its headquarters in Tanjung Pinang (25 miles south of Singapore), coordinated the efforts of twenty-four naval vessels, air force patrol craft, and ships of the Tax and Customs departments to force the new arrivals back to sea.

In Malaysia, Deputy Prime Minister Dr. Mahathir Mohamad announced measures aimed not only at preventing further arrivals but also at putting back to sea the estimated 73,000 Vietnamese in the country as soon as "we have the boats ready." The deputy prime minister is also reported to have said that the government might as a last resort consider shooting the Vietnamese as they entered Malaysian waters (ibid., June 16, 1979). This statement appeared all the more shocking in view of the controversy over the sinking, at the end of February 1979, of a boat with 230 Vietnamese off Pulau Pemanggil on the coast of Johore. The UNHCR representative in Kuala Lumpur said that one of the rescued Vietnamese had suffered a gunshot wound and implied that it had been the work of the Malaysian navy. Malaysia denied these allegations, but whatever the cause of the tragedy, the resulting row marred Malaysia's humanitarian image.

The deputy prime minister's statement drew extensive criticism abroad and led to an urgent cable from U.N. Secretary-General Kurt Waldheim. Prime Minister Hussein Onn's reply stated categorically that Malaysia's measures to prevent further inflow of the boat people did not include shooting them, but that "any boat carrying Vietnamese illegal immigrants, that tries to enter Malaysian waters or attempts to land, will be towed away and given assistance to proceed on its journey" (ibid., June 19, 1979). He also left open the possibility that unless there was a fall in the number of arrivals and a greater readiness by third nations to accept the refugees, those already in the country could find themselves expelled.

In the meantime, the government of the United Kingdom, facing an influx of Vietnamese refugees into Hong Kong, called for a U.N. conference on the refugee problem. In Washington, the House of Representatives unanimously approved a resolution urging President Carter to seek an emergency U.N. meeting. Despite opposition from Vietnam, Waldheim, obviously taken aback by the measures of the ASEAN countries, called a ministerial-level meeting in Geneva for July 1979.

At a private meeting with Malaysia's delegation leader two days prior to the conference, Hanoi's representative agreed to contain "for a while" the emigration of refugees, undertook to consider Malaysia's proposal that a processing center be set up in Vietnam to regulate the flow of refugees, and agreed to implement Hanoi's seven-point agreement with the UNHCR on a program of "orderly departures" from Vietnam. At the conference the Vietnamese suggested that processing centers could also be established in American-controlled Guam Island, Chinese-controlled Hainan Island, and on Japan's Okinawa. Without conceding anything, and indeed arguing that her free emigration policy was in accordance with basic principles of human rights, Vietnam thus used the conference to bargain for greater international aid.

The "orderly departure" program agreed between Vietnam and the UNHCR was of little relief. Under this arrangement, only those with children or relatives living abroad, who had been given entry visas by foreign governments, who were not awaiting trial in Vietnam, and who were not in important government positions were allowed to leave. Selection was based on lists given to the UNHCR by Vietnam and the receiving countries; only names on both lists qualified for exit. This could hardly satisfy the needs of the bulk of the aspiring emigrants. Those still in Vietnam were unlikely to receive priority, which would be given by first-asylum countries to those already on their soil. Leaving Vietnam by boats still appeared a better option, and thus the outflow continued.

Reflections on the Malaysian Experience

Malaysia's responses to asylum seekers from the Philippines and from Vietnam have differed markedly. Numbers, the nature of the relationship between Malaysia and the source countries of these arrivals, ethnicity, religious affiliation, labor requirements, and local political attitudes, rather than the plight of the asylum seekers, determine the response of Malaysian officials and society to these peoples. In an attempt to explain the inconsistency in dealing with the arrivals from Vietnam vis-à-vis those from the Philippines, the then-Malaysian Home Affairs Minister Tan Sri Ghazali Shafie told Parliament that:

> Filipinos who come to Sabah to seek sanctuary are given refugee status because their presence will not have adverse effects on the peace and order of the country . . . illegal immigrants from Vietnam could not be given similar status [and] protection because the government felt that their presence could have adverse consequences on the country [*The Daily Express*, November 24, 1979].

Malaysian immigration laws are designed to enable the government of the day to decide which groups will be granted asylum, regardless of the plight of the asylum seeker. Similar laws operate in most countries which are not signatories to international covenants and treaties pertaining to refugees. Reluctance to grant asylum and refugee status and failure to become a signatory of refugee conventions results from a number of considerations. To grant refugee status implies a new bond between the refugee and his new state of residence and imposes obligations on both. The 1951 Convention and the 1967 Protocol, for instance, oblige the state concerned to grant to the refugee rights no less than those of its own nationals in the following matters (UNHCR 1975b):

- Freedom to practice their religion and freedom as regards the religious education of their children (Art. 4);
- protection of industrial property, such as inventions, designs or models,

trade marks, trade names, and of rights in literary, artistic, and scientific works (Art. 14);

- access to the courts, legal assistance, and exemption from *cautio judicatum solvi* (Art. 16);
- the right to engage in wage-earning employment after three years of residence, or to have a spouse or child possessing the nationality of the country of residence (Art. 17);
- rationing (Art. 20);
- elementary education (Art. 22);
- public relief and assistance (Art. 23);
- labor legislation and social security (Art. 24); and
- duties, charges, or taxes (Art. 29).

The signatories of the conventions are obliged to extend in all other matters rights applicable to nationals of a foreign country or to aliens in general. In return for these obligations the refugee undertakes to conform to the host state's laws, regulations, and measures taken for the maintenance of public order (Art. 2). The contracting parties to the Convention clearly undertake responsibilities with political implications. When large numbers of refugees are involved, significant financial costs are incurred, plus local antagonism and the use of the refugee issue for political purposes. In such circumstances states can, and often will, refuse asylum to mass exoduses.

The U.N. Protocol on Refugees adopted in 1967 (resolution 2312 (XXII), recognizes that the granting of asylum to persons claiming persecution is a peaceful and humanitarian act and as such cannot be regarded as unfriendly by any other state. To many governments, however, the granting of asylum implies the recognition by one state of another's acts of persecution, and this cannot but strain relations. Often such a strained relationship leads to accusations and conflicts between neighboring states. For instance, the presence of Filipino refugees in large numbers in Malaysia led to Filipino charges that the Malaysians were harboring Filipino criminals and indeed assisting the separatist movement in the southern Philippines.

Because massive displacements of population have occurred within national boundaries and across them, demographic pressures in many parts of the world are leading to population dislocations that often produce interstate tensions. Mass exoduses are on the increase. Underlying all these movements are common problems of uprootedness, insecurity, and hardship. But it would be impossible to extend refugee status and the concomitant obligations to all categories of persons. It thus becomes necessary to differentiate refugees from the other categories of asylum seekers and migrants. Doing so would ensure that the special plight and circumstances of the refugees are not compromised by the considerations inevitably present when host nations are faced with mass exoduses.

The office of the U.N. High Commissioner for Refugees currently handles refugees and all mass exoduses. Yet when the U.N. General Assembly created UNHCR and gave it a mandate to protect and assist refugees, it was intended to be a short-term mandate to solve what was believed to be a residual problem resulting from World War II. Successive renewals of this and other mandates have kept the organization functioning, and have extended its competence to handling mass exoduses of persons other than refugees. A principal problem facing UNHCR has been a shortage of funds: when UNHCR was established in 1951, the General Assembly ruled that, except for a small regular budget subsidy for administrative costs (and which currently covers barely one-third of such costs), UNHCR should be totally dependent on voluntary contributions. This hand-to-mouth, precarious form of financing makes fund-raising difficult, particularly in view of the dramatic increase in requirements over the past few years. While in 1978 UNHCR spent voluntary funds totaling $135 million, in 1981 voluntary funds expenditure amounted to $474 million. The increased functions and the catering for the several categories of mass exoduses, cannot but exacerbate the plight of the refugee.

It would be an opportune moment to consider whether present funding for UNHCR is prudent and effective. To address the problem in all its dimensions would help apportion international aid rationally and arrive at a satisfactory methodology for facilitating solutions to the problems of the groups concerned. In this context it is encouraging to note that among the issues examined in the course of the 38th session of the U.N. Commission on Human Rights (1982) was the Human Rights and Massive Exoduses, a study by special Rapporteur Sadruddin Aga Khan, a former U.N. High Commissioner for Refugees. The Commission requested the secretary-general to transmit the study to the General Assembly for consideration, and has called for comments on the study.

The plight of the refugee is real and distressing. The compulsion to move from his home to an unknown future, often at short notice, by subterfuge and without protection, is sufficiently traumatic without his having to face rejection, and worse, *refoulement*. Yet this is the risk that refugees face when they are lumped along with other categories of asylum seekers and classified as illegal immigrants.

26

Thailand's Refugee Experience

Netnapis Nakavachara and
John Rogge

The recent massive forced migration of refugees into Thailand is but a continuation of a process of population displacement in Southeast Asia that has affected Thailand for nearly two centuries, and especially since resistance to French colonialism in Indochina developed in the early part of this century. Refugee migrations into Thailand have periodically surged, decreased, and reintensified in a seemingly endless repetitive pattern. Thailand's reaction to these in-migrations has likewise ranged from hospitality and acceptance to resistance and outright hostility. The purpose of this essay is to review briefly the historic influxes, to describe the scale and problems associated with the current Indochinese refugee crisis, and to evaluate the policy options now facing the Royal Thai government as it watches rates of third-country resettlement decline while the number of refugees being maintained in Thailand's holding camps remain constant.

Thailand's Refugees Prior to 1975

Thailand's refugee experience goes back for two centuries. At least four waves of Vietnamese refuge seekers had entered Thailand prior to World War II (Varophas 1966). As early as 1785, a group of Vietnamese sought "royal protection" in Thailand. They were followed in the 1820s and 1830s by religious refugees: Vietnamese Catholics who were fleeing persecution by the Vietnamese emperor Minh-Mang. In the closing decade of the century, when the French occupied parts of eastern Thailand during a campaign to induce Thailand to cede Lao territory to France, Vietnamese entered Thailand in the wake of the French forces. When the French finally withdrew, many Vietnamese remained.

A fourth Vietnamese migration into Thailand began in 1912, and over the following 30 years, as resistance to French colonialism grew, refugees from the conflict zones entered Thailand to settle in Nakhorn Phanom province. Until 1937 these migrants, like their predecessors, readily acquired Thai citizenship and in general became assimilated fully into Thai society. Their descendants are usually referred to as the "Old Vietnamese." Their number was estimated by Poole (1970) at around 20,000, and their degree of integration is evidenced by the fact that some attained high ranks in the Thai military or civil service (Poole 1967a). After 1937, however, a treaty between France and Thailand resulted in the refugees remaining French subjects, and as such, had to be registered as aliens.

Following World War II, Thailand once again was faced with accommodating persons seeking refuge from neighboring countries. When Thailand was forced to withdraw from western Cambodia, which Vichy France had ceded to it in 1940, departing Thais were joined by Vietnamese who had also settled in these territories. These migrants were followed by large waves of refugees who fled renewed fighting between the reestablished French colonial authorities and the much-strengthened Viet Mihn, as well as with the Lao Issara (Free Lao). As many as 46,700 refugees are believed to have entered Thailand between 1946 and 1949 (Poole 1967b).

During the 1950s, the number of Vietnamese in Thailand continued to grow as a consequence both of natural increase (estimated to have been in excess of 3 percent per annum) and from further influxes of refugees from both Laos and Cambodia in the dying days of the Franco-Indochina war. While in the early postwar years Thailand permitted refugees to settle, after 1949 its attitude toward the Vietnamese hardened; in the early 1950s they were restricted to only five northeastern provinces. Fears intensified that the Vietnamese, through their overt support of the Viet Minh, were creating a Communist fifth column within Thailand, and the security concern associated with refugees has continued to pervade Thai policy since then. Although some of these Vietnamese migrants were repatriated to North Vietnam in the early 1960s—some 35,000 returned—the repatriation process was brought to an abrupt halt by the Gulf of Tonkin incidence in 1964, so that by the end of the decade natural increase had almost made up for the numbers that had repatriated. Although no precise figures are readily available, it is commonly believed that as many as 80,000 Vietnamese were still in Thailand in 1975, when the current Indochinese refugee influx began.

Other refugee migrations also flowed into Thailand in the post–1945 period, from Burma, China, and even a small influx from Malaya. Chinese refugees began to arrive in Thailand in 1949 following Mao Tse Tung's victory. These were primarily remnants of Chiang Kai Shek's army, although some civilian refugees also arrived. The Kuomingtan forces—estimated at around 11,000 persons (Jones 1976)—settled in remote communities in the northern frontier areas, where they quickly established themselves as "war lords" controlling the "golden triangle's" opium trade. They created a serious security threat to Thai authorities, and even in the late 1970s, skirmishes between the Thai military and Chinese-controlled irregular forces were not infrequent. In contrast, most of the Chinese civilians that entered Thailand at that time quickly and successfully integrated into local Chinese urban communities.

Burmese have also entered Thailand as refugees in a number of waves. Since Ne Win's military takeover of Burma in 1959, insurgency has intensified throughout Burma. Many of the hill tribes that straddle the Thai–Burmese border continue to be engaged in guerrilla war with the Burmese central government, and consequently they periodically seek refuge across the Thai border when central government forces launch offensives against the guerrillas. The number of refugees waxes and waves, and few are ever assisted by either Thai or international agencies. There have been no official enumerations of these refugees, although in the late 1970s they were believed to have numbered around 13,000 (Thomson 1980). Thai authorities do not appear to be overly concerned about these hill tribe refugees.

The same cannot be said about the movement across Thailand's southern border with Malaya in the late 1950s. As the Communist emergency in Malaya was brought under control, a small number of guerrillas fled into southern Thailand, where they were able to blend among local Muslim and ethnic Malay populations. The ongoing insurgency in the southern border area plagues Thai authorities, and much of the blame for this continuing confrontation is placed upon the few migrants who sought refuge in southern Thailand in the late 1950s and early 1960s.

Thailand thus had a long history of refugee migrants prior to the post–Vietnam War influx of the late 1970s. Moreover, it had to cope with these past in-migrations without any external assistance. In spite of the threats that some of these migrations posed to its own security, Thailand was generally prepared to accept the migrants, at least until an opportunity for repatriation materialized. Given this historic experience, one may question why Thailand adopted its apparent intransigent position toward the contemporary Indochinese refugee dilemma. To understand this position, one must not only contemplate the scale of the post–1975 influx, but also appreciate the delicate balance that the Royal Thai government attempts to maintain between adherence to its humanitarian principals, on the one hand, and exercising its responsibility to the perceived security threat that the refugees pose, on the other hand.

The Post–1975 Refugee Problem

In contrast to other ASEAN countries, Thailand has had to cope not only with the post–1975 diaspora of boat people, but with a massive influx of land people from neighboring Laos and Kampuchea. In consequence, Thailand has carried the single largest refugee burden of any of the ASEAN states.

Arrivals

The current influx into Thailand began within days of the fall of Saigon in mid-1975. In the remaining months of that year, more than 75,000 Indochinese refugees entered Thailand, most coming from Laos (Table 26.1). In the following two years the rate of arrivals slowed to approximately 35,000 per annum, but in 1978 the rate of influx began to accelerate, peaking in 1979 at 200,000. The high rate of arrivals was maintained in 1981, but declined

dramatically after 1982. This surge during 1979–1980 in Thailand corre-
sponded with the crisis years of refugee influx experienced throughout the
region. Yet whereas other ASEAN countries were dealing exclusively with
the dispersion from Vietnam of boat people, Thailand was primarily concerned with refuge-seeking land people from Laos and Kampuchea, although the boat people influx was by no means small in Thailand, either.
Renewed warfare in Kampuchea after the fall of the Pol Pot regime in 1979,
together with the acute famine conditions that were the legacy of the years
of Khmer Rouge control, were responsible for the arrival of some 180,000
Khmer in Thailand in 1979 and 1980. As is shown in Table 26.1, during the
peak years of Indochinese refugee in-migration from 1975 to the end of 1982,
close to 600,000 refugees arrived in Thailand. Since then, some 60,000
additional refugees have arrived, bringing the total from 1975 to December
1985 to some 652,000 (see Table 26.2). This total is more than four times
greater than the total influx experienced by any other ASEAN country and
represents about half of the overall post–1975 Indochinese diaspora (Rogge
1985b).

Refugees in Thailand are enumerated by ethnicity: Vietnamese (no distinction is made between Sino-Vietnamese and ethnic Vietnamese, even
though the former dominated during the crisis years), Kampucheans,
lowland Lao, and highland or hill tribe Lao. Of these, the Kampucheans
have been by far the largest group (see Table 26.2). In addition to the
officially recognized Khmer refugees, another quarter-million are displaced
persons scattered in a number of camps along the Thai–Kampuchean
border. These do not feature in any data on Thailand's refugees, since their
sojourn is regarded as temporary only. Nor do these Khmer displacees
come under the jurisdiction of UNHCR: although they are assisted by the
United Nations Border Relief Organization (UNBRO), which is a subagency

Table 26.1   Arrival of Indochinese Refugees and Displaced Persons during the Peak

Category	Cumulative 1975 to Dec. 1982	1975	1976	1977
Kampuchean	215571	17038	6428	7045
Lowland Lao	167137	10195	19499	18070
Highland Lao (Hill tribe)	108727	44659	7266	3873
Vietnamese	95154	4446	5213	5328
Total arrivals	586589	76338	38406	34316
of which				
Boat people	71426	72	2627	4536
Land people	515163	76266	35779	29780
(Number of boats)	(2044)	(NA)	(NA)	(202)

Source: UNHCR, Bangkok.

of UNDP. Although regarded only as temporary sojourners, their presence in the border area is very real and adds to the prevailing tension and insecurity.

The lowland Lao have been the second most numerous group of refugees in Thailand (see Table 26.1). Moreover, while the rates of arrival of other groups declined dramatically after 1981, lowland Lao have continued to arrive in steady numbers: some 32,500 crossed into Thailand from 1983 to 1985, and lead to a serious questioning by Thai authorities of the legitimacy of their "refugee" status. Many are clearly economic migrants.

The arrival of hill tribe Lao was greatest immediately after the fall of Laos to the Pathet Lao in 1975, followed by a secondary wave in 1979. Some 116,000 hill tribe Lao have arrived in total, and although their influx is now only modest, the growth of this refugee community causes concern because of its inordinately high rates of natural increase and its lowest rates of third-country resettlement.

The smallest of the four groups of refugees have been the Vietnamese, of whom a little over 100,000 have arrived since 1975. Although they are Thailand's least numerous Indochinese refugee population, Thailand has been the third most important destination for Vietnamese after China and Malaysia. Only in 1981 did Vietnamese constitute the majority of refugees arriving in Thailand in a single year.

It is clear that Thailand continues to be a major destination for Indochinese refugees. In 1984 and 1985 it received close to half of the total Indochinese exodus, excluding Vietnamese leaving under the Orderly Departure Program (ODP): in 1984, 43,199 refugees left Indochina and 21,141 arrived in Thailand, and in 1985 the numbers were 45,539 and 22,592 respectively (UNHCR 1986). Such data contribute to Thailand's increasing concern and fear of long-term commitment to Indochina's refugees.

Years, 1975–1982

1978	1979	1980	1981	1982
3528	137894	43608	16	14
48781	22045	28967	16377	3203
8013	23943	14801	4356	1816
8818	16119	26491	22511	6228
69140	200001	113867	43260	11261
6301	11887	21549	18378	6076
62839	188114	92318	24882	5185
(212)	(282)	(573)	(556)	(219)

Table 26.2   Thailand's Total Refugee Influx, 1975 to December 1985

Total arrivals	652,397
Total departures[a]	−521,967
Balance Remaining December 1985	*130,430*
By Ethnic Origin	
Lowland Lao	199,668
Highland Lao (hill tribe)	116,217
Vietnamese	108,606
Kampucheans[b]	227,906

[a]Includes repatriation.
[b]Does not include displaced persons in border camps.

Source: UNHCR, Bangkok.

Departures

Of the 652,000 refugees who have entered Thailand since 1975, close to 80 percent subsequently departed (see Table 26.2), either for third-country resettlement (the greater majority) or for repatriation or "relocation." The Vietnamese have enjoyed the highest success rates in the resettlement process, with more than 90 percent having departed. Moreover, the interval between arrival and resettlement is shortest among Vietnamese, averaging less than one year (Public Affairs Foundation 1986). The lowland Lao have also experienced relatively high resettlement rates (77 percent), although rates of departure have slowed considerably in the last two years. Some 67 percent of the Khmer have been resettled, and the hill tribe refugees have experienced the poorest resettlement rate: only 57 percent have so far departed Thailand for permanent overseas asylum. They also appear to take the longest processing time, averaging three to four years (ibid.).

Resettlement opportunities in the traditional refugee receiving states have declined dramatically from the halcyon days of 1980 and 1981. "Compassion fatigue" is commonly cited as the reason for this decline, especially with regard to resettlement through private sponsorship. Nevertheless the growing competition from other refugee areas has contributed to this decline as more and more recipient countries create discrete regional quotas for their annual refugee intake. During 1985 a total of 53,493 refugees were resettled from Southeast Asian countries, yet this resulted in little or no overall decline in the region's refugee population, since 45,539 new refugees arrived and natural increase was high. In December 1985, the regional refugee population was 159,664, down only 543 from the previous year. Thailand's proportion of this "residual" population was 81.7 percent (Table 26.3).

Concern about reduction in resettlement rates was also increased by fear that arrivals throughout the region would again surge following Vietnam's unilateral termination of the Orderly Departure Program (ODP) in early 1986. Some 24,900 Vietnamese left Vietnam under the ODA in 1985 (and

Table 26.3   "Residual" Refugee Case-Load in Southeast Asia, December 1985

	Number of refugees remaining	Percent of total
Thailand	130,413	81.7
Hong Kong	9,443	5.9
Malaysia	8,456	5.3
Indonesia	6,568	4.1
Philippines	2,744	1.7
Japan	857	0.5
Macao	677	0.4
Singapore	235	0.1
Korea	208	0.1
China	63	0.03
Total, December 1985	159,664	100
(Total, December 1984	160,207)	

Source: Refugees, UNHCR, February 1986.

some 29,000 in 1984), and the specter that many more Vietnamese will once again escape by boat is becoming very real.

Thailand has also experienced some departures through repatriation and relocation. Although repatriation does not currently appear to be an attractive option for Vietnamese or hill tribe Lao, lowland Lao and Khmer have repatriated in some numbers. Up to December 1985, 2,835 Lao had voluntarily repatriated. Thailand has seen repatriation as the only viable option other than resettlement, and has been especially forceful in applying this concept to Khmer refugees. Shortly after the massive influx of Kampucheans commenced in 1979, some 42,900 refugees were forcibly relocated across the Kampuchean border, in an exercise aimed primarily at deterring other Khmer refugees from seeking refuge in Thailand. International outcry halted further relocations, but voluntary repatriation continues to be strongly promoted by Thai authorities. In total, 32,457 Khmer have returned voluntarily between 1980 and January 1986 (Public Affairs Foundation 1986). But the Vietnamese-controlled Heng Samrin government remains unsympathetic to large-scale repatriation, fearing that returning refugees will be hostile to it or even join opposition forces. The larger population of displaced Khmer that entered Thailand in early 1985, and who are temporarily accommodated in UNBRO-administered camps inside Thailand but close to the border, are all destined for relocation across the border as soon as the military situation there permits. Thailand is not a signatory of the U.N. Convention or Protocol on Refugees and hence is not bound by any of the international instruments dealing with *refoulement*. Thus there is growing concern among some relief agencies in Thailand that "residual" Khmer refugees at the Khao I Dang camp not accepted for resettlement by December 1986 will also be relocated to the UNBRO camps and thus destined for eventual repatriation.

Current Case Load

International response to the refugee problem during the crisis years of 1979 to 1981 resulted in most of the huge influx into Thailand and other ASEAN states being resettled by late 1982 or early 1983. By mid-1983, Thailand's case load had been reduced to less than 150,000 land people and a little less than 10,000 boat people. Also, the number of camps and reception centers had been greatly reduced: from more than thirty in 1981 to seven by 1986 (Figure 26.1). Yet the rate of reduction in the case load has slowed, partly because of reduced resettlement intake by the West, and partly because of high rates of natural increase among remaining camp refugees. The case load by mid-1986 was down by only about 4,000 from one year earlier (Figure 26.2). The largest group continues to be the hill tribe Lao (if the Khmer in the UNBRO camps are excluded), and the Vietnamese have declined to only 7,731. Several camps were closed during the first half of 1986, and their residual populations consolidated in other camps or at the Phanat Nikom processing center. While the total number of refugees declined by only 1.7 percent in the twelve-month period ending May 1986, the number of refugees accepted for resettlement and awaiting departure dropped from 9.8 percent to 7.7 percent in the same period (see Figure 26.2).

In consequence of this declining rate of departures, Thai authorities reassessed the policy in early 1986, the net effect of which has been a liberalization of rules regarding which refugees are eligible for resettlement. While the policy during 1985 continued to stress the need to focus resettlement on the backlog of earlier arriving refugees, and did not permit recent arrivals to be considered for resettlement, by mid-1986 virtually all refugees were eligible for interview by potential resettlement agencies, regardless of their date of arrival in Thailand. This policy modification was received favorably by agencies anxious to resettle "acceptable" refugees from the pool of hitherto restricted refugees, but it also has raised concern for the refugees who are not likely to be accepted in the current round of interviews, and that residual populations may be relocated to the border for eventual repatriation.

Political Versus "Economic" Refugees

An issue of increasing concern is that of distinguishing between legitimate political refugees, who are eligible for refugee status as defined by the U.N. Convention, and other migrants who have little or no well-founded fear of persecution, but are migrants whose motives are essentially economic. While "convention" refugees clearly fall into a category of migrants induced to move by political push factors, many refugees arriving in Thailand since the crisis years are migrants responding as much to economic pull factors in Thailand (and because of the prospect for resettlement, the pull factor of the West) as they are to political push factors in their home areas. In comparison to Indochina, Thailand's economy is very dynamic; it therefore acts as a magnet to migrants from less fortunate neighboring states.

Nowhere is this contrast more stark than along the two banks of the

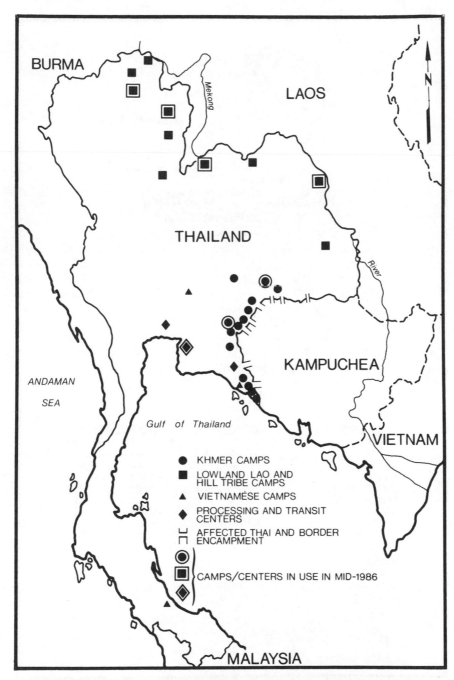

Figure 26.1   Location of Refugee Camps/Centers During Peak Influx Period

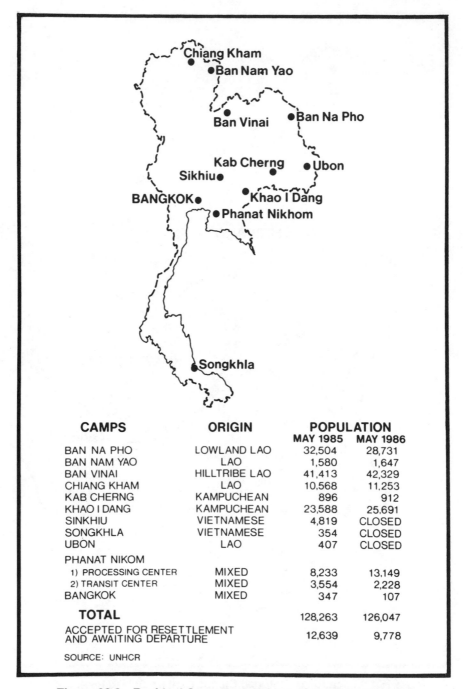

CAMPS	ORIGIN	POPULATION	
		MAY 1985	**MAY 1986**
BAN NA PHO	LOWLAND LAO	32,504	28,731
BAN NAM YAO	LAO	1,580	1,647
BAN VINAI	HILLTRIBE LAO	41,413	42,329
CHIANG KHAM	LAO	10,568	11,253
KAB CHERNG	KAMPUCHEAN	896	912
KHAO I DANG	KAMPUCHEAN	23,588	25,691
SINKHIU	VIETNAMESE	4,819	CLOSED
SONGKHLA	VIETNAMESE	354	CLOSED
UBON	LAO	407	CLOSED
PHANAT NIKOM			
1) PROCESSING CENTER	MIXED	8,233	13,149
2) TRANSIT CENTER	MIXED	3,554	2,228
BANGKOK	MIXED	347	107
TOTAL		128,263	126,047
ACCEPTED FOR RESETTLEMENT AND AWAITING DEPARTURE		12,639	9,778

SOURCE: UNHCR

Figure 26.2   Residual Camp Populations, May 1985 and 1986

Mekong River. The flow of migrants across the river from Laos to Thailand during 1984 and 1985 prompted Thai authorities to introduce individual screening of all Lao refugees to differentiate bona fide refugees from economic opportunists. In the first twelve months of this screening process, some 1,100 Lao were found not to be bona fide refugees and were promptly relocated to the border to await repatriation to Laos. The problem is complicated by the fact that many Lao attempt to integrate spontaneously among Thai ethnic Lao who live in the border areas. It is not often recognized by outsiders that there are more ethnic Lao living in Thailand than there are Lao living in Laos. Hence it becomes relatively easy for some Lao to establish themselves in Thailand, especially in the remote northern areas. As long as economic disparities between Thailand and its neighbors remain acute, the specter of further influx of economic refugees will remain real.

Policy Options

Because of its geographic location, Thailand will continue to remain a likely destination for refugees from Southeast Asia. This factor is appreciated by the Royal Thai government, and is the basis for the principal thrust of the current policy that emphasizes that third-country resettlement and repatriation are the only two acceptable options for refugees arriving in Thailand. This policy was succinctly summarized in May 1986 by Prasong Soonsiri, the secretary general of the National Security Council:

> that Thailand will give assistance to refugees in accordance with humanitarian principles so long as it does not adversely affect Thai sovereignty, national security, and national interests, and will provide temporary shelter while refugees await transfer to settlement in third countries or return to their homeland under the voluntary repatriation plan. The Thai government does not have any policy for refugees to have permanent residence in Thailand.

Thailand continues to pressure Western governments to increase resettlement quotas to clear the backlog of refugees. Periodic hints that residual refugees will be repatriated if not accepted for resettlement perhaps are made more to stimulate Western states to step up their rates of resettlement than as discreet policy objectives.

Moreover, one must appreciate that the prospects for resettlement or repatriation vary with each of the four ethnic refugee communities. The Vietnamese continue to have the highest success rates for resettlement and are seen as the refugees with the least prospects for repatriation. Success in resettling Vietnamese has resulted in the closure of the Sonkhla and Sikhiu camps in 1986. Lowland Lao also had reasonably high success rates for resettlement in the past, but this trend has changed recently. Fewer of the remaining Lao are of urban origin, educated, or skilled, and hence are less likely to be considered acceptable for resettlement. On the other hand, many of the residual Lao are regarded as having good prospects for repatriation. For many there appears to be no great risk of persecution should they opt to return to Laos.

For the Khmer, the prospects for resettlement vary, and for repatriation are intimately tied to the continuing political and military crisis in Kampuchea. Until early in 1986, Khmer refugees at Khao I Dang—the principal holding camp—were divided into three classes: (a) those arriving before 1981 and who were eligible for resettlement; (b) those arriving between 1981 and August 1984, who were legally entitled to be in the camp but were ineligible for resettlement until the backlog of earlier arrivals had been resettled; and (c) the arrivals after August 1984, who were in the camp illegally and, if caught, were transferred to the UNBRO-administered border camps. Most of those remaining in the camp since 1981 were refugees who had been rejected for resettlement; many had been rejected by more than one country. In contrast, many of the ineligible refugees would have been accepted for resettlement readily if permitted to apply. It is clear that Thailand implemented this policy because it was fearful that the cream of the refugees would be resettled and it would be left with the residuals: the orphans, the handicapped, the aged, the unskilled, and the politically suspect. This is a legitimate concern, and one not unique to Thailand. The relaxation of this policy in 1986 is resulting in more Khmer being accepted for resettlement, but will certainly result in a pool of residuals who face a very uncertain future.

There is also little prospect that the political climate in Kampuchea will change in the near future and permit the border camp population to repatriate. The Heng Samrin regime recognizes that some of its main opposition forces exist among displacees in the border camps, where all three factions of the opposition are represented: the Khmer Rouge, the nationalists under Sihanouk, and Sonn San's Khmer Peoples National Liberator Front. The risk of long-term border conflicts resulting from the existence of this opposition in the border camps is well founded, as shown by several incursions into Thailand by Vietnamese military during 1986. Analogies are beginning to be made with the Palestinians, and there is already talk of a "refugee nation" (van der Kroef 1984) situated along the Thai–Kampuchean border, its government being the U.N.–recognized "Democratic Kampuchea." It is understandable that Thailand is pressing the international community to do more to ensure that Kampuchea's political problem be resolved so that the displacees can return home.

The hill tribe refugees also present an intractable problem. While many of the residual Khmer wish to resettle but are simply not being accepted, many of the hill tribe refugees are unwilling to resettle, even though the U.S. has been especially lenient to this group in applying its selection criteria for resettlement. This reluctance to resettle is due both to a strong commitment to return to Laos, and staying close to the border reinforces this commitment, and to negative feedback from refugees who had earlier settled in the U.S. On the other hand, the Hmong, who make up the greater majority of the hill tribe refugees, have much to fear from repatriation. Having been intimately linked with the U.S. during the latter years of the Indochina war, the Hmong would almost certainly risk persecution by the present Laotian government if they were to return. Consequently, the Hmong present Thailand with a dilemma: they are unwilling to resettle, unable to repatriate, yet cannot stay in Thailand. In the meantime their population grows at an alarming rate due to inordinately high natural increase.

Thailand's emphasis on resettlement of refugees has also created a paradox. As long as resettlement to the West takes place, Thailand continues to be a magnet for refugees. Hence the introduction of the "humane deterrence" policy in mid-1981. Under this policy, newly arriving refugees were confined to austere prisonlike camps and were ineligible for resettlement until the backlog of earlier arrivals was cleared. While this policy was initially aimed primarily at the Vietnamese boat people, who would in theory then choose other destinations, it was subsequently applied to all arrivals. It achieved little in the way of reducing the inflow in Thailand, however, nor has it reduced the size of the residual refugee population, many of whom have now been in Thailand for more than five years, and among the Hmong, for as much as ten. At the same time the policy has tarnished Thailand's image as a country with a "humanitarian" philosophy. It is regrettable that Thailand's policy has often been condemned without first considering the context in which Thailand was pressured to adopt it. No sovereign state can indefinitely absorb displaced populations, especially when such migrations exacerbate existing economic or political difficulties.

The relaxation of the humane deterrence policy in 1986, and the extension of eligibility for resettlement to all refugees (but not the Khmer border-camp displacees) are steps that will clearly enhance Thailand's image, and may also increase rates of resettlement, at least temporarily. Yet it is unlikely to result in any massive decline of the overall number of refugees and displacees in the near future, and in the long term, Thailand will still face the problem of a residual refugee population. Whether Thailand will ever relax its stand on local settlement is a issue of considerable conjecture. Official policy suggests not; yet if the number of residuals were ever to be reduced through resettlement or repatriation to a more tolerable level, and on the basis of Thailand's historic responses to its displaced neighbor, at least some of the remaining refugees, such as the Hmong, might find permanent asylum in country.

27

Forgotten Refugees: Postwar Forced Migration Within Southeast Asian Countries

Graeme Hugo

Southeast Asians who have fled to havens within national boundaries have attracted little attention from researchers and international assistance agencies, although the problems and consequences associated with their movement have frequently been more significant than those created by the international movements. Many theoretical and applied issues relating to international refugee migrations are equally relevant and applicable to migrations that terminate within the country of origin. To understand forced migrations and to initiate policies and programs to cope with the associated problems, one gains a major advantage by viewing refugees as a subtype of a more ubiquitous form of involuntary mobility within Third World countries. The failure to do so is to compartmentalize the study of the phenomenon into internal and international migration and to hinder cross-fertilization of ideas between scholars working in the two fields.

Whereas the term "refugee" is used popularly to refer to all persons fleeing from war and civil strife, researchers and international agencies usually define a refugee as outside his country. This is one case where the popular conception of a social phenomenon seems eminently more reasonable than the professional one. Still, little or no attempt has been made to examine localized refugee movements within developing countries and regions. This essay reviews evidence drawn from a wide variety of sources regarding such migration in the Southeast Asian region, identifying the major types of forced internal relocations in Southeast Asian countries during the postwar period, and examining two case studies to denote the significance of internal refugee movements for social change and economic development within those countries. The final section explores significant similarities between intra- and international forced migrations with respect

to the problems and consequences that flow from these movements within
Southeast Asia.

One major difference between refugee migrations beyond national
boundaries and within national boundaries is the better quality of data
relating to the former, since some form of registration almost always occurs
upon the arrival of the refugee in the country of asylum. In contrast, no
large Southeast Asian country has an accurate population registration
system nor, since migration usually occurs in a time of crisis, is it surprising
that few accurate data are available regarding the scale and composition of
refugee movements within countries.

Postwar Refugee Migrations Within Indonesia

The largest country in Southeast Asia has experienced virtually the full
gamut of conflict-induced refugee flows during its three decades of independence. Several of the refugee movements discussed here occurred
during the 1950s and 1960s and were given particular prominence in the
main review of migration published during that period (McNicoll 1968).
Many of these conflict-induced refugee flows also led to the establishment,
when normalcy returned to the areas, of chain migration linkages between
areas of origin and refuge, which acted as conduits for much larger, later
migration flows.

The upheavals associated with World War II and the subsequent struggle
for independence produced substantial population dislocation in Indonesia
during the 1940s, as indicated by fluctuations in the population of the capital
city of Jakarta (Figure 27.1). The increase in population during the Japanese

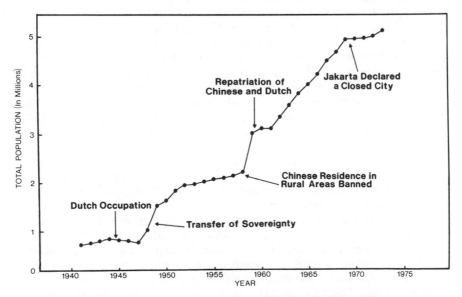

Figure 27.1   Jakarta: Population Growth, 1940–1975

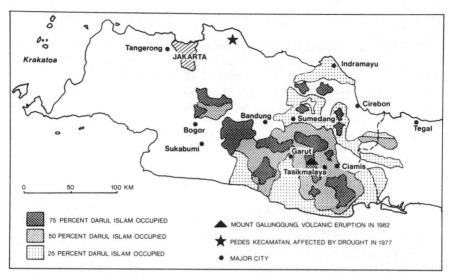

**Figure 27.2   West Java: Location of Areas under Darul Islam Control in
1954**

occupation (1942–45) resulted partly from an influx of rural dwellers from
nearby West Java (Figure 27.2), who were fleeing harsh requisitioning of
agricultural products and labor recruitment policies (Heeren 1955:704; van
der Kroef 1954: 157–58). A backflow to the villages occurred after the defeat
of the Japanese and the reestablishment of Dutch control.

With the transfer to sovereignty in December 1949, the city experienced
very rapid growth due to in-migration. The Chinese also migrated to Jakarta
due to financial uncertainty and maltreatment in the villages (van der Kroef
1954:158). This movement to the cities counterbalanced to some extent an
outflow of repatriated Chinese city dwellers to China. The decline after 1960
resulted partly from this emigration of Chinese aliens.

In his review of the growth of Indonesia's cities over the 1930 to 1961
period, Goantiang (1965) stresses the importance of refugee movements in
swelling the population of many of Indonesia's cities over that period. He
cites a 1954–55 field survey undertaken in Jakarta: "the findings prove that
the main reason why people move to Jakarta is the prevalence of lawless
disturbances in the interior." The case *par excellence* of refugee movement
being a major element in rapid urban and metropolitan growth in Indonesia
is that of Bandung in West Java.

Bandung was Indonesia's fastest growing city between 1930, when its
population was 166,815, and 1961, when it had reached 972,566. The
intervening period was marked by massive fluctuations. As in Jakarta,
Bandung experienced marked growth during the Japanese occupation due
to the push exerted by the social and economic disruption wrought by the
Japanese (Hugo 1975:252). In 1945–46 the Japanese surrender, the declaration of Indonesian independence, and the arrival of allied troops in Ban-

dung initiated much population movement. First was a massive in-movement from all over West Java of Dutch persons freed from Japanese internment camps, so that there were 60,000 Europeans in the city in November 1945 (Smail 1964:99), more than twice the prewar peak. For the following two years Bandung was effectively divided into two cities, separated by railway tracks passing through the city center. To the north was the European enclave guarded by British troops, and to the south the Indonesian section. Between November 1945 and March 1946, when fighting associated with the struggle for independence was at its height, 100,000 Indonesians moved out of the north sector, while Europeans and some Chinese settled in the north. In addition, there were substantial evacuations, mostly of women, children, and older people, from the southern sector into villages to the south. They were replaced by several thousand young men from all over Priangan taking part in the struggle against the Europeans. An additional group who moved to Bandung from surrounding rural areas at this time were village officials who were unpopular for having enacted oppressive Japanese policies and now sought refuge in the city (ibid.:122).

In March 1946, following an ultimatum by the British, Bandung was evacuated of Indonesians and large sections of it destroyed. Within four months approximately half a million people moved from Bandung and its environs into rural areas of Priangan. Bandung remained an essentially European-Chinese city until the beginning of 1948, when much of West Java was put under Dutch control. Many men followed the Republican army to Yogyakarta or joined guerrilla units operating in mountainous parts of the province. Despite these moves Bandung's population grew rapidly during the period of Dutch occupation.

With the transfer of sovereignty a decade of rapid growth began for Bandung, whose population almost doubled. Official figures of natural increase and net migration (Abdurachim 1970:5) show that, on average, 62.5 percent of each year's growth was due to net migration gain. Initially there was a return of soldiers and evacuees who had left when the Dutch reoccupied Bandung, as well as those who, after the excitement of life as a guerrilla, were unwilling to return to their villages. More important, particularly in the mid-1950s, was a population movement to Bandung (as well as to other West Java urban centers) caused by the insecurity of many rural areas due to the Darul Islam rebellion, which lasted from 1948 until 1962.

The Darul Islam revolt began when a group of soldiers, who had previously fought against the Dutch, rebelled against the newly independent government with the objective of making Indonesia an Islamic state. Similar revolts in south and southeast Sulawesi, Aceh, and South Kalimantan were loosely associated with the rebellion (McNicoll 1968:44). The rebellion established control over much of the eastern highland section of West Java and adjacent areas of Central Java, although at its height its impact was felt all over West Java. Figure 27.2 shows the Indonesian army's official view of the areas that were in rebel hands in May 1954. Initially Darul Islam adopted a campaign of terror and sabotage against the government but, as years went by, this degenerated into terrorizing and plundering gangs who could not return to normal life in society (Boland 1971:61). They caused much devastation of life and of property; economic opportunities inevitably shrank in rebel-threatened or rebel-controlled areas, as roads and railways became unsafe and as peasants limited their output of food crops in response to rebel requisitions (McNicoll 1968:44). This produced substantial refugee movement toward areas protected by the army. Accurate figures of the numbers are not available, but provincial authorities put the total number of refugees at 215,700 over the 1951 to 1956 period and at 52,672 in the last quarter of 1951 alone (ibid.).

The influx of refugees to West Java's cities in the 1950s resulted in their exceptionally rapid growth. The population registration figures for Bandung show the city increasing from 592,825 in 1949 to 1,028,245 in 1960 (Abdura-chim 1970:5). These figures undoubtedly understate the influx of refugees, however, since many did not register and others subsequently returned to their homes. The rapid increase in population and buildup of urban refu-gees placed great strain on Bandung's resources. Housing was under stress: in 1959, there were twelve persons in Bandung for every house (Rasjik 1972:4), and Lontoh (1964:51) estimated that in 1964 at least 11,000 houses in the city were illegally built without permission on government or private land. The seriousness of the growing pressure on city resources moved the authorities to attempt to stop the flow of people by declaring Bandung a "closed city" on March 1, 1954. Although the regulation stayed in force until September 1964, its major effect, like a more recent attempt in Jakarta, was to dissuade migrants from registering as permanent residents.

Figure 27.3 shows the impact of the refugee movements on Bandung's growth. The upper graph depicts net migration gains calculated by Abdura-chim (1970) from registration statistics maintained by the city. The lower graph presents results from a study undertaken in 1968 of population registers in the subdistricts of Bandung, in which was recorded the year of arrival in Bandung of migrants still living in those two subdistricts in 1969. While both sources are incomplete, they indicate the major patterns of forced migration to the city. Peaks of in-movement are evident at the time of the transfer of sovereignty from the Dutch, the onset of the Darul Islam rebellion in the early 1950s, and the mid-1950s decline in registration due to the closing of the city. An upswing occurred in 1965, again largely due to refugee movements—people displaced by the violence and disruption caused during the attempted coup—although the dislocation was not as great in West Java as elsewhere in Java and Bali.

The implications of the refugee movement to Bandung during the 1950s are considerable. The city experienced perhaps the most rapid rate of growth of any major city in Southeast Asia during the 1950s. In fact, population projections of the world's cities larger than 1 million by the U.N. Population Division (Bose 1974:40–41; Frejka 1974:10–11) designated Ban-dung as the fastest growing city in the world and projected that by 1985 its population would increase to 4.1 million. (This did not prove to be the case.) While the refugee movements were a major catalyst in the growth of Bandung, McNicoll (1968:45) suggests that the impact of such influxes of refugees is essentially temporary. Nonetheless, field investigation in Ban-

A. BANDUNG MUNICIPALITY: ANNUAL NET MIGRATION 1950-1968

B. BANDUNG MUNICIPALITY, KECAMATAN ASTANAANJAR AND LENGKONG: YEAR OF ARRIVAL OF RESIDENT LIFETIME MIGRANTS, 1969

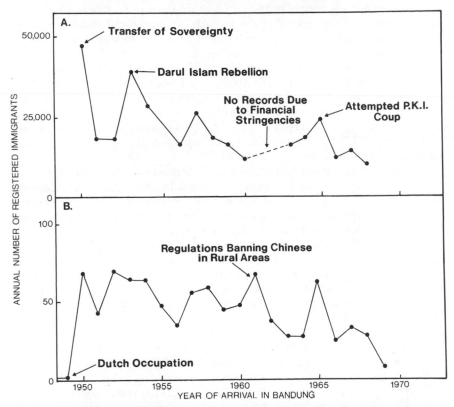

Figure 27.3 The Impact of Refugee Movements on Bandung

dung indicates the opposite. Although most rural-urban refugees moving to Bandung intended to return to their home villages when security was restored, the longer their period of insecurity away from their home place, the more likely they were to settle permanently in their urban refuge. Certainly, many refugees to Bandung returned to their villages as soon as security was restored, but Bandung registered no massive net migration loss when normalcy returned to its hinterland. Thus, at least among those refugees who were sufficiently committed to Bandung to register as citizens there, it was common to remain in the city after security was restored in their home villages. Indeed, many of the linkages between that city and particular parts of rural West Java were originally established by refugee moves during the 1950s. These consisted first of links with Bandung-based family members who had moved in as refugees, had settled and remained, but still maintained strong contacts with their natal villages. Second, even refugees who returned to their home villages commonly did so with a greatly enhanced knowledge of the city and of its opportunities, and with some contacts with urban-based people.

Other refugee movements were induced by ethnic-based conflict. The substantial displacement of ethnic Chinese refugees in postwar Indonesia is an example. It is apparent that the growth of Jakarta and Bandung in the 1950s was assisted by the displacement of Chinese from West Java. Chinese were subject to great pressure in several areas; indeed, at the end of the decade legislation was passed forbidding Chinese and other foreigners to operate a business or own land in rural parts of the province, thus forcing all remaining Chinese to migrate to the cities (Hugo 1978:53). In 1960, Chinese residents in Indonesia were forced to choose between Chinese and Indonesian citizenship, and as a result many Chinese returned to China. Of the net emigration of 142,653 Chinese nationals between 1952 and 1961, 102,197 emigrated in 1960 (Hugo et al. 1982:82).

As mentioned earlier, similar, although less substantial, movements to the Darul Islam–displaced refugees occurred in other parts of Indonesia during the 1950s. The smallest was in the province of South Kalimantan, where insecurity in the mountainous interior precipitated refugee migrations to the cities of Banjarmasin (McNicoll 1968:48) and Samarinda (Goantiang 1965:56). Both cities recorded very rapid rates of growth between the 1930 and 1961 Censuses, with Banjarmasin's population more than trebling and Samarinda growing by more than 600 percent. The rebellion in 1953 in Aceh created an estimated 60,000 refugees (McNicoll 1968:47) in neighboring North Sumatra. Although most returned to Aceh in the late 1950s, a significant minority remained and settled permanently.

The other area to experience an Islamic rebellion was South and Southeast Sulawesi, where insecurity extended from 1951 until 1965. This rebellion was accompanied by much terrorization of the local population, not only by rebels but also by wild gangs who roamed the countryside (Harvey 1974:268). At the peak of their power the Darul Islam controlled the bulk of the countryside and encircled the major cities, leaving only Makassar (now called Ujung Pandang) effectively under government control. During a single offensive in 1957 in Southeast Sulawesi, 40,000 refugees were forced to flee to the city of Kendari (ibid.:376). As with other internal refugee movements in Indonesia, much of the migration was directed toward the towns and cities remaining in government hands. Throughout the 1950s, for example, Makassar's annual rate of population growth approached 10 percent, due primarily to this influx of refugees. Similar rapid rates of growth were recorded in other local urban areas, and many of the migration chains, along which permanent and temporary migrants are currently moving to the city, were established by refugees during the years of the rebellion.

The latter applies also to much of the movement of Bugis and Makassarese out of South Sulawesi, especially to Jakarta and the east coasts of Sumatra and Kalimantan. McNicoll (1968:46) quotes reports of 10,000 Sulawesi-born refugees in the provinces of Jambi and Riau in 1956 and of another 5,000 along the coast of East Kalimantan. Lineton (1975a:180–81) quotes a Bugis businessman who arranged accommodation and transport for most Bugis migrants passing through Jakarta from the early 1950s, and who claimed that the rebellion led to a flood of emigration that peaked in 1955: in that year, more than 10,000 migrants passed through the port of Jakarta on their way to Sumatra, generally traveling in large parties of 45 or more.

Several other conflict-induced refugee migrations occurred in Indonesia, including several moves associated with the struggle for independence against the Dutch. In Java much movement focused on the capital of the guerrillas, Yogyakarta. Elsewhere, the typical pattern was for people to flee from the Dutch-controlled coastal areas to the interior, movements similar to those described by Naim (1973:135) in West Sumatra. Several short-lived rebellions immediately followed the granting of independence and initiated refugee flows, which involved former members of the colonial army of West Java, South Sulawesi, and Maluku (McNicoll 1968:43). Some 4,000 Ambonese (South Moluccan) soldiers and their families (totaling 12,500 persons) fled to the Netherlands, along with a larger number of Indonesians of mixed Dutch-Indonesian parentage. By the early 1980s, the South Moluccans in the Netherlands had grown to 35,000 (Woldring 1980:55). Other groups of refugee flows are associated with the Permesta rebellions in Central Sumatra and North/Central Sulawesi, respectively. These separatist rebellions were inspired by the belief that the Java-focused central government neglected the interests of numerically smaller groups located on the periphery. Although these conflicts were fairly shortlived, they initiated some significant refugee flows (Naim 1973:139). McNicoll (1968:49) points out that these flows tended to be dominated by the educated sections of the population, while those forced to move by the Darul Islam rebellions tended to be more representative of the total resident population in the conflict areas. Activities of separatist movements such as the Free Papua Movement (OPM) also initiated refugee flows from Irian Jaya, including a substantial flow into neighboring New Guinea (Garnaut and Manning 1974; Roosman 1980).

For many conflict-induced movements little or no information is available. In 1965, for example, the attempted coup by the Communist Party of Indonesia was quickly suppressed by the army, followed for several months afterwards by violent and widespread reprisals against communists and affiliated organizations (McNicoll and Mamas 1973:15), which led to significant refugee flows. More recently, Indonesia's annexation of East Timor in 1975 caused its inhabitants great violence and dislocation. In fact, its population, according to the 1980 Census, was considerably less than at the 1970 Census (552,954 compared to 610,541). Up to half of the population of East Timor was displaced during the second half of the 1970s, with some 20,000 fleeing overseas after the outbreak of violence in 1975, mostly to Portugal or Australia (Rodgers 1981:18). Others fled to West Timor, and in 1979 25,000 remained there (Rodgers 1979:5). In late 1978 an estimated 125,000 East Timorese had passed through or were still living in squalid refugee camps, and officials estimated that as many as 100,000 more could be hiding in the mountains (Jenkins 1979:29). By 1979 malnutrition and hunger were rife and death, commonplace, and the condition of more than

half the population living in East Timor was described by experienced relief
agency workers as "bad to critical" (ibid.:24).

Refugee Migrations in the Southern Philippines

In the Philippines, as in Indonesia, significant postwar conflict-induced
refugee movements have gained virtually no outside recognition, especially
in the migration literature. The largest of these movements was on the
island of Mindanao. Mindano has experienced considerable insecurity since
the declaration of martial law in 1972. The first official estimates of the extent
of the devastation resulting from the civil war were given by President
Marcos in 1977, when he indicated that 30,000 to 50,000 civilian deaths had
occurred, and from 500,000 to 1 million refugees had been displaced from
their homes and land. One of the provinces most influenced by the
devastation was Zamboanga Del Sur, which in 1980 held 1.18 million of
Mindanao's population of 10.9 million.

The causes of the insecurity over the last decade in Zamboanga Del Sur
are very complex and have evolved over a long time period. As Lewis
(1975:6) points out, the problem is generally and unfairly referred to as the
"Muslim problem," whereas "The major shortcoming in Mindanao is its
backward economy and the existence of a small affluent sector side by side
with a far larger subsistence group. The weak economy led to communal
misunderstandings and a breakdown in law and order, which spawned
hundreds of thousands of refugees and paralysed industry and commerce."

The origins of insecurity, therefore, are largely socioeconomic and political. This is reflected in the fact that although the Moro National Liberation
Front (MNLF) gains most publicity, other significant elements are in the
area. The Maoist New People's Army (NPA) is active in the northeast and
northwest of the province in remote areas geographically ideal for guerrilla
activity. Other more peripheral elements adding to local insecurity are
pirates and smugglers, and bandits in the mountainous interior. Moreover,
the activities of the army and of other military groups in declaring free-fire
zones and carrying out vengeance killings added greatly to the insecurity of
the residents of the region.

Migration is the most significant process shaping Zamboanga Del Sur's
contemporary social structure and ultimately underlying its major social
problems. Before the Spanish penetration of the Philippines, small Muslim
settlements were strung along the coast, and small inland groups of pagan
Subanon practiced slash-and-burn agriculture. The Spanish failure to subju-
gate the Muslims and endemic malaria combined to suppress Mindano's
population growth until the late nineteenth century, when some migrants
from the Visayas settled along the north coast. This movement increased
under American rule prior to World War II. Immediately after the war,
however, the growing pressure of population on land resources in the
Visayas and Luzon, the control of malaria, and the relative security of the
region produced a substantial in-movement into Mindanao, where, between 1948 and 1960, the population doubled to 5.4 million and increased
from 13.8 percent to 19.9 percent of the total Philippine population. For the

first time Zamboanga Del Sur was a major reception area for incoming migrants to Mindanao. It increased its population from 354,000 to 742,000 and its share of the total Philippine population from 1.84 percent to 2.74 percent. The migrants were overwhelmingly Visayan Christians (predominantly Cebuano).

Zamboanga Del Sur's rapid growth continued during the 1960s, with each year during the 1960s experiencing a net migration gain of more than 1 percent per annum. Thus in Zamboanga Del Sur more than half the population are either migrants from outside the province or children of such migrants. The Christian newcomers have come in such numbers in the postwar period that the former dominant groups of the province (the Muslims and the Subanon) have become minority groups locally.

The pattern of population movement in Zamboanga Del Sur has been transformed with the post–1972 deterioration in security. Although the in-movement of Visayans continued, one of the dominant forms of migration is now the movement, on both a long-and short-term basis, of refugees. The 1975 Census reported that the province's population had increased by 18 percent to 734,633, thus maintaining the growth rate of the 1960s. But the census enumerators were not able to enter several villages which were in MNLF or NPA hands, where estimates were made on the basis of 1970 figures; these almost certainly are overestimates, because these are precisely the areas the refugees have fled. Nevertheless, several municipalities located in the coastal regions where MNLF groups were most active did experience absolute population declines between 1970 and 1975. The location of critical areas can be determined from Figure 27.4, which shows villages where schools had to be closed in 1976 and where census enumerators could not enter in 1975.

The refugee movements initiated by the insecure situation have occurred both within and outside the province. It is clear, for example, that part of the rapid growth of the population of Pagadian City between 1970 and 1975 (17.2 percent) resulted from an influx of refugees, especially Visayan groups from the eastern sections of the Baganian peninsula. There have been other movements to safe areas. The total number of refugees is not known, but it is clear that the Visayan refugees have either relocated to another safer part of Zamboanga Del Sur or, less commonly, they have returned to relatives' houses in Misamis (in northern Mindanao) or even in the Visayas. This pattern clearly indicates the tenacity of family ties between Visayan migrants and their origins. These ties are the links along which much chain migration into Zamboanga Del Sur had occurred. They also are the links along which the refugee "retreat" from the settlement frontier has taken place.

The Muslim refugees are often in a worse situation, because they have been settled in the coastal areas for a much longer period and hence often have no relatives in safe areas to whom they can turn for shelter and assistance. Muslim refugees have tended to move outside the province of Zamboanga Del Sur to a far greater extent than the Visayans. The most significant movement, however, has been to Zamboanga City, where in July 1974 40,000 refugees were reported. At the time of the 1975 Census the city's

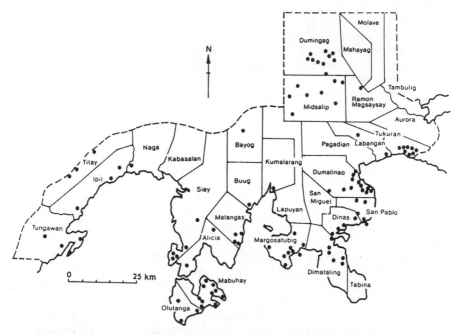

**Figure 27.4   Zamboanga del Sur: Location of Main Barangay with an
Unstable Peace and Order Situation, 1976**

population was 261,978, an increase of more than 31 percent over the 1970
population; much of the increase is attributable to the influx of refugees.
Newspaper reports since the Census have indicated an increase in the
refugee flow to the city.

A further destination of Muslim refugees is East Malaysia. During the
period 1972 to 1977, Sabah recorded the arrival of some 40,000 Muslim
refugees from the southern Philippines. In 1971, half of the population of
Sulu Province to the southwest of Zamboanga Del Sur had moved away,
mainly to Sabah. By 1980 an estimated 120,000 Filipino refugees were in
Sabah, and "the Filipinos, still pouring in, cannot be turned away, since
they have been given refugee status" (*Far Eastern Economic Review*, July 18,
1980).

The losses resulting from refugee migrations are of course enormous.
Once highly productive fields have been deserted and have become over-
grown with weeds. A few refugees in Pagadian make occasional daytime
trips to their fields to harvest their crops but return to Pagadian City at
night. The army frequently declares insecure barrios "no man's land,"
meaning that after a certain time anyone found in the barrio will be shot on
sight. This has meant that in some cases people have not only been forced to
evacuate, but also they are refused access to their lands and their crops rot
on the ground. Land owners and tenants are given no compensation and
are compelled to somehow survive, even though they have been forced

away from their source of livelihood. The influence of insecurity on agricultural production in many barrios has thus been very severe.

The displacement of refugees in the southern Philippines is not restricted to Zamboanga Del Sur. In all provinces of Mindanao in which there are significant numbers of Muslims there have been refugee flows. For example, in 1976 in Maguindanao 50,000 individuals had been made homeless, while in Davao the rapid growth of Davao City was facilitated by incoming refugees. The NPA activity and an intense army anti-guerilla campaign on the island of Samar in the eastern Visayas has also produced substantial refugee flows in recent years. Between 1978 and 1981 three major evacuation waves involved 600 families, 50,000 people, and 6,000 people, respectively, in which much of the displacement has been caused by search and destroy military offensives (Ocampo 1981:30).

The Significance of Internal Refugee Flows

The major postwar flows in Malaysia, Burma, Thailand, Laos, Kampuchea, Vietnam, Hong Kong, and Singapore have been reviewed elsewhere (Hugo 1983:49–67) and support the evidence presented here that internal refugee movements have occurred and are occurring on a very large scale in the Southeast Asian region, and that these movements are of considerable social, economic, and demographic significance. Moreover, there are many intrinsic similarities between these internal refugee movements and international refugee migrations in Southeast Asia. Speare (1974:89) suggests that one of the major differences between the two types of migration, and hence one of the reasons for differentiating between them, is that, were we to plot the distribution of moves along an involuntary-voluntary continuum, the internal moves would fall near the voluntary end of the continuum, whereas the international moves would be spread out with a larger number near the involuntary end.

An approach that lumps all types of international migration together and then compares them to internal movement imposes a structure on migration research that gives excessive importance to whether a migrant has crossed an international boundary. Instead, our understanding of the causes and consequences of population redistribution is more likely to be advanced if we adopt an alternative approach. This approach starts from the more fundamental and meaningful base of differentiating population movement according to the underlying forces that impel them. This does not mean that we ignore the significance of international boundaries, but it does suggest that we not impose a structure likely to distort the findings of our research. Migrations arising from conflict, as defined earlier in this essay, are frequently more appropriately studied as such, regardless if they happen to traverse an international boundary.

Pryor (1981:125) suggests five themes on which the possible integration of international and internal migration theories may be pursued:

1. Who are the migrants?
2. Why are they migrating?

3. What are the spatial or societal patterns of migration in terms of origin and destination?
4. What are the consequences of migration?
5. What are the policy and human rights issues associated with or influencing the migration?

On Pryor's first point we have little information for refugee migrants within countries, although this is not the case for international refugees, most of whome pass through international agencies and national immigration offices. Judging from the evidence in Southeast Asia, there may be similar patterns of differentials. Kunz (1981:49), for example, typifies anticipatory (international) refugee moves as being "composed almost solely of the well informed, well to do and well educated." Over time this selectivity is likely to be lessened somewhat. The difference is that conflict-induced refugee movements within countries are more likely than would international refugee flows to develop into mass flight involving little or no selectivity. The key element in selectivity appears to be whether the refugee migration is, in Kunz's (1973) terms, anticipatory or acute, not whether internal or international migration is involved. Selectivity on the basis of religion, ethnicity, and race is equally prevalent among both types of movement. An element of difference appears to apply more at the level of destination than of origin of the refugee flights. Third countries may apply (and be able to enforce) rigid criteria of health, education, occupation, skill, etc., in accepting international refugees for resettlement. A telling example is Thailand's acrimony over the non-acceptance by third countries of large numbers of unskilled Cambodian and Laotian refugees (McBeth 1982:49).

On Pryor's second point of the cases of migration, by definition no differences exist between internal and international refugee migration. The concept of conflict arising out of civil, political, religious, ethnic, and racial confrontation is central to the definition of a refugee and differentiates a refugee from other migrants, not whether he or she crosses an international boundary.

The third issue of the patterning of the flows is an interesting one. Kunz (1973) has produced an extremely useful set of models of refugee movements. Although his discussion is based on international refugee flows, almost all his lucidly presented schema have considerable application to internal refugee flows in Southeast Asia. The first model he presents is the flight-arrival pattern, in which he distinguishes anticipatory and acute movements. His first pattern of movement is the refugee anticipating conflict: "the person under apprehension of future calamities determinedly seeks out a possible country of settlement and as soon as he finds one willing to take him he makes his way there" (ibid.:132). This has an element of choice and of going through regular and legal channels, and applies to movements described by Rambo (1968) and Que et al. (1976) in Vietnam, as well as to much of the early movement in Indonesia's Darul Islam rebellions. The bulk of refugee moves, however, are the acute type—responding to great changes and pressures. The pattern is to move to a country of first asylum, and this has its internal equivalent in a place of refuge within the country (or, in many cases, a city). Thereafter several possibilities arise. First, the refugee may be able to and wish to stay at the place of first asylum (the push-pressure-stay-option). Or he may undertake resettlement elsewhere. Kunz (1973:134) describes this as push-pressure-plunge, because

> living under more deprivations than the anticipatory refugee before his departure, and in addition nudged and harassed both by the country of asylum and by international agencies, the refugee is usually unable to withstand pressure, and his final acceptance of an offer of settlement overseas is more the taking of a plunge than an enthusiastic reaction to a pull.

This is perhaps less applicable in internal refugee settlement, when in-country resettlement may surround the refugee in his or her new place of residence by familiar people, food, language, customs, etc. For example, in the southern Philippines many Christian refugees (who were first- or second-generation migrants in Mindanao) reversed their earlier migration (or that of their parents or even grandparents) to seek refuge with family in the Visayas or in larger settlement sections of Mindanao. The option of return is perhaps more frequent in within-country movements, although it is by no means universal, and the growing importance of repatriation in Indochina should be noted in this context. Kunz's (1973) model of forms of initial displacement in acute refugee situations also has equivalents among the types of internal refugee migrations considered earlier. In essence then, the structure and pattern of refugee flows are similar regardless of whether they are international or internal movements.

The fourth question posed by Pryor relates to the consequences of migration. This is a neglected area in migration research, and we have little empirical knowledge to guide us on the impact of migration upon refugee sending and receiving areas, or upon the refugees themselves. Nevertheless, there are some similarities in the experience of refugees in both international and internal migration situations. There is as much evidence of refugees settling successfully in international destinations as there is of refugees moving within countries. On the other hand, a refugee can be as socially isolated and economically deprived in a different part of his home country as he can in a foreign country. His family will feel his absence equally keenly whether he is in a distant part of his own country or overseas, although his destination may influence his ability to return for visits and to send money, as well as the frequency with which such visits or remittances can be made.

One issue of considerable significance relates to the consequences of refugee migrations for future non-refugee migrations. Refugee flows usually set up linkages between the place left behind and the place of refuge along which information, money, goods, and people can and do move. The latter is of particular importance in several of the Southeast Asian cases we have considered here. For example, the massive refugee flows to the city of Bandung initiated by the Darul Islam rebellion in the 1950s were important to the growth and expansion of that city. Yet this impact should not be measured only in terms of the large number of refugees who remained behind in the city, since it is clear that after security returned, "chain migration" of permanent and temporary movers continued to Bandung from the former Darul Islam areas and that the pioneers of these chains were refugees. Another example in Indonesia is the migration from Bali to the Outer Islands of Indonesia, especially Sulawesi and Southern Sumatra. The first major transmigration from Bali was the forced evacuation after the eruption of Mt. Agung in 1963, but the success of these transmigrants greatly encouraged family and friends to follow them. The information flow, money remittances, visits, etc., which followed the forced migration, led to a much larger spontaneous flow. Lineton's (1975a and b) study of Bugis migration from South Sulawesi to the east coast of Sumatra has produced similar findings. An equivalent pattern appears in international migration where countries of settlement have a "family reunion" immigration policy. In the United States, Canada, and Australia, for example, preference in selecting new settlers is given to the immediate family of former settlers. Neverthless, it is clear that the potential for forced refugee movements to become the pioneering phase of a larger spontaneous flow are more limited in international migrations than in the case of internal refugee displacements. Even so, the initial impetus of refugee flows in Southeast Asia to migration streams is undoubtedly important.

The role of refugee movements, both internal and international, in stimulating the level of urbanization should be mentioned, especially since much of this impetus occurred during the early postwar period when the levels of urbanization were very low in most countries of the region. In Indonesia during the 1950s, refugee flows played a major part in the massive growth of cities like Jakarta, Bandung, Ujung Pandang, and a host of smaller quickly growing cities. In Malaysia, the Briggs Plan produced a substantial concentration of population, and in Vietnam, the war produced massive urbanization between 1954 and 1975. Refugee migration has been a major urbanizing force in postwar Southeast Asia. This makes it all the more surprising that such mobility gets little if any attention in research relating to rural-urban migration and urbanization. As Goodwan and Franks (1975:199) point out, "Despite the fact that internal wars have occurred in every country in Southeast Asia, most research on urbanization does not access either the relative importance of internal warfare for overall rates of migration or the impact such warfare has on the pattern of urban growth."

The final question raised by Pryor relates to political and human rights issues associated with or influencing migration. At first sight this may appear to be the only one of the five dimensions where internal and international migration of refugees diverge completely. The refugees' freedom and ability to move is obviously greater within than beyond their country of origin. Although some countries have considerably restricted where nationals can choose to live, the restrictions on travel abroad are usually greater. Putting aside these considerations, however, we should remember that in the settlement and adjustment phase all refugees, internal and international, have the same basic needs—shelter, food, medical care and other basic services, and the opportunity to earn a living in some degree of security. Olson (1979a:131) points out that refugees usually require more assistance in meeting these needs than other migrants because they differ from other migrants in three crucial ways:

1. They tend to move suddenly in large numbers and hence overwhelm the usual channels of assistance.
2. Many are forced to leave money, assets, and belongings behind and hence are unable to meet costs of settlement and adjustment.
3. Many are ill-equipped to establish themselves at a new location since they have been forced to move into a new location whether or not they are suited to establishing a new life there.

These distinctions are between refugees and other migrants, not between internal and international refugees. The latter distinction becomes significant because most governments provide assistance to refugees only within their own national boundaries, although there are a number of intergovernmental organizations, the largest of which is UNHCR. UNHCR, however, is severely restricted in whom it can assist, in that "refugees who remain within their country and those fleeing from physical danger are not specified as being eligible for UNHCR assistance; however, specific cases of hardship resulting from these reasons sometimes receive UNHCR assistance under the 'good offices' of the High Commissioner" (Olson, 1979a:142)

Thus, internal refugees are usually denied UNHCR assistance even though their needs may be as great as, or greater than, international refugees. Still, there is an encouraging increase in the tendency of national governments to assist refugees in other countries, such as the bilateral funding being provided for refugee camps on the Thai–Kampuchea border.

Conclusion

During the postwar period Southeast Asia has been a region of conflict under the influence of processes of nation-building, internal and international power struggles, colonial and neo-colonial forces, and changing class, cultural, ethnic, and religious relationships. These conflicts have produced distinctive forms of displacement of population within and between countries in the region and outside of the region. The international displacement of refugees has attracted attention both among the international community generally and among social scientists. In addition, movements of refugees within the countries of the region have been both large in scale and profound in their impact, yet have attracted little attention or research. This represents a major oversight on many levels, since refugees displaced within their country can and frequently do suffer as much hardship and deprivation as those who cross an international boundary.

The inclusion of internal refugee migrations within international and national assistance guidelines and contingency strategies is essential, and this inclusion may already be occurring despite official definitions of refugees as being international migrants. In their regular reports of refugee statistics to the UNHCR, countries are increasingly including a category of "internal refugees" which is indicative of a growing recognition of the significance of internal refugees. Indeed, the UNHCR has already assisted persons displaced by civil war within their countries of origin (for example, Lebanon, Angola, and Vietnam), although it can do so only at the specific initiation of the country concerned.

At another level, Olson (1979b) has argued persuasively that the examination of refugee migrations in a developing country context can have significant implications for economic development and social change within those nations. A comprehensive understanding of these movements can inform the development and elaboration of population redistribution strategies that seek to redistribute population to achieve more equitable distributions of access to resources and wealth.

Another fact to emerge from this analysis is that the nature, causes, and impacts of forced migrations have been a neglected area of study in the Southeast Asian region. The significance of conflict as a cause of migration not only in itself, but also in initiating the establishment of patterns of chain migration, especially between rural and urban areas, has been underplayed.

This essay has also suggested that the exclusive focus upon international migration in refugee studies is conceptually artificial and often misleading, and may conceal interrelationships fundamental to a comprehensive understanding of the phenomenon. The material presented here tend to support Pryor (1978, 1981) that the artificial dichotomization of internal and international migration prevents the development of adequate theories relating to migration and its causes and consequences. On the basis of existing knowledge of the Southeast Asian region, the time seems ripe for the development of a more comprehensive analytical framework for the study and understanding of the impact and consequences of forced migrations that incorporate both internal and international refugee movements.

28

Indochinese Resettlement:
Cost and Adaptation in Canada,
the United States, and France

C. Michael Lanphier

This chapter examines short-term resettlement accommodation and long-term implications of Southeast Asian refugee resettlement since the 1979 wave into Canada, the U.S., and France. Although the expenditures appear moderately high, especially in France, they preponderantly provide front-loaded, relatively short-term items. Such concerns have overshadowed certain long-range implications of refugee adaptation. Difficulties have become apparent, especially during the past two years: protracted periods of delay before entering the labor force, low levels of adaptation to the language of the host country, and inadequate numbers of vacancies in job-training programs. Finally, the essay explores one of the few alternatives for long-term adaptation: assistance to ethnic (mutual-assistance) organizations as an initial step toward long-term intervention.

Costs of Resettlement

Costs of resettlement are difficult to state precisely. All receiving countries provide certain initial services that cannot be attributed directly to settlement, such as screening prior to arrival, medical examinations, and governmental infrastructure for selection. Thus, costs attributed to settlement underestimate total costs by an unknown proportion.[1] Contributions to refugees from the private sector, especially in North America from sponsors, often are made in kind (furniture, transportation, lodging, and food). These goods and services cannot be assigned a dollar value and often cannot even be attributed to a particular number of refugees.

Nevertheless, it is possible to examine types of expenditure incurred directly in resettlement of the recent wave of Indochinese refugees. Their fluctuations over time provide some indication of financial undertaking by the state in refugee resettlement. Moreover, expenditures across the three countries indicate certain differences in the kind of resettlement service deliveries characteristic of the particular receiving country.

Canada

Canada's Southeast Asian refugee wave has tapered quickly from the very large intake characteristic of 1979 to 1980, and aggregate costs have dropped correspondingly. The cost reduction occurred despite the fact that in certain areas service delivery has improved, especially with respect to classes in English or French. As Table 28.1 indicates, direct costs account for about half the total expenditures during the 1979–80 influx. The federal government assumed responsibility for increasingly larger proportions of the total refugee intake with each succeeding year.

Total costs sustained by government are higher than those enumerated in Table 28.1. Indirect costs sustained by the federal Department of Immigration (CEIC) have varied between Can$2.5 and $3.5 million per year (US$2.03 and $2.84 million). Moreover, other federal departments sustained indirect costs in terms of health, welfare, and other civil services.

Each province has contributed directly or indirectly to resettlement by providing language-training services, including special English as a second language and French as a second language classes both for children and adults, additional grants to nongovernmental agencies (NGOs), and certain social services provided directly by the province. Since each province has determined its own mix of services, it is not possible to provide a full range of additional costs, some of which are indirectly subsidized by the federal government through transfer payments or through specific subsidies/purchases of services.[2]

Table 28.1 Expenditures on Resettlement by Year, Canada (Can. $'000)

	1979–1980	1980–1981	1981–1982	1982–1983
Total costs (direct)[a]	50,284	84,282	30,294	24,763
Training subsidies	4,992	11,248	5,268	1,285
Number of refugees ('000)[a]	46.8	26.0	8.6	15.2
Government-assisted	13.0	14.8	6.2	10.4
Privately sponsored	23.8	11.2	2.4	4.8
Per-capita costs, average				
Government assisted: ($'000)[b]	—	2.4	—	2.5
Privately sponsored: ($'000)[c]	1.1	1.0	0.8	0.8

Sources: [a] *Indochinese Refugees: The Canadian Response, 1979 and 1980.* Ottawa, 1982.
[b] CEIC, Settlement Branch: includes allowances and language training.
[c] Refugee Documentation Centre, York University, "Refugees: Government/ Private Sponsorship," July 1983.

Per capita costs for the government-sponsored refugees are substantially higher than those for privately sponsored, even though the period during which government-assisted refugees were fully supported by the government has declined from an average of seven months during 1979–80 to about five months in 1982–83. By contrast, privately sponsored refugees benefit from a variety of nonaccountable donations. The magnitude of the difference (the privately sponsored refugee apparently costs about 48 percent less for the first seven month period for resettlement) represents a significant saving.[3]

United States

Expenditures for resettlement have been deployed in a certain front-loading of services and contracts awarded both for expenses upon arrival and for resettlement services, which are distributed either directly or by contract from a variety of federal departments. The decentralized nature of resettlement activities in the U.S. implies that costs sustained by the federal government "flow through" in services to refugees some time in the resettlement process, even though direct dollar subsidies to refugees occur only in cash assistance. Sponsors, as is the case in Canada, receive no funding.

The dramatic increase in expenditures during the fiscal year 1981, as indicated in Table 28.2, is attributable to the continuing assistance required during and after the first year of resettlement of the very large refugee cohort. These costs usually escalated through federal governmental departments, notably in case assistance and related social benefit programs. Moreover, costs rose as refugees gained eligibility to assistance programs faster than did their predecessors (North et al. 1982).

Fluctuation in resettlement costs has been remarkable within the past five years. The difference between expenditures sustained by federal and state governments rose some 440 percent from the fiscal year 1980 to the fiscal year 1981; the corresponding rise the next fiscal year, 1982, was only 12 percent. Apparently, a drop of some 67 percent was effected from the fiscal year 1982 to the fiscal year 1983. This reduction occurred principally through a reduction in the refugee's length of eligibility for categoric cash assistance (from 36 to 18 months, effective retroactively although beginning regionally at different periods throughout 1982) after arrival. Other economies correspondingly resulted in a cutback of federal sources.

Cost reductions are more apparent than real. Costs that otherwise might be attributed to the "lead" federal department, Health and Human Services, have been distributed into other federal, state, and local programs. Refugees gain eligibility for other cash and social assistance programs after termination of the initial benefits. As indicated in Table 28.2, the overall proportion of refugees receiving cash assistance stood at about 65 percent in 1982. On a per household basis, that proportion amounts to 40 percent (Bach et al. 1983). As the proportion of recipients in each cohort decreases with each successive year of residence, these costs will taper somewhat as each yearly arrival cohort diminishes in size. Nevertheless, the expendi-

Table 28.2   Expenditures on Resettlement by Year, United States (US $'000)

	Fiscal Years			
	1980[a]	1981	1982	1983
Sea arrival costs	274,000	261,059[b]	279,288[b]	194,500[c]
Resettlement costs[b]				
Department of State, Domestic	–	229,100	251,500	–
Office of Refugee Resettlement (ORR)	–	640,200	667,000	
Health and Human Services, others	–	267,300	326,900	390,500
Other federal departments	–	207,800	252,700	
State and local	–	251,300	294,700	
Subtotal	294,000	1,595,700	1,792,800	585,000[g]
Number of refugees ('000)[c]	207.1	159.3	97.3	90.0[e]
Average cost/arrival ($'000)	0.7	1.6	2.9	2.2
% receiving cash assistance	37%[d]	49%[d]	65%[f]	

[a] *Refugee Resettlement Resource Book.*
[b] *Report to Congress*, 1981.
[c] *Refugee Reports.*
[d] D. North, *Kaleidoscope*, June 1982.
[e] Ceiling fiscal year 1983. Intake at April = 27,400. *Refugee Reports*, IV, 6.
[f] GAO, Greater emphasis..., *Refugee Reports*, IV, 6.
[g] *Refugee Reports*, IV, 1.

tures will rise, especially in light of elevated unemployment rates, estimated for 1982 at 24 percent of refugees eligible for labor force participation (ibid.).

Overall, budgets for resettlement have been large, both in the immediate arrival costs and, even more impressive, for costs of long-term resettlement. Given the large volume of refugees, however, it does not necessarily follow that budgetary allocations meet any particular level of need. Rather, the high level of refugees receiving public assistance noted in Table 28.2 suggests that significant levels of unmet need exist, particularly in the first years of resettlement.

France

In contrast with North America, resettlement of refugees in France has proceeded as a rather smooth build up since 1975, with the commencement of the Southeast Asia wave (the third in France's history this century). Central government policy stabilized intake at around 12,000 persons per year, with the exception of 1979, when it rose to just over 15,000 persons. Intake returned to the prearranged level in 1980 and rose again toward the end of 1981, with the one-time acceptance of an additional contingent of some 8,000 Cambodian refugees of long duration, who were accepted over a period of some eighteen months.

Expenditures rose during the period, both in absolute amounts and on a per capita arrival or total basis, as indicated in Table 28.3. Although the expenditures during the late 1970s resemble those sustained during the first part of the wave in North America, they escalated quickly as numbers accumulated. The expenditures were particularly remarkable with respect to the centralized form of initial accommodation, *Centres provisoires d'heberge-ment* (temporary centers for lodging) (CPH).

Two reasons predominate in the recent increase in expenditures. First, greater numbers opted for this form of initial resettlement, rather than that for *solution individuelle*, where the refugee has prearranged accommodation with relatives or friends already established in France (usually in Paris). As a result, the number of refugees being lodged in CPH rose at least 35 percent by 1981. Second, the period of stay lengthened from the expected four months to the maximum allowed period of six months, so that a nearly 50 percent increase of expenditures was incurred: approximately French francs (FF) 110 (or US$19) per capita per day.

For refugees opting for *solution individuelle*, cash assistance is available in amounts approximating the daily living allowance in the CPH for equivalent periods. As some 75 percent of all such refugees have congregated in a certain southeast *quartier* of Paris, social service agencies report serious difficulties in securing housing and employment. Consequently, higher indirect costs accrue both for the independent and the government-sponsored refugee whose initial six-month allotment has expired.

From 1975 through 1981, the total cost of refugee assistance directly allocated by the French government amounted to FF 2.4 billion (approximately US$420 million). That amount includes an unspecified amount for prearrival costs, presumably much of the FF 685 million (US$118 million) noted as "Other" in Table 28.3. As CPH costs account for some 62 percent of

Table 28.3   Expenditures on Resettlement, France, 1975-1982 (FF '000)

	Pre-1977	1977-1978	1979-1981	Total
Nongovernmental organizations	20,184	16,020	76,400	114,000
Centres Provisoires d'hébergement (CPH)	34,917	449,828	1,026,255	1,511,000
Guyana (Hmong)			46,663	46,663
Training			80,518	80,518
Other			685,000	685,000
Total	55,101	465,848	1,914,836	2,437,181
Number Southeast Asian refugees ('000)	19.1	23.9	39.7	82.7
Expenditures/arrival (FF '000)	2.9	19.5	48.2	29.5

Source: Ministère de Relations extérieures, Ministère de Solidarité nationale, France Terre d'Asile.

the total costs, the expenditures appear to be more specifically allocated than those characteristic in North America in front-loaded assistance. Despite the relatively high level of expenditure, they do not include costs for language or skills training. Nor are indirect costs sustained by local prefectures and others in the community who are accountable in this record.

Several assistance programs have been established to develop long-range independence. An initial allotment of FF 3,000 to FF 4,000 (US$520 to $700) is specifically designated to help Southeast Asian refugees establish households. Terms for this grant have been narrowly interpreted, according to social service workers, so that only refugees in extreme situations of indigence have qualified. A fund for launching entrepreneurial activity was initiated in 1980. It met a relatively modest demand: some 123 applications, to whom only 39 awards were made. Yet these grants multiplied into nearly 180 jobs.

Training programs have been adapted primarily for younger persons. A two-step educational program, *pre-formation* and *formation,* provides workers with necessary language and quantitative background for a formal skill-training program. As the stage of *pre-formation* may require some two years of instruction, these programs have attracted mainly younger workers. They have operated almost exclusively in the region of Paris.

Programs for general cultural diffusion are minimal both in number and in allocation. Grants for employment of workers in cultural enterprises are made available through "Fonds d'Action Sociale." Application for the funds has resulted in bureaucratic difficulties for prospective recipients, with only about a four-month lead time. The smaller ethnic organizations that lack sufficient organizational infrastructure to respond effectively are at a distinct disadvantage.

A second distinct feature accounts for lack of visibility or influence of cultural organizations in France. Until the repeal of "Loi 1901" in 1981, no organization could receive a federal charter or official recognition unless it was composed of a majority of French nationals, who exclusively constituted its executive echelon. Whether cultural groups will now develop an autonomous status sufficient to organize services for refugees should become evident within the next few years.

Summary

Canada, the U.S., and France have all received large numbers of Southeast Asian refugees since the late 1970s. Canada and the U.S. both enacted a private sponsorship system to divide the labor of immediate resettlement. In addition, both governments have funded resettlement programs. In the U.S., these programs supplemented the contribution of sponsors, whose formal obligations terminated within the second month. Most programs, including cash assistance, have been available to all refugee arrivals, sometimes within days of landing in the U.S.

In Canada, by contrast, half of the refugees were assisted directly by the government without intervention of a private sponsor. Expenditures and programs are more elaborate than those characteristic of the U.S. system during the initial months. Several programs (for example, financial assistance to adults during language instruction) originally designed only for refugees assisted directly by the government, have recently been extended to privately sponsored refugees. Comparisons between per capita costs associated with aid for government-assisted and that for privately sponsored have indicated a significantly lower cost sustained by private sponsor groups in Canada. Although some of the difference may be explained by voluntary contributions on the part of sponsor group members, it is not clear whether the level of services or support provided by private sponsors has been equivalent. Likewise, as privately sponsored groups have been able to supplement their own resources with certain governmental assistance, several explanations for difference in expenditure levels exist without firm evidence to eliminate any of the alternatives just mentioned.

As sponsorship of the North American type lacks an exact French counterpart, most of the assistance to refugees depends upon governmental assistance, mediated through NGO service deliveries. Even those choosing *solution individuelle* are eligible for governmental assistance in amounts equivalent to that for the majority of refugees who begin their resettlement with the CPH experience. Therefore the role of government assistance is organizationally more centralized than that in North America.

Assistance from the government is the near-exclusive source both of financial support and of organization for the early stages of resettlement. While NGO and local governments modify or interpret central policy, financial constraint limits the range of independence. Local prefectures may temporarily refuse a certain planned quota, for example. But continued resistance could result in a contretemps with the national government well beyond the sphere of resettlement.

Centralized planning of resettlement activities has resulted in expenditures significantly higher than those in North America. Moreover, expenditures appear to have increased each year during the wave of Southeast Asia refugee resettlement. This higher level is due in the first instance to increased costs associated with the CPH, which provide the first six months of resettlement for most refugee arrivals. Limited evidence also indicates that higher levels of unemployment and concentration of Southeast Asia refugees within specific *quartiers* in Paris have led to higher costs for those entering community life directly upon arrival (Ajchenbaum 1981). Apparently, little detailed preparation for refugee accommodation is planned by receiving communities. Given the limited exposure to community life during refugees' stay in CPH, prolonged adjustment in the resettlement process remains a continuing concern for refugees and for host community alike.

Long-Term Resettlement

If rates of unemployment indicate a negative degree of collective success in adaptation, rates in the most recent years pose a double challenge. Earlier rates considered to be high (above 10 percent, for example) now appear as average or even moderate for the general population similar in age profile to refugee arrivals. Moreover, a comparative difference, such as a rate of 20 percent for refugees versus 15 percent for age peers, offers several interpretations. Relatively higher rates may appear to be normal for a newly arrived cohort. In addition, elevated rates were one of the most important consequences of the widespread economic recession. Yet the absolute level of unemployment rates implies that one refugee adult in five lacks the necessary means for independent survival. In these circumstances, the attainment of language or skill qualifications may not be sufficient for labor force participation.

No less ambiguous is the relation between the acquisition of cultural and language skills upon arrival and subsequent labor force participation. In the U.S., evidence appears to be positive (Bach and Bach 1980; Bach et al. 1983). Negative implications were attached to arrivals who were categorized in the first two years as "student" or "taking language courses," rather than as direct participants. More recently, that negative implication has reversed to positive: refugees with greater facility in English show commensurately higher rates of participation. Indeed, if any experience appears to affect degree of adaptation independent of the sheer number of years of resettlement, the degree of facility in English is uniquely salient (Whitmore 1983). If this relationship is borne out in the near future, lower rates of employment will appear among refugees in the U.S. who postponed their entry into the labor force until their language facility had improved significantly.

Data recently gathered in Quebec do not corroborate as strong an association between language instruction and labor force participation as appears in the American case. From the outset, Quebec resettlement policy has stressed cultural integration as requisite for success in resettlement (Ministère du Travail 1978). Accordingly, all heads of households and some proportion of spouses underwent intensive 36-week, full-time courses in the French language immediately upon arrival.

Unemployment rates during the first full year of resettlement (1981) appeared only somewhat higher than the average for age peers in Quebec, yet the effects of the intensive language and cultural training could not be assessed until a year had lapsed after arrival. In 1982, as rates of unemployment increased from 10 percent to more than 12 percent, the corresponding rates for refugee unemployment escalated above the 25 percent level. The reason for unemployment most often cited by the refugee ("no jobs available in this region") underscores the structural nature of their problem. Still, about a quarter of those unemployed during the second year (1982) attributed their difficulties with the French language as one cause of their unemployment.[4]

No single conclusion can be drawn from this comparison. The Quebec labor market has experienced an unusually high rate of unemployment, even when viewed against its average, which is characteristically higher than for Canada as a whole. Additional facility in adaptation, which language facility does afford refugees, may indeed appear only under conditions of low-to-moderate unemployment rates.

Labor force attachment among Southeast Asian refugees elsewhere in Canada has many features in common with those in Quebec. The rates of unemployment among refugees are considerably higher than those among other Canadians. In Ontario, a 1982 city-wide survey in Ottawa found a rate of unemployment of about 29 percent (S. E. Nguyen 1983). A survey among refugees living in Winnipeg during 1982 found a similar rate (Manitoba Division 1983). In both cases the high levels were attributed primarily to structural features of the Canadian economy and secondarily to lack of proficiency in English.

To date, studies of labor force attachment among refugees in the U.S. indicate that the largest single factor affecting degree of labor force participation is the number of years since arrival (Bach et al. 1983). Although the number of determinants is somewhat complex, "success" in occupational attainment is related to having more than one adult in the labor force and greater facility in English; these factors overshadow the level of formal education attained (Whitmore 1983).

By contrast, the relation between duration of stay and labor force attachment both in France and in Quebec is moderated by important intervening factors. Refugees of several years duration in France whose former occupation had been manual work found jobs more quickly than did former professionals. For the latter, their initial stay in CPH was prolonged (even beyond the maximum of six months) because of their inability to find work resembling that held in their country of origin. These refugees were the most fluent of all refugees in French, having improved their capabilities well beyond their initial rudimentary knowledge. Yet they were the least able to integrate into the labor force in the short term. Among the white-collar members who entered the labor force quickly, some 45 percent assumed manual or working-class jobs (Ajchenbaum 1981).

Similar to parallel data in North America, higher rates of labor force participation among refugees in France are related to status and class position; white-collar and professional cadres have much higher rates than do manual or working-class laborers (Ministère du Travail 1980). By implication, white-collar workers who waited for a suitable position prior to joining the labor force have been more successful in continuing their participation amid escalating rates of unemployment. Again parallel to the North American experience, the level of occupation upon entry to the labor force is the level where most refugees remain, at least in the immediate term. Although job change occurs with some frequency, subsequent jobs come from the same stratified job pool.

In sum, the immediate problems of large and sometimes massively high rates of unemployment of refugees in major receiving countries bear important implications for long-term resettlement. As noted elsewhere (Lanphier 1983b), sustained unemployment and lack of opportunities for job training may develop in refugees a consciousness of being disfavored as a class. Although evidence on this point awaits future events, it is pertinent that governmental assistance has been provided hesitantly to develop ethnic organizations that might forestall such an eventuality. Canada's policy of multiculturalism solicits applications for funding from such organizations. Certain provinces, especially Quebec, have in addition supported the formation of centers for ethnocultural activities, where several organizations often use the same physical plant.

Although the United States has provided funds for similar purposes, such as the development of mutual assistance associations, these have been awarded more on an ad hoc basis than as general policy implementation. Funding appears as seed money, with no promise of renewal, regardless of degree of success.

Unless a fairly comprehensive network of ethnic organizations is developed, it is difficult to predict whether support for assistance of newly arrived Southeast Asian refugees can be sustained beyond the networks of kin who have provided social and emotional mainstays, especially during the past decade of the turbulent lives of this wave of refugees. While the occupational structure has been the most universal and effective mode of immigrant absorption into mainstream social structure in industrialized countries during the twentieth century, its current failure to provide this function even for its native-born in lower occupational ranks leaves no confidence that it can fulfill that crucial and traditional function. Social and government support, however, has appeared to be ad hoc in the U.S., entirely new in France, and halting or slow in Canada.

It is clear that the recent wave of Southeast Asian refugees has provided a new challenge to immigrant absorption. This challenge is one that governments have dimly recognized. If the matter were solely one of preservation of the parent culture of refugees, a certain, if benign, indifference might have been expected, especially in an era of budget austerity. The challenge is quite otherwise: nothing less than the provision of instrumental means of absorption into the host culture. The indicators of high unemployment and low levels of acquisition of industrial job training and language facility are only surface manifestations of a problem that may be the greatest challenge in refugee resettlement.

Notes

1.   As governmental costs are attributed according to administrative category, rather than directly to particular function, pro-rata estimates of indirect governmental costs are variously attributed from country to country. For these reasons infrastructure costs will not be discussed. The discussion will treat instead only those that can be assessed as direct costs of resettlement.

2.   The province of Ontario, for example, which received the largest proportion (approximately 48 percent) of refugees arriving in Canada during the Southeast Asian wave, expended about Can $1.2 million of provincial monies during 1980–81 and about $825,000 in 1981–82 for services directly to refugees and to NGOs for refugee-related assistance. In addition, large metropolitan areas have provided additional subsidies to NGOs and have even launched certain services on their own initiatives. Because of the variability of these services from place to place and from time to time, they have not been taken into account for cost analysis.

3.   Expenditures by private sponsors vary widely. In the writer's personal experience, per capita costs sustained by sponsors in Toronto church groups were double those cited by the Refugee Documentation Project. Similar higher costs have also been recorded among private sponsors in Ottawa (G. Neuwirth, personal communication).

4.   By the second year, some three-quarters of Southeast Asian refugees in Quebec judged that, for a job search to be successful, it is important to be able to speak both French and English. Only about one-quarter of them had even a passable knowledge of both languages, however.

29

Forces of Dispersal and Forces of Concentration in Refugee Resettlement

Jacqueline Desbarats

Despite the federal recommendation that refugees entering the United States be evenly dispersed in the nation, the Indochinese refugees admitted since 1975 have rapidly concentrated themselves in only a few metropolitan areas. This unplanned geographic concentration of the refugee population implicitly calls into question the effectiveness and the desirability of the original dispersal policy.[1]

One important way in which the geographic distribution of a refugee population differs from that of a free immigrant population is that it reflects the interplay between a constrained and a voluntary component. The constrained component arises from the strict administrative control to which refugee admission and resettlement are subject. Yet, because refugees are free to "vote with their feet" after they have been resettled and thereby express their locational preferences through correction moves, free individual choices also play a role in shaping the aggregate distribution of refugee groups.

Superimposed on this distinction between constrained and voluntary processes is another distinction, relevant at the macro-scale, between influences fostering geographic dispersal and influences fostering geographic concentration, or clustering. What makes the case of Indochinese resettlement in the U.S. particularly interesting is that it clearly illustrates the spatial antagonism between a constrained resettlement process designed to foster population dispersal and voluntary individual decisions generating population concentration.

This essay analyzes the way in which the influences that guide and constrain the locational decisions of individual refugees have gradually evolved into a substantial redistribution of the refugee population as a whole. A dynamic framework is first proposed to describe the changing locational influences underlying the regional distribution of Indochinese refugees in the U.S. Next, the essay outlines the spatial consequences of the contradictions that have developed between the principles of resettlement policies and the realities of resettlement practices. In conclusion, it provides an empirical basis for reevaluating the effectiveness of the even dispersal policy and for assessing alternative resettlement policies.

Forces of Dispersal

Possibly every country offering permanent asylum to political refugees has manifested the desire to disperse the refugees over its national territory. In the U.S., as in most other Western countries, official resettlement policies have explicitly aimed at achieving a scattered distribution of the refugee population. To some extent, the rationale for dispersal may be traced back to conventional wisdom on immigrant adaptation, as expressed in the classic works of Eisenstadt (1954), Ex (1966), and L. W. Gordon (1964), in which immigrant adjustment is viewed as dependent on the newcomers' opportunities to participate in the social, economic, and cultural institutions of the host society. Thus, it is generally thought that the greater the interaction of a new immigrant group with members of the host society, the more rapid and thorough its adaptation will be. One obvious geographic implication of this viewpoint is that the settlement pattern most conducive to adaptation and assimilation should be one that reduces opportunities for contact among the members of the immigrant group while promoting maximum contact with native-born Americans. Such a settlement pattern would involve a distribution as similar as possible to that of the native population.

A second reason for trying to achieve maximum dispersal of a refugee population relates to the effect that a large influx of newcomers might have on their communities of settlement. Dense concentrations of immigrants inevitably alter the social and economic fabric of local communities, in ways sometimes beneficial and sometimes less so. When the first Southeast Asian refugees entered the U.S. in 1975, the American economy was in recession. It was therefore important to minimize the social and economic disruptions that a refugee influx might produce in individual states and localities, and to ensure that no community would be required to bear a disproportionate burden of the refugee costs. In particular, federal refugee officials were determined to avoid the extreme geographic concentration manifested by Cuban refugees in the 1960s. The Interagency Task Force, responsible for coordinating the activities of all U.S. groups participating in the Indochina Refugee Program, operated under the assumption that scattering the refugees in a variety of communities would both encourage their assimilation and reduce their local economic impact. Consequently, it made the geographic dispersal of the refugee population one of the primary goals of the resettlement program (L. W. Gordon 1980; Taft et al. 1979).

Implementation of the Dispersal Policy

Assistance to refugees in the U.S. has traditionally been provided by voluntary agencies—private, nonprofit charitable organizations, either religious or secular. After four temporary processing camps had been established at U.S. military bases for sheltering and processing the refugees, resettlement itself was undertaken by the voluntary agencies, which operated as autonomous entities, using resettlement methods established by their respective headquarters.[2] During the initial resettlement period the voluntary agencies made deliberate efforts to scatter the refugees around the country, especially to places where employment prospects were good, through their assignment to sponsors such as individuals and church or community groups.

Although occasionally some refugees rejected their assigned sponsors in the hope of avoiding cold climates or isolated locations, most, in their desire to be released from the camps, accepted what was offered to them. As individuals, then, the refugees participated only marginally in their own resettlement. As a group they likewise had very little control over their geographic distribution, which was determined essentially by the operation of the voluntary sponsorship system. This system, generally praised for its inexpensiveness and for its efficiency in speedily clearing the refugees out of the camps, has nonetheless been the object of some criticism regarding its haphazard methods and its lack of accountability to federal, state, and local governments. In particular, the voluntary agencies' apparent disregard for the long-term locational consequences of their resettlement methods has been blamed for compounding the problems arising from the absence of national planning and from the lack of coordination between states and local communities (California Department of Social Services 1980:24).

Because sponsorship may involve a substantial personal and financial responsibility, only a limited number of groups or individuals were able to meet sponsorship requirements in any one community. This factor helped contribute to the partial success of the early dispersal policy. By the end of 1975, the geographic distribution of the 130,000 Indochinese refugees already in the country, although not perfectly balanced, was not markedly clustered. The density of resettled refugees varied from a low of 149 per 100,000 state residents in West Virginia, to a high of 2,778 in Hawaii. In general, higher refugee densities were found in the states where the four processing camps had been located and in states west of the Mississippi. Elsewhere, densities higher than the national average bore witness to an especially successful effort by a specific voluntary agency. While large variations existed in the density of refugees resettled by state, overall refugee distribution was relatively even. Twenty percent of all refugees were in California.

Forces of Concentration

From the onset, the locational influences expected to foster an even distribution of the refugee population through the application by the voluntary agencies of explicit federal guidelines were themselves counterbalanced by a set of powerful concentration forces. Most important among these was the spontaneous tendency of immigrants to seek others of the same national origin and to form geographically localized ethnic communities. This agglomerative propensity of immigrants has long been noted by researchers as a major constant in the history of American settlement, as has the tendency of established immigrant clusters to act as magnets for later arrivals, through migration chains. Agglomeration in ethnically defined concentrations provides the psychological support of a group of compatriots, as well as the more tangible help ethnic networks can lend to newcomers who seek work or housing in an alien environment. Repeatedly, the experience of successive waves of European immigrants settling in America has drawn attention to the facilitating role of ethnic enclaves in the adaptation process (Fitzpatrick 1966; Thomas and Znaniecki 1958). More recently, work on the experience of Cuban exiles has again confirmed the significant role played by ethnic enclaves in the process of economic adaptation (Wilson and Portes 1981).

As could have been predicted, the well-documented forces that lead to the establishment of immigrant clusters have been swift to operate among Indochinese refugees. Not unlike most contemporary immigrants, the Indochinese are forced to cope with temporary downward occupational and social mobility, a problem more easily handled within the context of a familiar culture and value system. Like most Third World immigrants, they originate from cultures characterized by tightly knit familial and social systems, whose members are bound by a complex web of mutual obligations and aid. But in contrast to most voluntary immigrants, the Indochinese who are "acute" political refugees also have to cope with the trauma of flight and permanent exile and associated psychological stress. These circumstances have increased the refugees' emotional dependence on the support provided by the family and the ethnic community beyond what would be expected with voluntary immigrants. Such dependence has significant consequences for the geographic mobility of individual refugees and, inevitably, for the spatial distribution of the refugee group as a whole.

Processes of Concentration

The regrouping of the Indochinese population began as soon as the first-wave refugees were sponsored out of the transit camps. It gathered momentum in the following years, with the three separate processes of secondary migration, family reunification, and free case allocation compounding one another's effects.

The significant secondary migration of the refugees after resettlement has been a major contributor to the redistribution of the refugee population away from the ideally dispersed pattern envisaged by the Task Force. Some refugees moved across the country, while others, isolated in small towns and rural areas, left for large metropolitan areas. Far from affecting all regions equally, this movement reinforced the trend toward agglomeration: from 1978 to 1980, the three years for which data on refugee interstate migration are available, only one fifth of the states registered positive net migration balances (U.S. Department of Health, Education, and Welfare 1979; U.S. Department of Health and Human Services 1981.) Most notable was the movement of refugees from snowbelt states to sunbelt and Pacific

Coast states, in particular to Texas, Washington, and California. In 1980, for instance, the California Department of Social Services estimated that one out of four refugees initially resettled elsewhere had moved to California (California Department of Social Services 1980.) Since 1980, migration trends have been marked by a net refugee movement into the upper Midwest, and a net outflow from Texas, Oregon, and Washington into California.

Among students of Indochinese resettlement exists a high level of agreement concerning the hardship and distress caused by the fragmentation of extended families brought about by the initial dispersal strategy (Haines et al. 1981; Tran 1976). Indeed, much secondary migration was a tangible manifestation of the refugees' paramount concern for family reunification. Geographic mobility serves the purpose of bringing together not only close members of nuclear families dislocated in the exodus, but also members of the traditional Asian extended family separated in the resettlement process. Thus, the early dispersal policy has been an indirect, if unwitting, cause of secondary migration. At the same time, post-resettlement moves represented, at least initially, a rational response to adverse climatic conditions and a solution to the health problems exacerbated by these conditions. The severe winter of 1977, for instance, triggered off a mass movement of refugees from northern and northeastern states to regions with milder climates. Some movement was also noted from states where refugees had difficulty securing satisfactory entry-level employment; in Florida, for instance, they had to contend with stiff competition from Cubans.

The consequences of secondary movement have raised as much concern as their motivations raised speculation. Voluntary agencies were the first to express a preoccupation with the unexpected and unplanned refugee movement, which interfered with their ability to follow up on refugee progress. As the process of regional cluster formation progressed, the local communities most affected by the spontaneous redistribution of the refugee population expressed concern, in turn. They voiced fears that rapid, uncontrolled refugee inflow, by saturating existing services, might overtax their capacity to absorb the newcomers into their social and economic fabric (see Desbarats and Holland 1983 for an example of refugee impact on a local community). Following the recent publication of several reports showing secondary migration to be associated with higher rates of dependency on public assistance, this concern has also spread to federal refugee program officials and to some government officials in the states most affected by refugee movement.

Simultaneously, the population redistribution generated by secondary migration is being perpetuated by the humanitarian policy of admitting new refugees on the basis of family ties. By 1979, when the second large wave of Southeast Asian refugees began to enter the country, most of the newcomers consisted of family reunification cases sponsored into the U.S. by previously resettled relatives. With both admission and initial placement depending on an anchor relative acting as a sponsor, the initial placement locations of newcomers became automatically predetermined by the locations of the sponsoring relatives. Inevitably, the pattern of initial placements became increasingly concentrated in a few regions, reflecting the increasingly concentrated pattern of the sponsoring relatives.

Obviously, the spatial implications of the family reunification policy are no different now than they were at the beginning of the resettlement effort, at least in theory. Nonetheless, the consequences of family resettlement became much more visible as sponsorship offers, which in the initial phase originated mostly from American families, largely became the responsibility of previously resettled refugees. The significance of this evolution is highlighted in a report of the U.S. Department of Health and Human Services, which indicates that the proportion of Vietnamese sponsors in all individual and family sponsorships of Vietnamese refugees increased from 15 to 90 percent between 1975 and 1979 (U.S. Department of Health and Human Services 1982: 31.) As the proportion of kin-sponsored refugees increased, so also did the geographic concentration of initial placements. For instance, 31 percent of all incoming refugees were resettled in California in 1981, as opposed to 19 percent in 1975. As time went on, then, the resettlement with family members of a growing proportion of incoming refugees perpetuated the concentration of the Indochinese in a few states.

In addition, the trend toward spatial concentration was encouraged by the placement of free cases, those refugees who do not have close relatives in the U.S. and who are resettled under a category other than family reunification. There are indications that even refugees without family links have been resettled in a disproportionately concentrated pattern. For instance, of the 1,800 refugees processed for resettlement through the Kuala Lumpur office in May and June 1981, 34 percent were destined for California, a surprisingly high proportion in view of the fact that less than half of them—a small proportion compared to the totality of new entrants that year—were being reunited with family members.[3] Thus, the resettlement of free cases also appears to have contributed to the growing spatial concentration of the refugee population, above and beyond the level due to the family reunification policy.

Characteristics of Refugee Concentrations

The redistribution of the refugee population in a more clustered pattern results from a complex interaction among the forces of dispersal and the forces of concentration described above. Concentrations have developed primarily in California, in the Pacific Coast states, in Texas, and in the upper Midwest, a spatial pattern that raises the question of specific features making some states, but not others, attractive destinations for the Indochinese. Statistical analyses throw some light on this question by helping identify state characteristics most likely to be associated with high rates of initial resettlement, with large inflows of secondary migrants, and with dense refugee populations.[4]

In 1975, higher rates of initial placement were more likely to be found in states that had large Oriental populations prior to the beginning of the resettlement program and unemployment levels relatively lower than those in the rest of the country. Such associations are not unexpected, as they attest to the voluntary agencies' efforts to place refugees in areas with above average employment opportunities, and hint at a disproportionate role of Asian-Americans in volunteering as sponsors. Over time, however, as sponsorship increasingly became the responsibility of the established refugee community, liberal public assistance programs turned out to be the most prominent characteristic of states with high resettlement levels. Since 1978, initial resettlement densities have been consistently higher in states that tolerate high rates of public assistance dependency among the refugee population, although this may be to some extent a spurious connection in light of the distribution of first-wave refugees at that time.

The decrease in employment-related determinants with a simultaneous increase in benefits-related determinants mirrors the substantial growth in the use of cash assistance by the refugee population nationwide. In the early phase of resettlement, most of the incoming refugees were resettled with private American sponsors, whose initial willingness to assume financial responsibility alleviated the burden of welfare institutions. As kin sponsorship spread, the more limited resources of Indochinese sponsors led to a greater reliance on welfare institutions. This shift in the composition of the sponsor population coincided with a change in the socioeconomic profile of the incoming refugees. Second-wave refugees, entering since 1979, have generally had fewer marketable skills and less linguistic competency, and have therefore needed to spend longer periods of time in cash-assistance-supported language and job-training programs. This shift occurred at the very time the deepening recession was exacerbating the difficulties of potentially employable refugees in obtaining and keeping employment.

The effect of interstate differences in the implementation of refugee assistance programs on the distribution of the refugee population is readily apparent when one considers the factors accounting for differential rates of post-secondary migration among the states. Net outflows of secondary migrants characterize states where public assistance eligibility requirements are strict and where benefits levels are low. Net inflows characterize states which not only provide liberal assistance programs, but also have high per capita incomes and low unemployment levels and appear to offer the promise of economic prosperity. These results raise the controversial question of the extent to which refugee secondary migration might be encouraged, rather than simply facilitated, by interstate differentials in eligibility criteria and benefit levels for cash and medical assistance.

As for refugee population densities, which represent the cumulative result of initial placement and secondary migration, they are likely to be higher, other things being equal, in states with milder winters, with lower unemployment rates, with less stringent eligibility requirements for public assistance, and with higher public assistance benefit levels. Here again, it is interesting to note the marked increase between 1975 and 1983 in the significance of factors related to refugee assistance relative to climatic and economic factors.

Overall, then, statistical results repeatedly highlight the attraction of Indochinese refugees to areas of the country where they can both meet their needs for family and community and find acceptable alternatives to entry-level employment. As the practice of resettlement evolved, the refugees became increasingly responsive to specific locational attractions: kin and friends, and public assistance. The influences fostering refugee concentrations in specific regions of the country have gradually reinforced one another's effects. The obstacles that federal policies have attempted to place in the way of development of refugee communities have succeeded only in slowing down the formation of Indochinese clusters. They have failed to prevent it.

Conclusion

Although statistical analyses performed at the aggregate level do not necessarily constitute a strong basis for drawing inferences about individual residential motivations, these results nonetheless provide a broader context in which to evaluate alternative resettlement policies presently considered by the U.S. Office of Refugee Resettlement. They also suggest specific hypotheses that should be tested in survey research.

Most significant among these findings is the conclusion that interstate variations in public assistance regulations consistently emerge as the most important potential explanatory factor, both for migration patterns and for population distribution. This finding indicates that the future evolution of refugee settlement patterns will most likely be affected by shifts in the allocation of fiscal responsibility for refugee programs among various levels of government. Since the effect of government income-transfer programs on the locational choices of lower-income groups has already received some attention from economists and migration specialists (Cebula 1979; De Jong and Donelly 1973), it seems urgent to extend this work to determine the extent to which short-term welfare dependency is viewed by recent political refugees as a legitimate part of long-term strategies of economic adaptation. Closely linked to this question is the issue of the higher dependency rate of secondary migrants. On the one hand, the mere disruption caused by a move that is genuinely motivated by climatic or family reasons would in itself explain why migrants seem to have a greater tendency to rely on cash assistance than do stable refugees. On the other hand, it is also necessary to understand the circumstances in which cash assistance availability becomes an initial motivator of secondary moves.

The practical significance of the issues raised by these results is highlighted in the current preoccupations of refugee resettlement officials at all levels with the geographic aspects of resettlement. The Office of Refugee Resettlement, sensitive to the need to direct new refugees away from areas already showing substantial refugee concentrations, intends to effect the required changes in geographic distribution (U.S. Department of Health and Human Services 1982). Simultaneously, voluntary agencies are searching for ways to develop new placement opportunities, to encourage refugees to stay in their places of initial resettlement, and to deflect secondary migrants from impacted communities.

Overall, the American experience with Indochinese resettlement suggests that attempts to induce the rapid assimilation of an immigrant group through government-dictated dispersal policies can be expected to come to loggerheads with the culturally ingrained adjustment and adaptation strategies typically found in the immigrant group. This experience also highlights the critical importance of the initial stages of ethnic cluster formation in polarizing later population redistribution, and demonstrates the great difficulty involved in slowing down the formation of immigrant clusters once they have reached critical mass.

From a practical perspective, one major conclusion to emerge from eight years of Indochinese resettlement is that voluntary agencies, states, and local governments need to coordinate their efforts from the very beginning of a refugee program if they are to be effective in influencing the distribution of refugee populations. Another relevant implication is that planned cluster resettlement in carefully selected sites, along the lines of the Khmer Guided Placement project, might be a desirable alternative to the unplanned clustering brought about by the failure of the dispersal policy. But it would not be realistic to expect a cluster resettlement policy promoted belatedly, after geographic patterns have been allowed to crystallize, to reverse the self-perpetuating trend of Indochinese concentration that has emerged unchecked since 1975.

Notes

1.   The author wishes to acknowledge the support of the National Science Foundation in funding this research.

2.   The four camps were Camp Pendleton, California; Fort Chaffee, Arkansas; Fort Indianton Gap, Pennsylvania; and Eglin Air Force Base, Florida.

3.   Personal communication from Mr. V. Mahan, Resettlement representative, U.S. Embassy, Kuala Lumpur, Malaysia, August 14, 1981.

4.   The results presented below summarize a series of regression analyses in which the dependent variables were initial placement density, net interstate secondary migration rate, and refugee population density. The independent variables included a comprehensive set of variables measuring the ecological, social, political, and economic characteristics of states. Complete analyses may be found in Desbarats 1981.

30

Social Science Research on Southeast Asian Refugee Settlement in Canada

Doreen Marie Indra

People from Vietnam, Laos, and Kampuchea do not have a long tradition of immigration to Canada.[1] Approximately 1,000 Southeast Asian immigrants had come to Canada prior to 1975, most of them either students or highly trained professionals living in Quebec. Until then Indochinese Canadians attracted almost no academic attention. With the fall of the Thieu regime, about 6,000 Vietnamese refugees came to Canada, chiefly from refugee centers established in Hong Kong, Guam, and the United States. Many were middle-class people involved in government work, the military, or the professions. Half were relatives of former students in Canada. Refugees tended to go to Quebec and Ontario, but some were attracted elsewhere by better job prospects. Small communities of Vietnamese thus became established in Calgary, Edmonton, and Vancouver. Since virtually no Vietnamese had settled in these cities earlier, community-based settlement assistance was minimal. Nevertheless, settlement generally proceeded smoothly (see Indra 1983, on Alberta settlement; Nguyen and Dorais 1979, on Quebec) because of the congruence of several factors: refugees were generally very skilled, were comparatively bicultural, and came when the economy was buoyant.

The second wave of immigrants attracted little academic interest between 1975 and 1978, although some programmatic work was done on psychological adjustment (Chan 1977), settlement problems (Q.B. Nguyen 1977), and peripherally on refugee policy (Dirks 1977). The lack of research activity was chiefly a result of refugee settlement having fallen between the cracks of the disciplinary division of labor. Canada's well-established community of East and Southeast Asian studies scholars generally lacked both the interest in and the methodological tools for investigating Southeast Asian settlement in Canada. Nor did Vietnamese communities in Canada attract the attention of sociologists or urban anthropologists, for their settlement had not yet become a social issue.

After a hiatus of a few years, refugees again began arriving in 1978. This was initiated in part by the now-famous *Hai Hong* incident, when Canada airlifted 604 people from a stranded freighter (Canada Employment and Immigration Commission [hereafter CEIC] 1982a; Pappone 1982). Refugees were soon arriving in large numbers. The government of Canada quickly developed its unique refugee sponsorship program. For each refugee that private sponsorship groups brought in and settled, the government agreed to support the settlement of one more (Adelman 1980; CEIC 1982a and b). Some 60,000 Indochinese came to Canada between 1977 and 1982, and there are now about 80,000 Indochinese in Canada.

In several respects the settlement of refugees between 1978 and 1981 matched that in the U.S. The immigration and settlement services infrastructure was at first ill adapted for dealing with either the volume or the unique cultural demands of Indochinese. Little information was available on any of the ethnocultural groups that were arriving, nor on their countries of origin. No Canadian refugee program in recent times had dealt with so many individuals so suddenly. In most places to which refugees went there were no established ethnocultural communities, hence little community support for the settlement process. There were several crucial differences between how settlement proceeded in Canada and in the U.S. Canada developed an extensive system whereby groups of private citizens could sponsor refugees and agree to support them for up to a year, if necessary. Private sponsorship gave many refugees significant advantages in becoming established. It also resulted in an initially high degree of geographical dispersal, as refugees were sent wherever sponsorship groups were established.

Government-sponsored refugees were primarily assisted through a complex network of governmental and nongovernmental agencies in a rather different fashion than was done in the U.S. (CEIC 1981a and b, 1982a; Lanphier 1981a and b, 1983a). Voluntary organizations ranging from ongoing immigrant settlement agencies to church to temporary groups provided a wide range of services. Also, Indochinese refugees came to Canada at a time when comparatively greater economic possibilities were available to them than was the case in the U.S. (Alberta Advanced Education & Manpower 1982). Because most of their communities were relatively small and institutionally incomplete, they were not the target of racism or antiimmigrant prejudice (Breakspear 1980), although some job discrimination in Toronto has been documented (Siu 1980a).

The first phase of Canadian research on Indochinese settlement (1978–1981) was prompted by the immediate need for practical information on refugee culture, needs, and source country situations. City, provincial, and federal governments as well as many private organizations actively assembled and disseminated such information. As one of the most active groups in the private sponsorship of refugees, Canadian Mennonites generated several important background papers for potential sponsors. They also produced orientation materials for Indochinese still in camps and waiting to come to Canada (Saunders 1981). Thus arose a host of background papers on Southeast Asian source countries and the refugee condition.[2] At the same time, a few studies by academics described aspects of the settlement process (Chan 1977; Drudi 1979; Indra 1979; Nguyen and Dorais 1979). Some of these were also oriented primarily toward the social service community, policy-makers, and sponsors (Adelman 1980; Tepper 1980). In this respect, the edited book by Tepper (1980) is noteworthy as the first systematic academic attempt to present what was then available about Indochinese refugee settlement.

The year 1980 saw the rise of many small-scale studies of refugee settlement, typically conducted by either one or two researchers with limited financial support and with highly localized empirical and topical focuses. Analyses of mental health problems were common (Chan 1977; Chan and Lam 1981, 1983; Li et al 1980; S.D. Nguyen 1979, 1981, 1982a and b; Suh 1980; Tyhurst 1980) and a consensus developed that there was a high frequency of mental illness among Indochinese refugees (Suh 1980). Rather predictably, many psychological problems were seen to be directly derivative from the refugee experience (Chan and Lam 1983a and b). Much published research on mental health was derived from ongoing psychiatric work and was consequently highly applied (Li et al. 1980; S.D. Nguyen 1979). Some theoretical models of refugee uprooting and mental responses developed out of this work (S.D. Nguyen 1982b). Mooney (1982) has produced a bibliography of mental health research and Indochinese refugees, including both Canadian and American material.

A few studies of this variety dealt with refugee health needs. In general, discussion of Indochinese health problems mirrored that in the U.S., noting the special disease problems of refugees (Keystone 1979; Tan and Tan 1980) and culturally based attitudes toward medicine and health (Alberta Advanced Education and Manpower 1980a). At the same time, Lees and Doliszney (1982) argued on clinical evidence that Southeast Asian utilization of health care services quickly matched that of the general population in frequency of use and type of needs.

Numerous studies noted the consequences of refugee flight and sudden settlement on family structure (Chan and Lam 1981; Indra 1979, 1983; Neuwirth and Clark 1981; Poon 1977). These stressed the vital role the family plays in maintenance of personal identity and sense of stability, both of which were highly stressed by the flight from Indochina and by consequent socioeconomic and cultural adaptation (Chan and Lam 1983). Although the special needs of such groups as young unattached men and women have been noted, these groups have not been the target of concerted research; S.D. Nguyen's (1980) work with these groups has established the importance of the development of community-based, fictive kinship networks in easing the disorientation of personal identity caused by uprooting and flight. In a similar vein, the importance of having a strong social service provision system tailored to Southeast Asian needs is well recognized, but research on the actual implementation of such services by agencies other than government is very sketchy.[3]

One national study of immigrant social service needs was initiated at that time by the government of Canada and is now in the process of completion (Newman 1983). This study addresses government programs and voluntary agency opinions of refugee needs and extant social service provision. Another government research project assessed the impact of the 1979–80 influx of Indochinese refugees on Canada Immigration Centres and Canada Employment Centres (CEIC 1981b).

Because of its importance (and international uniqueness), private sponsorship has been the target of numerous investigations. For example, Fuhr (1981) surveyed the attitudes of people to their roles as private sponsors, as did Kehler (1980). There is now strong evidence that refugees who were privately sponsored tended to have considerably fewer settlement difficulties than those who were government-sponsored. Sponsorship groups affiliated with larger (chiefly church) organizations seem to have functioned considerably more efficiently than ad hoc sponsorship groups; the latter often complained of having been "left to flounder" by both the federal and provincial governments (CEIC 1982b). The study by DPA Consulting (1982) provides a relatively complete background to the government's refugee settlement programs, and provides several models of settlement based on a study of voluntary private-sector participation in the resettlement process.

Published studies of sociocultural adaptation have been sufficiently numerous to produce a few basic generalities. Southeast Asians who came to Canada after 1977 often have significant acculturation problems. Indochinese refugees frequently faced grave language difficulties, and some research has been devoted to detailing these (Q. B. Nguyen 1980; Nguyen and Dorais 1979). In addition, Dorais and Nguyen have completed a large-scale sociolinguistic study of language use in Quebec (1983). Access to English and French language training has varied enormously from province to province and from individual to individual. Yet the effect of this unequal access on people's life chances is still largely unknown, despite a growing literature on refugees and second language education (Kaley 1980).

Because no Southeast Asian Canadian community is large enough for a significant proportion of individuals to derive their income from working within the community, economic adaptation consequently results in considerable cultural adaptation. In addition, cultural adaptation is made somewhat easier because Southeast Asians are neither ghettoized nor highly discriminated against. Moreover, many are eager to learn more about Canada and develop greater contacts with other Canadians (Gee and McKim 1980; Nyguyen and Dorais 1979).

Wherever Southeast Asians have settled in any number they have been quick to develop a range of community institutions, which thereafter have played many important roles. For example, Canada's multicultural policy has encouraged the establishment of Southeast Asian community-based ethnocultural associations (Indra 1983). Informal community social networks are strongly maintained and are a vital part of individual adaptation (Li et al. 1980); however, such networks have not received much research attention. Neither has the rise of religious institutions, cultural celebrations, or community-level attempts at cultural maintenance.

Successful economic adaptation is crucial to the long-range success of

Southeast Asian settlement in Canada. Again, this has been well recognized, but has not resulted in a commensurate level of research activity. Some initial work has been done on general questions of economic adaptation (Buchignani 1980; Samuel 1986), job discrimination (Siu 1980b), the occupational adjustment of military personnel (MacRury 1979), and the economic benefits of private sponsorship (CEIC 1981a, 1982a; DPA Consulting 1982a and b; Neuwirth and Clark 1981). There is a developing consensus (as seen in the above studies) that English or French language facility has a strong determinant effect on economic adaptation. An important piece of research on economic adaptation was directed by the Canada Employment and Immigration Commission. This was a national longitudinal study of the economic adjustment of refugees over the period 1981–1983 (see Samuel 1986 for details).

In addition, a large number of papers and reports addressed aspects of Canada's rapidly evolving policy on Indochinese refugee settlement (Adelman 1980; Adelman et al. 1980; Knott 1981; Lanphier 1981a, 1981b, 1983a).

Several other large-scale projects on Indochinese refugee settlement began in late 1980 or 1981, but some have not yet found their way into print. These include a multidisciplinary study of individual immigrant adaptation in Vancouver (Nann et al. 1984), an Ottawa-centered analysis of sponsorship and occupational adjustment (by Neuwirth and Clark), and a research project on the legal difficulties of Indochinese refugees (with particular reference to unaccompanied minors), which compares Canada to the U.S. (Pask 1983).

In overview, the literature on Southeast Asian settlement in Canada can be looked at in two ways. To take the more optimistic side, one could argue that there are now a fair number of studies on this process; the literature on Southeast Asians in Canada is now substantially larger than it is for most of Canada's ethnocultural populations of comparable size. Policy analysis is well developed, and sufficient information now exists to put together a broad sketch of Southeast Asian life in Canada.

At the same time, there are enormous gaps and omissions in the literature. For example, virtually all research has been on Vietnamese or Vietnamese Chinese, while Lao and Khmer have been systematically ignored. There have been almost no transnational studies linking immigrants with their source countries or with their source-country kin; an exception is Allen's work (1983) on the logic of deciding to leave Vietnam. Very little has been done on the structure of Indochinese communities (for an exception, see Lam 1983). Almost no account has been taken of the effects of the 1981–83 economic downturn on refugees, despite the fact that in some cities, such as Calgary and Edmonton, the present refugee unemployment rate is informally figured to be 40 percent. Indochinese use of social, health, and educational services remains largely unknown. Language problems for many individuals remain profound, yet these also have received insufficient attention. After a spate of interest in family and mental health problems, activity in this area seems to have prematurely flagged. As in so many areas of social science, very little research is done specifically on Indochinese women in Canada.

Many so-called refugees are refugees no longer. They are Vietnamese, Vietnamese Chinese, Lao, and Khmer Canadians. Increasingly, their commitment is to Canada, yet almost no research has been devoted to the direction their long-term integration into Canadian society will take. Finally, few researchers have considered the fundamental question of what specifically is Southeast Asian about the settlement of Southeast Asian refugees in Canada. That is, what aspects of their settlement saga can be attributed to their "Southeast Asian-ness," and what aspects result from their refugee status?

It is difficult to predict the future course of research on Southeast Asians in Canada. Southeast Asians have largely dropped out of the news, and they are not ethnocultural groups that are likely to protest even the most acute community problems. Consequently, it is unlikely that many academics not already involved in Southeast Asian Canadian settlement research will be attracted to it. As Southeast Asian communities become more established, however, they are likely to receive somewhat greater attention through other research orientations. For example, they will be a natural focus of studies concerned with social and cultural pluralism in Canada.

Notes

1. This essay is an abstracted version of another containing almost all available studies involving research on Southeast Asian settlement in Canada. It was supported in part by the Canadian Asian Studies Association. The latter paper is available upon request.

2. It should be also noted that Refuge, Canada's periodical on refugee affairs, was established at this time. It is a good reference for current issues in Indochinese refugee settlement.

3. For a bibliography, see Abraham et al. (1980); Calgary Sponsor and Refugee Society (1982) on perceived refugee legal needs and their attitudes toward the law; Ottawa-Carleton Immigrant Southeast Asian Refugee Steering Committee (1983) on settlement needs in their area; and Vietnamese Association (1979) on Vietnamese social service needs.

31

Socioeconomic Adjustment of Southeast Asian Refugees in Canada

Gertrud Neuwirth

The mass exodus of Southeast Asians in 1979 and 1980 marks a turning point in the history of refugee resettlement in Western societies. Southeast Asians have been admitted not only to the United States but also to other countries, including Canada, France, Australia, England, and the Federal Republic of West Germany. In Canada alone some 60,000 were accepted between 1979 and 1980, and more than half were resettled by the private sector. The arrival of thousands of refugees from Vietnam, Cambodia, and Laos not only changed our perception of refugees but made us realize that it is refugees from the Third World rather than from eastern Europe who require resettlement.

It is unfortunate that the technologically developed societies of the west are still ill prepared to cope with the settlement of the "new refugees." Since so little is known about their social and cultural background, the trauma of their escape, and their experiences in refugee camps, we are not able to offer the specific assistance they need to ease their adaptation to the host society or to faciliate their social and economic integration. Most settlement programs and services in immigration countries such as Canada are still designed for the needs of European immigrants and, for this reason alone, are inadequate for refugees and other immigrants from the Third World.

Since so many Southeast Asians have been resettled in the West, their adaptation should be closely monitored over several years if only to learn about their culture-specific problems. Since, in terms of their social and demographic characteristics, they are quite representative of the population in their home countries, a longitudinal study would also yield findings that might well apply to refugees from other parts of the Third World. Thus it may be possible to arrive at some generalizations concerning the difficulties these refugees experience in their economic and occupational transition to their societies of resettlement.

By placing the adaptation of Southeast Asians in the wider context of the transition from a technologically less developed to a technologically developed society, it also becomes apparent that when current sociological theories of immigrant adaptation and assimilation are applied to them, they have little explanatory significance. The theories are based on the experience of European immigrants to North America who came in the early part of the twentieth century under rather different structural conditions. As Rex (1973:191) pointed out, their arrival coincided with the industrialization of Canada and the U.S. when the technological gap between receiving and sender societies was not yet wide. Indeed, these immigrants in effect made industrialization possible and, together with their descendants, eventually formed the main labor force in both countries. Since they came mostly from the eastern and southern parts of Europe, sociological theories focused on their linguistic and other ethnic differences, and thus emphasized their cultural assimilation and adaptation to a dominant English culture.

In contrast, refugees and immigrants from the Third World arrive at a time when the technological gap between their native and Western societies has become considerable, and when jobs are not as readily available as they once were. New theoretical approaches are therefore needed to take into account the structural constraints that circumscribe the integration of refugees and immigrants from the Third World. Whatever their final formulation might be, such theories will have to treat "adaptation" as a multidimensional concept including, for instance, economic, social, and cultural adjustment.

Economic Adaptation

The concept of economic adaptation can be used in two different senses. In the wider sense it refers to refugees' ability to find employment and to become self-sufficient. In the narrower sense it is equivalent to occupational adjustment, which, following Stein (1979), can be defined as the ability to transfer occupational skills acquired in the home country to the new society, or to obtain a job of a status similar to that of the one previously held. Economic adaptation in the first sense is relatively easily attained, although the jobs that refugees initially obtain usually involve severe downward mobility and low incomes. Refugees are not fluent in the new language, and they lack information about available jobs. Since their occupational skills and degrees are not formally recognized, they have little choice between jobs.

Occupational adjustment—that is, economic adaptation in the narrower sense—is much more difficult to accomplish. Yet, as Stein argued, this adjustment is the most important dimension of a refugee's overall adaptation, such that the other two dimensions of social and cultural adjustment are contingent upon it. As several studies have shown, refugees who have been able to transfer their former occupational skills, or to assume an occupational status commensurate with their previous one, have more quickly adapted culturally than those whose occupational adjustment was poor. Through language courses and vocational upgrading and retraining programs, as well as through sheer determination and hard work, eventually they may be able to enter the same or similar occupations. The period of occupational adjustment appears to be shortest for blue-collar workers and longest for those with technical or professional qualifications. But as Stein pointed out, if a refugee is not able to effect his occupational adjustment during the first three or four years of resettlement, the chances of doing so subsequently are greatly reduced. Any job changes that occur later no longer tend to lead to an improvement in the refugee's occupational status. As time goes by, family obligations increase, and determination begins to wane as hopes and ambitions are transferred to children.

Regardless of which dimension is emphasized, all four dimensions of adaptation are based on the value orientations of the host society. The dimension of social adaptation taps the immigrant's willingess or ability to include members of the dominant groups among his friends and acquaintances. The cultural dimension implicitly devalues the immigrant's cultural heritage and traditions by basically measuring the degree to which they have adopted the dominant cultural practices and thus abandoned their customary ones. Economic adjustment in both of its senses, however, is based on the quintessential value orientation of Western capitalist societies. Imbued with an achievement ideology, a person's social status is determined primarily by his position within the occupational structure. Moreover, as ideological thinking will have it, the occupational position is attained primarily through personal achievement and not through the accident of birth or family connections. Thus, lack of achievement or even unemployment still tends to be attributed largely to personal failure rather than to structural constraints.

One can therefore argue that by emphasizing economic adjustment, refugees' adaptation is assessed on the basis of much more stringent criteria than those underlying cultural and social adjustment. For refugees at least can choose to some extent whether, and to what degree, they want to become socially and culturally adjusted. Nevertheless, they are severely constrained in their economic adjustment by conditions beyond their control. Although they may wish to attain their previous occupational status, they can do so only if, apart from their own determination and personal sacrifices, they are given the opportunity to upgrade their occupational skills. They may aspire only to self-sufficiency, yet they can attain it only if they are given a job enabling them to support their family. Hence, the success or failure that refugees experience in their economic adjustment is as much, if not more so, an indicator of the host society's openness in integrating them economically as it is of the refugees' own abilities.

Economic Adjustment of Southeast Asians in Canada

Several social scientists have studied the sociocultural adjustment of Southeast Asian refugees (Dunnigan 1982; Haines et al 1981). But with the exception of Bach's work (1985) and a Michigan study (Whitmore 1984), not much research has been undertaken that focuses specifically on refugees' economic adjustment. The findings of these two studies, as well as of Stein's analysis, suggest that Southeast Asians experience much greater difficulties than did earlier refugees from Europe. In Canada two research projects specifically address this issue. The first is a comprehensive longitudinal survey of Southeast Asians by Employment and Immigration, which, among other topics, contains information on refugees' economic as well as occupational adjustment. The second is this author's research, which is specifically designed to ascertain differences in the resettlement and multi-dimensional adaptation between government-assisted and privately sponsored refugees during their first fifteen to eighteen months in Canada.[1] The study explores, in some detail, refugees' occupational background and their occupational trajectory for this period.

The government survey was carried out through mailed questionnaires in three separate waves in 1981, 1982, and 1983, and thus allows for cross-sectional data analysis for each year separately, as well as for a longitudinal panel analysis based on those respondents who answered all three questionnaires (Neuwirth et al. 1985). This author's own research was conducted in Ottawa, Toronto, and in two counties of eastern Ontario during the summer and fall of 1981.[2] The sample consisted of about 120 privately and 50 government-assisted refugee households in each city. The rural area component included 35 of the 50 privately sponsored families who had originally been settled in the two counties. Because of lack of employment opportunities, several had moved, and only some were located in Ottawa and Toronto. Interviews were conducted with heads of household in the refugee's native tongue, but information was obtained for all male and female family members who were part of the officially sponsored unit.[3]

The analysis and discussion of the refugees' economic adjustment in both its wider and narrower sense will be based mostly on the Ottawa–Toronto–rural area study. It will also incorporate, whenever appropriate, findings of the government survey, including both the cross-sectional and the panel analysis of the data. Despite differences in the formulation of questions and in the data-collecting techniques, the findings of the two projects supplement each other. Any inferences drawn from them regarding the difficulties other Third World refugees are likely to face will therefore be considerably strengthened.

The combined sample of all three research sites (Ottawa, Toronto, and the rural areas) yielded a total of 1645 persons. The number of refugees over 15 years of age for whom information on occupational background is available, and who did not resume their education in Canada, is 743.[4] More than two-thirds of these respondents came from Vietnam and the balance from Cambodia and Laos. But according to the respondents' ethnic self-identification, Sino-Vietnamese from both North and South Vietnam constitute about 50 percent, and ethnic Vietnamese only 17 percent of the sample; ethnic Chinese are, however, in the minority among refugees from Cambodia and particularly from Laos (Table 31.1). Using a different indicator of ethnicity—language most often spoken at home—the government survey's sample shows a similar preponderance of ethnic Chinese among refugees from Vietnam. Both these findings contradict popular perceptions of refugees from Vietnam: by referring to them as "boat people" it is still widely

Table 31.1   Education of Combined Sample by Ethnicity

	South Vietnamese	South Vietnamese Chinese	North Vietnamese	Cambodian
Primary education	8	64	49	36
	(6.6)	(25.2)	(31.4)	(57.1)
Some secondary education	28	113	68	17
	(23.1)	(44.5)	(43.6)	(27.0)
Completed secondary education	33	55	19	5
	(27.3)	(21.7)	(12.2)	(7.9)
University/Technical incomplete	21	12	7	1
	(17.4)	(4.7)	(4.5)	(1.6)
University/Technical complete	24	4	5	
	(19.8)	(1.6)	(3.2)	
Not specified	7	6	8	4
	(5.8)	(2.4)	(5.1)	(6.3)
	121	254	156	63
Total	(16.3)	(34.2)	(21.0)	(8.5)

Note: Figures in parentheses denote percentages of ethnic group (body of table) and of total Indochinese refugees (bottom line).

believed that most are ethnic Vietnamese; hence the Sino-Vietnamese who constitute the majority are ignored.

The educational levels of respondents in our combined sample are generally low. Fully two-thirds had been only in grade school or had attained only some secondary education. Seventeen percent completed high school, 7 percent had some post-secondary education, but only 4 percent had obtained at least one degree from a university or technical school. Ethnic South Vietnamese have generally higher levels of education: only 7 percent did not go beyond grade school, but more than one-third had some post-secondary education or at least one degree. The overall educational levels of Sino–South Vietnamese rank second: about two-thirds had some secondary education or had completed it, and a few continued their education further. The educational distribution of ethnic Lao is relatively extreme: over one-third had not gone beyond grade school, yet one-fourth had graduated from high school or had some post-secondary education. Refugees from Cambodia have the lowest levels of education: more than half of both ethnic and Sino-Cambodians did not go beyond grade school. When interpreting these data, however, one should keep in mind that Cambodians suffer from an educational deficit. Since schools were closed down in 1975, the education of many young Cambodians was forcibly interrupted. Thus, their educational levels are not, strictly speaking, comparable to those of other Southeast Asian refugees in the same age groups, as the latter at least were able to leave school on their own accord.

The refugees' relatively low levels of formal education are reflected in

Cambodian Chinese	Laotian	Laotian Chinese	Laotian Hmong	Laotian Cambodian	Total
32	22	7	2		220
(57.1)	(36.1)	(25.0)	(100.0)		(29.6)
18	16	16			276
(32.1)	(26.2)	(57.1)			(37.1)
3	11	2			128
(5.4)	(18.0)	(7.1)			(17.2)
1	4	2			48
(1.8)	(6.6)	(7.1)			(6.5)
					33
					(4.4)
2	8	1		2	38
(3.6)	(13.1)	(3.6)		(100.0)	(5.1)
56	61	28	2	2	743
(7.5)	(8.2)	(3.8)	(.3)	(.3)	(100.0)

their former occupational status. According to Table 31.2 which lists occupations in some detail, relatively few respondents were administrators or in the army (5.1 percent), had been professionals (6.7 percent), or in white-collar and sales occupations (6.5 percent). Eighteen percent had been students, and close to 10 percent were in retail or wholesale businesses. Blue-collar workers (32 percent) are distributed over a wide variety of occupations, with the highest concentrations in textiles and other product processing and assembling. Quite a few women either helped their husbands at work and in business or were housewives, while 18 percent had been students. Ethnic South Vietnamese and ethnic Lao, with one-third each, show the highest concentration in nonmanual occupations, while Sino–South Vietnamese and Sino-Lao have been in retail or wholesale businesses more frequently than any other ethnic group.

It should be emphasized, however, that the refugees' occupations have been classified according to the Canadian Classification and Dictionary of Occupations and thus according to North American criteria. This classification conceals the very real differences between credentials and skills demanded for seemingly similar occupations in Western societies vis-à-vis the technologically underdeveloped countries of Southeast Asia. The discrepancy in formal occupational requirements between Canada and Southeast Asia becomes apparent when respondents' educational level is analyzed separately for each major occupational group.

As is to be expected, the discrepancy is most pronounced for former professionals, administrators, managers, and army personnel. Of profes-

Table 31.2   Occupation of Combined Sample by Education

	Primary education	Some secondary education	Completed secondary education	University /Technical incomplete	University /Technical complete	Not specified	Total
Government, Army, Managers	4 (10.5)	9 (23.7)	9 (23.7)	7 (18.4)	7 (18.4)	2 (5.3)	38 (5.1)
Professional	4 (8.0)	13 (26.0)	7 (14.0)	9 (18.0)	16 (32.0)	1 (2.0)	50 (6.7)
Artists	2 (28.6)	3 (42.9)	2 (28.6)				7 (.9)
Technicians	l (14.3)	1 (14.3)	3 (42.9)	1 (14.3)	1 (14.3)		7 (.9)
Sales and clerical	4 (8.3)	20 (41.7)	22 (45.8)	1 (2.1)		1 (2.1)	48 (6.5)
Service occupations	8 (38.1)	10 (47.6)	1 (4.8)	1 (4.8)		1 (4.8)	21 (2.8)
Food and beverage production	12 (75.0)	3 (18.8)	1 (6.3)				16 (2.2)
Transport	6 (27.3)	7 (31.8)	6 (27.3)			2 (13.6)	22 (3.0)
Crafts	5 (31.3)	9 (56.3)	2 (12.5)				16 (2.2)
Textile	26 (41.9)	27 (43.5)	5 (8.1)	1 (1.6)		3 (4.8)	62 (8.3)
Processing and assembly	13 (29.5)	23 (52.3)	4 (9.1)	2 (4.5)	1 (2.3)	1 (2.3)	44 (5.9)
Mechanics	7 (22.6)	15 (48.4)	8 (25.8)	1 (3.2)			31 (4.2)
Construction	3 (21.4)	6 (42.9)	2 (14.3)	1 (7.1)		2 (14.3)	14 (1.9)
Farmers	18 (72.0)	3 (12.0)				4 (16.0)	25 (3.4)
Wholesale and retail	23 (31.9)	32 (44.4)	9 (12.5)	2 (2.8)	2 (2.8)	4 (5.6)	72 (9.7)
Street vendors	9 (60.0)	6 (40.0)					15 (2.0)
Helper wives	5 (26.3)	9 (47.4)	3 (15.8)			2 (10.5)	19 (2.6)
Housewives	47 (63.5)	17 (23.0)	1 (1.4)	1 (1.4)		8 (10.8)	74 (10.0)
Students	14 (10.4)	56 (41.8)	35 (26.1)	20 (14.9)	5 (3.7)	4 (3.0)	134 (18.0)
Not worked	2 (66.7)	1 (33.3)					3 (.4)
Not specified	7 (28.0)	6 (24.0)	8 (32.0)	1 (4.0)	1 (4.0)	2 (8.0)	25 (3.4)
Total	220 (29.6)	276 (37.1)	128 (17.2)	48 (6.5)	33 (4.4)	38 (5.1)	743 (100.0)

sionals included in our combined sample, about one-third had obtained one or more university degrees, and an additional 18 percent had some post-secondary education. Yet nearly half the sample had no post-secondary education and 8 percent had not even gone beyond grade school. Except for the lower proportion of respondents with a post-secondary degree (18 percent), the educational qualifications of former administrators and army personnel are rather similar to those of professionals. Most white-collar and sales employees had attended or graduated from high school (87 percent). But few respondents who owned their own business and, with the exception of transport workers and mechanics, few manual workers had completed their secondary education. The educational levels are lowest for respondents in food and beverage processing, followed by farmers, housewives, and street vendors, such that between three-fourths and mroe than 60 percent in each category had attended grade school only.

Even though somewhat different educational and occupational categories were used, very similar findings have been obtained in the government survey, both as far as respondents' occupational distribution and their educational qualifications are concerned.[5] Since the government survey does not have a separate category for completed post-secondary education, it is likely that educational qualifications of professionals and administrators combined may be even lower than those ascertained in our study. Only slightly more than one-third of respondents in the survey had at least fourteen years of education, but 30 percent have the equivalent of junior high school, and 9 percent had only been in grade school. Primarily as a result of the different combination of occupational categories, manual workers seem to be somewhat better educated than those in our study. Refugees in sales (including street vendors who have been separately classified in our study), in food and beverage preparation, and in textile processing have generally the lowest levels of education: close to half of the respondents in each of these occupational categories had attended only grade school or less.

Based on formal educational qualifications alone, it becomes obvious that most refugees who had been in professional, administrative, and even some in white-collar occupations will require additional training if they intend to resume their careers in Canada. Former blue-collar workers are handicapped as well. Formal licensing of skilled workers and craftsmen is practically unknown in all three countries. Few of them had any formal on-the-job training; most acquired their skills either informally or simply by watching other, more experienced workers. Because of the restrictive trade practices in Canada (and in other Western societies), many of these refugees will not be able to reenter their occupations on similar skill levels unless they first undertake some vocational training or acquire necessary licenses.

The refugees' problems are further compounded by the fact that, although several speak at least one other Southeast Asian language, they have no familiarity with a European language. Owing to differences in script or pronounciation, particularly of consonants, refugees have experienced near insurmountable difficulties in acquiring English or French language skills. Second-language courses in Canada, which have been designed for immigrants speaking other European languages, have not been very useful in this respect. Even though most refugees were enrolled for language courses, the results are most discouraging.

For example, when respondents in our study who had been enrolled in language training were asked whether they could now function in a job requiring English, only 16 percent said yes, and more than 50 percent categorically said no. The remaining 30 percent qualified their replies to the effect that they could function only if very little knowledge of English was required. The respondents' self-ratings are strongly related to their level of education. Respondents who have a university degree and are thus likely to speak some French are most optimistic in their evaluation, while those who attended only grade school or had some secondary education are least optimistic in their evaluation. Of the former, 42 percent agreed and 37 percent denied that they could function in such a job; of the latter, only slightly more than 10 percent gave an unqualified positive response, and more than half an unqualified negative response.

The findings of the government study are even more telling. In all three surveys, respondents were asked to rate their present ability to speak and understand English or French on a 5-point scale ranging from "fluent" to "none." The cross-sectional analysis shows that over the three-year period, refugees living outside Quebec acquired at least a basic ability to communicate in English, but few became fluent. The proportion of respondents who did not speak the language decreased from 6.5 percent in the first wave to 2.7 percent in the third, and those who rated their ability as "poor," from 44.1 percent to 35 percent. The ratings of "fluent" increased only from 1.3 to 2.3, and the ratings of "good" from 10 percent to 18 percent. Yet in the third year, three-fourths of the respondents still rated their ability as being only poor or fair. The association between education and the level of fluency is similarly strong and monotonic for each of the three years. In the third wave, however, only 36 percent of the respondents with at least fourteen years of education rated their ability to speak and understand English as "fluent" or "good", compared to 8 percent of those with up to six years of education (Neuwirth et al. 1985:184–89).

Refugees are therefore doubly handicapped in their economic and particularly their occupational adjustment. They did not possess readily transferable occupational skills, and most of them had at best a poor working knowledge of English. Moreover, the linguistic handicap was especially pronounced for refugees who, because of their limited formal education, will also have limited job opportunities in Canada. Yet if employability in the new labor market is taken as one of the indicators of economic adjustment in the wider sense of the term, then the respondents in both studies have done surprisingly well. They found jobs very quickly, either shortly after arrival or after having left the English Secondary Language Courses. The high employment rate among Southeast Asians has to be attributed, at least in part, to the fact that sponsors have been a valuable source of job referrals for the refugees they sponsored. Through their contacts with friends and acquaintances, sponsors were able to access jobs that would not normally be registered with the local Employment Centres, and thus might not have been offered to refugees. Moreover, sponsors continued to be the most important source of job referrals in subsequent years. According to the government survey, in the first year 46 percent, in the second year 39 percent, and in the third year still 36 percent of refugees found jobs through them. In each of the three years, government-assisted refugees relied primarily on friends and relatives, and secondarily on their own initiative, while referrals by Employment Centres rank third (Neuwirth et al. 1985:86).

With few exceptions, refugees found only manual work at the bottom rungs of the occupational ladder. The 656 respondents in our combined sample for whom the first job is known show particularly high concentrations in service occupations (27 percent), nontextile (21 percent) and textile processing (16 percent), and unskilled work (14 percent). Only 7 percent had found white-collar jobs. Most of these have been employed as clerks and in auxiliary technical occupations, and a few found jobs in arts and recreation, although not necessarily white-collar work. A very similar picture emerges from the government survey. The proportion of respondents whose first job was nonmanual is about the same as in our study. Since blue-collar occupations are somewhat differently classified, no direct comparison is possible with our study; however, the rather high proportion of refugees in unskilled work (22 percent) should be noted. Most of the jobs were also poorly paid. According to our study, with an hourly wage of up to $3.49, one-third of the refugees received less than the minimum wage at that time. The wages of 18 percent each fell either between $3.50 to $3.99 or $4.00 to $4.99 an hour. Only 9 percent received hourly wages of $5.00 or more; the wages of the remaining one-fifth are not known.

Since there is so little variation in the kinds of jobs respondents initially obtained, none of the traditional sociological background variables, such as previous occupation and level of education, is at this stage related to their occupations. There is, however, one exception, which concerns the differential placement and payment of men and women. Women are more heavily concentrated in occupations such as chambermaids or seamstresses, and thus are in low-paying jobs, while men work primarily in construction, as mechanics, and in service occupations and product processing and fabrication. It is worth noting at this point that seven of the nine respondents who started out in auxiliary technical occupations had been former administrators and professionals, and six had either completed high school or continued beyond it. The placements are so few, however, that they cannot be interpreted as indicating a beginning occupational adjustment; instead they should be ascribed to chance alone. Former professionals and administrators as well as respondents with post-secondary education are scattered over the whole range of manual jobs, as are former blue-collar workers and respondents with fewer years of education.

Wages received at the first job tend to be related to level of education and to the respondents' gender. The proportion of respondents who received less than $3.49 an hour decreases consistently from 50 percent for those with elementary education, to 27 percent for university graduates and postgraduates. The wage differentials based on gender are similarly significant. For instance, over half the women, but less than one-third of the men, receive wages of up to $3.49 per hour, that is, the minimum wage or below. Although differences in employment prospects and earning potential between immigrant men and immigrant women are well documented (and apply to Canadian-born men and women as well), it is somewhat surprising that Southeast Asians should be exposed to them in their first jobs (Boyd 1985:Chap. 11). Well-intentioned sponsors and employment counselors may have inadvertently contributed to these differences. In their attempt to help refugee families become self-sufficient, they concentrated primarily on finding jobs for the husband and head of household, and viewed the women as only secondary contributor to the family income.

Based on research findings for other refugee populations, the initial concentration in low-level and low-paying jobs was to be expected. The two questions to be addressed are therefore whether Southeast Asians have been able to attain some upward mobility through subsequent job changes, which would enhance their economic adjustment in both of its senses, and to what extent they may have even experienced downward mobility that impeded or blocked their adjustment. Job changes that involve primarily an increase in pay will be interpreted as being indicative of the refugees' continuing economic adjustment in the wider sense of the term, since they presuppose that the refugees have at least acquired some knowledge of the Canadian labor market, and some familiarity with conditions and practices in the workplace. Such job changes, however, do not necessarily lead to occupational adjustment, that is, reentry into their previous occupation. Unfortunately, the analysis of occupational adjustment has to be confined to the job changes of nonmanual workers, as it is impossible to make any reliable inferences that the respondents work at a skill level equivalent to their occupational self-designation of jobs held in Canada.

The employment changes of respondents (333) in our study who went on to second jobs demonstrate considerable mobility between occupational categories. Among manual workers, most movements occurred out of traditionally low-paying occupations, such as food and beverage preparation, textile fabrication, unskilled work, and farming. More than half the respondents in each of these occupational categories left their first job, and very few performed the same kind of work in their second job. Workers in textile fabrication are the exception, with 28 percent of job-leavers reentering it with a different employer. Moreover, fewer respondents entered occupations in each of these industries for the first time than had left them. Apart from the occupational turn-over, most second jobs gave respondents longer working hours than their previous one. For example, four-fifths of the respondents who held part-time jobs with less than 30 hours a week were able to find employment in which they could now work full time or at least longer hours than before. Yet, over one-fourth of those repondents who at first had worked 40 hours or more a week no longer had the same hours in their second job.

A comparison of wage rates confirms that six out of every ten respondents have indeed found better paying jobs (Table 31.3), with most of them receiving from $1.00 to $1.50 more per hour. It is rather striking that such improvement was mostly confined to refugees who had originally received

Table 31.3 Comparison between Wages Received in First and Second Jobs

Hourly wage in first job	Hourly wage in second job (percent)			Number changing jobs[a]	Proportion of persons changing jobs (percent)
	Lower	Same	Higher		
$0–$2.99	—	—	100	9	64.3
$3–$3.24	1.0	21.6	77.4	102	65.9
$3.25–$3.49	6.1	18.4	75.5	49	51.0
$3.50–$3.99	14.9	29.9	55.2	67	47.3
$4.00–$4.99	26.7	40.0	33.3	45	33.2
$5.00–$5.99	46.7	26.7	26.7	15	
$6.00–$20.00	51.1	42.9	—	7	26.9
More than $20.00	100.0	—	—	3	100.0
				297	

[a] Includes only those for whom the wage is known.

very low wages. The tendency toward higher wages is strongest for respondents who at first received less than the minimum wage, and becomes progressively weaker for each subsequent category, until it finally is reversed for those who earned at least $6.00 an hour. While all the respondents who had earned less than $3.00 an hour have been able to find better paying jobs, seven of the ten respondents in the last category had to take a cut in pay, and only three were able to find a job with similar wages.

Some noteworthy changes are also apparent among the few respondents who had started out in nonmanual work. Four of the nine respondents who were placed in auxiliary occupations left their first job, but only two found a similar one. The turn-over is highest among refugees who had been employed in arts and recreation, which includes some manual occupations: three out of four left their original employment, but only one reentered a similar occupation. There is also some downward mobility among white-collar workers. About one-fourth of them left their previous job, but only one-third of these job leavers remained at that level. Except for auxiliary technical occupations, only eight respondents were able to enter non-manual, mostly clerical, employment the first time.

These findings demonstrate that at least during the first fifteen months or so, refugees' upward mobility was basically limited to minor improvements in wages. The wages at the second job are again related to respondents' level of education, as well as their gender. Compared to the first job, both tendencies have become somewhat stronger. For example, the proportion of respondents who now receive less than $4.00 decreases successively from 64 percent for those with grade school education, to 27 percent for university graduates. Similarly, 32 percent of the men, but nearly twice as many women, receive wages that fall in the same range. In this sense the economic adjustment, particularly of the better educated respondents, has somewhat improved. Except for the movement of a few white-collar workers into nonmanual work, there have been no indications of a beginning occupational adjustment. No additional respondents have suceeded in entering auxiliary technical employment as a possible first step toward resuming their previous occupation. Moreover, as far as the second job is concerned, several of the few former administrators, professionals, and white-collar workers who started out in similar occupations have become downwardly mobile. It is also worth noting that respondents with elementary education tend to gravitate toward service and textile occupations, while respondents with post-secondary education begin to concentrate in processing occupations other than textile, machining, and product fabricating.

Since the government survey covers the three-year period considered crucial for occupational adjustment, the question can be addressed whether the refugees' subsequent job changes are indicative of continuing economic and beginning occupational adjustment. An evaluation of the relevant findings is compounded by the fact that in 1981, in the refugees' second year, Canada entered one of its worst economic recessions in recent history. Although the precise impact cannot be assessed, the onset of the recession certainly slowed down the progress refugees might otherwise have made, and it also had a particularly adverse effect on the most vulnerable groups among them.

If, for instance, employability is used as the most basic indicator of economic adjustment, one would normally expect that over time, as refugees become more familiar with the job market and with new work practices, their chances of becoming employed will be enhanced. In fact the opposite is the case. Their unemployment rate not only rose consistently from 9 percent in the first year, to 15 percent in the second year, to 20 percent in the third year, but it was also higher than the rate for Canadians, which increased from 9 percent to 10 percent and 14 percent during the same period. Furthermore, even though there were similar changes in the unemployment rate between men and women, and a similar widening of the gender gap for both refugees and Canadians, Southeast Asian men were particularly adversely affected. In the third year, for example, the unemployment rate for refugees was 21 percent for men and 15 percent for women, as compared to 15 percent and 13 percent, respectively, in the overall population. Further analysis also showed that unemploment was higher among older refugees and, as is to be expected, among refugees with limited formal education (Neuwirth et al 1985:96–138). The increase in unemployment can be attributed mainly to the recession.

As the cross-sectional analysis of gross weekly earnings indicates, the refugees were unable to improve their economic adjustment by obtaining better paying jobs over the three-year period. Although a few have reported substantially larger earnings, the majority of refugees, particularly between the second and third years, experienced only a very modest increase, if any at all. Using the Consumer Price Index as correction factor for inflation, the median earnings increased by 8 percent from $192 per week in year-one to $207 in year-two, but by only 3 percent to $214 in year-three. According to the panel analysis performed on those respondents who participated in all three waves, there was little uniform improvement in earnings over the period. In quite a few cases the refugees' economic situation in fact deteriorated, such that earnings reported in the subsequent year are frequently lower than those in the previous one. Similar to the findings of our study, the tendency toward downward mobility was more pronounced among respondents in the higher earning brackets. For instance, 10 percent and 17 percent, respectively of those who had weekly earnings of up to $100, or between $101 to $150 in year-one, reported a lower income in year-two, compared to 45 percent of those who, with earnings of over $300, fall into the highest bracket. The tendency is less pronounced for the third year; yet the difference between those in the lowest and highest earning categories who experienced a reduction in earnings still comes to 28 percentage points.

The regression analysis performed by Gilles Grenier on cross-sectional data also shows that, with the exception of gender, the factors that could be expected to affect earnings have in fact very little impact on them. Education and previous work experience have a small effect on earnings over time, such that the better-educated report slightly higher incomes in the third year. As is to be expected, English and French language skills have a similar positive effect, while contrary to expectations, language training did not increase earnings and appears even to have decreased them. Women, however, have much lower earnings than do men, such that this difference still persists after we control for other variables in the regression. Since the independent variables explain so little of the variance, Grenier suggests that other factors that cannot be measured, such as motivation and simple chance, must have had a major influence on earnings (Neuwirth et al 1985:234–38, 267–69).

The modest increases in earnings alone would indicate that refugees' occupational mobility was rather limited during the three-year period. The cross-sectional analysis that due to a declining participation of blue-collar workers, is based on successively smaller samples and does not necessarily include the same respondents, demonstrates this lack of mobility even more starkly. Compared to year-one, the absolute number of refugees who in year-three have entered professions or white-collar occupations has increased only by three additional cases each. Among respondents who started out in manual work, only the proportion of unskilled laborers has decreased by seven percentage points (ibid.:78–84, 94).

The panel analysis (Table 31.4) that traces in some detail the occupational trajectory of former administrators, various professionals, and white-collar workers similarly shows that few respondents have been able to affect some occupational adjustment. Excluding former white-collar workers and sales persons, only 12 percent of 147 former professionals and administrators have been able, by the third year, to enter the same or similar occupations. This mobility is confined primarily to respondents in two occupational categories: medical professionals (which also includes herbal doctors, veterinarians, and dentists), and scientists and engineers. In the third year, eight of the twelve medical professionals have begun to work in the same and related occupations; of the fifteen scientists, six are in related fields, and two have moved into administrative work. The few refugees in other science and engineering occupations, as well as in fine arts, who initially started out in the same occupations, experienced downward mobility. The government report also notes that "a respondent's initial placement in year-one is of some importance for his subsequent career. Few of the respondents who began in blue-collar work were able to leave it, and if they did so at all, such a move occurs only in the second year but not later on" (Neuwirth et al. 1985:230–34).

Table 31.4   Previous Occupations by Occupation in Canada for Professionals, White Collar, and Sales

Previous occupations	Same	Related	Other
Administrative and manager	1	—	1
Science and engineering	4	2	1
Technicians	3	—	—
Teachers	—	1	1
Other education	—	1	1
Professional, medicine	—	4	3
Nursing, other medicine	3	—	—
Fine arts	2	—	—
Clerical	3	2	—
Sales	1	—	—
Total	17	10	7
Administrative and managers	—	—	1
Science and Engineering	3	4	1
Technicians	—	—	—
Teachers	—	2	1
Other education	—	1	—
Professional, medicine	2	5	1
Nursing, other medicine	3	1	—
Fine arts	1	—	—
White collar	3	2	—
Sales	1	1	—
Total	13	16	4
Administrative managers	1	1	—
Technicians	—	6	1
Other science and engineering	—	—	—
Teachers	—	—	3
Other education	—	—	3
Professional, medicine	4	4	—
Nursing, other medicine	5	1	—
Fine arts	—	—	—
Clerical	4	—	5
Sales	—	—	—
Total	14	12	12

Conclusions

Southeast Asian refugees showed so little improvement in their earning capacity, and in their occupational placements over the three-year period, that even with the beginning economic recovery, any later substantial progress seems to be most unlikely. Although the economic recession has aggravated their economic adjustment to some extent by contributing to their unemployment, it cannot entirely account for their heavy concentra-

Occupations in Canada: Year One

White collar	Sales	Blue collar	Unskilled labor	Total	Proportion in manual work (percent)
5	1	9	7	24	67
—	1	4	1	13	38
—	—	1	3	7	71
2	—	15	7	26	85
4	—	10	4	20	70
—	—	4	1	12	42
—	1	14	8	26	85
—	—	11	4	17	88
—	1	25	15	46	87
—	—	17	6	24	96
11	4	110	56	215	77

Occupations in Canada: Year Two

White collar	Sales	Blue collar	Unskilled labor	Total	Proportion in manual work (percent)
9	—	10	1	21	52
1	1	2	2	14	28
—	—	7	3	10	100
2	1	14	5	25	76
2	1	16	2	22	82
1	—	3	—	12	25
3	—	13	6	26	73
—	—	11	3	15	93
—	1	36	7	49	88
1	—	19	3	25	88
19	4	131	32	219	74

Occupations in Canada: Year Three

White collar	Sales	Blue collar	Unskilled labor	Total	Proportion in manual work (percent)
8	2	9	2	23	48
—	1	6	1	15	47
—	—	10	1	11	100
3	1	11	5	23	70
2	—	14	2	21	76
—	—	4	—	12	33
2	—	16	3	27	70
—	—	13	2	15	100
—	1	32	8	50	80
2	—	19	6	27	93
17	5	134	30	224	73

tion in low-paying jobs. Their lack of progress has to be attributed primarily to the fact that without vocational training or upgrading courses, they cannot capitalize on their educational qualifications and previous work experience; thus they remain locked into the bottom rungs of the occupational ladder. As the government survey suggests, if they are given the opportunity to attend such courses soon after arrival, they are indeed able to move up the occupational ladder. The panel analysis, for instance, shows that the few respondents, mostly refugees with post-secondary education, who were fortunate enough to attend a secondary language as well as another course during their first year, are five times as likely to enter job skill-training programs in the second year, and more than three times as likely to do so in the third year, than are those who did not have the same initial opportunity. The regression analysis of lagged effects of language and other training courses on subsequent years also suggests that attendance of courses other than lanuage training in the first year, but not later, may affect the earnings in the subsequent years (Neuwirth et al. 1985:227–30, 238–39, and 269).

Refugees themselves are keenly aware of the handicaps that prevent their integration into the labor market and the utilization of their previous skills. According to the government survey, the needs for language training and job skills training occupy the first and second rank among reasons given by respondents for their difficulties in finding employment or finding the jobs they would like to have (Neuwirth et al. 1985:118). The findings of both studies suggest that refugees from Third World countries will need vocational training and up-grading programs soon after arrival, and on a much larger scale than was the case for Southeast Asians. Since it has yet to be established that formal education received in the home country influences significantly the refugees' performance in the occupations for which they are trained or retrained, such programs should be particularly available to refugees with lower levels of education. By assuming that years of formal education do have such an influence, we may again impose our own standards upon others for whom it may not be appropriate.

Notes

1. The federal government agreed initially to resettle 50,000 refugees provided the private sector would sponsor, and thus bear the expenses, for at least half of them. But because of the overwhelming response by Canadians across the country, the private sector's quota was soon exceeded. As a result, between 1979 and 1980, more than 60,000 refugees were admitted. In inviting the participation of the private sector, the government made use of a provision in the 1978 Immigration Act, which introduced the concept of private sponsorship. According to the act, locally incorporated organizations or groups of at least five Canadian citizens and/or permanent residents were able to sponsor refugees provided they agree to assume the "financial and moral responsibility" for the refugees during their first year of resettlement. Sponsors have to provide the refugees with housing and furniture and assist them financially until they become self-sufficient, but no longer than for the length of this period. Sponsors are also responsible for helping refugees become acquainted with, and adjust to, their new surroundings and way of life. Government-assisted refugees are aided in their resettlement by the local Canadian Employment and Immigration Centres and nongovernmental immigrant service organizations.

2. Roberta Markus, Ryerson College, was the research director of the Toronto

segment of the study. The data collection phase of the research was funded, under the aegis of the Institute for Research on Public Policy, by Employment and Immigration, Canada, the Ministry of Culture and Recreation for Ontario, the Multicultural Historical Society, and the Institute. Data analyses have since been made possible through grants by the Multicultural Directorate, Secretary of State, and the Social Sciences and Humanities Research Council of Canada.

3. Households consisting of large extended families often were sponsored partly by government and partly by private groups, particularly if the relatives did not arrive in Canada together. The restriction to officially sponsored family members was, therefore, necessary to separate the impact of the mode of sponsorship on adaptation.

4. It was not possible to obtain revelant data for every adult refugee. Since many families consisted of six or more persons, interviewers sometimes forgot to ask entire questions for each of the members of the household, and at other times interviewees were unable to provide the answers for some relatives. This applies particularly to the interview sections dealing with respondents' occupational background in their home country, and employment history in Canada. Depending on the variables used in the analysis, the number of cases is, therefore, different.

5. Since only principal applicants, that is, heads of households or unattached individuals who were at least fifteen years old, were sampled, the survey does not include, as our study does, housewives and students who are dependents.

Bibliography

Abdurachim, I. 1970. "Migration from Rural Areas into Bandung." Paper presented at the seminar on Southeast Asian Studies, IKIP Bandung.

Abraham, D. M. G., and D. C. Herberg, compilers. 1980. *Cross-cultural Social Work in Canada: An Annotated Bibliography*. Toronto: The Multicultural Workers' Network.

Adelman, H., ed. 1980. *The Indochinese Refugee Movement: The Canadian Experience*. Toronto: Operation Lifeline.

Adelman, H., C. LeBlanc, and J. P. Thorien. 1980. "Canadian Policy on Indochinese Refugees." In *Southeast Asian Exodus: From Tradition to Resettlement*, edited by E. L. Tepper. Ottawa: Canadian Asian Studies Association.

Adepoju, A. 1982. "The Dimensions of the Refugee Problem in Africa." *African Affairs* 81:21–25.

Aga Khan, S. 1971. "The One Million Refugees in Africa." *Migration News* 20(4):3–12.

———. 1981. "Study on Human Rights and Massive Exoduses." *Report to the Commission on Human Rights*. E/CN/ 4/1503.

Ahmed, A. S. 1980. "Resettlement of Afghan Refugees and the Social Sciences." *Journal of South Asian and Middle Eastern Studies* 4(1): 77–89.

Aiboni, S. A. 1978. *Protection of Refugees in Africa*. Uppsala: Svenska Institutet for Internationell Ratt.

Ajchenbaum, Y. 1981. *Les Populations originaires d'Asie de Sud-est Accueillies en France au Sein des Centres Provisoires d'Hebergement: 1975–1979*. Paris: France Terre d'Asile.

Akhtar, R., ed. 1981. *Pakistan Year Book*. Karachi: East and West Publishing Company.

Akol, J. O. 1986. "Refugee Migration and Repatriation: Case-Studies of Some Affected Rural Communities in Southern Sudan." Ph.D. diss., University of Manitoba, Winnipeg.

Alberta, Advanced Education and Manpower, Edmonton. 1980. *A Health Workers Guide to Indochinese Refugees*. Alberta: Advanced Education and Manpower.

Alberta, Advanced Education and Manpower (Settlement Services) and Canada, Employment and Immigration Commission (Alberta Region). 1982. *Guide to Indo-Chinese Refugees and Employment*. Edmonton.

Ali, T. 1970. *Pakistan: Military Rule or People's Power*. London: Jonathan Cape.

Alier, A. 1976. "Speech to the People's Regional Assembly on the Process of Integration." Southern Region, Juba, May 12.

Alla, N. 1976. *Report on Socio-Economic Survey Among Refugees in Wad el Hileiew*. UNHCR and COR.

Allen, R. 1983. "The Social Organization of Uprooting and Flight." Master's thesis, University of Calgary.

Allen, R., and H. H. Hiller. 1983. "The Social Organization of Migration: An Analysis of the Uprooting and Flight of Vietnamese Refugees." Paper presented at the Annual Meeting of the Canadian Sociology and Anthropology Association, Vancouver, B.C., June 4.

Amin, S. 1974. *Modern Migrations in Western Africa*. London: Oxford University Press.

Anandan, S. 1983 "Refugees in Their Homeland." *The Illustrated Weekly of India* 104 (May 22): 10–11.

Asomani, K. 1982. "Belize Settlement Project." *Refugees Magazine* 1 (September): 22.

Australian Population and Immigration Council. 1979. "Refugees and Australia." *Population Report* No. 3.

Awanohara, S. 1983. "In the Shadow of Death." *Far Eastern Economic Review*, July 14: 38

Azam, S. 1983. "The Bangla-Burma Bridge." *Bangladesh Today* (Dhaka), June 1.

Bach, R. L. 1985. *Labour Force Participation and Employment Among Southeast Asian Refugees in the United States*. U.S. Department of Health and Human Services, Office of Refugee Settlement.

Bach, R., and J. Bach. 1980. "Employment Patterns of Southeast Asian Refugees." *Monthly Labor Review* (October): 31–38.

Bach, R., L. W. Gordon, D. W. Haines, and D. R. Howell. 1983. "The Economic Adjustment of Southeast Asian Refugees in the U.S.." *World Refugee Survey 1983*. New York: American Council for Nationalities Service.

Barbour, K. M. 1961. *The Republic of the Sudan: A Regional Geography*. London: University of London Press.

Barton, M. S. 1986. "Refugees in Central America: What Lies Ahead?" *Refugees* 31: 19–27.

Baster, N. 1972. "Development Indicators: An Introduction." *Journal of Development Studies* 8: 1–20.

Beck, K. S. 1982. "Refugee Emergencies in Africa: 1980–1982." Paper presented at seminar on the Refugee Problems on Universal, Regional and National Levels, Institute of Public International Law and International Relations, Thessaloniki, August 30–September 17.

Beijer, G. 1969. "Modern Patterns of International Migratory Movements." In *Migration*, edited by J. A. Jackson. London: Cambridge University Press.

Beshir, M. O. 1968. *The Southern Sudan: Background to Conflict*. New York: F. A. Praeger.

———. 1975. *The Southern Sudan: From Conflict to Peace*. London: C. Hurst & Co.

Betts, T. R. 1966a. "Refugees in Eastern Africa: A Comparative Study." Unpublished manuscript.

———. 1966b. "Zonal Rural Development in Africa." *Journal of Modern African Studies* 7(1): 149–53.

———. 1980. "The Spontaneous Settlement of Rural Refugees in Africa." Paper for Euro-Action ACORD, London.

———. 1981. *Spontaneous Settlement of Rural Refugees in Africa*. London: Euro-Action ACORD.

Billard, A. 1983a. "The Closed Camps of Hong Kong." *Refugees Magazine* 3: 21–22.

———. 1983b. "Khao-I-Dang Holding Centre." *Refugees Magazine* 3: 12–13.

———. 1983c. "Pirates of the Siam Gulf." *Refugees Magazine* 3: 24–26.

Birido, O. Y. 1983. "International Conference on Assistance to Refugees in Africa (ICARA) and Its Aftermath." Paper presented at the seminar on Refugees, Khartoum, September 11–14.

Blood, H. 1950. "British Honduras: Land of Opportunity." *Journal of the Royal Commonwealth Society* 3(3): 83–86.

Boesch, E. E. 1975. *Zwischen Angst und Triumph*. Bern: Humber Verlag.

———. 1976. *Psychopathologie des Alltags*. Bern: Humber Verlag.

———. 1980. *Kulture und Handlung*. Bern: Humber Verlag.

———. 1983a. *Zum Konzept der "Identitat" aus kulturpsychologischer Sicht*. Saarbruecken: Socio-Psychological Research Center, University of the Saar.

———. 1983b. *From Expulsion to Hospitality: A Psychologist's Look at the Refugee Problem*. Saarbruecken: Socio-Psychological Research Center, University of the Saar.

Boland, B. J. 1971. *The Struggle of Islam in Modern Indonesia*. The Hague: Martinus Nijhoff.

Bolland, O. N. 1977. *The Formation of a Colonial Society: Belize from Conquest to Crown Colony*. Baltimore and London: Johns Hopkins University Press.

Bonavia, D. 1979. "Slowing Down the Exodus." *Far Eastern Economic Review*, July 13: 22.

Bose, A. 1974. "Exodus to the City." *UNESCO Courier* 27: 39–41.

Boyd, M., ed. 1985. *Mobility and Status Attainment in Canada*. Ottawa: Carleton University Press.

Breakspear, A. 1980. "Community Support and Backlash—A Commentary." In *The

Indochinese Refugee Movement—The Canadian Experience, edited by H. Adelman. Toronto: Operation Lifeline.

Brooks, H. C., and Y. El-Ayouty, eds. 1970. *Refugees South of the Sahara: An African Dilemma*. Westport, Conn.: Negro Universities Press.

Brukdown: The Magazine of Belize.

Buchignani, N. 1980. "The Economic Adaptation of Southeast Asian Refugees in Canada." In *Southeast Asian Exodus: From Tradition to Resettlement*, edited by E. L. Tepper. Ottawa: Canadian Asian Studies Association.

Buehrig, E. 1971. *The United Nation and the Palestinian Refugees: A Study in Non-territorial Administration*. Bloomington: Indiana University Press.

Buhler, R., n.d. "A Refugee of the War of the Castes Makes Belize His Home: The Memoirs of J.M. Rosado." *Occasional Publications of the Belize Institute for Social Research and Action*, no. 2. Belize: The Benex Press.

Bushra, J. A. 1982. "Education and Training Needs for Refugees." Paper presented at the Khartoum Refugee Seminar, Khartoum, September.

Cabib, A. 1982. "Central American Refugees: The Flight from El Salvador." *Intercom* 10(1): 12.

Calgary Sponsor and Refugee Society. 1982. *Legal Needs of Southeast Asian Refugees: A Survey*. Calgary: Calgary Sponsor and Refugee Society.

California Department of Social Services. 1980. *Refugees: The Challenge of the 80's*. Sacramento: Report of Hearings Conducted by the California State Social Services Advisory Board.

Canada, Employment and Immigration Commission (CEIC). 1981a. *Longitudinal Survey of Indochinese Refugees of Labour Force Participation Rate and Unemployment Rate by Sponsorship Mode and Selected Characteristics*. Ottawa: Canada Employment and Immigration Commission, Immigration and Demographic Analysis Division.

———. 1981b. *Study of the Impact of the 1979–80 Indochinese Refugee Program on Canada Immigration Centre (CIC) and Canada Employment Centre (CEC) Operations*. Ottawa: Canada Employment and Immigration Commission, Immigration Program Division, Program Evaluation Branch, Strategic Policy and Planning.

———. 1982a. *Indochinese Refugees: The Canadian Response, 1979 and 1980*. Ottawa: Ministry of Supply and Services.

———. 1982b. *Evaluation of the 1979–80 Indochinese Refugee Program*. Ottawa: Canada Employment and Immigration Commission.

———. 1984. *A Longitudinal Survey of Indochinese Refugees, 1981–1983*. Ottawa: Canada Employment and Immigration Commission.

Canadian Mental Health Association. 1983. "Mental Health Needs of Southeast Asian Refugees." Manitoba division. (Mimeo).

Cebula, R. J. 1979. "A Survey of the Literature on the Migration Impact of State and Local Government Policies." *Public Finance* 34(1): 69–84.

Chambers, R. 1975. *Rural Refugees in Africa: Observations of UNHCR Policies and Practice*. UNHCR Document 140/18/75.

———. 1976a. "Rural Refugees After Arusha." Paper for UNHCR.

———. 1976b. *Report on Workshop/Seminar on Rural Refugees in Africa Held in Arusha, Tanzania (February 16–19, 1976)*. UNHCR Document 140/14/76.

———. 1976c. "UNHCR Crisis, Choices and Future." Paper for UNHCR.

———. 1979. "Rural Refugees in Africa: What the Eye Does Not See." *Disasters* 4: 381–92.

Chan, K. B. 1977. "Individual Differences in Reactions to Stress and Their Personality and Situational Determinants: Some Implications for Community Mental Health." *Social Science and Medicine* 11: 89–103.

———. 1983. "Mental Health Needs of Indochinese Refugees: Toward a National Refugee Resettlement Policy and Strategy in Canada." In *Community Mental Health Action: Primary Prevention Programming in Canada*, edited by D. P. Lumsden. Ottawa: Canadian Mental Health Association.

Chan, K. B., and L. Lam. 1981. "Resettlement of Vietnamese-Chinese Refugees in Montreal: Some Socio-psychological Problems and Dilemmas." In *Asian Canadians: Regional Perspectives. Selections from the Proceedings, Asian Canadian Symposium V of the Canadian Asian Studies Association*. Halifax: Mount Saint Vincent University. Reprinted 1983 in Canadian Ethnic Studies 15(1): 1–17.

————. 1983a. *Psychosocial Adaptation: Some Psychological Dilemmas of the Resettlement Process.* Montreal (Mimeo).

Chanda, N. 1977. "Hanoi Comes Down to Earth." *Far Eastern Economic Review,* February 4: 28–33.

Christensen, H. 1978. *The Progress of Refugee Settlements in Africa.* Geneva: International University Exchange Fund.

————. 1982. *Survival Strategies for and by Camp Refugees. Report on a Six-Week Exploratory Sociological Field Study into the Food Situation of Refugees in Camps in Somalia.* Report No. 82.3, UNRISD, Geneva.

————. 1983. *Sustaining Afghan Refugees in Pakistan. Report on the Food Situation and Related Social Aspects.* Report No. 83.3, UNRISD, Geneva.

Coat, P. 1978. "Material Assistance: Some Policy Problems Reviewed in the Light of Robert Chambers." *Evaluation Reports.* Paper for UNHCR.

Cobus, M. 1977. "A Look Back at Chile: Canada's Attitude Towards Refugees and Immigrants." *Rights and Freedoms* (Ottawa) 27.

Collins, C. O. n.d. "Nation Building and Political Geography: The Case of Belize." *Graduate Studies on Latin America* 3: 23–45.

Commissioner of Refugees (COR). 1980. "COR Memoranadum on the Repatraition of Ethiopian Refugees." No. 46/B/1, September 1, Khartoum (in Arabic).

Cox, R., and H. Jacobson. 1975. *Patterns of Influence: Decision Making in International Organizations.* New Haven: Yale University Press.

Crisp, J. F. 1984. "Voluntary Repatraition Programmes for African Refugees: A Critical Examination." *Refugee Issues* 1(2): 23.

Crosbie, A. J., and P. A. Furley. 1967. "The New Belize—Prospects for British Honduras." *Scottish Geographical Magazine* 83(1): 53–63.

Dak, O. 1974. *A Geographical Analysis of the Distribution of Migrants in Uganda.* Makerere University, Department of Geography, Occasional Paper no. 11.

Das, K. 1983. "The End Is Not in Sight." *Far Eastern Economic Review.* July 14: 37–38.

Das, K., and G. Sacerdoti. 1978. "Economics of Human Cargo." *Far Eastern Economic Review,* December 22: 10–12.

Davico, L. 1983. "Boat, Land and Other People." *Refugees Magazine* 3: 5.

David, H. P. 1969. "Involuntary International Migration: Adaptation of Refugees." *International Migration Review* 7(3/4): 67–105.

Davidson, W. V. 1983. *Historical-Cultural Geography of Belize.* Report prepared for Country Environmental Profile, Belize City, Belize.

DeJong, G. F., and W. L. Donelly. 1973. "Public Welfare and Migration." *Social Science Quarterly* 54: 329–44.

Desbarats, J. M., and L. Holland. 1983. "Indochinese Settlement Patterns in Orange County." *Amerasia Journal* 11(1).

Deschamps, G. 1982. *Etude Longitudinale sur l'Adaptation Socio-economique des Refugies Indochinois au Quebec: Bilan apres un an de Sejour.* Quebec: Ministere des Communautés Culturelles et de l'Immigration, Septembre.

Desmond, C. 1971. *The Discarded People.* Harmondsworth: Penguin.

Deutsche Stiftung fur Internationale Entwicklung (DSE). 1982. *Fluchtlinge und Entwicklung.* Berlin: DSE.

Dev, B. J., and D. K. Lahiri. 1978. "The Line System in Assam: A Study of the Role of Moulana Bhasani." *Journal of the Asiatic Society of Bangladesh* 23(2): 65–98.

de Voe, D. M. 1980. "Framing Refugees and Clients." *International Migration Review* 15.

Diegues, A. C. S. 1981. "UNHCR Experience with Rural Settlement Planning for Refugees in Africa." Paper presented at the workshop on Rural Refugee Settlements, Dar es Salaam, September 1–10.

Dirks, G. F. 1977. *Canada's Refugee Policy: Indifference or Opportunism?* Montreal: McGill–Queen's University Press.

Dobson, N. 1973. *A History of Belize.* Trinidad and Jamaica: Longman Caribbean Ltd.

Dorais, L. J., and Q. B. Nguyen. 1983. *The Vietnamese of Quebec: A Socio-linguistic Profile.* Quebec City: Laval University Anthropology Department.

Downie, J. 1959. *An Economic Policy for British Honduras.* Belize: Government Printer.

DPA Consulting Limited, in Association with Maxwell Brem. 1982. *Evaluation of the Indochinese Refugee Group Sponsorship Program: Executive Summary*. Prepared for the Program Evaluation Branch, Employment and Immigration Canada, Ottawa.

Drudi, G. 1979. "Les refugies vietnamiens: accueil ou tolerance?" *L'ecoutille*. March.

D'Souza, F. 1980. *The Refugee Dilemma: International Recognition and Acceptance*. London: Minority Rights Group Report No. 43.

Dunnigan, T. 1982. "Segmentary Kinship in an Urban Society: The Hmong of St. Paul–Minneapolis." *Anthropological Quarterly* 55(3): 126–34.

Eisenstadt, S. N. 1954. *The Absorption of Immigrants*. London: Routledge & Kegan Paul.

Elahi, K. M., and S. Sultana. 1980. "Population Redistribution and Settlement Changes in South Asia." Paper presented at the symposium on Development and Population Redistribution in South Asia, Commission on Population Geography, International Geographical Union, Karachi, January 4–10.

El Badry, M. A. 1965. "Trends in the Components of Population Growth in the Arab Countries of the Middle East: A Survey of Present Information." *Demography* 2: 140–86.

Elmandjra, M. 1973. *The United Nations System: An Analysis*. London: Faber & Faber.

Emergency Committee for African Refugees. 1982. "U.S. Policy and the Current Refugee Crisis in Africa." Issue 12(1/2): 10–12.

Eriksson, L-G., G. Melander, and P. Nobel, eds. 1981. *An Analysing Account of the Conference on the African Refugee Problem: Arusha, May 1979*. Uppsala: Scandinavian Institute of African Studies.

Evans, G. 1948. "Report of the British Guiana and British Honduras Settlement Commission." Presented by the Secretary of State for the Colonies to Parliament by Command of His Majesty, September 1948. Colonial Office. CMD. 7533. London: His Majesty's Stationery Office.

Everitt, J. C. 1970. "Terra Incognita: An Analysis of a Geographical Anachronism and an Historical Accident." Master's thesis, Simon Fraser University, British Columbia.

———. 1982. "Changing Patterns of Cultural Imperialism in a Developing Country." Paper presented to the Annual Meeting of the Association of American Geographers, San Antonio, Texas.

———. 1983. "Mennonites in Belize." *Journal of Cultural Geography* 3(2): 82–93.

Ex, J. 1966. *Adjustment after Migration*. The Hague: Martinus Nijhoff.

Farah, A. B. 1983. Statement by the United Nations Under-Secretary-General. Meeting of OAU Secretariat and Voluntary Agencies, Arusha, Tanzania, March 21–26.

Finnan, C. R. 1981. "Occupational Assimilation of Refugees." *International Migration Review* 15(1): 292–309.

"Fire in Asssam, South Asia's Arc of Crisis." 1983. *Asiaweek* 9 (September): 11–16.

Fischer, C. 1976. *The Urban Experience*. New York: Harcourt-Brace Jovanovich.

Fitzpatrick, J. P. 1966. "The Importance of Community in the Process of Immigrant Assimilation." *International Migration Review* 1(1): 5–16.

Fondation pour la recherche sociale. 1980. "L'insertion des Refugies du Sud-est Asiatique en Region Parisienne." *Migrations/Etudes* 31. Paris: Ministere du Travail et de la Participation.

Forbes, D. 1981. "Petty Commodity Production and Underdevelopment: The Case of Pedlars and Trishaw Riders in Ujang Pandong, Indonesia." *Progress in Planning* 16.

Foreign Broadcast Information Service (FBIS). 1983a. *Daily Report, South Asia*, Vol. 8. May 5.

———. 1983b. *Daily Report, South Asia*, Vol. 8. May 24.

———. 1983c. *Daily Report, South Asia*, Vol. 8. June 8.

Fox, D. J. 1962. "Recent Work on British Honduras." *Geographical Review* 52(1): 112–17.

Frejka, T. 1974. "Which Road Will Population Take on the Way to the Twenty First Century?" *People (UNESCO)* 1(4): 5–11.

"From Serf-Owner to Refugee: The Story of One Ethiopian Woman Refugee." 1985. *The Weekly Review* (Nairobi), February 22: 16–17.

Fuhr, A. L. 1981. *Sponsorship of South-East Asian Refugees in Edmonton and Adjoining Area: The Sponsors' Perspective*. Report prepared for Community Aid to Refugees Today (C.A.R.T.), Edmonton.

Gaafar, M. O., and C. Ramchandran. 1982. *Impact of Development Projects on Population Redistribution: A Case Study for Gedaref Town in Eastern Sudan*. Khartoum: ECA/PD/WP/ 1982/1, Statistics Department.

Gankovsksy, Y. V., and L. R. Gordon-Polonskaya. 1964. *A History of Pakistan*. Moscow: U.S.S.R. Academy of Science.

Garnaut, R., and C. Manning. 1974. *Irian Jaya*. Canberra: Australian National University Press.

Gasarasi, C. P. 1976. *The Life of a Refugee Settlement: The Case of Muyenzi in Ngara District, Tanzania*. Master's thesis, University of Dar es Salaam.

Gee, J., and M. K. McKim. 1980. "Cultural Conflicts of Chinese Canadian Adolescents." In *Selections from the Proceedings, Asian Canadian Symposium IV*, edited by K. V. Ujimoto and G. Hirasayashi. Quebec: University of Montreal.

George, T. J. S. 1980. *Revolt in Mindanao: The Rise of Islam in Philippine Politics*. Kuala Lumpur: Oxford University Press.

Gerry, C. 1974. "Petty Producers and the Urban Economy: A Case Study of Debar." Geneva: International Labour Office, World Employment Programme Research Working Paper.

Gleek, L. E., Jr. 1974. *Americans on the Philippine Frontier*. Manila: Carmelo & Banermann.

Goantiang, T. 1965. "Growth of Cities in Indonesia 1930–1961." *Tijdschrift Voor Economische en Sociale Geografie* 56: 103–8.

Goodwan, A. E., and L. M. Franks. 1975. "The Dynamics of Migration to Saigon 1964– 1972." *Pacific Affairs* 48: 199–214.

Gordenker, L. 1971. "The United Nations and Economic and Social Change." In *The United Nations in International Politics*, edited by L. Gordeneker. Princeton: Princeton University Press.

———. 1982. "Causes of Forced Migrations." Paper presented at the Columbia University Seminar on Human Rights, New York.

———. 1983. "Refugees in Developing Countries and Transnational Organization." *The Annals* 467: 62–77.

Gordon, L. W. 1980. "Settlement Patterns of Indochinese Refugees in the United States." *INS Reporter* 28(1): 6–10.

Gordon, M. M. 1964. *Assimilation in American Life*. New York: Oxford University Press.

Gosling, L. A. P. 1979a. "Population Redistribution: Patterns, Policies and Prospects." In *World Population and Development: Challenges and Prospects*, edited by P. M. Hauser. New York: United Nations Fund for Population Activities.

———. 1979b. *Population Resettlement in the Mekong River Basin*. Studies in Geography, Vol. 10. Chapel Hill: University of North Carolina.

Gould, W. T. S. 1974. "Refugees in Tropical Africa." *International Migration Review* 8(3): 413– 30.

Goundaim, O. 1970. "African Refugee Convention." *Migration News* 2: 1–12.

Government of Pakistan. 1951. *Census of Pakistan, 1951*. Karachi: Ministry of Home and Kashmir Affairs.

———. 1982. *Pakistan Economic Survey, 1981–1982*. Islamabad: Finance Division, Economic Advisors Wing.

Government of Southern Region of Sudan. 1973. *Peace and Progress, 1972–73: A Report*. Juba: Regional Ministry of Information and Culture.

Government of the Southern Region of Sudan, Secretariat-General of the High Executive Council. 1974. *Progress Report, April 1972–October 1973*. Juba, January.

Government of the Southern Region of Sudan, Regional Ministry of Finance and Economic Planning, Directorate of Planning. 1977a. *The Six-Year Plan for Economic and Social Development, 1977/78–1982/83*. Juba, June.

Government of the Southern Region of Sudan, Regional Ministry of Health and Social Welfare. 1977b. "Progress Report for the Period April 1972–March 1977." Juba, September.

Government of Sudan. 1972a. *Projects for Relief and Reconstruction in the Southern Region*. Khartoum: Government Printing Press.

———. 1972b. "The Addis Ababa Agreement on the Problem of South Sudan." Khartoum, March 12 (pamphlet).

Government of Sudan, Ministry of State for Southern Affairs. 1972c. *Proceedings of the Relief and Resettlement Conference on Southern Region.* Khartoum: Government Printing Press, February 21–23.

Gowing, P. G. 1977. *Mandate in Moroland: The American Government of Muslim Philippinos, 1899–1920.* Quezon City: University of the Philippines.

Grigg, D. B. 1980. "Migration and Overpopulation." In *The Geographical Impact of Migration,* edited by P. E. White and R. I. Woods. London and New York: Longman.

Habibullah, M. 1968. "Communal Virus." In *Mainstream,* August 15 (Independence Day Issue).

Hagopian, E., and A. Zahlan. 1974. "Palestine's Arab Population: The Demography of the Palestinians." *Journal of Palestine Studies* 3(4): 32–73.

Haines, D., D. Rutherford, and P. Thomas. 1981. "Family and Community Among Vietnamese Refugees." *International Migration Review* 15(1/2): 310–19.

Hamrell, S., ed. 1967. *Refugee Problems in Africa.* Uppsala: The Scandinavian Institute of African Studies.

Hansen, A. 1979. "Once the Running Stops: Assimilation of Angloan Refugees into Zambian Border Villages." *Disasters* 3(4): 369–74.

———. 1981. "Refugee Dynamics: Angolans in Zambia from 1966–1972." *International Migration Review* 15 (1/2): 175–94.

———. 1982. "Self-Settled Rural Refugees in Africa." In *Involuntary Migration and Resettlement: The Problems and Responses of Dislocated Peoples,* edited by A. Hansen and A. Oliver-Smith. Boulder: Westview Press.

Harris, D.W. 1982. "Southeast Asian Refugees in the United States: Interaction and Kinship and Public Policy." *Anthropological Quarterly* 55(3): 170–81.

Harris, W. 1978. "Refugees and Settlers: Geographical Implications of the Arab-Israeli Conflict 1967–1978." Ph.D. diss., Durham University.

Hart, T. and C. M. Rogerson. 1982. "The Geography of International Refugee Movements in Southern Africa." *South African Geographical Journal* 64(2): 126–37.

Hartling, P. 1983. Opening Statement by the High Commissioner for Refugees to the 34th Session of the Executive Committee of the High Commissioner's Programme. October 10.

Harvey, B. 1974. "Tradition, Islam and Rebellion: South Sulawesi 1950–1965." Ph.D. diss, Cornell University, Ithaca.

Haub, C. 1982. *World Population Data Sheet.* Washington, D.C.: Population Reference Bureau.

Heeren, H. J., ed. 1955. "Urbanization of Djakarta." *EKI* 8: 696–736.

Holborn, L. W. 1975. *Refugees: A Problem of Our Time: The Work of the United Nations High Commissioner for Refugees, 1951–1972.* 2 vols. Metuchen, N.J.: Scarecrow Press.

Holdridge, D. T. 1940. "Toledo: A Tropical Refugee Settlement in British Honduras." *Geographical Review* 30(3): 376–93.

Hombee, P. M. 1981. "Refugee Settlement Administration in Tanzania." Paper presented at the workshop on Rural Refugee Settlements, Dar es Salaam, September 1–10.

Homeida, M., and A. Kabosh. 1980. "Educational Survey: Port Sudan, Kassala and Gedaref." MOE/COR, Khartoum.

Howard, M. C. 1975. *Ethnicity in Southern Belize: The Kekchi and the Mopan, Museum Brief No. 21,* Museum of Anthropology. Columbia: The Curator of the University of Missouri.

Hugo, G. J. 1975. "Population Mobility in West Java, Indonesia." Ph.D. diss., Australian National University, Canberra.

———. 1978. *Population Mobility in West Java.* Yogyakarta: Gadjah Mada University Press.

———. 1982. "Report on The 1981 Socio Economic Survey of Zamboanga Del Sur." (Mimeo).

———. 1983. "Postwar Involuntary Migrations Within and Between Southeast Asian Countries: A Review." Paper presented at the symposium on the Problems and Consequences of Refugee Migrations in the Developing World, Manitoba, August 29–September 1.

Hugo, G. J., H. Sigit, and S. Suharto. 1982. *Migration, Urbanization and Development in Indonesia.* Bangkok: United Nations Economic and Social Commission for Asia and the Pacific.

Hugo, G. J., and M. Tolentino. 1977. *The Social Impact of the Philippine-Australian Develop-*

ment Assistance Programme, Zamboanga Del Sur Development Project. Pagadian City: Co-
lombo Plan, Government of Australia-Republic of the Philippines.
Indian Statutory Commission. 1930. *Report of the Indian Statutory Commission, Vol. 15.*
London.
Indra, D. 1979. "Vietnamese Settlement in Edmonton." In *Asian Canadians in a Multicultural
Society,* edited by K. V. Ujimoto and G. Hirabayshi. Ottawa: Secretary of State.
————. 1983. "Khmer, Lao, Vietnamese and Vietnamese Chinese in Alberta." In *Ethnic
Groups in Alberta,* edited by H. Palmer. Calgary: Western Producer.
International Labour Office (ILO). 1959. *International Migration 1947–1957.* Geneva: ILO.
Jackson, J. A. 1979. *Migration.* Sociological Studies 2. Cambridge: Cambridge University
Press.
Jackson, K. D., and J. Meoliono. 1973. "Participation in Rebellion: The Daru'l Islam in West
Java." In *Political Participation in Modern Indonesia,* edited by R. W. Liddle. New Haven:
Yale University Southeast Asian Studies Monograph Series 19.
Jenkins, D. 1979. "A New Row Over East Timor." *Far Eastern Economic Review,* November
2: 29.
Jilil, M. Y. 1979. *Matinya Parti Berjaya.* Kuala Lumpur.
Jones, P. 1976. "Old Soldiers Worry Thais." *Far Eastern Economic Review,* October 15.
Jung, A. 1983. "Afghan Refugees: They Wait with God." *The Illustrated Weekly of India,* April
17.
Kabera, J. B. 1982. "Rural Population Redistribution in Uganda since 1900." In *Redistribu-
tion of Population in Africa,* edited by J. I. Clarke and L. A. Kosinski. London: Heinemann.
Kaley, R. B. 1980. "L'adaptation des enfants vietnamiens en milieu scolaire quebecios."
Ph.D. diss., Department of Anthropology, Laval University.
Kamaluddin, A. F. M. 1980. "Refugee Problems in Bangladesh." Paper presented at the
Symposium on Development and Population Redistribution in South Asia, Commission
on Population Geography, International Geographical Union, Karachi, January 4–10.
Karadawi, A. 1977. "Political Refugees in Africa: A Case Study from Sudan, 1964–1972."
Master's thesis, Reading University.
————. 1980. "Urban Refugees in the Sudan." Paper presented at a conference on
Refugees in the Sudan, Commissioner for Refugees, Khartoum, Sudan. June.
————. 1982. "Definition of a Refugee Changing Concepts." Paper presented at the
Khartoum Refugee Seminar, Khartoum, September.
Kaul, J. M. 1961. *Problems of National Integration.* New Delhi: Vikash Publications.
Keely, C. B. 1981. *Global Refugee Policy: The Case for a Development Oriented Strategy.* New
York: The Population Council, Public Issues Papers on Population.
Keesing's Publications. 1973. *Keesing's Contemporary Archives,* Vol. 19. Bristol: Longman
Group Ltd.
Kehler, L. 1980. *Making Room for "Strangers."* A Review of the Refugee Assistance Program
of MCC (Canada) and the Provincial MCCs. Winnipeg: Mennonite Central Committee.
Keller, E. J., ed. 1982. *Issue: A Journal of Africanist Opinion* 12(1/2): Spring/Summer (Special
Issue on African Refugees).
Keller, S. L. 1975. *Uprooting and Social Change: The Role of Refugees in Development.* Delhi:
Manohar Book Service.
Keystone, J. S. 1979. "Imported Disease in Vietnam Refugees." *Ontario Medical Review*
46(8): 369–70.
Khan, M. R. 1974. "Pattern of External Migration to and from Bangladesh, 1901–1961." *The
Bangladesh Economic Review* 2(2): 599–631.
Khumalo, E. N. 1981. "Case Study: Refugee Rural Settlements in Swaziland." Paper
presented at the workshop on Rural Refugee Settlements, Dar es Salaam, September 1–
10.
Kibreab, G. 1985. *African Refugees: Reflections on the African Refugee Problem.* Trenton, N.J.:
Africa World Press.
Knott, Y. 1981. "A Case Study of a Canadian Policy and Calgary Community Response to
the Southeast Asian Refugees, 1979–80." Master's thesis, University of Calgary.
Kraak, J. H. 1957. "The Repatriation of Netherlands Citizens and Ambonese Soldiers from
Indonesia." *Indonesia* 4(4): 348–55.

Kroef, J. M. van der. 1954. "The City: Its Culture and Evolution." In *Indonesia in the Modern World I*, edited by J. M. van der Kroef. Bandung Masa Baru.

Kunz, E. F. 1973. "The Refugees in Flight: Kenetic Models and Forms of Displacement." *International Migration Review* 7(2): 125–46.

———. 1981. "Exile and Resettlement: Refugee Theory." *International Migration Review* 15(1/2): 42–51.

Kureshy, K. U. 1978. *A Geography of Pakistan*. Karachi: Oxford University Press.

Labour and Immigration, Belize. 1977. *Belize City*. Belize Development Finance Corporation.

Lam, L. 1983. "Vietnamese Chinese Refugees in Montreal." Ph.D. diss., York University, Toronto.

Lanphier, C. M. 1981a. "Canada's Response to Refugees." *International Migration Review* 15(1/2): 113–30.

———. 1981b. "Dilemma of Decentralization: Voluntary Agencies and Refugee Resettlement in the United States and Canada." Paper presented at the Canadian Council for Southeast Asian Studies, annual proceedings, Calgary, Alberta, November 14.

———. 1983a. "Indochinese Resettlement and the Development of Canadian Refugee Policy." In *Two Nations, Many Cultures, Ethnic Groups in Canada*. 2nd. edition, edited by J. L. Elliot. Scarborough, Ontario: Prentice-Hall Canada.

———. 1983b. "Refugee Resettlement as Mass Movement: Governmental Policy Implications: United States, Canada and France." Paper presented at symposium on Refugee Resettlement: Indochinese in Transition, Vancouver, B.C. (Mimeo).

Lederer, K. 1980. *Human Needs*. Cambridge, Mass.: Oelgeschlager, Gunn & Hain, and Verlag Anton Hain.

Lee, R. 1980. "Sabah Frets About Consequences of Open Door Policy for Filipinos." *The Asia Record* 2(4): 7–27.

Lees, R. E. M., and K. Doliszny. 1982. "Utilization of Ontario Health Care Services by Southeast Asian Refugees." *Canadian Family Physician* 28(1): 56–62.

Lewis, O. D. 1975. "The Philippines: Promises and Some Progress." *Orientations*, November 5–10.

Li, K. C., D. B. Coates, L. R. Buckley, and H. Luk. 1980. "Vietnamese Refugees in British Columbia: Their Psychological Adaptation." Paper presented at the Canadian Psychiatric Association Annual Meeting, Toronto, Ontario, October 1.

Lineton, J. A. 1975a. "Pasompe Ugi: Bugis Migrants and Wanderers." *Archipel* 10: 173–204.

———. 1975b. "An Indonesian Society and Its Universe: A Study of the Bugis of South Sulawesi and Their Role Within the Wider Social and Economic System." Ph.D. diss., University of London.

Lippman, L., and S. Diaz-Briquets. 1981. "Latin America and Caribbean Migration: A Regional View." *Intercom* 9(7): 8–11.

Lontoh, S. W. 1964. "Sumbungsih Jang Mendasari Pertimbangan Perentijanaan Perlusan Kolu Bandung." Ph.D. diss., IKPP Bandung.

Lowenthal, D. 1961. "The Range and Variation of Caribbean Societies." In *Readings in Cultural Geography*, edited by P. L. Wagner and M. W. Mikesell. Chicago: University of Chicago Press.

Lumby, E. W. R. 1954. *The Transfer of Power in India*. London: Allen & Unwin.

Lyons, G., D. Baldwin, and D. McNemar. 1977. "The 'Politicization' Issue in the U.N. Specialized Agencies." In *The Changing United Nations: Options for the United States*, edited by David Kay. New York: Academy of Political Science.

Macauley, S. 1983. "The Sudanaid Vulnerable Groups Approach." *Migration News* 2: 3–9.

MacRury, K. A. 1979. *The Occupational Adjustment of Vietnamese Refugees in Edmonton, Canada*. Master's thesis, University of Alberta, Edmonton.

Mahdi el Tom, A. 1975. *The Rains of Sudan*. Khartoum: University of Khartoum Press.

Majul, C. M. 1978. *Muslims in the Philippines*. Manila: Saint Mary's Publishing.

Marie de Val, D. 1981. "Framing Refugees as Clients." *International Migration Review* 15(1): 88–94.

Marks, S. 1980. "From Difaquane to Discarded People: South Africa's Internal Refugees." *African Research and Domination* 22: 2–12.

McBeth, J. 1979. "Take a Figure and Double It." *Far Eastern Economic Review*, November 16: 25–28.

———. 1982a. "An Exodus to Order." *Far Eastern Economic Review*, May 14: 25–26.

———. 1982b. "Hard Times Are Coming." *Far Eastern Economic Review*, October 22: 48.

———. 1982c. "Frustration Builds Up." *Far Eastern Economic Review*, October 22: 48–50.

———. 1983a. "Homeward Bound." *Far Eastern Economic Review*, August ll: 23.

———. 1983b. "A New Exodus." *Far Eastern Economic Review*, August 25: 24–26.

———. 1983c. "Revolution to Evolution." *Far Eastern Economic Review*, May 12: 24–25.

McCorguodale, B. 1981. *Greater Toronto Southeast Asian Refugee Task Force Report*. Toronto: Greater Toronto Southeast Asian Refugee Task Force.

McNicoll, G. 1968. "Internal Migration in Indonesia." *Indonesia* 5: 29–92.

McNicoll, G., and S. G. M. Mamas. 1973. "The Demographic Situation in Indonesia." *East West Population Institute Papers*, no. 28.

Melander, G. 1978. *Refugees in Orbit*. Geneva: International University Exchange Fund.

———. 1981. "Refugees and International Cooperation." *International Migration Review* 15(1/2): 35–41.

Mengers, C. C. 1980. *A Study of Mexican Foreign Policy*. Indianapolis: The Hudson Institute.

Meng-Try, E. 1981. "Kampuchea: A Country Adrift." *Population and Development Review* 7(2): 209–28.

Mills, L. R. 1977. *Population and Manpower in the Southern Sudan*. Research Paper No. 1. University of Juba, Population and Manpower Unit.

———. 1982. "Trends and Implications of Recent Population Redistribution and Urban Growth in the Southern Sudan: The Case of Juba, The Regional Capital." Paper presented at the International Geographical Union Symposium, Khartoum, March 8–12.

Ministère du Travail et de la Participation (Quebec). 1980. *Etude No. 31*, Quebec.

Moi, A. 1983. Opening speech at the opening session of the 19th OAU Heads of States Meeting, Addis Ababa, Ethiopia, June 8.

Mooney, M. C. 1983. *Mental Health and Southeast Asian Refugees: A Bibliography*. Toronto: Ministry of Citizenship and Culture.

Moussalli, M. 1983. Statement of Mr. Michel Moussalli, Director of International Protection, to the Executive Committee on the occasion of the debate on the International Protection of Refugees. Executive Committee of the High Commissioner's Programme, October 13.

Mtewa, M., ed. 1982. *Science, Technology and Development: Options and Policies*. Washington: University Press of America.

Mujahid, S. A. 1947. "Muslim India Demands: Eviction Must Go." *The Weekly Observer*, Allahabad, May 9.

Murray, C. 1980. "Defining the Unit of Study: Notes on the Orange Free State." Paper presented at the conference on the Interactions of History and Anthropology in Southern Africa, Manchester University, September 21–24.

———. 1981. "Ethnic Nationalism and Structured Unemployment: Refugees in the Orange Free State." *Disasters* 5: 132–41.

Naim, M. 1973. "Merantau, Minangkabau Voluntary Migration." Ph.D. diss., University of Singapore.

Nann, R. C., P. J. Johnson, and M. Beiser, eds. 1984. *Refugee Resettlement: Southeast Asians in Transition*. Vancouver: University of British Columbia Refugee Resettlement Project.

National Committee for Aid to Refugees. 1980. *Documentation for June 20–23 Conference, Khartoum*. 4 Volumes. Khartoum: Government of Sudan.

Nations, R. 1978. "The Forgotten 140,000." *Far Eastern Economic Review*, December 22: 12.

Neuwirth, G., and L. Clark. 1981. "Indochinese Refugees in Canada: Sponsorship and Adjustment." *International Migration Review* 15(1/2): 131–40.

Neuwirth, G., and G. Grenier, J. Devries, and W. Watkins. 1985. *Southeast Asian Refugee Study: A Report on the Three Year Study of the Social and Economic Adaptation of Southeast Asian Refugees to Life in Canada, 1981–1983*. Ottawa: Employment and Immigration Canada.

The New Belize. 1980: Vol. 10, No. 9. 1981: Vol. 11, Nos. 1 and 12. 1982: Vol. 12, No. 7. Belmopan: Government Information Service.

Newland, K. 1981. *Refugees: The New International Politics of Displacement.* Worldwatch Paper 43.

Newman, L. 1983. *Needs Assessment of Southeast Asian Refugees with Reference to Social Service Agencies and Other Government Programs.* Ottawa: Canada Employment and Immigration Commission.

Nguyen, Q. B. 1977. "The Vietnamese in Canada: Some Settlement Problems." In *Visible Minorities and Multiculturalism: Asians in Canada,* edited by K. V. Ujimoto and G. Hirabayashi. Toronto: Butterworths.

————. 1980. "Education and Adaptation." In *The Indochinese Refugee Movement—The Canadian Experience,* edited by H. Adelman. Toronto: Operation Lifeline.

Nguyen, Q. B., and L. J. Dorais. 1979. *Monograph on the Vietnamese in Eastern Canada.* Ottawa: Minister of State for Multiculturalism.

Nguyen, S. D. 1979. *Rapport sur les resultats de l'etude sociale effectuee aupres de la communaute des Vietnamiens a Montreal.* Programme de service communautaire etudiant, Secretariat d'Etat, Montreal.

————. 1980. "The Refugee Experience: A Conceptual Model of Social Disintegration." Paper presented at the 1980 Refugee Consultation Conference, Toronto.

————. 1981. "Psychiatric and Psychosomatic Problems among Southeast Asian Refugees." Paper presented at the Sixth World Congress of the International College of Psychosomatic Medicine, Montreal, September 13–18.

————. 1982a. "Psychiatric and Psychosomatic Problems among Southeast Asian Refugees." *Psychiatric Journal of the University of Ottawa* 7(1): 26–35.

————. 1982b. "The Psycho-social Adjustment and the Mental Health Needs of Southeast Asian Refugees." *The Psychiatric Journal of the University of Ottawa* 7(1): 26–35.

————. 1983. *Ottawa-Carleton Refugee Needs Assessment.* Ottawa: Ottawa-Carleton Southeast Asian Refugee Project. Royal Ottawa Project.

Nilssen, E. S. W. 1981. "Implementation and Management of a Settlement Project." Paper presented at the workshop on Rural Refugee Settlements, Dar es Salaam, September 1–10.

Noble, L. 1976. "The Moro National Liberation Front in the Philippines." *Pacific Affairs* 49(3): 405–24.

North, D. 1982. *Kaleidoscope: The Resettlement of Refugees in the U.S. by the Voluntary Agencies.* Washington, D.C.: New TransCentury Foundation.

Novicki, M. A. 1983. "The Economic Outlook." *Africa Report,* February: 8–14.

Nyerere, J. K. 1979. "Settling Refugees: The Story of Five Loaves, Two Fishes." A speech at the 1979 Pan African Conference on Refugees, Arusha; Daily News, May 8.

Nyrop, R. F. 1974. *Area Hand Book for Pakistan.* Washington: Government Printing Office.

Obrecht, T. 1983. "More than 260,000 Vietnamese in China." *Refugees Magazine* 3: 30–31.

Ocampo, S. 1981. "An Island in Death's Shadow." *Far Eastern Economic Review,* March 27: 30–33.

Oliver-Smith, A., and A. Hansen. 1982. "Involuntary Migration and Resettlement: Causes and Contexts." In *Involuntary Migration and Resettlement: The Problems and Responses of Dislocated Peoples,* edited by A. Hansen and A. Oliver-Smith. Boulder: Westview Press.

Olson, M. E. 1978. "Flight, Settlement and Adjustment: Refugees in Laos and Other Developing Countries." Ph.D. diss., University of Michigan, Ann Arbor.

————. 1979a. "Refugees as a Special Case of Population Redistribution." In *Population Redistribution: Patterns, Policies and Prospects,* edited by L. S. P. Gosling and L. Y. C. Lim. New York: United Nations Fund for Population Activities.

————. 1979b. "Village Cohesion in Laos: The Effect of the War Refugee Experience." In *Population Resettlement in the Mekong River Basin,* edited by L. A. P. Gosling. Chapel Hill: University of North Carolina.

O'Shaughnessy, T. J. 1975. "How Many Muslims Has the Philippines?" *Philippines Studies* 23(3): 375–82.

Palmer, I. 1982. "Employment Among Refugee Women." Paper presented at the Khartoum Refugee Seminar, Khartoum, September.

Pappone, R. 1982. *The Hai Hong: Profit, Tears and Joy.* Ottawa: Employment and Immigration Canada.

Pask, E. D. 1983. "Issues in Child Welfare: The Refugee Child." *Child Welfare Forum* 1: 68–80.

"People Are Coming Like ə Deluge in the Naaf." *Bichitra*, May 12, 1978. Dhaka.

Perez de Cuellar, J. 1983. Secretary-General's Statement to Meeting of African Countries of Asylsum Concerning 1984 Conference on Refugees in Africa. United Nations Press Release, SG/SM/3386, REF/902, February 23.

Peterson, W. A. 1985. "A General Typology of Migration." *American Sociological Review* 23(3): 256–66.

Poole, P. A. 1967a. "Thailand's Vietnamese Minority." *Asian Survey* 7(12): 886–95.

———. 1967b. "Thailand's Vietnamese Refugees: Can They Be Assimilated?" *Pacific Affairs* 15(3–4): 324–32.

———. 1970. *The Vietnamese in Thailand: An Historical Perspective.* Ithaca: Cornell University Press.

Poon, P. M. 1977. "Successful and Troubled Function of Chinese Families." Master's thesis, McGill University, Montreal.

Pryor, R. J. 1978. "The Interrelations Between Internal and International Migration with Some Evidence from Australia." Paper presented at the conference on Economic and Demographic Change: Issues for the 1980's. Lige: International Union for the Scientific Study of Population.

———. 1981. "Integrating International and Internal Migation Theories." In *Global Trends in Migration: Theory and Research on International Population Movements,* edited by M. M. Kritz, C. B. Keely, and S. M. Tomasi. New York: Center for Migration Studies.

Public Affairs Foundation. 1986. *Report on Thai Refugee Research.* Bangkok.

Que, L. T., A. T. Rambo, and G. P. Murlin. 1976. "Why They Fled: Refugee Movement During the Spring 1975 Communist Offensive in South Vietnam." *Asian Survey* 16: 855–63.

Quebec. 1978. *Le Refugie: Un Etranger Malgre Lui.* Quebec: Minister of Immigration.

Rambo, A. T. 1968. *Refugee Movement in Revolutionary War: A Study of the Causes and Characteristics of Civilian Population Displacement in Viet-Nam.* McLean, Va: Human Sciences Research.

Rasjik, A. W. 1972. "Masalah Perumahan Di Kotamadya Bandung Dalam Hubungannya Dengan Perkembangan Penduduk." Ph.D. diss., IKIP, Bandung.

Refugee Documentation Project. 1983. "Refugees: Government/Private Sponsorship." Toronto: York University (Mimeo).

Refugee Policy Group. 1983. *Refugee Assistance in Developing Countries.* Washington, March.

Repatriation and Resettlement Commission. 1974. *Final Report, May 1972–April 1974.* Juba: Government of the Southern Region of Sudan.

Rex, J. 1973. *Race Relations in Sociological Theory.* 2nd edition. London: Routledge & Kegan Paul.

Rizvi, M. 1978. "The Problems of the Burmese Muslims." *Pakistan Horizon* 31 (4).

Rodgers, P. 1979 "Where Have All the People Gone?" *Advertiser* (Adelaide), November 5.

———. 1981. "The Timor Debate Goes On." *Far Eastern Economic Review,* February 6: 16–18.

Rogge, J. R. 1975. "The Qala en Nahal Refugee Settlement Scheme." *Sudan Notes and Records* 56: 130–46.

———. 1977. "A Geography of Refugees: Some Illustrations from Africa." *The Professional Geographer* 29(2): 186–93.

———. 1981. "Africa's Resettlement Strategies." *International Migration Review* 15: 195–212.

———. 1982. "Refugee Migration and Resettlement." In *Redistribution of Population in Africa,* edited by J. I. Clarke and L. A. Kosinski. London: Heinemann.

———. 1983. "New Roots." *Refugees* 15:7.

———. 1985a. *Too Many, Too Long: Sudan's Twenty-Year Refugee Dilemma.* Totowa, N.J.: Rowman & Allanheld.

———. 1985b. "The Indo-Chinese Diaspora: Where Have All the Refugees Gone?" *Canadian Geographer* 29(1): 65–72.

———. 1986. "Africa's Displaced Population: Dependency or Self-Sufficiency?" In *Population and Development Projects in Africa,* edited by J. I. Clarke, M. Khogali, and L. Kosinski. Cambridge: Cambridge University Press.

Roosman, R. S. 1980. "Irian Jaya Refugees: The Problem of Shared Responsibility." *Indonesian Quarterly* 8(2): 83–89.

Ross, N. 1983. Refugee Aid and Development. Statement of Australian Delegation to the Executive Committee of the High Commissioner's Programme, Geneva, October.

Ross-Larson, B. 1976. *The Politics of Federalism: Syed Kechik in East Malaysia,* Singapore: Ross Larson.

Sakir, M. 1972. *Muslims in Free India.* New Delhi: Kalamkar Prakashan.

Salih, M. A. 1971. "The Round Table Conference and the Search for a Solution to the Problem of the Southern Sudan, 1964–69." Master's thesis, University of Khartoum.

Samha, M. 1979. "Migration to Amman: Patterns of Movement and Population Structure." Ph.D. diss., Durham University.

Samuel, T. J. 1986. "Economic Adaptation of Indochinese Refugees in Canada." In *Uprooting, Loss and Adaptation: The Resettlement of Indochinese in Canada,* edited by K. Chan and D. Indra. Toronto: Canadian Public Health Association.

Sandhu, K. S. 1964. "Emergency Resettlement in Malaya." *Journal of Tropical Geography* 18: 157–83.

Sathyamurty, T. V. 1979. "Language, Religion and Political Economy: The Case of Bangladesh." In *Political Identity in South Asia,* edited by D. Taylor and M. Yapp. London: Curzon Press.

Saunders, E. 1981. *Vocational Counselling with Indo-Chinese Refugees.* Bangkok: Mennonite Central Committee.

Silva, R. D. 1979. *Two Hills of the Same Land: Truth Behind the Mindanao Problem.* Mindano: Sulu Critical Studies and Research Group.

Siu, B. 1980a. "The Employment of Indochinese Refugees in Toronto." In *Living and Growing in Canada,* edited by I. Chu, C. K. Fong, and J. M. Seung. Toronto: Council of Chinese Canadians in Ontario.

———. 1980b. "Underemployment of Indochinese Refugees: U.S.A. and Canada." In *The Indochinese Refugee Movement: The Canadian Experience,* edited by H. Adelman. Toronto: Operation Lifeline.

Smail, J. R. W. 1964. *Bandung in the Early Revolution, 1945–46.* Modern Indonesia Project. Ithaca: Cornell University.

Smock, D. 1982. "Eritrean Refugees in the Sudan." *The Journal of Modern African Studies* 20(3): 451–65.

Solien, N. L. 1971. "West Indian Characteristics of the Black Carib." In *Peoples and Cultures of the Caribbean,* edited by M. M. Horowitz. Garden City, N.Y.: The Natural History Press.

Sommer, J. W. 1968. "The Sudan: A Geographical Investigation of the Historical and Social Roots of Political Dissension." Ph.D. diss., Boston University.

Soonsiri, P. 1986. Address to the Committee for Coordination of Services to Displaced Persons in Thailand (CCSDPT), Narai Hotel, Bangkok, July 11.

South African Institute of Race Relations (SAIRR). 1981. *A Survey of Race Relations in South Africa 1980.* Johannesburg: SAIRR.

Speare, A. 1974. "The Relevance of Models of Internal Migration for the Study of Internal Migration." In *International Migration: Proceedings of a Seminar on Demographic Research in Relation to International Migration,* edited by G. Tapinos. Paris: CICRED.

———. 1974. "The Relevance of Models of Internal Migration for the Study of International Migration." In *International Migration Proceedings of a Seminar on Demographic Research in Relation to International Migration,* edited by G. Tapinos. Paris: CICRED.

Stavrakis, O. and M. L. Marshall. 1978. "Women, Agriculture and Development in the Maya Lowlands: Profit or Progress." In *Proceedings and Papers of the International Conference on Women and Food.* Tucson: University of Arizona.

Stein, B. N. 1979. "Occupational Adjustment of Refugees: The Vietnamese in the U.S." *International Migration Review* 13(1): 25–45.

———. 1980. "The Refugee Experience: An Overview of Refugee Research." Paper presented at the conference on the Refugee Experience, The Royal Anthropological Institute and the Minority Rights Group, London.

———. 1981a. "Documentary Note—Refugee Research Bibliography." *International Migration Review* 15(1/2): 331–93.

————. 1981b. "Refugees and Economic Activities in Africa." Paper presented at the Refugee Seminar, Erkowit, Sudan.

Suh, M. 1980a. "Psychiatric Problems of Immigrants and Refugees." In *Southeast Asian Exodus: From Tradition to Resettlement*, edited by E. L. Tepper. Ottawa: Canadian Asian Studies Association.

Suhrke, A. 1981. "Global Refugee Movements and Strategies: An Overview." Paper presented to the Wingspread Workshop on Immigration and Refugees, sponsored by the Rockefeller, Ford, and Johnson Foundations.

————. 1983. "Global Refugee movements and Strategies of Response." In *U.S. Immigration and Refugee Policy: Global and Domestic Issues*, edited by Mary Kritz. Lexington, Mass.: Lexington Books.

Surplus People Project (SPP). 1983. *Forced Removals in South Africa*. Cape Town and Pietermaritzburg: SPP.

Symonds, R. 1951. *The Making of Pakistan*. London: Faber & Faber.

Taft, J. V., D. S. North and D. A. Ford. 1979. *Refugee Resettlement in the U.S.: Time for a New Focus*. Washington, D.C.: New Transcentury Foundation.

Tan, S. K. 1968. *Sulu under American Military Rule, 1899–1913*. Quezon City: University of the Philippines.

————. 1977. *The Filippino Muslim Armed Struggle, 1900–1972*. Filipinos Foundation.

Tan, S. K., and K. L. Tan. 1980. "Health Problems of Vietnamese Refugees." *Canadian Family Physician* 26.

Taylor, D. M. 1951. "The Black Caribs of British Honduras." *Viking Fund Publications in Anthropology*, no. 17. New York: Wenner-Gren Foundation for Anthropological Research.

Teitelbaum, M. S. 1983. "Immigration: A Popular Answer Is No Answer." *Los Angeles Times*, May 25, Part II: 13.

Tepper, E. L., ed. 1980. *Southeast Asian Exodus: From Tradition to Resettlement. Understanding Refugees from Laos, Kampuchea and Vietnam in Canada*. Ottawa: The Canadian Asian Studies Association.

Terrill, C. F. F. 1983. "The Creation of the Acholi Minority of the Southern Sudan: Their Dispersal as Refugees, Repatriation and Resettlement." Paper presented at the IGU Commission on Population Geography Symposium on the Problems and Consequences of Refugee Migrations in the Developing World, Hecla Island, Manitoba, August 29–September 1.

Thomas, W. I., and F. Znaniecki. 1958. *The Polish Peasant in Europe and America*. New York: Dover Books.

Thompson, J. E. S. 1972. *The Maya of Belize: Historical Chapters since Columbus*. Belize: The Benex Press.

Thomson, S. 1980. "Refugees in Thailand: Relief, Development, and Integration." In *Southeast Asian Exodus: From Tradition to Resettlement*, edited by Elliot L. Tepper. Ottawa: Canadian Asian Studies Association.

Tran, T. N. 1976. "Vietnamese Refugees: The Trauma of Exile." *Civil Rights Digest* 9: 59–62.

Tuker, F. 1950. *While Memory Serves*. London: Cassel.

Turley, W. 1976. "Urban Transformation in South Vietnam." *Pacific Affairs* 49(4): 406–24.

Tyhurst, L. 1980. "Refugee Resettlement—The Role of Community Oriented Social Psychiatry in the Integration of Aid." Paper presented at the Second Pacific Congress of Psychiatry, Manila, Philippines, May 13.

United Nations, Economic and Social Council (UNECOSOC). 1974. *Assistance to Southern Sudanese Returnees and Displaced Persons—Final Report of the UNHCR*. Geneva, June.

United Nations High Commissioner for Refugees (UNHCR). 1965a. *Report on the 14th Session of the Executive Committee*. A/AC.96/313, November.

————. 1965b. "UNHCR Operations in 1964." A/AC.96/277, March.

————. 1966. *UNHCR Program for 1966: New Projects*. A/AC.96/310, May.

————. 1969. *The Promise of M'boki*. Geneva, March.

————. 1972. *The Water Road: Highway to Regional Development at Qala en Nahal, Sudan*. Geneva.

————. 1973a. *UNHCR Newsletter*. 6.

————. 1973b. *Nursing a Miracle: The Role of the Office of the UNHCR in United Nations Emergency Relief Operations in the South Sudan.* Geneva, September.

————. 1974. *Report on UNHCR Assistance Activities in 1973–74 and Proposed Voluntary Funds Program and Budget for 1975.* A/AC.96/506, August 28.

————. 1975a. *Report on UNHCR Assistance Activities in 1974–75 and Proposed Voluntary Funds Program and Budget for 1976.* A/AC.96/516, August 13.

————. 1975b. *United Nations Resolutions and Decisions Relating to the Office of the United Nations High Commissioner for Refugees.* 3rd edition. HCR/INF/48/Rev. 2.

————. 1979. *Report of the Conference on the Situation of Refugees in Africa, Arusha, Tanzania, 7–17 May.* REF/AR/CONF/Rpt. I, HCR/140/12/79.

————. 1982. *Report on UNHCR Assistance Activities in 1981–1982 and Proposed Voluntary Funds, Programmes and Budget for 1983,* United Nations General Assembly, No. A/AC.96/606, 23 August.

————. 1983a. Second International Conference on Assistance to Refugees in Africa (ICARA II). Guidelines for the Identification and Submission of Assistance Proposals. Inter-office Memorandum No. 13/83, February 11.

————. 1983b. *Report on UNHCR Assistance Activities since 1982–1983 and Proposed Voluntary Fund Programmes and Budget for 1984.* United Nations A/AC.96/620, August 1.

————. 1983c. *Refugee Aid and Development.* United Nations A/AC.96/627, September 12.

————. 1983d. "International Conference on Assistance to Refugees in Africa ICARA II." *Mimeo for the Information of the Executive Committee,* February 22.

————. 1983e. *UNHCR Fact Sheet.* Geneva: June 8.

————. 1983f. Guidelines for Country Submissions on the Impact of Refugee Problems on National Economies and Possible Development Assistance Required to Alleviate these Problems. Office of the Under-Secretary-General for Special Political Questions, SO 564 (1), March 25.

————. 1985. *Report on UNHCR Assistance Activities in 1984–85 and Proposed Voluntary Funds, Programmes and Budget for 1986.* Geneva: UNHCR.

————. 1986. "Indochinese: 1985 Statistics." *Refugees* 26: 7.

UNHCR/ILO. 1982. *Income Generating Activities for Refugees in the Sudan.* Report of the UNHCR/ILO Interdiscipclinary Mission on Employment, Income Generation and Training of Refugees in the Sudan. 80-82/AF/VAR/AR/I/ARV/B. Geneva.

United States. 1980. *Refugee Resettlement Resource Book.* Washington, D.C.: U.S. Coordinator for Refugee Affairs.

————. 1981. *Proposed Refugee Admissions and Allocations for Fiscal Year 1982: Report to Congress: Summary.* Washington, D.C.: U.S. Coordinator for Refugee Affairs.

U.S. Committee for Refugees. 1964–1982. *World Refugee Survey.* New York: American Council for Nationalities Services.

————. 1980. *World Refugee Survey 1980.* Washington, D.C.

————. 1984. *World Refugee Survey 1984.* Washington, D.C.

U.S. Department of Health, Education, and Welfare. Social Security Administration. Office of Refugee Affairs. 1979. *Indochinese Refugee Assistance Program.* Washington, D.C.: Report to Congress.

U.S. Department of Health and Human Services. Social Security Administration. Office of Refugee Resettlement. 1981. *Refugee Resettlement Program.* Washington, D.C.: Report to Congress.

————. 1982. *Refugee Resettlement Program.* Washington, D.C.: Report to Congress.

————. Office of Policy/Office of Research and Statistics. 1982. *Survey of the Social, Psychological, and Economic Adaptation of Vietnamese Refugees in the U.S. 1975–1979.* Washington, D.C. No. 13-11755.

U.S. Department of State. 1981. *Country Reports on the World Refugee Situation.* Washington, D.C.: Office of the Coordinator for Refugee Affairs.

————. 1983. *Country Reports on the World Refugee Situation, Report to the Congress.*

————. 1984. *Country Reports on the World Refugee Situation, Report to the Congress.*

U.S. General Accounting Office. 1982. *International Assistance to Refugees in Africa Can Be Improved.* Report by the Comptroller General to the Congress, GAO/ID-83-2.

van der Kroef, J.M. 1979. "The Vietnamese Refugee Problem." *World Affairs* 142(1): 3–16.

———. 1984. "Thailand's Refugee Dilemma: Another Lebanon?" *Internationales Asienforum* 15(1/2): 117–36.

Varophas, J. 1966. "The Vietnamese Refugees in Thailand." *World Affairs* 128(4): 233–38.

Vietnamese Association. 1979. *A Profile of the Vietnamese Community in Toronto*. Toronto: The Vietnamese Association.

Visaria, P. M. 1969. "Migration between India and Pakistan, 1951-61." *Demography* 6(3): 323-34.

Waddell, D. A. G. 1961. *British Honduras—A Historical and Contemporary Survey*. London: Oxford University Press.

Wain, B. 1981. *The Refused: The Agony of the Indochina Refugees*. Hong Kong: Dow Jones Pub. Co. (Asia).

Weeks, J. R. 1981. *Population: An Introduction to Concepts and Issues*. 2nd edition. Belmont, Calif.: Wadsworth.

Weintraub, P. 1978. "The Exodus and the Agony." *Far Eastern Economic Review* December 22: 8-13.

Weis, P. 1982. "The Development of Refugee Law." *Michigan Yearbook of International Legal Studies*. New York: Clark Boardman.

Whitaker, B. 1972. *The Biharis in Bangladesh*. London: Minority Rights Group.

Whitmore, J. K. 1984. "Economic Self-Sufficiency Among Recent Southeast Asian Refugees in the U.S.: A Summary." In *Refugee Resettlement: SE Asians in Transition*, edited by R. C. Nann, P. J. Johnson, and M. Beiser. Vancouver: University of British Columbia.

Wilson, K. L., and A. Portes. 1981. "Immigrant Enclaves: An Analysis of the Labor Market Experiences of Cubans in Miami." *American Journal of Sociology* 82: 295-319.

Woldring, K. 1980. "Ethnic Minorities in Holland Today: The South Moluccans and Suriname People." *Journal of Inter Cultural Studies* 6(2): 50-66.

World Bank. 1981. *Accelerated Development in Sub-Saharan Africa: An Agenda for Action*. Washington, D.C.

———. 1982. *World Development Report, 1982*. New York: Oxford University Press.

Yughi, H. 1973. "Refugees' Problems in the Jordanian Camps as Seen by Their Children in the UNRWA Training Center in Amman." Master's thesis, University of Jordan.

Zolberg, A. 1983. "Contemporary Transnational Migrations in Historical Perspective: Patterns and Dilemmas." In *U.S. Immigration and Refugee Policy: Global and Domestic Issues*, edited by Mary Kritz. Lexington, Mass.: Lexington Books.

Index

Contributors

Akol, Joshua O.	University of Juba, Juba, Sudan
Christensen, Hanne	United Nations Research Institute for Social Development, Geneva, Switzerland
Desbarats, Jaqueline	University of California, Irvine, California, U.S.A.
Elahi, K. Maudood	Jahangirnagar University, Savar, Dhaka, Bangladesh
Everitt, John	Brandon University, Brandon, Canada
Ferris, Elizabeth	World Council of Churches, Geneva, Switzerland
Gasarasi, Charles	University of Dar es Salaam, Dar es Salaam, Tanzania
Goitom, Eyob	University of British Columbia, Vancouver, Canada
Greenway, Dan	University of Chicago, Chicago, Illinois, U.S.A.
Haque, Chowdhury	University of Manitoba, Winnipeg, Canada
Harris, Bruce	Fundación para el Desarollo de la Communidad y Ayuda Infantil, Alamos, Mexico
Hugo, Graeme	Flinders University, Bedford Park, Australia
Indra, Doreen	University of Lethbridge, Lethbridge, Canada
Kabera, John	Makarere University, Kampala, Uganda
Kamaluddin, A. F. M.	Jahangirnagar University, Savar, Dhaka, Bangladesh
Karadawi, Ahmed	Office of the Commissioner for Refugees, Khartoum, Sudan
Lamphier, Michael	York University, Toronto, Canada
Mabin, Alan	Witwatersrand University, Johannesburg, R.S.A.
Melander, Goran	University of Lund, Lund, Sweden
Nakavachara, Netnapis	Chulalongkorn University, Bangkok, Thailand
Neuwirth, Gertrud	Carleton University, Ottawa, Canada
Pitterman, Shelly	Northwestern University, Evanston, Illinois, U.S.A.
Rachagan, Sothi	University Malaya, Kuala Lumpur, Malaysia
Rogge, John R.	University of Manitoba, Winnipeg, Canada
Samha, Musa	University of Jordan, Amman, Jordan

Schoenmeier, H. W.	Universität des Saarlandes, Saarbrücken, West Germany
Simmance, Alan	United Nations High Commission for Refugees, Geneva, Switzerland
Smythe, Mabel M.	Northwestern University, Evanston, Illinois, U.S.A.
Stein, Barry	University of Michigan, East Lansing, Michigan, U.S.A.
Ugalde, Miguel	Fundación para el Desarollo de la Communidad y Ayuda Infantil, Alamos, Mexico